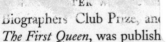

Biographers Club Prize, and ...
The First Queen, was publish ...
She is a regular contributor to *BBC History Magazine* and *History Today*. She lives in Kent.

'Linda Porter's fascinating portrayal of Katherine Parr contradicts much of what we thought we knew about her. Far from being a matronly sort who spent much of her time tending to Henry's various diseases, she was passionate, radical and highly intelligent, the only one of the women who followed Katherine of Aragon, who seemed truly to have anything of the queen about her'   *Beautiful Britain*

'Katherine Parr, Henry VIII's sixth and final wife, has long been regarded as a homely, matronly woman who had little impact on our history . . . In a new biography, *Katherine the Queen*, by Linda Porter this theory is turned on its head, and Katherine – who was only 30 when she married Henry – is revealed as feisty and radical'   *Choice*

'Porter's vividly written biography confirms her belief that Katherine was an influential woman. As stepmother she shaped Elizabeth I, one of England's most successful monarchs. More importantly, Porter presents a portrait of an attractive woman more than capable of navigating the treacherous waters of life at the duplicitous Tudor court'   PETER BURTON, *Daily Express*

'Katherine Parr is presented here as an intelligent, wily woman of passions . . . It's a story of high Tudor intrigue, confidently told by a good historian in a lively style'
IAIN FINLAYSON, *Saga*

Linda Porter

Katherine the Queen

The Remarkable Life of Katherine Parr

PAN BOOKS

First published 2010 by Macmillan

First published in paperback 2011 by Pan Books
an imprint of Pan Macmillan, a division of Macmillan Publishers Limited
Pan Macmillan, 20 New Wharf Road, London N1 9RR
Basingstoke and Oxford
Associated companies throughout the world
www.panmacmillan.com

ISBN 978-0-330-46080-4

The acknowledgements on pages 371–2 constitute an extension of
this copyright page.

Inside front cover: letter from Katherine Parr to Thomas Seymour accepting his marriage proposal,
reproduced by kind permission of Sudeley Castle, Gloucestershire.

Every effort has been made to contact copyright holders of material
reproduced in this book. If any have been inadvertently overlooked, the publishers
will be pleased to make restitution at the earliest opportunity.

1 3 5 7 9 8 6 4 2

A CIP catalogue record for this book is available from
the British Library.

Typeset by SetSystems Ltd, Saffon Walden, Essex
Printed in the UK by CPI Mackays, Chatham ME5 8TD

Visit **www.panmacmillan.com** to read more about all our books
and to buy them. You will also find features, author interviews and
news of any author events, and you can sign up for e-newsletters
so that you're always first to hear about our new releases.

For Anna

Contents

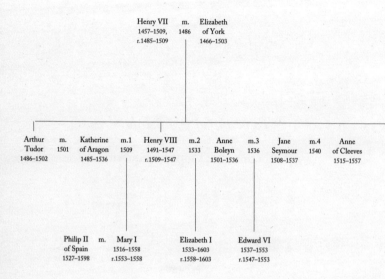

Henry VII m. Elizabeth
1457–1509, 1486 of York
r.1485–1509 1466–1503

Arthur m. Katherine m.1 Henry VIII m.2 Anne m.3 Jane m.4 Anne
Tudor 1501 of Aragon 1509 1491–1547 1533 Boleyn 1536 Seymour 1540 of Cleeves
1486–1502 1485–1536 r.1509–1547 1501–1536 1508–1537 1515–1557

Philip II m. Mary I Elizabeth I Edward VI
of Spain 1516–1558 1533–1603 1537–1553
1527–1598 r.1553–1558 r.1558–1603 r.1547–1553

The Tudors

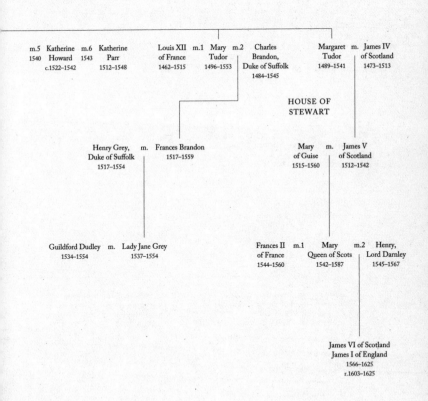

m.5	Katherine	m.6	Katherine		Louis XII	m.1	Mary	m.2	Charles		Margaret	m.	James IV
1540	Howard	1543	Parr		of France		Tudor		Brandon,		Tudor		of Scotland
	c.1522–1542		1512–1548		1462–1515		1496–1553		Duke of Suffolk		1489–1541		1473–1513
									1484–1545				

HOUSE OF
STEWART

	Henry Grey,	m.	Frances Brandon			Mary	m.	James V
	Duke of Suffolk		1517–1559			of Guise		of Scotland
	1517–1554					1515–1560		1512–1542

Guildford Dudley	m.	Lady Jane Grey		Frances II	m.1	Mary	m.2	Henry,
1534–1554		1537–1554		of France		Queen of Scots		Lord Darnley
				1544–1560		1542–1587		1545–1567

James VI of Scotland
James I of England
1566–1625
r.1603–1625

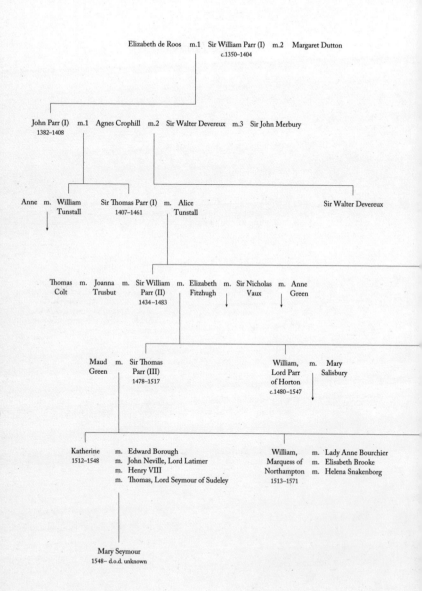

Elizabeth de Roos   m.1   Sir William Parr (I)   m.2   Margaret Dutton
                                 c.1350–1404

John Parr (I)   m.1   Agnes Crophill   m.2   Sir Walter Devereux   m.3   Sir John Merbury
1382–1408

Anne   m.   William   Sir Thomas Parr (I)   m.   Alice   Sir Walter Devereux
             Tunstall   1407–1461   Tunstall

Thomas   m.   Joanna   m.   Sir William   m.   Elizabeth   m.   Sir Nicholas   m.   Anne
Colt   Trusbut   Parr (II)   Fitzhugh   Vaux   Green
                            1434–1483

Maud   m.   Sir Thomas   William,   m.   Mary
Green   Parr (III)   Lord Parr   Salisbury
             1478–1517   of Horton
                                                    c.1480–1547

Katherine   m.   Edward Borough   William,   m.   Lady Anne Bourchier
1512–1548   m.   John Neville, Lord Latimer   Marquess of   m.   Elisabeth Brooke
            m.   Henry VIII   Northampton   m.   Helena Snakenborg
            m.   Thomas, Lord Seymour of Sudeley   1513–1571

Mary Seymour
1548– d.o.d. unknown

The Parrs

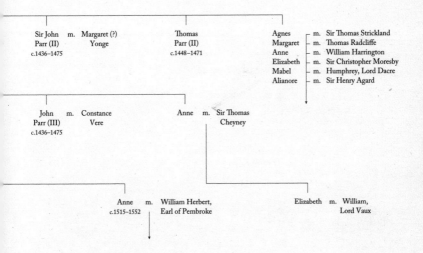

Sir John Parr (II) c.1436–1475	m.	Margaret (?) Yonge		Thomas Parr (II) c.1448–1471		Agnes	— m.	Sir Thomas Strickland

Agnes — m. Sir Thomas Strickland
Margaret — m. Thomas Radcliffe
Anne — m. William Harrington
Elizabeth — m. Sir Christopher Moresby
Mabel — m. Humphrey, Lord Dacre
Alianore — m. Sir Henry Agard

John Parr (III) c.1436–1475   m.   Constance Vere

Anne   m.   Sir Thomas Cheyney

Anne c.1515–1552   m.   William Herbert, Earl of Pembroke

Elizabeth   m.   William, Lord Vaux

indicates
other
descendants

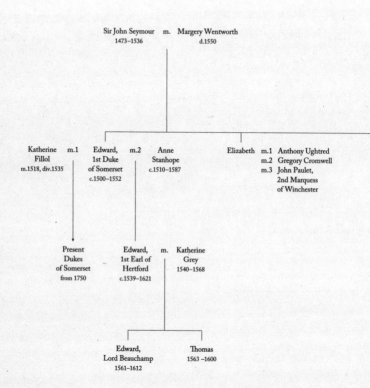

Sir John Seymour m. Margery Wentworth
1473–1536   d.1550

Katherine m.1 Edward, m.2 Anne   Elizabeth m.1 Anthony Ughtred
Fillol   1st Duke   Stanhope   m.2 Gregory Cromwell
m.1518, div.1535 of Somerset c.1510–1587   m.3 John Paulet,
              c.1500–1552   2nd Marquess
                                                        of Winchester

Present   Edward,   m. Katherine
Dukes   1st Earl of   Grey
of Somerset   Hertford   1540–1568
from 1750   c.1539–1621

              Edward,   Thomas
              Lord Beauchamp 1563–1600
              1561–1612

coming. It was not one she particularly feared, since it would bring her freedom, or so she hoped.

But for Katherine this anxious time was only the culmination of a difficult and unnerving year. The halcyon early days of her marriage had begun to seem far behind her in the summer of 1546, when she was afraid that she had lost the affection of her husband and might be in great danger. There were those among his ministers who whispered against her, quite prepared to sacrifice her in the struggle between the supporters of the old and new religious ideas. Henry's health declined dramatically at that time, and he became more cunning and unpredictable. Almost too late, she realized that he disapproved heartily of her writing, was irritated by her conversation and opinions, disappointed (as was she) by her childlessness. She had been too confident in her influence over him. All that was over now. They had kissed and made up. His indulgence and generosity returned and, as if to recompense her for her demotion to being merely his consort, no longer his close adviser, he filled her wardrobes and jewel-caskets with all the finest things that money could buy. Katherine was reassured, at least for her personal safety, but she was not fooled.

She was relieved to be allowed to return to Whitehall in the second week of January, knowing that at least she would be in the same palace as her husband. But he did not send for her; her enquiries were politely but firmly turned aside. And yet, given her positive and outgoing nature, hope had never entirely gone away. She knew that her period as regent in 1544 had been a success and she still expected to be appointed to that role for her young stepson when the unmentionable did finally happen and Henry left this life. Edward would need her greatly then, to protect him from the greedy and ambitious men raised up by his father, who all looked, in one way or another, to improve their position. She believed the boy would trust her, since she was the only mother he had ever known. The other marriages were so brief that her predecessors had not established any place in the child's affections, while she was secure in his devotion, at least.

They exchanged letters regularly, but her most recent one to him, while reminding him of his father's virtues, made no mention of the king's physical condition. Edward was at Hertford Castle with Elizabeth, and Katherine knew better than to raise alarm.

The worries, though, remained. She was not the prince's natural mother and the Seymour brothers, his uncles, were clearly manoeuvring for power. The elder, Edward, earl of Hertford, was said to be closeted almost permanently with the king, the chief of the coterie that had made an impenetrable ring around her husband. They ensured that access to the king was closely controlled, and she was not included in their counsel. She knew all these men, of course, and their wives. Sitting in her own apartments were the ladies of her court whose husbands would, in all probability, decide her future. She would not reveal any-thing to them and, besides, she doubted that they knew anything of material importance. Except, perhaps, for Anne Seymour, who was finding it hard to conceal a very slight air of triumphant satisfaction. Katherine did not like this over-confident woman – few did, except for Mary – and she sensed that the countess expected further elevation for her husband. But these things were never discussed in the open. The household's daily routine of morning prayers, scripture reading, needlework and musical entertainment continued as smoothly as ever. Katherine was queen of England and attended as such. Even if some thought her days as Henry's wife would soon be past, nothing was said. Only to the women of her immediate family, her sister and cousin, could she give vent to her dissatisfaction and frustration. Their constant advice was to be patient and she could not disagree.

Sometimes, she thought of Thomas Seymour, Hertford's younger brother, the suitor she had been required to abandon when the king made his own intentions plain. Tom was still unmarried, despite the renewed attempt last summer to forge a marital alliance between the Seymours and the Howards. Would he renew his wooing when she herself was once more a widow, and, if so, how might she respond? As queen regent, she could probably not afford to indulge her own desires, though he might be a useful ally as well as a handsome bedfellow.

In Katherine's more optimistic moments, with her dogs at her feet beside the hearth, she did not abandon the belief that Henry would, yet again, keep death at bay for a while. The summons would come at last and she would, once more, be enfolded in that massive bulk, his beloved Kate, as she had been that July day in 1543 when she became his sixth wife. Despite her anguish and misgivings when she succumbed to family pressures and accepted the king's proposal – for who, as had been made quite clear to her, could refuse their sovereign? – she was bound to acknowledge to herself that she enjoyed being Henry VIII's queen. His loss would diminish her status unless she secured the regency immediately. The uncertainty over her position once the old king was gone would not go away, however brave a face she presented to her ladies.

After she had risen and dressed, then worshipped and breakfasted, she learned of a rumour that Dr Cranmer had been summoned to see the king late the previous night from his house south of London. It crossed her mind to send for Cranmer, on the pretext of discussing religion, but he was her husband's servant first, not hers, and she knew Cranmer well enough to realize that she would get no confidence out of him that touched on secret matters of state. Meanwhile, everything, so it appeared, continued as normal in the functioning of the king's Privy Chamber. His advisers came and went, and meals were still being taken in and out at the appointed hour, with due fanfare and ceremony. Yet something told her that the tidings she so dreaded to hear could not be long delayed.

Part One

The Northern Inheritance
1512–1529

CHAPTER ONE

The Courtiers of the White Rose

> *'The final end of a Courtier, where to all his good conditions and honest qualities tend, is to become an Instructor and Teacher of his Prince.'*
>
> Baldassare Castiglione, *The Book of the Courtier*, 1528

WHITEHALL PALACE is a long way from Westmoreland. In the sixteenth century the contrast between this opulent mansion on the busy river Thames and the wild country of the Lake District was even more pronounced. It took two weeks to travel between London and Kendal, the area's main town; a daunting prospect indeed and one seldom attempted in winter. Westmoreland was border country and its landowners and men of influence, often viewed as somewhat crude by their southern counterparts, were nevertheless expected to protect the king and the realm of England from the depredations of the country's neighbour, the violent, unpredictable kingdom of the Scots. But there was a lingering air of unreliability about the English nobility in this part of the kingdom. The Percy family's loyalty, in particular, was often in doubt, as was that of the other great northern clan, the Nevilles.[1] The prospect of rebellion was never far away.

And yet, even in this hostile environment, it was possible to prosper and to gain for one's family the prospect of influence and a better future. The family of Henry VIII's sixth wife had built their wealth, and thus their place in society, on the backs of the hardy sheep who grazed their lands on England's northern fringes. The famous Kendal Green wool produced by their flocks was much in demand and made them money. Though not of the aristocracy, service in the household of John of Gaunt and a marriage alliance with the prominent de Roos family enhanced their standing.[2] Knighthoods followed and they began to hope for ennoblement, that most cherished of medieval social aspirations. In the late fourteenth century, they took their first steps on the path that promised advancement: they became courtiers and servants of the Crown. The Parr family motto, 'love with loyalty', seemed entirely apt.

Over the next fifty years, the wealth of the Parrs grew. They acquired more lands and began to develop the complex web of local patronage and political presence that underpinned the fabric of rural England in the declining years of feudalism. But as the fifteenth century passed its midway point, with dissatisfaction growing against the inept rule of Henry VI, the Parrs had to consider exactly what 'loyalty' meant. In 1455, following the lead of the ambitious Nevilles, his powerful neighbours, Sir Thomas Parr, the head of the family, made a decision that had profound implications for his three sons. He would align himself with the party of Richard, duke of York, against the queen, Margaret of Anjou, and the clique of nobles who were manipulating the king and ruining the country.

He did not know then what confusion, mayhem and sorrow lay ahead for the ruling class of his country, as it slipped into the troubled time known to history as the Wars of the Roses. Sir Thomas Parr fought alongside Richard Neville, earl of Warwick, and Warwick's father, the earl of Salisbury, at the battle of St Albans in 1455 and four years later at the battle of Ludlow. Here the Yorkists came off very much second best and Sir Thomas fled south, with the future Edward IV, and eventually took a ship from the Devon coast to France to await happier times. His action left him an attainted traitor, the future of his family very much in doubt.

On his return, things at first went from bad to worse. He and his sons fought at the battle of Wakefield in December 1460, which saw the summary execution of the duke of York by the Lancastrians, led by the duke of Somerset. Sir Thomas himself was listed as dead but survived for another year. By that time, the pendulum had swung again and the Yorkists emerged victorious from the carnage of Towton in Yorkshire, on Palm Sunday, 1461. It was one of the bloodiest battles ever fought on English soil. When William Parr, the eldest son, assumed responsibility for the family's lands and future, there was no question that the Parrs were confirmed supporters of the White Rose.

Nothing, however, was straightforward in those confusing times. As many of the old aristocracy perished in the convulsions of the next twenty-five years, so new opportunities arose for men who were willing to serve the monarchy in their stead. The Parrs were shrewd when they decided to divide their efforts. William stayed mostly in the north, managing the family estates and trying to combat the decline of law and order brought about by civil war and the continued menace of Scottish armies. He became, despite all the challenges, a very active local business-man, expanding his flocks, building new fulling mills to boost cloth production and, by the 1470s, controlling the net fishing industries of Windermere and other major sources of local food supply.

His younger brothers, John and Thomas, meanwhile, went south to London, intent on establishing themselves at court. John became an esquire of the body in Edward IV's household and Thomas a retainer of Richard, duke of Gloucester. Yet the brothers were themselves to experience the tensions that ripped families apart during the Wars of the Roses. William was, unavoidably given his position in the north, Warwick's man. As the 'Kingmaker' grew into the fearsome overmighty subject who would challenge the young king himself, William Parr found himself on the opposite side from his siblings.

The year 1470–1 has been described as one of the most confusing in English history. Opposed by the man who had helped put him on the throne, and by his own brother, the duke of Clarence, Edward IV fled to Burgundy, leaving his queen, Elizabeth Woodville, to take sanctuary in Westminster Abbey, where she gave birth to her first son. Edward was not exactly welcome in Burgundy – fugitive monarchs are always an embarrassment to their reluctant hosts – but he was determined that he would not stay there long. Henry VI was briefly restored, but the move smacked of desperation, for his sanity was clearly compromised. And despite the chaotic times, when shifting allegiances were commonplace, Warwick and Margaret of Anjou made strange allies. In reality, the earl had overstretched himself. His domination of English politics was at last broken on the battlefield of Barnet on Easter Sunday 1471, and he himself despatched by Edward's soldiers.

William Parr had deserted Warwick by that time. In March, when Edward returned to reclaim his throne, the eldest Parr brother met him at Nottingham with 600 of his own men 'well arrayed and habled [prepared] for war'. It must have been a difficult decision to break with the Nevilles, and the anxiety that he might have miscalculated stayed with William Parr until Warwick was dead. That his gamble eventually paid off was no comfort for the loss of his youngest brother. Thomas Parr fell fighting beside the duke of Gloucester at Barnet. So the Parrs were not, in the end, immune to the sorrows experienced by many families in those unquiet days. Finally, on 4 May 1471, Edward IV inflicted a comprehensive defeat on Queen Margaret and her son at Tewkesbury. There was to be no sentiment for the vanquished. Henry VI may have been saintly but he was too dangerous as a figurehead to be kept alive any longer. His murder in the Tower swiftly followed the death at Tewkesbury of his only son.[3] Edward had, at last, gained undisputed control of

England. William and John Parr were with him at the climax of the Wars of the Roses. However much they mourned their brother and feared for their own survival, they did not waver in the end. The victorious king knighted John Parr on the battlefield. At last, the brothers would reap the full rewards offered by a grateful king.

RECOGNITION came quickly. Only weeks after Tewkesbury, Sir William Parr was appointed comptroller of the royal household, a key role in which essentially he managed all the king's personal expenditure. He also became a royal councillor. Sir John Parr was named master of the horse and constable of Kenilworth Castle. These were no mere decorative functions. The master of the horse controlled all the king's stables, horses, hounds and the paraphernalia that went with them. Both Parrs were given properties in the north that had belonged to the fallen earl of Warwick and John's position at Kenilworth, together with other grants of lands in Warwickshire, suggests that the king intended to build up a role for him in the heart of England.

It was, however, in their frequent and physical proximity to the king that the Parrs enjoyed the greatest influence. They were typical of the kind of men, sound in outlook and loyalty, conscious of where they had come from and also where they hoped to go, whom Edward encouraged. He was suspicious of what remained of the old nobility and was under pressure from the tensions produced by the rivalries between his own brothers and the relatives of his wife, Elizabeth Woodville. The counsel and company of men he could trust and speak with freely were highly valued. These were true courtiers, not vainglorious aristocrats. And Edward, with his mixture of energy and laziness, his affability often masking a steely resolve when it came to his own survival, could not have been an easy man to serve.

The year 1474 was perhaps the high point of Sir William Parr's life. He became a Knight of the Garter, one of only two members of the gentry to receive this honour in the second part of Edward IV's reign. By this time he held more than a dozen offices and had recouped the financial losses of the previous decade, when even his business acumen could not cover his mounting debts to the Crown.[4] His successes enabled him to make an impressive second marriage in the same year that he received the Garter. On the death of his first wife, Joanna, William married Elizabeth Fitzhugh, niece of the late earl of Warwick and became, through her, a cousin to the king himself. William was forty by then and his new bride a mere twelve years old. A significant, though not quite so large, difference in age was to become a feature of Parr marital unions in the sixteenth century. Initially, the marriage was perhaps nothing more than in name. Elizabeth Parr did not give birth to her first child until she was sixteen years old. It was the dynastic alliance itself that mattered in such arrangements.

Yet just one year after he wed Elizabeth, Sir William resigned from his role as comptroller and went back up to Westmoreland. This move may have been necessitated by the unexpected death of Sir John Parr, whose affairs required management. The elder Parr was with Edward IV in France for the campaign of the summer of 1475, but, that period apart, he did not return permanently to court and the personal service of the king again until the end of 1481. His reinstatement in the same office he had held before suggests that his stock had remained high with his royal master. In the six years of his absence, Sir William had worked mainly with Richard, duke of Gloucester, by now the king's only surviving brother.[5] Gloucester had built up a power base in the north during his time as the visible presence of monarchy there and Sir William Parr was, effectively, his lieutenant. Parr's experience of dealing with the Scots was also important as relations between Edward IV and Scotland declined again in the last years of the king's reign. Whether Sir William was personally close to the duke, as his brother Thomas had been, is another matter. The unfolding of events in 1483 suggests that

William Parr's loyalty was first and foremost to the Crown and to legitimate descent.

Although the pursuit of pleasure had broadened Edward IV's girth and coarsened his youthful bloom, there is nothing to suggest that his health was giving rise to alarm. As late as Christmas 1482 he presided over sumptuous celebrations with his usual hedonistic enjoyment, in the company of his large family, 'frequently appearing clad in a great variety of most costly garments, of quite a different cut to those which had been usually seen hitherto in our kingdom', according to the *Croyland* chronicler. Ever conscious of his public image, Edward would have taken satisfaction in the comment that his dress gave him 'a new and distinguished air to beholders, he being a person of most elegant appearance, and remarkable beyond all others for the attractions of his person'.[6] Even allowing for some judicious flattery, this was clearly a monarch to be noticed and admired. So the sudden onset of serious illness in late March 1483 caused consternation. It may well be that Edward IV suffered a stroke. For eleven days after being stricken he lingered, alert enough mentally to try to reconcile his feuding relatives, aware as he must have been of the difficulties that would ensue for the minority of his son. But there was little doubt that he would not survive, and he died on 9 April, aged only forty. At his funeral, Parr was chosen to play the ceremonial role of man of arms: 'Sir William Parr, arrayed in full armour, save that his head was bare, and holding in his hand an axe, poll downward, rode up to the choir and, after alighting, was escorted into the church to make his offering as the man of arms'.[7] It was Parr's last service to the king who had contributed so much to the rise of his family.

The unexpected death of Edward IV plunged England into a deep political crisis that has been the stuff of drama, romance and divided opinion for more than five hundred years. The struggle for power that culminated in the disappearance of two young boys is one of the most fascinating in English history and the mystery that lies at its heart has never been solved. It remains an emotive issue to this day. But it is easy to overlook the impact that the events of the spring and summer of 1483 had on men like Sir William Parr, torn between conscience and expediency as they watched events unfold. In Parr's case, this led to a decision which could have caused a rift with his wife and her family.

In the immediate aftermath of Edward's death it became apparent why, in the colourful language of the late fifteenth century, the collective term for a group of courtiers was a 'threat'.[8] As his struggle with the Woodvilles and the queen became more bitter, the duke of Gloucester, nominated Protector of the Realm, had the full support of Sir William Parr. Lady Fitzhugh, Parr's mother-in-law, also put pressure on him to follow the duke's lead, perhaps because she and Elizabeth Parr were close to Gloucester's wife, Anne Neville, herself the daughter of Parr's old commander, the earl of Warwick. But these complex family networks were not, eventually, sufficient to persuade Parr that Gloucester's determination to gain the throne for himself was justified. The ruthless murder, on 13 June 1483, of William, Lord Hastings, one of the late king's closest friends and most trusted advisers, was the tipping point. Parr was loyal to the institution of monarchy but baulked at the idea of such a usurpation, however much it could be justified in terms of political expediency. He was wise enough to keep such thoughts to himself, though, and his attendance at the coronation of Richard III on 26 June was expected – indeed, he was listed as one of those who would carry a canopy during proceedings. But when the ceremony took place, he was absent. His womenfolk, however, were most definitely there, Lady Parr resplendent in the seven yards of cloth of gold and silk given 'by the King's special gift'. Her mother had been provided with material for two gowns, one of blue velvet and crimson satin as well as one of crimson velvet with white damask. It is not known which she wore as she rode behind Queen Anne, one of seven noble ladies given this honour. Elizabeth Parr was swiftly appointed as one of the queen's ladies-in-waiting, a further sign of royal favour.

But while his wife seemed set to uphold the family's tradition of service in the new regime, Sir William Parr returned, for the last time, to Kendal. He personally wanted no part in King Richard III's regime. This does not mean that he and Elizabeth had fallen out; they may simply have felt it sensible for her to stay close to those in power, when he could not bring himself to do so. But it is not known whether she ever saw him again. He died in late autumn 1483, aged forty-nine, the last member of his family to reside in Kendal Castle. He had lived through a prolonged period of civil strife and still there seemed no permanent resolution of the dynastic problems that had beset England during his lifetime. He left behind four children, three sons and a daughter, the eldest of whom, his heir, Thomas, was five years old. When Richard III fell at Bosworth Field just two years later, in 1485, Lady Parr, still only twenty-three, faced a most uncertain future.

Her destiny and that of her young family very much in her own hands, Elizabeth Parr demonstrated very quickly the capacity for balancing pragmatism with personal contentment that characterized her granddaughter sixty years later. She made a second marriage, some time early in the reign of Henry VII. It proved both happy and fruitful for her and gave her children by Parr a settled childhood, as well as improving their prospects in the uncertain landscape of the new Tudor England. Sir Nicholas Vaux of Harrowden in Northamptonshire, her second husband, was a member of an old Lancastrian family. His mother, a Frenchwoman, had been one of Margaret of Anjou's ladies and his father had died fighting for the queen at Tewkesbury. He had close links to the countess of Richmond, mother of Henry VII. In the new order, he cancelled out Elizabeth Parr's awkward Yorkist past perfectly. It was an inspired match.

Thomas Parr and his siblings thrived in the congenial atmosphere of their extended family. Three daughters were born to Elizabeth and Nicholas, but no boys, and Thomas grew close to his stepfather. As the years went by, and Henry VII's hold on his throne, shaky at first, was tightened, Thomas was carefully educated and prepared to take his place at court. Nicholas Vaux had been brought up in the household of the king's mother, Margaret Beaufort, a woman of outstanding intellect and strong character, who was a notable patron of humanist scholars. The endowments she gave to Cambridge University, and St John's College in particular, helped develop the ideas of many of the leading intellectuals of the last two decades of Henry VIII's reign, men who would play a significant part in shaping religious reform and the education of Henry VIII's younger children. It has been suggested that Thomas Parr himself was placed in Margaret Beaufort's establishment at Colyweston, Northamptonshire, where other young gentlemen were sent to be educated by the Oxford scholar Maurice Westbury. Colyweston was close to Vaux's estates and his own connection with Margaret Beaufort during his childhood makes it entirely possible that he would have wanted his stepson to follow in his footsteps.

Thomas Parr was given a classical education in Latin and Greek, and he also acquired all the polish and poise that would be required by a courtier. He may well have spoken French and other European languages, as was expected of gently-bred young men. All this would no doubt have pleased his father, though Sir William might have regretted his son's lack of interest in the steadily crumbling castle of Kendal itself. When he came into his inheritance in 1499, Thomas Parr was well aware that most of what his family had gained from their Yorkist connections had been taken back by the Crown. He would need to use his very considerable charm and courtly skills to stay close to those in power. But as the new century dawned he had reason to be optimistic. England was changing, and constant upheaval seemed to be a thing of the past. He could rebuild the family fortunes. And a first step on that road was to make, as both his parents had done, a good marriage.

✄

FORTUNE FAVOURED Thomas Parr in his search for a suitable heiress. The opportunity that came his way was brought about by the death in the Tower of London in 1506 of Sir Thomas Green, a landowner from Northamptonshire whose curmudgeonly nature had led to charges of treason against Henry VII. The accusations may well have been unjustified. It was a time when disputes with neighbours were commonplace and frequently turned violent. Recourse to law to settle differences kept the legal profession busy. The blustering Sir Thomas had clearly miscalculated the effect of his aggressive behaviour and his health failed during his captivity. He left behind him two orphaned daughters, Anne and Matilda, heiresses to considerable wealth and an uncertain future. Within a year of her father's death, Thomas Parr purchased the wardship and marriage of the younger girl, fifteen-year-old Matilda, known as Maud. In 1508 he married her and, at about the same time, his stepfather Nicholas Vaux, by then himself a widower, married Maud's sister, Anne. This arrangement may appear calculated and no doubt it was, but it also brought happiness and security to the Green sisters, whose children grew up and were educated together in the close family relationship that Thomas Parr had enjoyed as a child. Through several generations, the intricate ties of their cousins and half-siblings would underpin the social standing of the Parr and Vaux families in Tudor England.

Maud Green came from good Yorkist stock. Her maternal great-grandfather, Sir John Fogge, had been treasurer of the royal household between 1461 and 1468, in the first part of Edward IV's reign and would have known Thomas Parr's father, though it is unlikely they had been friends. Fogge was a Woodville henchman and liked to throw his weight around in a manner bordering on intimidation. On both sides, Maud's male forebears were an unpleasant lot. Yet she, happily, inherited the positive side of her father's attributes, all his confidence and passion and determination, without the tendency to make enemies. Thomas Parr must have known from the moment they met that her education and spirit, as well as her inheritance, were a good match for him. For despite Sir Thomas Green's inability to get on with his neighbours, he had not neglected the education of his daughters. Maud was fluent in French and probably read Latin as well. The age difference mattered much less than what she had in common with her husband. Certainly he did not treat her like a chattel and she no doubt appreciated the fact that this man twice her age, who had literally bought her, was refined enough not to rush her into the marriage bed before she had got used to him. It was clear that they would complement one another well. But their destiny depended on others. The key to their future together lay in Thomas Parr's careful cultivation of the teenage Prince Henry, the heir to the throne.

The Parrs' situation was transformed by the death of the old king in April 1509. As part of Henry VIII's coronation honours, Thomas was created a Knight of the Bath. This social recognition no doubt pleased the new Lady Parr but, more crucially, it was soon followed by the waiving of some of the huge debt which had bound her husband (and many others of his background) to the Tudor dynasty. At the time of Henry VIII's accession, Thomas Parr owed the Crown almost £9,000, the equivalent of £4.5 million today. Much of this was for title to lands in Westmoreland, but part, of course, was for Maud herself. The king's generosity brought most welcome relief. Such actions may have endeared Henry VIII to his debtor lords, but his father, who had built a full Treasury on calling in these feudal rights, would not have approved.

Henry VIII's relationship with his courtiers was all together different. They were companions and friends, only slightly less gorgeous than the handsome prince himself. He loved display and he wanted his court to reflect his youthful energy and love of magnificence. In this respect, he owed much to the flair and love of public show exhibited by his grandfather, Edward IV. The young king was determined to enjoy himself, to find outlets for his restive physicality and his love of music and composition. In these early days of the reign, during the summer progress of 1510, he passed his days 'shooting [archery], singing, dancing, wrestling, casting of the bar, playing at the recorders, flute, virginals, and in setting of songs, making of ballads, and did set two goodly masses, every of them of five parts, which were sung oftentimes in his chapel and afterwards in diverse other places. And when he came to Woking, there were kept both jousts and tournays. The rest of this progress was spent in hawking, hunting and shooting.'⁹

Henry's court was soon provided with that other prerequisite of the medieval ideal to which he aspired: a queen and her ladies. Katherine of Aragon married Henry in a private ceremony on 11 June. Their joint coronation followed on Midsummer's Day. The Spanish princess, marooned in England since the death of Henry's elder brother, Prince Arthur, some seven years earlier, now became the wife of the boy who had escorted her into St Paul's Cathedral on her first wedding day. This sounds romantic, but the truth was much less so. Katherine did not know the young king well and had been kept apart from him during the prolonged wrangling over her future between her own father, Ferdinand of Aragon, and Henry VII. There had been hard bargaining over the payment of the long overdue remainder of her marriage portion before vows were finally exchanged. She was nearly six years older than Henry VIII; not a huge difference, but he was barely eighteen when he ascended the throne and Katherine seems to have thought, with justification, that she knew more of the world than he did. She was never prepared to play the role of invisible queen consort, as Elizabeth of York, so briefly her mother-in-law, had done in the previous reign. But she was happy to wear the king's favours as he jousted, to worry over the injuries he sustained (which were to cause him great pain many years later) and to be his consort. Petite and golden-haired, she was an attractive young woman with an unmistakable air of regality. Katherine was the perfect foil to her husband's exuberance. Her contentment, with just a hint of indulgence, is apparent in the letter she wrote to her father, telling him that the days were passed 'in continual festival'.

So these were good times for those families accustomed to serve. Both Sir Thomas and Lady Maud Parr were able to take full advantage of the openings for people of their background and social skills. They were often at court, participating in entertainments and disguisings, enjoying life to the full. Thomas and his younger brother, William Parr, were close companions of the king, part of the charmed circle surrounding the new monarch. They kept company with the Staffords and the Nevilles, the Carews and a diplomat-knight of Norfolk origin, Sir Thomas Boleyn. Amusement was constant, luxury unabashed. Henry had an innate grasp of the importance of image. The Venetian ambassador described his glittering appearance with awe: 'his fingers were one mass of jewelled rings and around his neck he wore a gold collar from which hung a diamond as big as a walnut'.[10] The business of government he found irksome, but the possibilities of diversion were ever present. Typical of his rumbustious approach to life was his foray into the queen's chambers in Westminster one January morning in 1510, his entourage dressed as Robin Hood's men, bent on getting the ladies to dance. There was always about him something of the air of a practical joker (he used the same approach to impress a startled Anne of Cleves at their first meeting thirty years later, with such unfortunate results), but if the king's determination for such good cheer was occasionally oppressive, his companions knew better than to criticize. All seemed set fair for the Parrs. They preferred to follow the court rather than establish their residence in any one place.

While her husband used his charm and courtier's training, Maud became a lady-in-waiting to Queen Katherine and served her faithfully for the rest of her life, from the heady early days of the reign through the testing time of the 1520s, until Maud's death in 1531. Theirs was a relationship that went much deeper than giddy pleasure. Both women knew what it was like to lose children in stillbirths and in infancy. During the first year of her marriage, Katherine had a late miscarriage, which pride and gynaecological ignorance refused to acknowledge. It began a pattern of failed pregnancies and infant deaths for which only the Princess Mary, born in 1516, was an exception. And Maud, too, suffered as many mothers did in those days. She conceived shortly after she married Thomas Parr and bore him a son. But any happiness at the arrival of an heir was fleeting; the child died young and not even his name is known. Then, between 1512 and 1515, three healthy children came in close succession. The eldest of these was a girl. She was christened Katherine, after the queen, who may also have been her godmother.

THE PRECISE DATE of Katherine Parr's birth is not known but there is general agreement that it was probably some time in August 1512. The following year saw the arrival of her brother, William. Two years later a second daughter, Anne, was born. Despite their father's northern background, the Parrs grew up in the south of England. Kendal Castle was already falling into disrepair and it is not likely that Maud Parr would have struggled to the north of England for the birth. Her husband, though mindful of his family's origins in Westmoreland, never wanted to live there. It was too far from the centre of things. Nor does he seem to have desired to establish a pre-eminent residence among the properties he owned elsewhere. His base was very much London and the house he owned in Blackfriars, which was probably where Katherine was born.

His reluctance to establish himself as a provincial grandee had nothing to do with monetary difficulties. At the beginning of 1512 he inherited half of the estates of his Fitzhugh cousin, Lord Fitzhugh of Ravenworth, making him a major landowner in the north-east of England as well as the north-west. Combined with the cancellation of the rest of his debt to the Crown the following year, Sir Thomas could be much more confident about his situation than he had been a mere four years earlier. But still no hereditary title came his way. Sir Thomas Parr accepted that, if he was ever to achieve this goal, he must continue to look for office and stay close to the royal family. Opportunities would present themselves, and he had a good eye for them. In 1515 he journeyed to Newcastle, ready to accompany the king's sister, Queen Margaret of Scotland, on her return to England. Margaret, who had a weakness for attractive men, seems to have been charmed by her gallant escort and stayed close to him throughout her month-long progress south to London. There was no hint of anything improper; Parr was merely demonstrating how perfectly he had mastered the courtier's arts.

He knew, however, that acting the gallant to royal ladies was only part of the secret of success for a gentleman in his position. The following year he was offered a more prosaic but potentially lucrative role by his cousin Sir Thomas Lovell, a former chancellor of the exchequer. It was a new office – associate master of the wards – and Parr took it gratefully. Family connections thus helped to tie him to the growing civil service as well as the court. He also moved in the humanist, educated circles of his day and had a direct link to Thomas More, the renowned scholar and later Lord Chancellor. Thomas More's first wife was the daughter of Parr's stepbrother. Popularity, erudition and loyalty were important in the court milieu; but what he wanted, above all else, was to be Lord Parr and to pass the title on to his son.

Thomas died without fulfilling his dream, at the age of thirty-nine, in the autumn of 1517. The onset of his illness appears to have been sudden and its outcome unavoidable, as he made his will only four days before his death. In it, he left marriage portions of £400 (£160,000) each to his two daughters, five-year-old Katherine and her little sister, Anne. This was not an overly generous amount and it suggests that he expected them to marry respectably rather than impressively. Maud, who was pregnant again at the time of his demise, was instructed that if she produced another daughter, the girl was to be married at her

mother's expense. This seems a sour farewell to a woman who
had been such a lively and committed helpmate, though it may
reveal him as nothing more or less than a typical man of the early
sixteenth century. His son, predictably, was left with much better
provision, inheriting most of the estate. Still, he did nominate his
wife as executor, along with Cuthbert Tunstall, the archdeacon
of Chester (who was his kinsman), his brother, Sir William Parr
of Horton, and Dr Melton, his household chaplain.

He was buried close to his London home, at the church of
St Anne's, Blackfriars. The inscription on his tomb read: 'Pray
for the soul of Sir Thomas Parr, knight of the king's body, Henry
the Eighth, master of his wards ... and ... sheriff ... who
deceased the 11th day of November in the 9th year of the reign
of our said sovereign lord at London, in the Black Friars . . .'[11]
His will, with its mention of a signet ring given to him by the
king, illustrates how close he was to Henry VIII. But this was
only bleak comfort to Maud Parr, pregnant, grieving and left, at
the age of twenty-five, a widow with three small children to bring
up in a difficult world.

CHAPTER TWO

A Formidable Mother

*'Remembering the wisdom of my said Lady Parr ... I
assure you he might learn with her as well as in any place
that I know.'*

Lord Dacre's advice on the education of his grandson

IT MUST BE ASSUMED that Maud Parr lost the child she was
carrying, whether through miscarriage, stillbirth or death in early
infancy we do not know. Nothing more is heard of it. But
whatever the cause, the outcome of Maud's last pregnancy, even
if it caused further distress at a difficult time, may also have been
something of a relief. It enabled this clear-headed woman to
concentrate her efforts on the family that Sir Thomas Parr had
left behind and on her responsibilities as chief executor of his
will. In devoting herself to her children, Maud amply fulfilled the
promise that her husband had detected in her a decade earlier.

Despite her undoubted eligibility, she did not marry again.
There is no record of offers made and refused, but the most likely
explanation is that Maud came to realize that widowhood was an
opportunity and not merely a regret. In this she was typical of
other well-born women of her time, who had sufficient confidence to manage their own affairs (though not, it should be made
clear, without the assistance of male members of the family and
friends) and to experience the independence that would be lost in

subservience to a second husband. Educated, energetic and determined to do her best for her young family, it is unlikely that Maud would have turned down an offer of remarriage that could have notably enhanced their prospects. She possessed good judgement and ambition in equal measure. Evidently no suitable candidate for her hand presented himself. Yet the Parr children did not suffer from the absence of a prominent stepfather; instead they benefited from their mother's attention, and seem to have loved her greatly.

Maud had considerable strengths where the upbringing of her children was concerned. Her own position at court continued, as one of Katherine of Aragon's household, and she was able to combine the role successfully with the demands of her family. The queen's ladies worked on a rota basis (as they still do), so the requirement to be away from home could be balanced with a continuing personal presence in their children's lives. Royal attendants were fed and clothed at the monarch's expense but their undivided attention was expected while they served their turn. The court was no place for children. Princess Mary, who was born in 1516, had her own household, though she did frequently spend Christmas and other holidays under the same roof as her parents in the early years of her life.

Katherine Parr's early experience of the Tudor court would have been indirect, gleaned through the descriptions of her mother. If, as has been assumed, Queen Katherine was indeed her godmother, the christening was probably the only time that she came into direct contact with the royal family as a child. But her mother's presence ensured that the Parr name was well known at court and that Maud's children might hope to derive advantage from such service in the future. There is no doubt that Maud remained close to the queen, even as Katherine's relationship with Henry VIII declined and her position became much more difficult. In her will, Maud Parr made mention of several items given by Katherine of Aragon, notably the 'beads of lacquer allemagne dressed with gold which the said Queen's grace gave me'.[1] These tokens of intimacy and favour were extremely important to royal servants.

Maud's daily life at court, most often passed at Greenwich but sometimes also at other palaces, such as Eltham, revolved around providing companionship to Katherine of Aragon and performing a variety of tasks to ensure the queen's comfort. The role of ladies-in-waiting was largely social. They were there to provide conversation, to entertain, to play cards to wile away the time, to sew and to pray with the queen. Official occasions, such as the great feast days of the Church calendar and diplomatic visits from Henry VIII's fellow European princes, required the queen's attendance, and she herself would be supported by some of her ladies. But the reality of life for women like Maud in Katherine's service was often more mundane than these great occasions of state. They were not expected to undertake menial tasks (laundry, cleaning and cooking were, of course, left to a different class of servants) but they assisted with the queen's toilette night and morning, helped choose her clothes and jewels, ensured that everything was where it should be, supervised packing and unpacking as the court moved from place to place, consulted with apothecaries and doctors when necessary and generally formed a barrier of protection around their queen when they felt it appropriate. They watched as Katherine's husband became more distant, saw his infatuation with Anne Boleyn, who was, after all, one of them, and inevitably began to take sides. Henry's first wife never lost the loyalty and affection of women like Maud Parr, Gertrude Courtenay and Elizabeth Howard, who had been with her since the first years of the reign. Yet it would be wrong to confuse access, which these women undoubtedly had, with true intimacy. Katherine of Aragon was a proud woman, very conscious of the fact that she was the daughter and wife of monarchs, and there were lines not to be overstepped. In a fiercely hierarchical society, Maud Parr knew her place. It was at the queen's side, certainly, but that does not mean that she was privy to Katherine's innermost thoughts as Henry VIII sought to put her aside.

WHILE THEIR MOTHER was away, the Parr children were well cared for by servants at Rye House in Hertfordshire, which came to be their permanent home not long before their father's death. It was leased from one of Sir Thomas Parr's many cousins and was their fixed establishment until Maud's own death fourteen years later.[2] Here Katherine and her brother and sister began their education, under the supervision of their mother but with considerable input from two people who were to play important roles in Katherine's development. For, though fatherless, Katherine and her younger siblings were by no means deprived of male influence: Maud, very much a woman of her day, understood well the importance of male protection and involvement in her children's lives. She was fortunate to be able to call upon her late husband's brother, Sir William Parr of Horton, and Cuthbert Tunstall, a distant Parr kinsman who was to become one of the most prominent churchmen and diplomats of the first half of the sixteenth century. Together, they provided a powerful further resource, far beyond what Maud's own role at court could bring, for the future of her family.

Katherine's uncle had, like her father, flourished under the care of Sir Nicholas Vaux. His ties to Northamptonshire remained close throughout his life and were strengthened by his marriage (several years before that of Thomas and Maud Parr) to Mary Salisbury, daughter of a local landowner. Mary brought as part of her dowry the manor of Horton, and William Parr styled himself accordingly. It was a happy marriage that produced four daughters, and so Katherine Parr grew up in the company of her cousins, especially the eldest girl, Maud, who shared her lessons and was to become a lifelong friend and confidante. Combining the education of the children was no doubt appealing for both family and financial reasons, and the younger generation of Parrs were joined by another cousin, Elizabeth Cheyney, in their studies.[3]

William Parr of Horton was of more military bent than his brother and had fought with distinction in both France (where he was knighted by Henry VIII in Tournai Cathedral the year after Katherine's birth) and in Scotland. But he was less adept as a courtier and politician. Though he came to recognize that valour was admired but seldom rewarded by financial gain, he does not ever seem to have been comfortable in court circles. His lack of finesse would not have been well received there. Insecure in developing relationships with others in an atmosphere where everyone was jockeying to be noticed, he nevertheless accompanied the king at the celebrated 'Field of Cloth of Gold' in northern France in 1520. His awkwardness was compounded by incompetence in handling his own financial affairs. This may have been exacerbated by the additional responsibilities he took on in assisting his sister-in-law, for while Maud managed her estates in the south of England, William Parr dealt with her lands in the north.

As a family man, however, he seems to have been held in genuine affection. Katherine Parr wrote a dedication to him in her father's Latin *Book of Hours*, used by the Parr children as a Latin primer, which shows that he was an important presence in her life as a child: 'Uncle, when you do on this look, I pray you remember who wrote this in your book. Your loving niece, Katheryn Parr.'[4] The rhyme may be rudimentary, but the sentiment is clear, and the bond between uncle and niece was to last for the rest of William Parr's life.

The precise nature of Cuthbert Tunstall's influence is harder to determine, but Maud Parr herself acknowledged that she consulted him on matters relating to her children and that she valued his advice greatly. The extent of their contact can perhaps be gauged by the fact that she made him the chief executor of her will and left him a ring with a large ruby. Sir William Parr of

Horton was the anchor of Maud's fatherless family, but Cuthbert Tunstall, archdeacon of Chester when Katherine's father died, was an international figure, a prominent humanist, churchman, educator and diplomat who was to become one of the great survivors of sixteenth-century England. Maud could not have imagined, when she made her will in 1530, that Tunstall would outlive her daughter by eleven years. He was, by then, already over fifty years old.

Tunstall was illegitimate at birth, although his parents later married and the irregular circumstances of his background were never held against him. The connection with the Parrs was that he and Katherine's father shared a grandmother (Alice Tunstall), as well as a northern background. Like his cousin, Tunstall was an engaging man who learned to thread his way through unpredictable times, but he rose to far greater prominence. An outstanding scholar and mathematician, he had been educated in England, spending time at both Oxford and Cambridge, before a six-year spell at the University of Padua in Italy, from which he received two degrees. His Church career began in 1505, the year after he returned to England. He was not ordained until four years later, by which time he had come to the attention of the Archbishop of Canterbury, William Warham, who sponsored his early advancement and brought him to court. He was also close to Wolsey, Henry VIII's chief minister, who recognized in this urbane, polished man the potential to serve his country well in diplomacy. Such confidence was not misplaced, and at the time of Sir Thomas Parr's death Tunstall had only recently returned from a mission to Burgundy, where he had met the future Holy Roman Emperor, Charles V. The knowledge that this well-connected kinsman could assist his wife and children must have been a comfort to Sir Thomas as he lay dying in the autumn of 1517.

In both the ecclesiastical and international spheres, Cuthbert Tunstall was already an influential person when Katherine Parr lost her father. But it was his distinction as a humanist, his

reputation for virtue and intellect, and the circle of friends he had
known for many years that were even more important to her
upbringing. He was close to all the great names of English
humanism in the early sixteenth century: to Thomas More,
John Colet, William Grocyn and Thomas Linacre and, on the
wider European stage, to Erasmus. The Dutch thinker, so greatly
revered by his contemporaries, admired Tunstall's modesty, scholarship and charm – the latter quality apparently one that the
Parrs and their relatives possessed to a notable degree. Tunstall
helped Erasmus in the preparation of the second edition of his
Greek Testament, with its Latin translation and notes. When it
appeared in March 1519, he wrote to Erasmus: 'You have opened
the sources of Greek learning to our age, and the splendour of
your achievement has for ever thrown into the shade the work of
earlier scholars as the rising sun blots out the stars.'[5]

And there was no shortage of approbation for Tunstall
himself, particularly from Thomas More, who wrote of him in
the introduction to *Utopia*: 'his virtue and learning be greater and
of more excellency than I am able to praise them'. Almost twenty
years after the publication of what is perhaps the best known of
all humanist writings, More composed the inscription for his own
tomb. By then, he anticipated the likely outcome of the stand he
was taking against Henry VIII and he also knew that his old
friend had made the decision to side with the king. Yet he wrote
of his association movingly, describing Tunstall as 'then bishop
of London, but soon after of Durham ... . than whom the world
contains today scarcely anyone more learned, sagacious or good'.[6]

Tunstall also seems to have had a genuine fondness for
children and an interest in their progress. 'How great is the joy
of a father,' he wrote, 'when his little ones recognize him and
come to him with smiles, when in their first attempts to speak
they utter ridiculous sounds in their effort to mimic our
words ...' Perhaps it was his interest in children, as well as his
position in the Church, which caused him to be chosen to deliver
the Latin oration, *In Praise of Matrimony*, at the betrothal of the

two-and-a-half-year-old Princess Mary to the Dauphin of France in 1518. The splendidly attired little Mary, whose marriageability was to become a staple of Henry VIII's diplomacy throughout his reign (though he never did find a husband for her) apparently sat through the ceremony with remarkable patience for one so young. Tunstall had, however, anticipated a degree of fidgeting, even in a princess, for he had shrewdly built into his speech the observation: 'See how catching sight of her father she springs forward from her nurse's lap.'[7] This allowed gave Mary's grateful nurse to breathe a sigh of relief whilst also flattering the king's ego.

There is, however, no evidence that Katherine Parr was educated with Mary Tudor, as has been suggested in the past.[8] She was four years older than the princess, her requirements were much more modest in terms of her expectations and future role, and, tellingly, neither she nor anyone else in her family ever made mention of such a connection. But the two girls may well have benefited individually from Cuthbert Tunstall's enthusiasm for mathematics. In 1522, shortly before he was consecrated as bishop of London, Tunstall published a treatise on arithmetic, *De arte supputandi*, which enhanced his reputation among the leading thinkers of Europe.

In a letter to Thomas More, Tunstall explained that he had begun the work some years earlier, after he suspected that he was being swindled by money-changers: 'I was forced to look rather more closely into methods of ready reckoning and to apply myself again to the art of arithmetic with which as a youth I had made some acquaintance.' He had, he said, struggled to complete his treatise over several years – it had not come easily – and he had more than once thought of abandoning his efforts all together. Now, the responsibilities he would face as bishop of London had spurred him on to consider what to do with 'the labours of so many nights', and, in the hope that 'something not without value might be found in these writings for those intending to study arithmetic', he dedicated the work to his friend More, 'you who can also pass the book on to your children for them to read . . .

for them it might be most specially beneficial ... since by nothing are the abilities of young folk more invigorated than by the
study of mathematics'.[9] Here Tunstall revealed that the *De arte
supputandi* was intended above all to be a practical aid to young
people. He believed that facility with arithmetic helped train the
mind, and his book was the first that dealt with the subject in
the modern sense, in contrast to earlier, more abstract studies
of the properties, rather than the applications, of numbers. The
uses of such guidance in the real world were obvious. In the
running of a household, a good grasp of arithmetic played an
important part. Later, both Mary Tudor as princess and Katherine Parr as queen would sign their own accounts.

Like their fellow humanists, Tunstall and More shared a keen
interest in education, and the wider influence of both men can be
seen in the schoolroom of Katherine Parr. Anne Parr, Katherine's
younger sister, herself later said that the children's education was
based on the approach used in the family of Thomas More.[10]
Here boys and girls were educated together, as was the case with
the Parrs until William left home in 1525 to join the household
of Henry VIII's bastard son, the duke of Richmond. By that time
he was twelve years old and the foundation of his education was
already laid.

More's views on the education of women were eloquently
expressed to his children's tutor:

> Though I prefer learning joined with virtue to all the
> treasures of kings, yet renown for learning, when it is not
> united with the good life, is nothing else than splendid and
> notorious ignominy; this would be especially the case in a
> woman. Since erudition in a woman is a new thing and a
> reproach to the sloth of men, many will gladly assail it, and
> impute to literature what is really the fault of nature, think-
> ing from the virtues of the learned to get their own ignorance
> esteemed as virtue. On the other hand, if a woman (and this
> I desire and hope with you as their teacher for all my
> daughters) to eminent virtue should add an outwork of even

moderate skill in literature, I think she will have more profit than if she obtained the riches of Croesus and the beauty of Helen.

He went on to emphasize his belief that there should be no distinction between the education of daughters and sons:

Nor do I think that the harvest will be affected whether it is a man or a woman who sows the field. They both have the same human nature and the power of reasoning differentiates them from the beasts; both, therefore, are equally suited for those studies by which reason is cultivated, and is productive like a ploughed field on which the seed of good lessons has been sown.[11]

This mix of classical allusion and agricultural metaphor was typical of the man and his times, and More's insistence that learning, especially in women, was not an end in itself but could only be fully effective as part of a morally centred approach to life, was a theme found generally among writers on the education of women. The Spanish humanist Juan Luis Vives, in *The Education of a Christian Woman*, a work dedicated to Katherine of Aragon and offered as a blueprint for the upbringing of Princess Mary, emphasized the importance of virtue, domestic skills and womanly restraint, while sharing More's views that women could – and, indeed, should – learn as effectively as men. He held that it was the roles of men and women in society, not their basic intellects, that were different.

In our age, where women's view of themselves has been greatly influenced by the debates on feminism of the second half of the twentieth century, these views sound patronizing rather than progressive. But the sixteenth century had never heard of feminism, and though much has undoubtedly been learned from studying women of the period, 'gender studies' is a modern invention and has become a growth industry. Like all constructs projected on to the past it can be enlightening but also misleading. Maud Parr's approach to the education of her family was

evidently admired by Lord Dacre, who thought it would benefit
his grandson, but the mixed schoolroom at Rye House was also a
product of Maud Parr's situation as a widow who needed to live
within her means. By including pupils from the wider family,
better quality tuition was more affordable and ties of kinship were
reinforced. Families with the right combination of wealth and
social standing had long been able, if they so desired, to educate
their daughters, at least to competent standards of literacy. Much
depended on the aptitude of the girls themselves and the attitude
of the head of the family, who, in Tudor times, was almost
always male. Maud Parr was an exception – not unique, for other
women of her time recognized the benefits of widowhood – and
she undoubtedly wanted the best for her daughters, within the
framework of the society in which she lived. But her son, as we
shall see, was always her priority.

Katherine Parr grew up well aware of this reality. Scripture
told her that women were, indeed, the weaker vessel, fashioned
from Adam's rib, and less perfect than men. St Paul certainly
thought so and the Church establishment over the centuries,
overlooking the more liberal attitude of Jesus himself, had followed suit. Most commentators on the subject considered the
female to be diminished by her sexuality. She existed to bear
children and be a helpmate. In the running of a household this
latter expectation was of considerable importance and was no
lightweight responsibility. Marriage was a partnership of sorts,
but not an equal one. A successful and loving marriage nevertheless allowed scope for the development of personal interests, such
as Katherine herself would welcome in adulthood, and it also
provided security. Meanwhile, her education would equip her to
function fully as a lady of her class.

We do not know who Katherine Parr's tutors were or precisely
what she studied, though an overall impression can be gained
from looking at her interests and attainments as an adult and
from the sort of programme followed by her contemporaries. Her

literacy in English was clearly of a high standard, as she was to demonstrate in her writings as queen of England. The growth of humanism, however, with its concept of 'New Learning', did not itself promote the desirability of the vernacular as the basis of good education, or, indeed, of a worthy life. Rather, it emphasized the need to return to a better, direct understanding of the classical languages of Greece and Rome, so that the scriptures could be read without the interpretation placed on them by centuries of commentary by leading figures of the Church. This belief, that the word of God should be read directly, and applied to civic duty and personal piety, was eventually to be transformed into a conviction that the Bible should be available in the vernacular. Katherine Parr became one of the keenest exponents of this belief, although during her girlhood the leap had not yet been made.

But though the study of classical languages was fundamental for young men, its place in the education of women was less clear. While Mary Tudor learned Latin to a high standard and her younger sister, Elizabeth, studied Greek as well, ideas on education were changing by the time Elizabeth began to learn and both were, of course, the daughters of a king. Their opportunities and expectations were different from those of other young women, even those who were well born. Katherine Parr evidently learned some Latin, but there is still debate about the extent of her abilities in the language. What seems likely is that she acquired a basic knowledge as a child, and that circumstances allowed her to improve significantly as an adult. Few high-born women in the early sixteenth century, no matter how pious, had an extensive knowledge of Latin. Margaret Roper, Thomas More's much-loved daughter, was unusually gifted in the language, but this is hardly surprising with such a father. Other ladies tended to have more modest achievements. Lady Margaret Beaufort, mother of Henry VII, is a good example. She was a clever and influential woman, the benefactress of

St John's College, Cambridge and other academic institutions, but she herself acknowledged that her reading ability in Latin was limited to the headings in her religious books.

Modern languages, however, were a different matter. Katherine learned French and could probably read Italian. At her death, her library contained a copy in Italian of Petrarch's sonnets. This could, of course, indicate merely a desire to have such a book in her possession, as a collector, but she was definitely learning Spanish while married to Henry VIII so it seems quite possible that she was already competent in Italian. Both Katherine's parents could speak French. This was considered a desirable attribute in court circles.

The basic curriculum proposed for children by Tunstall and Vives embraced the leading classical thinkers and writers: Quintilian, Plutarch, Cicero, Homer (in Latin translation) and Aristotle. Erasmus, the English Latinist and medical expert Thomas Linacre and the French scholar Guillaume Budé completed the list. Budé, the founder of the Collège de France, was a prolific writer; diplomat and royal librarian to Francis I, he was regarded by many as the leading Greek scholar of his day. Study of the scriptures was, of course, an essential part of learning. Familiarity with classical scholarship and humanist writers trained the mind, exposing children to ideas and revealing to them first hand the richness of their European inheritance. It also gave to women like Katherine Parr confidence to discuss philosophy and religion and the independence of thought that goes with regular study. In so doing, it produced a tension between the accepted wisdom that even educated women would never play more than a secondary and submissive role in life and the experience of the lives they in fact led. The Tudor queens, Mary and Elizabeth, are prime examples of this dichotomy. Katherine Parr felt it too, and from an early age. She had only to look at her mother to see that being female did not equate to weakness. And Katherine, like a number of other intelligent, well-born girls, does not seem to have been burdened by a feeling of inferiority.

Outside the schoolroom, Katherine Parr developed other interests and enjoyed a variety of pastimes. She liked country pursuits (perhaps encouraged by her uncle) and was a keen rider and hunter. She collected coins, played chess and loved music and dancing. Hers was a comfortable and stimulating upbringing, bounded by strong bonds of family affection. Perhaps she had ambitions, or daydreams, of a much greater future. The story she told her mother that she was not interested in needlework because her hands were made for sceptres is almost certainly apocryphal. But as she left childhood behind, she would have known that her prospects were unlikely to be brilliant. She had no great fortune and no title. Only marriage could bring her those attributes.

LADY PARR began the quest for a husband for Katherine when her daughter was eleven years old. If this seems startlingly young, it should be remembered that the process could take time and, even after the wedding ceremony itself, cohabitation often did not take place until both parties were about sixteen years old. In the recent past, Katherine's female relatives had tended to marry much older men. This was a common-enough occurrence when death in childbirth was frequent and men found themselves widowers not just once, but often several times. It could also be the outcome of the underlying imperative to gain financial and social advancement through marriage wherever possible. Maud Parr knew that she did not have anything outstanding to offer a prospective son-in-law and that she would therefore be unlikely to find a match for Katherine in court circles. The most obvious solution was to find someone from among her extensive network of relatives. Here an opportunity presented itself in the spring of 1523, whether by chance or design we do not know, to take the matter forward.

While the court was at Greenwich, and Maud evidently in attendance on the queen, she discussed Katherine's future with Lord Dacre, Sir Thomas Parr's first cousin. Dacre was a northern

lord of influence and wealth who spent much of his life holding
the borders of England against the Scots for successive kings far
away in London. A Yorkist, like the Parrs and many other
northerners, he accepted the Tudors and fought well for them,
at Flodden and in continuing border skirmishes; but the relationship was always uneasy. His military prowess and local power
was praised by the poet earl of Surrey, whose admiration was
not easily won. In April 1523 Lord Dacre was at court but had
to leave to deal with yet another threatened Scottish invasion.
There must have been many calls on his time and patience, but
somehow Maud Parr managed to get his attention before his
departure to talk to him about finding a suitable candidate for
the hand of her elder daughter. This says a great deal about
Maud's powers of persuasion and the ties of family. The outcome was that Dacre agreed to try to facilitate a marriage between
his grandson, Henry Scrope, and Katherine Parr. He evidently
responded with enthusiasm to the idea of a union that would
strengthen family links in the north and, with his encouragement, negotiations began between Lady Parr and Lord Scrope of
Bolton.

They did not fare well. Dacre may have been a formidable
soldier and scourge of the Scots, but his son-in-law resisted
doing his bidding. Scrope's disdain for the match is palpable;
Katherine Parr was neither rich enough nor good enough for his
son. Still, his response was not one of outright refusal; instead,
he stalled and then put forward terms that were unacceptable
to Maud Parr. She thought that she had agreed the detail with
Lord Dacre, but Scrope did not like what had been proposed.
Maud was understandably irritated. 'Where it pleased you at your
last being here,' she wrote to Dacre in July 1523,

> to take pain in the matter in consideration of marriage
> between Lord Scrope's son and my daughter Katherine, for
> the which I heartily thank you; at which time I thought the
> matter in good furtherance. Howbeit, I perceive that my said
> Lord Scrope is not agreeable to the consideration, as more

plainly may appear unto you by certain articles sent to me
. . . the copy of which articles I send you herein enclosed.[12]

Scrope wanted a full answer to his counter-proposals by the
beginning of August, and she needed Dacre's help.

She disliked several aspects of Scrope's proposed articles and
made it clear that she wanted to stick to what had been agreed
with Lord Dacre. 'Glad I would be to have the matter go forth if
might be conveniently: if it please you to call to remembrance the
matter before you at Greenwich was that I should pay at your
desire 1,100 marks, whereof 100 marks in hand, and every year
after 100 marks, which is as much as I can spare, as you know.'
Scrope wanted his money in too much of a hurry: 'I am content
with the first day, but the residue of his days of payment be too
short for me.' She was also perturbed that, as Scrope's conditions spelled out, 'The said Lord Scrope will not agree to repay
no money after the marriage is solemnized and executed, nor
to enter into no covenant especially for the governance of the
children during the nonage of them.' As the children were not to
live together until Henry Scrope was fourteen and Katherine Parr
twelve, Maud recognized that she would lose her money if death
or disagreement intervened. Meanwhile, she still had to feed,
clothe and educate her daughter at her own expense.

Maud was by no means impoverished; the amount she was
willing to offer at her daughter's marriage is the equivalent of
about £323,000 today. But she had always been prudent and
could not afford to write this off as Lord Scrope was insisting
she must if, for any reason, the marriage should be solemnized
but nothing more. There is something in her tone that suggests
she already suspected nothing would come of her overtures, but
she could not bring herself to back down yet. Though she might
be a widow, she was not willing to give up without seeing if the
application of further pressure would swing matters her way.

Lord Dacre was in Newcastle when he replied on 30 July. He
was disappointed, even slightly harassed, but he promised that
he would pursue the question of Katherine Parr's marriage:

Cousin, since my departure from you I assure you I was not two nights together in mine own house, by reason whereof I never had leisure to labour in these matters. And I do think, seeing my Lord Scrope cannot be content with the communications that was had at my last being with you, which was thought reasonable to me ... that this matter cannot be brought to no perfect end without mutual communication to be had with my said lord, either by myself, my son or my brother. Wherefore, as soon as conveniently any of us may be spared, this matter shall be laboured.

He remained confident of a satisfactory outcome for the Parr–Dacre–Scrope connection, having extracted (or so he then believed) a promise from his daughter and son-in-law 'that they shall not marry their son without my consent, which they shall not have to no person but unto you'. He counselled patience: 'be not overhasty', he concluded, 'but suffer and finally ye shall be well assured that I shall do in this matter, or in any other that is or may be either pleasure, profit, or surety, to you or my said cousin, your daughter, that lieth in my power'.[13]

This was a hearty assurance and an eloquent witness of the abiding strength of family in sixteenth-century England. But it did not suffice to bring about a wedding between young Katherine Parr and Henry Scrope. At the end of 1523 Lord Dacre was still in the north of England. He wrote to his son-in-law recognizing that there was too large a distance between Scrope's demands and what Lady Parr would accept, desiring him to re-open negotiations. He urged the importance of family ties, 'the wisdom of my said Lady, and the good wise stock of the Greenes whereof she is come, and also the wise stock of the Parrs of Kendal'. He understood Scrope's concerns, acknowledging that 'your son and heir is the greatest jewel that ye can have', but he fully believed that the lad would fare extremely well if he was educated in the Parr household with his young bride. There he could learn 'French and other languages, which meseems were a commodious thing for him'. And Dacre further dangled as a carrot the possibility that, were Katherine Parr to die, her younger sister Anne would have her marriage portion as well.

None of this was sufficient to change Lord Scrope's mind. Perhaps he did not care whether his son became a competent linguist. In Wharfedale, where he lived and where his son would inherit, it was much less of an attraction than in the court at Greenwich. Maud became progressively frustrated and disenchanted. Eventually, she turned to Cuthbert Tunstall for advice and his view was unequivocal: the matter should be dropped. So Maud wrote to Lord Dacre in March 1524, thanking him for his 'manifold pains' but saying that 'I have taken advice of my Lord of London and divers others of my husband's friends and mine, who think that my said Lord Scrope's offer . . . is so little and so far from the customs of the country, and his demand is so great and so large of me, with short payment, that my said friends will in no wise that I shall meddle with the said bargain after my Lord Scrope's offer and demand.'

The matter had, she went on, 'been so long in cogitation, I am right sorry on my part it cannot take effect'.[14] She had wanted this marriage above all for Katherine and was extremely disappointed that it would not now take place.

Lord Dacre was clearly offended by the outcome, sending a terse reply and pointing out that 'Lord Scrope demanded nothing but it that ye were content without the meddling of any person to give' – presumably a dig at Cuthbert Tunstall. But the truth was that he had not been able to influence the outcome to the satisfaction of either party. The following year Henry Scrope died and Maud's concerns were fully vindicated. By this time she was turning her attention to her son's future. His marriage, she naturally thought, was the key to ensuring the family's fortunes. Katherine would have to wait.

⤬

MAUD'S RESILIENT SPIRIT did not allow her to remain disheart-
ened over the setback to Katherine's prospects. She believed she
had reason to be much more optimistic over William. In 1525,
at the age of twelve, Katherine's brother joined the household of
the duke of Richmond, the six-year-old illegitimate son of Henry
VIII and Elizabeth Blount. His entrée was easily arranged: Sir
William Parr of Horton, his uncle, had been appointed chamberlain of the child's separate establishment, which was to be based
at Sheriff Hutton Castle in Yorkshire. Here Richmond would
preside, at least nominally, over the Council of the North, an
institution that existed to manage the king's affairs in this unruly
and distant part of England. It was thought desirable to include
other young boys in the little duke's entourage, and so William
Parr, though much older, prepared to leave his mother and sisters,
in the company of his uncle. It seemed like a stroke of good luck.
William's education would be completed by the very best tutors
and he would mix with the sons of other prominent families,
under the attentive eye of his uncle. Maud herself entertained the
retinue on the second stage of its journey north, and it was
recorded that at her house 'his Grace was marvellously well
intreated and had good cheer'.[15] Lady Parr also gave Richmond a
pony, a 'grey ambling nag', with which he was clearly delighted,
preferring to ride on it rather than sit in his splendid litter and
be carried to Yorkshire.

    It soon became apparent, however, that being part of the
Richmond household was not the great passport to success that
Parr of Horton had anticipated for himself and his nephew.
Henry VIII was very fond of his bastard son but he never had
any intention of naming him as his heir. The king was a stickler
for legitimacy when it came to his dynasty. His determination to
pursue his divorce from Katherine of Aragon took shape while
Richmond was in the north, and, despite setbacks and frustrations, he held firm over a period of six years. It has been claimed
that Maud Parr and her brother-in-law coached William to make
sure that he ingratiated himself with Richmond, in case the duke

ever became the official heir, but there is no evidence to support this.[16] In fact, the family association with Richmond may have been some embarrassment to Maud in her relationship with Katherine of Aragon, who had bitterly opposed the granting of a title and personal household to her husband's illegitimate off-spring.

Nor, as Sir William was soon to discover, were there great opportunities for financial benefit or wider influence. The house-hold was controlled by Wolsey from London and he expected it to be run tightly. It was he, not Richmond's chamberlain, who granted access, office and additional benefits that normally came with such a role. There were limited possibilities for supple-menting Parr of Horton's basic salary of £26 13s and 4d (about £12,500 today). And there were also other, daily frustrations. Almost from the moment that the household arrived at Sheriff Hutton, tensions developed between the duke of Richmond's tutors and the household officers under Parr of Horton.

In essence these had to do with a difference of opinion on the balance between recreation and study for the duke and his schoolfellows. Sir William was a countryman who thought it perfectly natural for boys to prefer hunting and sports to the boring recitation of Latin and Greek verbs from dawn till dusk. The increasingly unruly behaviour of Richmond and the other boys, who included two of the duke's maternal uncles and John Scrope, the only surviving junior member of the family that had rejected Katherine Parr, seems to have been viewed with amuse-ment by Parr and his colleagues. After six months, John Pals-grave, Richmond's first tutor, felt he could no longer take being undermined and belittled, and resigned his post. He had been schoolmaster to Princess Mary Tudor, Henry VIII's sister, and was a prominent scholar of French, with excellent links among the leading humanists of his day. Although he understood the still-feudal attraction of leading from the front, he defended the fundamental importance of education: 'Some think that learning doth make one cowardish but Alexander's and Caesar's acts prove the contrary.'[17] He could not endure the poisonous atmosphere at Sheriff Hutton. His successor, Richard Croke, ran into even greater difficulties, of which he complained loud and long. An ordained priest (as were many tutors at that time), Croke encountered derision and anticlericalism. He soon found that he had no control over his charge at all. Even the threat of corporal punishment was countered with 'Master, if you beat me, I will beat you.'[18]

Such was the household over which Parr of Horton presided as chamberlain. Suspicious of schoolmaster priests, and contemptuous of anyone he considered of lesser birth, though he was not, of course, a nobleman himself, the spell in Yorkshire showed another, less amiable side of Katherine Parr's uncle. For her brother, the experience was a far cry from the pleasant schoolroom and family atmosphere of Rye House. Though it introduced young William to a select circle whose friendship was important later in his life (Edward Seymour, brother of Queen Jane Seymour, was master of the horse to Richmond), it did nothing for the immediate fortunes of the Parr family. If Parr of Horton had spent less time in acrimonious struggles with Richmond's tutors and devoted more attention to his own responsibilities, he might have escaped censure. A disorganized and incomplete approach to accounting could not conceal that the household was overmanned and too expensive. Reductions were made but, by the time Richmond was ordered back from Yorkshire in the summer of 1529, Sir William Parr of Horton was suitably embittered by his failure to find any personal profit or advancement out of his sojourn in the north.

The episode was, however, less negative in its impact on young William Parr. His uncle may not have covered the family name in glory or added to its influence, but his mother was very active in pursuing a splendid marriage for him. In February 1527, at the age of thirteen, William Parr, a good-looking boy of affable disposition, was married to Anne Bourchier (pronounced

Bowser), the only daughter and heiress of the elderly earl of Essex, in the chapel of Essex's country seat, Stansted Hall. Maud Parr, who lived close to the family home of the earl's wife, had cajoled, pressured and bought her son's way into the English aristocracy. The earl of Essex was in debt and he asked a high price for his daughter's hand; Maud had to borrow from Cuthbert Tunstall, several other of her late husband's close friends, the guild of mercers and even the king himself, to meet the asking price for Lady Anne. Apart from the lands she stood to inherit, the hope must also have been that William Parr's child-bride would bring him her father's title when the earl died.

William Parr did, eventually, become earl of Essex in 1543, the year his sister Katherine became Henry VIII's last queen; it was her elevation, not his marriage, that brought him the long-coveted title. By then, it was obvious that his relationship with Anne Bourchier was beyond repair. The union was one of the most unhappy marriages of the sixteenth century on record. Perhaps Anne resented being married so young – she was only nine at the time – to a boy of inferior rank; their interests and intellects were widely divergent and her childhood dislike turned into full-blown hatred as an adult. Maud Parr died before the rift between them became fully obvious, and her bequest of jewellery to her daughter-in-law to be received 'when she lyeth with my son', often cited as an inducement to the recalcitrant girl, is more readily explained by the fact that Anne was still only fourteen years old and a year or so below the age when she would be expected to cohabit with her spouse.

We do not know whether Katherine Parr attended her brother's wedding in Essex. They were always close and she would, no doubt, have wished him well. But she must also have known that her mother had nothing left to find her a husband of comparable rank. She could expect to be married respectably, but nothing more. Two more years passed before her future was decided. Then, in the spring of 1529, at the age of nearly

Part Two

Wife and Widow

1529–1543

CHAPTER THREE

The Marriage Game

'I am indebted to Sir Thomas Borough, knight, for the marriage of my daughter.'

Maud Parr's will, May 1529

GAINSBOROUGH WAS a port on the river Trent, already steeped in history when Katherine Parr arrived there as a young bride. 'Then runneth the Trent down to Gainsborough, a town ennobled by reason of the Danes ships that lay there at rode,' wrote the celebrated sixteenth-century antiquary William Camden. It was also, he added, notorious for the death of the colourfully named Danish tyrant Sweyn Tings-Kege, 'who after he had robbed and spoiled the country . . . being here stabbed to death by an unknown man, suffered due punishment . . . Many a year after this it became the possession of Sir William de Valence, Earl of Pembroke, who obtained for it of King Edward I the liberty to keep a fair. From which earl by the Scottish earls of Athol and the Percies, descended from the Barons of Borough who here dwelt . . .'[1]

Katherine's new home was in one of the most isolated of all English shires. Both topographically and culturally, Lincolnshire was a distinctive place, its agricultural flatlands, marshes and coastline contrasted with the range of hills known as the Wolds. It was the most distant county to be ruled directly from London;

the rest of the north of England came under the administration of the Council of the North. To Katherine, it must have seemed a very different place from the more prosperous, populated south, a world away from the stimulation of court gossip and intrigues which she had known, indirectly through her parents, all her life. Most southerners viewed this part of the world with a prejudice based on ignorance. Inhabitants of the fenlands, for example, were thought to be slightly less than human and Henry VIII famously described the common people of his second largest county as 'one of the most brute and beastly of the whole kingdom'.[2] This attitude clearly communicated itself to his successors. There was no royal visit to Lincolnshire between 1541 and 1617. Unloved and remote, it was almost frontier territory. There was only one major overland access from the south, via the Great North Road at Stamford. Otherwise, it had to be reached by coastal voyage to ports such as Grimsby or Skegness. Two of its largest towns, Lincoln itself and Boston, were in decline during the Tudor period.

Though rich agriculturally, Lincolnshire had few major landowners at the time that Katherine Parr married into the Borough family. The Boroughs, like many of their neighbours, were knighted gentry. This absence of an obvious rallying point for royal authority added a further dimension to the area's perceived awkwardness and isolation. Not until the mid-1530s, when Charles Brandon, duke of Suffolk, married his ward, the local heiress Katherine Willoughby, was there a great lord in Lincolnshire. Brandon's second duchess (his first had been the king's sister, Princess Mary Tudor), was to become, by a strange coincidence, a close friend of Katherine Parr in the next decade.

The rural landscape of Lincolnshire was not marked by major castles but it had a deep-rooted monastic heritage. Fifty-one monasteries, covering all the great orders except the Cluniacs, bore witness to the enduring importance of religion in the east midlands. The Gilbertines, the only religious order originating in England, had been founded by St Gilbert of Sempringham (a village in the Lincolnshire fens) in 1131. Not all the houses were wealthy but most, despite the inevitable lapses into apathy and occasional sexual irregularity uncovered in visitations, were respected by local people.

Life in this part of England continued to be dominated by the cycles of the agricultural year, the need for self-sufficiency and a straightforward faith in God. These all contributed to a strong sense of local identity. The area was noted for the independence of mind of its inhabitants and their capacity for rebellion. Lincolnshire folk by no means did what they were told and they could carry much of the rest of the north of England with them, an uncomfortable truth insufficiently appreciated by the king and government in London. From the perspective of an outsider like Katherine Parr, even though her mother owned a number of manors not far from Gainsborough, it was a very different environment from the one she had known. There was much to be learned and a great deal of adapting to do.

ONE SOURCE of pleasure, amidst all this uncertainty, must have been her new home itself. Her surroundings, at least, were gracious, comfortable and even opulent, certainly by local standards. The mansion of the Boroughs dominated the small town of Gainsborough and today is one of the most impressive fifteenth-century manor houses surviving in Britain. It was built of red brick and timber, a style that became increasingly popular during Tudor times, and originally it had a moat and a gatehouse, which have long since disappeared. Rebuilt after its destruction during the Wars of the Roses by a Lancastrian army that included many of the first Lord Borough's personal enemies, the house rose up even grander than before. An inventory recorded that it consisted of '[a] hall, a parlour, an inner parlour, a withdrawing room, a great chamber with another next to it, a chamber in the tower and in the gallery'.[3] There were further rooms originally described but part of the inventory is long since lost. The west wing had three floors of lodgings, with brick walls at the back and a fireplace and privy for each room.[4] This early version of 'en-suite accommodation' shows how much the Boroughs anticipated entertaining. Certainly their great, open high-vaulted hall and the well-designed kitchen were amply suited to feed even a king. The house received two royal visitors, Richard III during his brief reign and, later, Henry VIII and Katherine Howard. Gainsborough Old Hall may have been a long journey from London, but it was not lacking in sophistication. 'Almost every room was hung with tapestries and the bed in the lower chamber had a canopy of chequered velvet and cloth of gold.'[5]

The Borough family themselves, distant kin of the Parrs, had a history as eventful as that of the building in which they sought to display their wealth and influence. Their rise through the turmoil of the Wars of the Roses mirrored that of Katherine's family. The first Lord Borough, great-grandfather of Katherine's husband, had been an esquire of the body and master of the horse to Edward IV, as well as a royal councillor, roles which had also been held at different times by Katherine's grandfather and great-uncle. The success of the Boroughs and the Parrs was ample evidence of the truth of the old dictum about servants of the Privy Chamber: 'theyre business is many secretes'. Like Sir William Parr, Thomas Borough was well rewarded by Edward IV and he, too, married a rich widow, was given extensive local responsibilities and negotiated the regime change smoothly when Henry VII came to the throne. In fact, in one crucial respect, he outdid the Parrs. In 1487 he became a lord and was given the title of baron of Gainsborough. So Katherine Parr was marrying into a family that had already achieved a title, with the prospect, in due course, of becoming Lady Borough herself. What the Boroughs had not done, however, was consolidate their personal standing with the Tudors by service at court.

In fact, the positive relationship that had benefited the first Lord Borough was already declining at the time of his death in the mid-1490s. It seems likely that the family already met considerable problems with the fragile mental state of Edward, the second Lord Borough. He had certainly attended court, where his prowess as a horseman was noted at a tournament to honour the young Prince Henry, and he enhanced the family fortunes by marrying a wealthy Kentish heiress; but all was not well. In late 1495 he had been made to bind himself in legal recognizance to the king and was placed in the custody of the lord chamberlain. Perhaps the dispute was initially about money – Henry VII valued his aristocracy more for their purses than their equestrian skills – but, whatever the cause, Edward Borough ended up in the Fleet prison. His escape from that institution put him in debt to the Crown to the tune of £3,000, which had a catastrophic effect on his family's immediate prospects.

If Edward Borough had been emotionally unstable at the time of his dispute with Henry VII, the outcome only made him worse. By 1510 he was judged as 'having unsound mind with lucid intervals'. His estates were administered by the Crown and the profits from them helped to repay debts from Henry VIII's French wars. Edward continued to live at Gainsborough Old Hall, but it fell to his eldest son, Sir Thomas Borough, to put all the effort into restoring the family's estates and local standing. It was Sir Thomas, who, as Maud Parr acknowledged in her will, became the relatively young father-in-law of Katherine Parr less than a year after the death of his own, troubled parent.

A lot of nonsense has been written in historical novels about Katherine Parr's first marriage. Even her most recent biographer, while making quite clear that her husband was not the elderly Lord Edward Borough but his young grandson, refers to Katherine's life at Gainsborough Hall with 'a lunatic rattling his chains in the attic'. It is a colourful image, but Lord Edward died in August 1528, well before Katherine's wedding to his namesake. If there were noises of chains in the attic, they must have been from the tragic lord's ghost.[6]

It was, though, a difficult situation for a young woman from a happy and stable background, dominated by a very competent mother, to find herself in a troubled family tightly governed by a strong-willed and opinionated father. Sir Thomas Borough had been compelled to take over the day-to-day running of his family's affairs at an early age. He had seen his father disgraced and removed from society and his own prospects compromised as a result. Not for him the courtly entertainments of Greenwich that had figured so largely in the lives of Sir Thomas and Lady Maud Parr. Though personally brave (he was knighted after the battle of Flodden) and appointed one of the king's aristocratic bodyguards, the King's Spears, he was not close to Henry VIII and was seldom at court. The responsibility of keeping his family together meant that he spent most of his time in Lincolnshire, where he married Agnes Tyrwhit, the daughter of another leading family in the county, produced sons of his own and devoted himself to giving his offspring the direction of a strong father-figure that he himself had never known.

That he comes across through the centuries as harsh and over-bearing is not surprising. He was certainly a difficult man, but he was not some ancient tyrant. Born in 1494, he was thirty-five at the time of his eldest son's wedding, which surely means that Katherine Parr's bridegroom could not have been, at the most, more than a few years older than she. It must have been clear to an intelligent young woman like Katherine, right from the outset of her marriage, that if she could not establish a reasonable relationship with Lord Borough, then life at Gainsborough would be a struggle.[7] Her father-in-law was a man of his times and, as master of the household, he expected obedience. He does not seem to have mellowed as he grew older. In 1537 Lady Elizabeth Borough, wife of his second son, wrote in despair to Thomas Cromwell, the Lord Privy Seal, complaining of the 'trouble she is put to by Lord Borough, who always lies in wait to put her to shame'. She had heard that her father-in-law had complained of her to the Privy Council, declaring that her child was not his son's. She begged Cromwell to prevent the little boy from being disinherited, adding that her husband 'dare do nothing but as his father will have him'.[8] But Borough was implacable. Elizabeth was thrown out and her children declared illegitimate.

Katherine evidently managed the irascible Thomas Borough more successfully. What he thought of her upbringing and scholastic attainments we do not know. Perhaps she did not parade them too openly, but there is no reason to assume that her father-in-law did not value learning as such. Indeed, he was himself interested in the new religious ideas and kept a reforming chaplain in his household. He did not want his children to question him, but on spiritual matters he had a much more open mind. And he was also sufficiently proud of his wife, and sensitive to the power of the court and its connexions, to arrange for her to be painted by Hans Holbein. He became Anne Boleyn's chamberlain after Katherine had left his care, and a dedicated supporter of the Royal Supremacy and the suppression of the Pilgrimage of Grace of 1536. His household when Katherine lived there must have been an uneasy place, but it was by no means sterile.

She did not live under his roof for long, and the fact that she escaped it at all, without recriminations, says much for her powers of persuasion. It also suggests that Thomas Borough could be flexible when he chose. About two years after their marriage, Katherine and her husband were permitted to set up their own household at Kirton-in-Lindsey, a dozen miles from Gainsborough. Perhaps Thomas Borough felt that it was appropriate for his eldest son and heir to live independently by then. If so, he must have had considerable confidence in Katherine as well. No doubt he hoped they would produce children to carry on the Borough name, but none appeared. If Katherine was ever pregnant by Edward Borough (and it is possible that she was expecting a child when the idea of a separate household was raised), then clearly none survived to full term, or certainly past early infancy. The historical record is completely silent on this point, and though her immediate family must have known, they never seem to have spoken of it and neither did Katherine herself.

The indirect evidence is contradictory but what can be said is that her subsequent husbands all seem to have believed that she could bear children. Whether this was based on optimism as opposed to her past history we cannot know, but it is, of course, indisputable that almost two decades after she and Edward Borough were married, she bore a healthy child.

It was not birth, but death that coloured Katherine's life over the next few years. At the end of 1531, Maud Parr died in London. She was laid to rest beside the husband whose interests she had so ably supported all her adult life. She was only thirty-nine and her passing was a great sadness for her children. In her will she left Katherine Borough, her eldest child, seventeen different items of jewellery, including 'a ring with a great pointed diamond set with black enamel', a 'pair of bracelets, chain fashion, with two jacinths [garnets] in them' and a 'tablet with pictures of the king and queen'.[9] At the time of her death Maud, like everyone else, must have known that the marriage of Henry VIII and Katherine of Aragon was probably beyond repair. The king was already four years into the process of seeking a divorce. But King Henry and Katherine of Aragon had been the most important people in her life after her husband and children, and the portrait of them was very dear to her. She wanted her own Katherine to have it. Typical of the kind of woman she was, Maud also left monies for the founding of schools and the marrying of maidens, the latter bequest intended to help the less fortunate members of her wider family.

Scarcely before she had accustomed herself to life without her mother's guiding hand, Katherine also lost her husband. Edward had begun to establish a local role for himself at Kirton-in-Lindsey, serving as a justice of the peace, but by the early spring of 1533 he was dead. Katherine, at the age of twenty, found herself a widow with no child or significant wealth to give her comfort in life. She had little claim on her in-laws and neither they nor Katherine seem to have wanted her to return to reside with them. Thomas Borough did not, though, just cast her aside.

He provided Katherine with a small income from three of his southern manors (two in Surrey and one in Kent), but with this his generosity was at an end. He was, in any case, probably much more concerned with the new position he had been given as Anne Boleyn's chamberlain and in the arrangements for her coronation, in which he played a prominent part. Determined to show that he was a strong supporter of the Boleyns, he was in London for much of the heady summer of 1533. Katherine's future could not have greatly preoccupied him.

FACING AN uncertain future and with no home to call her own, Katherine Parr disappeared, briefly, from public record. But she had friends in the north, and they were people of influence. Cuthbert Tunstall, an important figure in her childhood, had been appointed bishop of Durham and president of the Council of the North in 1530. His presence must have been a comfort and she would have undoubtedly looked to him for guidance. His careful positioning on delicate matters such as the royal divorce demonstrated his grasp of political reality. By 1533 he had accepted that Katherine of Aragon's cause was hopeless, whatever his personal disapproval of the king's actions. This pragmatism (some would call it trimming) ensured his survival when the consciences of others, like his friend Thomas More, took them to the executioner's block. To Katherine Parr he was of far more help alive and still exercising his influence with his contacts than he would have been as a glorious martyr.

She also had her own resilient character, inherited from both her parents, to see her through these uncertain times, and the comfort that her brother William and sister Anne were making their own way in life. Anne Parr had arrived at the court, family connections no doubt helping to find her a place, and she was to serve all Henry's queens from the mid-1530s. William, meanwhile, was starting to move with as much assurance at court as his father had done at the beginning of Henry VIII's reign,

helped by the people he had known as a boy in the household of
the duke of Richmond. His charm and sociability brought him
many friends, including the earl of Surrey and Sir Thomas Wyatt,
the poet who had been in love with Anne Boleyn. It was evident
that the fortunes of the Parrs were still rising and that Katherine
would eventually benefit from this.

So her life had changed, but not necessarily for the worse.
She was not abandoned, merely waiting to see what opportunities
would present themselves. Tradition has it that she passed the
twelve months after Edward Borough's death at Sizergh Castle
in Cumbria, the imposing ancestral home of the Strickland
family. This beautiful castle outside Kendal would have been a
wonderful place to recover from grief and consider the direction
her life might take. Sizergh was already nearly 350 years old at
the time of Katherine's reputed residence there. The house and
grounds were on a much larger scale than the Old Hall in
Gainsborough, providing many opportunities for quiet contem-
plation. But it seems that the young widow was not idle during
her stay; a piece of embroidery, which can still be seen at the
castle, is said to be her work.

The dowager Lady Strickland, born Katherine Neville, was
one of Katherine's many cousins on her father's side and was also
related to the Boroughs. Perhaps she felt she had a double
obligation to provide temporary shelter. The later appointment
of William Kynyatt, Lady Strickland's third husband, as auditor
to Katherine Parr when she became queen, is evidence of the
closeness of the two women. These family ties, and the way they
were used, are one of the most distinctive features of sixteenth-
century life. They provided a network of support and reward that
went far beyond the limits of the modern, more confined family
relationships to which we are accustomed. And they could be
particularly valuable to a woman like Katherine, whose immediate
kin were geographically distant and not yet quite well enough
placed, in the case of either of her siblings, to help launch her
back into the wider marriage market.

For a second marriage, and a better one, if possible, was the only option for Katherine Parr, a fact she would undoubtedly have known. She was clever, attractive and good-natured, not rich, but well born and well connected. Circumstances made it unlikely that a southern gentleman would suddenly appear to claim her. In this respect her brother could not help her. Indeed, there were already signs that he might be in need of marital advice himself, as attempts at cohabiting with his wife, now she had reached the age of sixteen, had not been successful.

Yet in Tudor England, a woman of Katherine Parr's quality was unlikely to remain single for long. By the summer of 1534 a suitable husband had been found for her, probably through the combined efforts of Lady Strickland and Bishop Tunstall. The man was John Neville, Lord Latimer, a relative of both Katherine and her hostess at Sizergh. Twice married and twice widowed, he had a title, a castle at Snape in North Yorkshire and an established role in northern politics. And he was also father to a fourteen-year-old son and nine-year-old daughter, who had been without a maternal figure in their lives for four years, following the death of a previous stepmother in 1530. Now they were to have an even younger woman to fill that role. Katherine Parr was barely twenty-two when she became Latimer's third wife and moved to a new life in the pleasant countryside of the Yorkshire Dales.

CHAPTER FOUR

Lady Latimer

'I am never able to render to her grace sufficient thanks for
the godly education and tender love and bountiful goodness
which I have ever more found in her highness.'

Margaret Neville's generous tribute to her stepmother,
Queen Katherine Parr, in her will of 1545

IT WOULD BE EASY to be cynical, to say that it could not possibly
have been a love match, this alliance between a very young and
financially insecure widow and a northern baron twice her age
who needed companionship and wanted a woman's presence in
the lives of his two children. In the Tudor age, love was a
relatively minor consideration where marriage was concerned.
The cementing of family ties, the enhancement of wealth and
social prospects, these all figured much more prominently. In
balancing decisions on such an important step, romance seldom
figured. A sensible marriage, based on a proper understanding of
what both parties brought to the union and their shared values,
was more desirable than the unpredictable consequences of falling
in love, which seldom fitted into the scheme of things in the
sixteenth century.

This does not mean, however, that love was not a factor at all
in the marriage of Katherine and Lord Latimer. She may have
felt little more than a fondness tinged with gratitude at the

outset, but Katherine developed a genuine affection for her
husband over the nine years of their marriage. When she died,
she still had a copy of his New Testament with his name
inscribed in it. On his side, in particular, the attractions of his
third bride seem to have outweighed any concerns he might have
harboured about her ability to manage his home and help shape
the lives of his son and daughter.

The earliest known portrait of Katherine dates from the
period of her marriage to Lord Latimer. It is a striking image.
The young woman in the picture is blessed with good features,
an oval-shaped face with a firm jawline and a clear complexion.
But it is the overall impression of intelligence and intensity that
is so compelling. She is not quite beautiful but there is an inner
strength in the face that commands attention. Katherine looks
confident and resolute without seeming imperious. This is no
giddy girl, rather a woman of grace and a maturity that belies her
years. The portrait is carefully composed and Katherine evidently
gave a great deal of thought to how she wished to look and what
she would wear. The final result must have met with the approval
both of Katherine and her husband. She is very much the
aristocratic lady, expensively dressed and already demonstrating a
love of jewels and fashion that was to develop over the years. Her
clothing is red and gold, with the hood perfectly matching the
gown. Interestingly, although the gown has fashionable slashed
undersleeves and a gauzy partlet, covering the throat and chest,
the coifed gable hood that Katherine is wearing was a more
conservative choice. Anne Boleyn had made popular the French
hood, which showed more of the hair, but in some circles it was
still considered rather unseemly. Jane Seymour favoured the gable
hood, though this may have been less a personal preference than
a conscious decision to differentiate herself from her more flighty,
disgraced predecessor. In Katherine Parr's case, she had married
a man whose overall outlook was conservative and it is possible
that her head-wear reflected his taste. Her jewels, three ropes of
pearls and a large, round gold, pearl and ruby brooch, are also a

sign of wealth without ostentation. In this portrait, Katherine is very much the elegant nobleman's wife.

Yet she is clearly also a woman of depth of character, and it was this, as much as her undoubted style, that Latimer had perceived. Perhaps he detected in her what others were to remark upon later, a serenity that was not without passion when aroused, a good mind and a steadiness of purpose that would serve their relationship well. He knew that the Borough marriage and life at Gainsborough Hall could not have been full of merriment, but Katherine's essential vivacity had survived a stern test. She would undoubtedly face other trials in her new life at Snape Castle, Latimer's principal residence.

He had certainly not rushed into finding a new wife. Elizabeth Musgrave, his second spouse, had died in 1530 after barely two years of marriage. The gap between her death and Latimer's wedding to Katherine suggests that he was more concerned to find the right woman than merely to fill the empty place in his bed. It must have been a difficult time, as political duties called him away frequently, sometimes to attend meetings of the Council of the North and sometimes further afield, to London, where attendance at parliamentary sessions was required. His children were left at home in Yorkshire, presumably under the care of tutors and household staff. We know little of his family arrangements during the early 1530s, but as one of two members for Yorkshire in the House of Commons during the Reformation Parliament in 1529 and then as a member of the House of Lords two years later, after he had succeeded to the Latimer barony he was not always present in person to supervise his home and family. A new wife could be a proper helpmate to him and Katherine Parr's reappearance on the marriage market provided him with the opportunity to fill that role.

What sort of a man had Katherine taken as her second husband? Certainly John Neville, who became Baron Latimer at the end of 1530 following the death of his father, Richard

Neville, was a complete contrast to Edward Borough. He was over forty years old, an experienced man of the world, a soldier, legislator and administrator. His was one of the oldest and most powerful families in northern England, with a long tradition of military service and a reputation for seeking power at the cost of loyalty to the Crown, best exemplified by Warwick the King-maker. The Parrs' relationship with the Nevilles had always been that of a client family rather than one of equals, and Katherine's grandfather, William Parr, had, as we have seen, found it extremely difficult to extricate himself from this connection back in 1471. It might appear that Katherine's marriage to John Neville continued the tradition of the Parr obligation to their ennobled kin. But times were changing and the Parrs, through circumstance and intelligent appraisal of their situation, were better placed to reap the rewards of political and religious turmoil. They represented the new and Lord Latimer the old, though this was not yet fully apparent.

So Katherine had married a much older man who, despite his frequent sojourns in the capital, was very much the provincial nobleman. He was, at heart, a Yorkshireman who was uncomfort-able with the foetid air of intrigue that hung over court and parliament in London. He preferred the quiet life, the traditional ways of Church worship, the day-to-day challenge of managing an estate that was already in financial difficulties. In April 1534, with his new marriage very close, he wrote to Thomas Cromwell, the king's chief minister, about the problems he was encountering in paying off family debts:

> As I have been at every prorogation of Parliament nearly these four years, which has been very painful and chargeable to me, as I have not yet paid the king all that is due for the livery of my lands, nor all the sums I am bound to pay by the wills of my father and mother-in-law, I beg you will give me leave to tarry at home and be absent from the next prorogation. I shall be in better readiness to do the king

service against the Scots when we in these parts are called
upon.[1]

In these few sentences, Latimer summed up the problems
that beset many of the Tudor nobility: the expenses incurred in
inheriting a title, the duties of involvement in national legislation
and the obligation to defend the monarch from foreign enemies.
Cromwell received so many of these begging letters that he
seldom took any notice of them, even when they were accompanied by 'gifts' such as the gelding that Latimer provided on
this occasion. The horse may have added to Cromwell's stable,
but not necessarily his respect for Lord Latimer. In time, he
would ask for considerably more.

Latimer knew the leading politicians and noblemen of the
realm but does not seem to have liked many of them, or been
able to influence them. He had few friends at court beyond
William Fitzwilliam, the son of a Yorkshire knight, who was a
Neville on his mother's side. Fitzwilliam grew up as Henry VIII's
companion and was very close to both the king and Cromwell;
these connections may well have saved Latimer's life in 1537 in
the aftermath of the Pilgrimage of Grace. For Katherine's husband was not very effective at pleading his own cause. He was
inclined to compromise, avoiding confrontation. This may seem
sensible, but it was not what was expected of the nobility; strong
leadership and unquestioning devotion to the king were highly
prized in the 1530s. It could only have been a matter of time
before Katherine realized she had married a man who worried a
lot, an endearing ditherer who viewed soldiering as a duty rather
than an opportunity for heroism, though he had been knighted
in Lille during the French campaign of 1513. Her new husband
was also slow to make decisions. When he did, they often
betrayed a lack of judgement.

Yet Latimer had many positive attributes. He was neither
cruel nor vindictive – he was no wife-beater, like the duke of
Norfolk – and he was not controlling or unfaithful. He strove to

be a good provider, even if he was not always a valiant protector. And in fairness to Latimer, his life was very far from straightforward. He was the eldest of fifteen children, with many younger brothers over whom he was supposed (but often failed) to exercise some degree of restraint. They were a quarrelsome tribe and gave him a great deal of difficulty. After his father's death, two of Latimer's brothers had wasted no time in pursuing him through the law courts for property they believed was rightfully theirs. A few years later, there was more embarrassment when another brother, William, dabbled in the occult and got himself arrested. He seems to have been looking for supernatural encouragement that the head of the family might die or be killed in battle, enabling William to replace Lord Latimer as the head of their branch of the Nevilles and thus be in line for the earldom of Warwick, vacant since the demise of the Kingmaker. It could not have been very comforting to Latimer to know that one of his siblings was resorting to the black arts to gain his title, but William's involvement with wizards and soothsayers had also led to charges of sedition, as Henry VIII's death was prophesied as well. In the end, nothing came of this strange episode but it was an indication of the jealousy and irrationality that pervaded the Neville family's dealings with each other, and a further source of stress for Latimer.

At home, his own two children were also in need of guidance and stability. John Neville, then fourteen years old, had had little parental presence in his life. This was by no means uncommon in those days but his subsequent behaviour, as a violent and unpredictable adult and Katherine Parr's own, indirect comments about young people, point to the fact that he was a very difficult stepson. There was an urgent need for direction, for proper attention to be paid to his education and for inculcating some sense of responsibility in one apparently prone to blame others for his misdemeanours. When, more than a decade later, Katherine Parr wrote *Lamentation of a Sinner*, she harked back to the frustrations of dealing with her stepson, though she does not, of course, name him personally:

younglings and unperfect are offended at small trifles, taking
everything in evil part, grudging and murmuring against
their neighbour ... when [they] see that it is reputed and
esteemed holy to commit sin ... they learn to do that, and
worse, and wax cold in doing good and confirm themselves
in evil, and then they excuse their wicked life, publishing the
same with the slander of their neighbour. If any man reprove
them, they say such a man did thus and worse ... their
affections dispose their eyes to see through other men and
they see nothing in themselves ...[2]

Although the sixteenth century did not have a separate
category for 'teenagers' it is very easy for any modern parent to
sympathize with Katherine Parr's experience, so eloquently
expressed, in dealing with difficult youngsters. When first confronted with Latimer's son and heir, she was not quite twenty-
two. She might have been forgiven for wondering whether the
confidence of this sulking, lying, over-sensitive boy could ever be
won. Yet during her tenure as his stepmother, he does seem, at
least, to have avoided the disgrace which subsequent allegations
of rape and murder brought to the name of Latimer. Nor did she
abandon him after his father's death; the younger John Neville's
wife, Lucy, was one of Katherine's ladies-in-waiting when she
became queen.

Thankfully for Katherine, her stepdaughter, Margaret, then
a girl of nine, was all together different. Theirs quickly became a
close and loving relationship. Margaret had never really known
a mother but that gap in her young life was filled by her father's
third wife, who supervised her education, encouraged a love of
learning and a devotion to religion which mirrored Katherine's
own journey into spiritual awareness. They were never parted for
any length of time until Margaret's premature death at the age of
twenty-one. The child watched her stepmother support her father
and appreciated the attention and guidance that she received. She
also witnessed Katherine's personal courage and coolness at times
of crisis. Margaret was an apt pupil and her upbringing seems to

have given Katherine great satisfaction. The experience undoubtedly stood Katherine in good stead when, in 1543, she became
stepmother to another nine-year-old girl, Elizabeth Tudor, on
whom her lasting influence would be profound.

There is some indication that Margaret Neville may have
been her father's favourite. If so, this might partly explain her
brother's truculence. Or it may simply be that John was an
awkward youth and she a biddable and intelligent little girl, eager
to get on with her new mother rather than oppose her. Certainly,
her father had grand plans for her, for within months of his
marriage to Katherine, he paid a Yorkshire neighbour, Sir Francis
Bigod, 700 marks for Margaret's marriage to Bigod's infant son,
Ralph. This put further strain on Latimer's finances and actually
promised less than might have been apparent at the time. True,
Bigod was the master of two impressive residences in Yorkshire,
Settrington and Mulgrave, and he had been the ward of Cardinal
Wolsey. But he was himself heavily over-extended financially, the
result of mismanagement of what had been a debt-free inheritance and a reckless programme of building on his various estates.
He may have looked a sound prospect as Margaret's father-in-
law, but he was also enmeshed in borrowing his way out of debt
(his letters to Cromwell were even more desperate than Latimer's)
and he was already known for embracing new religious ideas,
though this apparently did not trouble Katherine's more conservative husband. There was ample evidence that he could be an
unpredictable ally, though Latimer could not have foreseen, in
October 1534, just how dangerous and compromising his connection with this man might be.

AS KATHERINE got to know the Latimers, she also had to
accustom herself to a change of scene and a new home. Her
husband lived principally at Snape Castle in Richmondshire, a
name for this part of north Yorkshire only revived in the late
twentieth century. It was a charming location. Far from being

isolated or surrounded by inhospitable terrain, Snape sits in a verdant valley, in gently undulating countryside, surrounded by fields which then, perhaps even more so than now, were full of sheep. A stream flows through the village, dividing it in two, and it is only a short distance to the market towns of Masham (whose charter was awarded in 1250), Leyburn and Bedale. Ripon, with its ancient cathedral dating back to the seventh century, is only ten miles away, and the Cistercian abbey at Jervaulx, one of the great monastic houses of the region, about the same distance.

It is certainly dramatic to imagine Katherine stuck in the wilderness of the more remote dales, but it is also completely inaccurate. Defensive castles might be found in outlying locations, but Lord Latimer, like others of his class, preferred to live in more comfortable, accessible surroundings. There would certainly have been good hunting, a pastime Katherine always enjoyed, nearby, and Snape (which means boggy pasture) was not an uncivilized place. It was within a day's ride of York, then the second city in England and very much its northern capital. The social life of north Yorkshire could not, of course, match that of the court in London, but as the wife of a prominent local nobleman, Katherine had a certain position to occupy, and a role that was all together grander, and offered far more opportunities for meeting people of her own class, than that of her first marriage.

The grey stone castle in which Katherine lived as Lady Latimer probably dated from the 1420s, though there had been a manor house on the same site as far back as the mid-thirteenth century. It is not in any way a forbidding edifice, of the sort that inspires stories of prisoners languishing in dungeons. It was intended as a home, rather than a military outpost against the marauding Scots, and though there was a long association with the Neville family, the ill-fated Richard III was briefly its overlord. No details of its interior survive from this period, but we can assume that it was comfortably appointed, if perhaps somewhat lacking a feminine touch in the years that Lord Latimer had been a widower. Katherine's later interest in making alterations to her accommodation as queen suggests that she could have made changes at Snape, if money permitted.

Today, Snape Castle is privately owned but its chapel continues to serve the village. This little-known, rare example of a pre-Reformation chapel was first mentioned in the early sixteenth century and is marvellously evocative of the past. It occupies an upper floor on the south side of the castle, reached nowadays by a flight of steps from an outer door. In the 1530s, however, direct access from within the castle would probably have existed. Prayer and the offices of the Church shaped the lives of everyone in those days, in ways which our secular society can no longer appreciate. Their lovely chapel would have been an integral part of family life for the Latimers. One can easily picture Katherine and her husband worshipping in its peace and stillness, perhaps finding solace there from the cares of the world.[3] For cares there were aplenty. Katherine's life at Snape was peaceful, even gentle, for a brief period, despite John Neville's tantrums. But in the wider context of English politics and society there were great changes with each passing year. The Latimers may have lived far from London, but they were not immune to the effect of what was happening at the centre of power.

WHEN KATHERINE and Lord Latimer were married it was already apparent that major change was sweeping England. At the heart of the transformation was Henry VIII himself. The king's worries about the future of his dynasty had been fuelled, in the late 1520s, by his obsession with Anne Boleyn. He wanted a new wife, one who could provide him with male heirs, and Anne was determined that she would be that woman. Henry was equally determined that the process of freeing himself from Katherine of Aragon, and making Anne his queen, should follow the proper legal course. It is ironic that a monarch who began the painful process of the divorce with a wholly unjustified confidence that the pope in Rome would grant him a speedy end to his first marriage, finished six years of convoluted disputation with the religious authorities by declaring the Church in England independent of Rome and nominating himself as its Supreme Head. There had been rulers who clashed with the papacy before, and not just in England. It was quite possible to consider oneself a good Catholic and to defy the pope. The Emperor Charles V did so constantly, and, for good measure, his troops had sacked Rome in 1526. But he was not excommunicated, and he was never accused of fomenting heresy. Henry's search for a male heir was both convulsive and divisive, opening doors to new religious ideas that the anti-Lutheran monarch himself had never anticipated. Events unfolded at a frightening speed, and, as the power of the monarchy increased, so new men appeared to uphold Henry VIII, hoping for advancement. In such an unpredictable climate, political and Church careers were put in jeopardy, consciences examined and lives sacrificed for what some men saw as a higher ideal and Henry viewed as treachery. By this time his own religious beliefs were probably developing along reforming lines; he disliked superstition, idolatry and anything that came between him and those he governed. For a while, until he realized its implications, he supported the translation of the Bible into English and a more straightforward form of religious service. Thus were the doors opened for the word of God to be brought to all men – and, indeed, to all women who were literate, including educated ladies like Katherine. For some, it was an exhilarating time of much-needed change, promising an end to the primacy of the priesthood and the beginning of a direct relationship with God. The slavish subjection to the papacy was at an end. But many others, perhaps the majority of the population, felt a profound sense of dislocation. Their doubts could not be assuaged by legislation, no matter how far-reaching it might be.

It had been acknowledged for years that the king wanted to

put aside Katherine of Aragon. At the time that Katherine married Lord Latimer, Henry VIII's first wife, now known as the Princess Dowager (a title so patronizing that one cannot blame her for despising it), was banished from court and living at Kimbolton Castle on the edge of the fens in Huntingdonshire. She had not seen her daughter, Mary (also banished from court and living in the household of Anne Boleyn's daughter, Elizabeth) for three years. Some of the nobility, particularly women, had been brave enough to support her openly, but despite her continued defiance, Anne Boleyn's triumph over her would have seemed a reality in 1534. Mary, bastardized and disinherited when Elizabeth was born, had suffered severe stress and psychological harassment, as well as serious bouts of illness. But she was still refusing to acknowledge the change to her status or the invalidity of her parents' marriage. Her position must have seemed all but hopeless to outside, but not necessarily disinterested, observers like the Latimers. Lord Latimer had conformed sufficiently to sign the letter of the nobility to Rome supporting the divorce and he had sat in parliament as the programme of reform was pushed through, but the substance of it was against his own personal inclinations. At this stage, like others, he kept his doubts to himself.

The legislative process that led to the complete break with Rome had begun in 1532 but reached its height in the year that Katherine Parr married Lord Latimer. In 1534 were passed the Act of Supremacy, a new Act of Succession (which ignored Mary), supported by the leading nobility of England, the Ecclesiastical Licences Act, which upheld English as opposed to papal law, and an act that banned the payment of Church taxation to Rome; henceforward, the Crown would take one-tenth of clerical income. In a sweeping move to stifle dissent, further legislation made criticism of the Boleyn marriage treasonable, as were accusations of heresy or schism against the king. It was in this atmosphere of ruthless determination and suppression of opponents that the Latimers and their relatives lived their daily

lives. There were quite evidently advantages to be had if opportunity and care were skilfully combined. But there was also danger
and difficulty, particularly for anyone suspected of being less than
completely loyal. Cuthbert Tunstall, Katherine's distant cousin,
knew this only too well.

Katherine's second marriage must have been a minor consideration to her kinsman, the bishop of Durham, in the year
1534. Or perhaps he found his involvement in it a welcome relief
from the extreme pressure that he was put under to conform to
the king's will. For three years, he had been trying to balance his
conscience with political expediency. He had defended Katherine
of Aragon, but not with the vigour or absolute conviction of the
bishop of Rochester, John Fisher. He had been bold enough to
tell Henry that he could not be Head of the Church in spiritual
matters and he may well have been one of the four bishops of the
northern convocation who voted against the divorce (direct evidence is lacking), but he recognized that the queen's cause was
hopeless, and never attempted to lead any organized opposition
to Henry. In fact, he attended Anne Boleyn's coronation. But it
did not end there. On a personal level, he felt he could not just
keep quiet. There was too much at stake; he dreaded rejection by
the whole of Christendom and exposure to the predations of
foreign powers seeking to take advantage of England, as, he
pointed out in a letter to the king, Henry himself had done when
he invaded France more than twenty years before. Henry refuted
Tunstall's points line by line. Yet this was much more than an
academic difference of opinion that could be confined to written
exchanges. It made the king realize that he must bring Tunstall
to heel.

The bishop had expected to attend parliament in early 1534
but he was directed to stay in the north; Henry did not want
dissidents present while vital legislation was being passed. But
once that legislation was on the statute books, Cuthbert Tunstall
was summoned south to take the oath to the Act of Succession.
In his absence, his home at Bishop Auckland in County Durham

was searched, by order of the king, but no incriminating documents or books were found, mainly because Tunstall had been forewarned to remove anything that might endanger himself. Once he took the oath (however unwillingly) he found that there was no going back. Both he and Archbishop Lee of York were required to explain to the imperial ambassador, Eustace Chapuys, and subsequently to the very angry Katherine of Aragon herself, the justification for the annulment of her marriage. They did not succeed in getting her to agree or to acknowledge that she would cease to use the title of queen.

Tunstall's experience at the time of Katherine Parr's second marriage must have been a harrowing one. Fisher and Thomas More, with whom he essentially agreed on all points concerning the divorce and the break from Rome, were in the Tower. His own loyalty was highly suspect, as the secret raids on his property showed. There is some indication that More advised him not to endanger himself any further, because it would achieve nothing. Perhaps he thought that, by staying alive, he could at least keep the worst excesses of Lutheranism out of England. He knew he was no martyr yet he bridled at the accusation of infirmity aimed at him by the diplomat and theologian Reginald Pole in 1536: 'where ye do find fault with me, that I fainted in my heart, and would not die for the Bishop of Rome['s] authority; when this matter was first purposed unto me, surely it was no fainting that made me agreeable thereunto'.[4] He had struggled, one cannot know how much, with his conscience and he emerged from a perilous time alive, but compromised. The politician in Tunstall had survived; he retained his post as bishop of Durham and president of the Council of the North. Above all, like many of the upper ranks of the clergy and the aristocracy, he put loyalty to the king first. But Henry never really trusted him again. For the king, it was a simple matter. Those who were not fully committed to his break with Rome, the new Royal Supremacy and all the raft of legislation that underpinned his Reformation, were against him. They could submit, or die. A few, like Thomas

More, saw it as a clear choice. A man like Tunstall, a seasoned diplomat but also long-standing churchman, found the predicament agonizing.

He could only watch as More and Fisher went to the block in the summer of 1535 and the attack on the religious orders gained momentum. Any hopes that the final outcome of the divorce and the split with Rome would see an end to instability were crushed as it became apparent that the government's religious policy was still evolving. The king and Cromwell needed to be sure that the split from Rome could not be undone insidiously. They were well aware that there were many important men (such as Tunstall) and many sectors of the community where acquiescence to the royal command did not equate to conviction. And where these doubts lingered, there was the potential for undermining the achievements so purposefully put in place in London. Two obvious sources of concern were the attitude of the universities and, more crucially still, that of the monasteries, whose first loyalty had so recently been to Rome and not to Henry VIII. It has been suggested that too much has been read into the assessment of monastic wealth, the *Valor Ecclesiasticus*, ordered by Cromwell early in 1535 and completed by the autumn of that year.[5] But even if this exercise was not the first step in a far-reaching plan to gain hold of monastic property and wealth – and, with hindsight, it certainly looks that way, but it is easy to confuse cause with effect – its underlying assumption that the religious houses were not to be trusted, that many of them had strayed far from the simple path laid out by St Bernard of Clairvaux in the eleventh century, pointed to an uncomfortable, uncertain future. It remained to be seen who would benefit by reform of the monastic way of life, yet one thing was clear: whatever course was followed, it would be dictated by the Crown.

A year after the completion of the *Valor Ecclesiasticus*, after the high-profile deaths of his former chancellor, the bishop of Rochester and leading members of the Carthusian monastic order, Henry was more determined than ever to extend his authority.

Thus far he had dealt successfully with dissidents. The Latimers, living unremarkably at Snape, would nevertheless have been aware of Cuthbert Tunstall's dilemma and may have known of the opposition to the king's divorce by Sir George Throckmorton, a Warwickshire knight who was Katherine's uncle by marriage. William and Anne Parr, though silent on national affairs and well connected at court, had themselves crossed Thomas Cromwell in 1533, when he tried to help himself to lands that they owned. These kind of indirect embarrassments were not, however, unique to the Latimers and they might have managed to avoid criticism had calm prevailed. But there was no tranquillity for England in 1536. Voices of resistance were not silenced; in fact, they were growing stronger. Nowhere were these louder than in the north.

CHAPTER FIVE

The Pilgrimage of Grace

'When time enlarged villainy to commit all profane and sinister acts, no thing was spared, how holy soever it was. All was turned upside down, and the bodies of saints and other heroical persons being wrapped in lead were turned out thereof, and lead sold to plumbers, books and pictures were burned, evidences not regarded; all was subject to violence and rapine.'

Yorkshireman Thomas Meynell's view
of the assault on traditional religion[1]

THE YEAR 1536, the most momentous of Henry VIII's reign, started quietly enough. Yet by 8 June 1536, when the brief parliament of that year opened in London, the king's first two wives were dead and he was already married to a third. Katherine of Aragon had succumbed to failing health and heartbreak at the beginning of January, her love of Henry undiminished. She was buried with muted ceremony in Peterborough Cathedral. The position of the queen who had supplanted her was, however, far from secure. Anne Boleyn was a mercurial, difficult woman who made enemies easily. She had certainly made one of Thomas Cromwell, the chief minister, who knew her well enough to realize that the breach between them threatened his career and possibly his life as well. But despite her volatile relationship with

Henry VIII, made more uneasy still by the fact that she had not born him a male heir, had recently miscarried and was now in her mid-thirties, Anne does not seem to have understood that her husband could become her enemy as well. The loss of the king's love, whether or not it amounted to actual hatred, combined with Cromwell's belief that she stood in his way. For Anne, it was a fatal brew. On 19 May she went to the block on trumped-up charges of adultery, ruthlessly abandoned by those who had fawned on her during the long years of the divorce from Katherine of Aragon. Only ten days later Henry married Jane Seymour, carefully groomed as the meek, blonde successor to Anne, the brunette termagant. By 22 June he had finally suppressed the one woman of his family who remained defiant, his elder daughter, Mary, forcing her to acknowledge that her mother's marriage was unlawful and that she herself was illegitimate. Her supporters, threatened with death, fell quiet.

Henry was now truly master in his own country and could concentrate on pushing through his programme of religious reform. Whether this encompassed, as early as 1536, the total suppression of the monasteries, seems unlikely. But the act of March 1536 did close many (though by no means all, there were significant exemptions) of the smaller monasteries whose annual income fell below £200. In the same month that he was bringing his daughter to heel after some three years of disobedience, the king's views on religious purification and the need for unity in the Church (his Church, as it now was) were published as the Ten Articles. These attacked superstition, holy days and pilgrimages and idolatry but retained the Mass and refused to embrace the Lutheran doctrine of justification by faith alone. In August, injunctions were issued to the clergy as to how the Ten Articles should be used in preaching and day-to-day religious life. Some degree of unpopularity was anticipated but it was hoped that the force of good argument would prevail. Meanwhile, the visitations of monasteries continued, even after the smaller ones were closed.

If there was no far-reaching plan as yet in place, there was equally
no intention to stand still on matters of religion.

All of this Lord Latimer knew well enough. He had first
attended parliament in 1529 as a member of the House of
Commons, representing Yorkshire, but had moved up to the
House of Lords the following year, on the death of his father.
The Reformation Parliament, as it is known, actually sat for
seven years, through eight different sessions, until it was finally
dissolved in mid-April 1536. The Journal of the House of Lords
is missing for much of this period, though we do know that
Latimer regularly attended in the first part of 1534, shortly before
his marriage to Katherine Parr. Since he also wrote to Cromwell
in 1536 asking for leave of absence, the inference must be that he
was normally a conscientious attendee. As he also had duties to
fulfil on the Council of the North, his time at home in Snape
could only have been limited. And there were other matters
requiring his presence outside Yorkshire. He missed the beginning of the brief parliament of 1536, which began in June,
because of business connected with his estates in Worcestershire.
Subsequently, he journeyed to London, but was absent again
when parliament was dissolved in July. The likelihood is that his
affairs in Worcester were not completed and he felt compelled to
leave early. By the autumn, he was back in Snape. It must have
seemed a welcome break from his travels. But there were storm
clouds all around.

THE FIRST SIGNS of serious discontent in northern England
were reported by Sir Francis Bigod (the intended father-in-
law of Katherine's stepdaughter) to Cromwell at the end of
September. Little did Bigod know then the role he would
play in unfolding events. The king's commissioners who were
carrying out monastic visitations in Northumberland wrote, at
the same time, of the outright defiance they met in Hexham,
where 'the convent had prepared guns and artillery to defend

themselves ... many armed persons [were] in the streets ...
there were twenty brethren in the house who would all die before
the commissioners should have it'.[2] Here is an indication of a
deep-seated concern, of suspicion of the motives of the government's representatives and a festering hostility that could suddenly
translate to violence. Yet few could have anticipated the wide-
spread northern uprising of 1536, which its participants called
the Pilgrimage of Grace.

It has been described as the rebellion that shook Henry VIII's
throne. Yet despite the large numbers of men (and some women),
of varying social groups and backgrounds who were caught up in
the Pilgrimage, none of them wanted to overthrow the king.
Throughout the winter of 1536 and on into the next year, when
a further uprising fatally compromised those who had put their
faith in Henry VIII, protestations of loyalty were constant,
consistent and genuine. Also consistent was the king's utter
disdain for those who had dared to rise against him and his
determination to take revenge on their 'leaders', men like Lord
Latimer who were probably coerced by the pilgrims, but who
were by no means out of sympathy with their demands. For there
was a fundamental difference between the rebels and the king.
They believed all along that he was influenced by heretic, greedy
upstarts and was merely ill-advised, and that, as a just prince, he
would listen to their demands. It was, in truth, a naive viewpoint,
based on a completely false reading of Henry VIII's personality
and his increasingly dictatorial interpretation of kingship. Perhaps
there was also a degree of defensive thinking behind the pilgrims'
stance, as the uprising grew. Rebels seldom found favour with
monarchs in the long run and Henry had given ample indication
of how he dealt with those who stood in his way. The king had
one straightforward objective in dealing with the Pilgrimage of
Grace: to defeat it utterly, by any means. An early victory would
be better but he was astute enough to accept that he might have
to bide his time.

The Pilgrimage affected the lives of many of those close to

Katherine Parr. Ranged against her husband and his perhaps unwilling colleagues in the great castle of Pontefract, which became the headquarters of the Pilgrimage, were her brother and uncle and her former father-in-law, Lord Borough. Cuthbert Tunstall, determined to remove himself from danger and the taint of suspicion that still hung over him, fled to his castle in Norham-on-Tweed as the pilgrims advanced on Auckland and stayed put there until it was all over. He did refuse the king's request for him to come to London, but made sure that he was in no way implicated in this conflagration on his doorstep. Such a course, as we shall see, was not open to Lord Latimer.

Other important names of the court and the Church, men whom Katherine would come to know in the aftermath of the events of 1536–7, were also caught up in the rebellion. The dukes of Norfolk and Suffolk commanded the king's armed forces and Norfolk was chief negotiator with the pilgrims, a role he filled with his unique combination of guile and whining complaint. But it was the northern aristocracy, represented by the Darcys, the Constables, the Percys and the Nevilles themselves, who faced the most difficult dilemma during the Pilgrimage. Viewed as traitors in London and untrustworthy, potential turncoats by the rebels, they would pay the highest price of all. And at the centre of events remains one of the most mysterious figures of sixteenth-century England, the one-eyed lawyer Robert Aske, who set out in early October 1536 from his east Yorkshire home to return to legal practice in London and was executed the following summer, hanged in chains in York, his trust in Henry VIII rewarded by a terrible death.

For the Pilgrimage of Grace was more than a clash between the old and the new. It went to the heart of the order of things in Tudor England and how the monarch should govern and be advised. It was a popular uprising with a veneer of aristocratic leadership, because the lords of the north could not ultimately let themselves be led by the commons. The intention was not to remove the king, but to make him better. Instead, it made him worse.

THE REPORTS from Northumberland indicate that a climate of suspicion had settled over much of northern England by the autumn of 1536, but it was in Lincolnshire, thirty-five miles from Katherine Parr's former home, that opposition first erupted in full force. On Sunday 1 October, Thomas Kendall, vicar of Louth, preached an arousing sermon in his parish church of St James. An Oxford-educated theologian, he had no time for new religious ideas: 'My desire', he later said, 'was never other but for the establishment of our faith and putting down the schismatic english books wherein the unlearned persons taketh many errors.'[3] Kendall's words were not, however, spoken merely to instil in his flock a devotion to the way they had always worshipped. They also put them in mind of the pride they felt in their church, with its high spire, only finished in 1515, and its impressive collection of plate, vestments, books and processional crosses, built up over many years. To the Louth faithful, as to many others, these were visible signs of the glory of God, not gaudy decorations that distracted them from true piety. But a visitation from the king's commissioners, now systematically assessing the wealth of the Church throughout northern England, was expected the next day. Already there were rumours circulating in other parishes that the commissioners intended to confiscate church silver. One of Cromwell's officials in Louth had even made ill-advised comments that one of their silver dishes was more appropriate for a king than for ordinary men such as they. Kendall advised his listeners 'to get together and look well upon such things as should be required of them in the said visitation'. This they certainly did, keeping an overnight vigil at the church to ensure that its contents were safe.

The determination of the men of Louth to defend their

church proved a powerful catalyst. Lincolnshire was ripe with rumours that all parish churches were to be targeted by the king's agents, and dismay was spreading. The next day, before the commissioners could begin their work, the bells were rung in Louth, an ancient call to rebellion, and crowds began to gather. Their leader was a shoemaker. Other men involved in the disturbances he began to orchestrate were also of humble origin, blacksmiths, weavers, sawyers and labourers. They were typical of those known as 'the commons', ordinary working people, viewed with suspicion by the local gentry and despised by the government. While their betters never believed that they could organize themselves or produce coherent demands, they were much feared.

The disorder soon spread to neighbouring towns. Lord Borough's experience of the extent of the problem was direct and chilling, as he reported immediately to the king himself. He said he had been at the town of Caistor with a number of other gentlemen summoned by the king's commissioners when

> suddenly there came a great multitude of people from Louth and was within a mile of us. Thereupon the inhabitants made us direct answer that they would pay no more silver and caused the bells to be rung . . . There was no remedy but to return to our houses and the people so fast pursued that they have taken Sir Robert Tyrwhit, Sir William Askew [and others] . . . I hear the commonality increase to them and I fear will do more, because they have taken the gentlemen who have the governance in these parts under your Highness. I have sent to my Lord Steward [the earl of Shrewsbury] the Lord Darcy and others to be in readiness . . .[4]

Lord Borough omitted to mention that he had, in fact, ridden hell for leather to get away from the mob, abandoning his servant, who was so badly beaten up by the angry crowd that he later died of his injuries. Nor did he stay at Gainsborough Old Hall for long. After issuing orders to his tenants that they were not to join the rebels, he escaped across the Trent to join Lord Shrewsbury at Newark.

On a personal level, Borough was unsympathetic to the rebels' concerns about religion and his authoritarian nature was too uncompromising to consider any accommodation with them. He was always the king's man. But his letter is interesting not just for what it reveals (and conceals) about his own part in the events at Caistor but because it touches on a number of common aspects of the rising as it spread beyond Lincolnshire: the determination and anger of the rebels, their resentment of the government's demands on them and their tactic of taking hostages from among the local gentry and minor aristocracy – many of whom privately shared their misgivings. Some may not even have confronted their consciences until compelled to do so by force. One such man, indeed, eventually became their leader.

ROBERT ASKE was the third son of Sir Robert Aske, a landowner from south Yorkshire. On his mother's side he was connected to the Clifford family (his cousin was the first earl of Cumberland) and he was evidently well educated. A fellow of Gray's Inn, he had probably been working for some years as a lawyer in London, but there are only glimpses of him before the fateful day in early October 1536 when he left the family home at Aughton, near Selby, to cross the river Humber into Lincolnshire. It was the first stage of a long journey that would take him back to London for the start of the Michaelmas law term. If he had heard of the troubles, he was certainly not deterred by them. Perhaps his mind was fixed on his work. There was no reason to suppose that his journey would be interrupted by anything beyond the normal hazards of travel in those days. He took the ferry on 4 October unimpeded. But the next morning, at the little town of Sawcliffe, he was intercepted by a band of commons who gave him the stark choice of taking the oath to their cause, or dying. Thus menaced, Aske swore 'to be true to god and the king and the

commonwealth'. This was a minor variant of an oath used
throughout Lincolnshire during the rising there. Others specifically mentioned the 'holy church' or 'Christ's catholic church' and
some substituted the word 'commonalty' for 'commonwealth', but
their underlying meaning was the same. God, Henry VIII and
the common people were spoken of in one breath. It was not a
trinity that pleased the king.

In that one moment, as he sat on his horse surrounded by the
angry men of north Lincolnshire, Robert Aske's life was changed.
It could be argued that an oath taken under duress is not binding,
but the sixteenth-century mind believed that oaths were a moral
force that could not be lightly abandoned, whatever the circumstances in which they had been administered. Not all men
thought that way, of course. There were opportunists and time-
servers then as now, and it was not, in the context of rebellion, a
defence that the government acknowledged. Henry VIII and his
supporters had no truck with such knavery, as they saw it. But
Aske felt differently.

We do not know what went through his mind at Sawcliffe or
why, instead of trying to fade quietly into the background, he
stayed with this group of rebels and began to coordinate communications between them and others who had risen further
south in Lincolnshire. Their concerns must have struck a chord
in him and perhaps he felt, with his lawyer's training, that he
could give voice to them in an effective way. A younger son
without, apparently, any great prospects, he may also have relished the opportunity for leadership that had accidentally come
his way. His life was outwardly unremarkable. He was unmarried
but close to his family, a good brother and uncle. Perhaps the
loss of one of his eyes marked him out as physically different and
he had felt the effect of this. But he led an ordered existence, if
somewhat lacking in stimulation. Suddenly, here was an opportunity to play a part on a much larger stage, in pursuit of worthy
ideals. He had been a counsel on cases in the court of Star
Chamber. Now he could speak for the defence of the Church

and the commons, for the preservation of a way of life that was deemed to be under attack. Around him, he could see the smaller monasteries suppressed and traditional worship denigrated. His world was out of joint.

The Lincolnshire revolt subsided in the space of a fortnight. The men of Louth had sent written demands to Henry VIII which he rejected with furious contempt. From the outset of the troubles in the north, the king was uncompromising in tone. He would not be told what to do by the common people: 'We take it as a great unkindness that our common and inferior subjects rise against us without any ground: for, first, as to the taking away of the goods of parish churches, it was never intended; Yet, if it had been, true subjects would not have treated with Us, their prince, in such violent sort, but would have humbly sued for their purpose.' He would throw the might of a huge military force at them: '100,000 men, horse and foot, in harness, with munitions and artillery, which they cannot resist. We have also appointed another great army to invade their countries as soon as they come out of them, and to burn, spoil, and destroy their goods, wives and children with all extremity, to the fearful example of lewd subjects.'[5]

This was sufficient to break the spirit of the men of Lincolnshire. They had no wish to confront the duke of Suffolk and his approaching horde, which was much smaller in reality than the king claimed. But it was not enough to deter Robert Aske. Already he had raised Marshland and adjacent districts of Yorkshire on the other side of the Humber. Clearly Aske was not alone, but the risks he was running were high. When he came to Lincoln to hear the king's pronouncement, he was warned that he was a marked man. He knew then that there was no point in hesitating. If it was rumoured in London that he was a leader of the commons, then that was what he would become. In Yorkshire, he believed, there would not be such easy capitulation.

His confidence and powers of organization proved formidable. On 16 October he entered the city of York with 10,000 followers and heard Mass at the Minster. It must have been an emotional occasion. Honourably received and lodged with a local alderman, he spent two days in York, and it was here he composed the 'Oath of the Honourable Men' that was sworn by all those who massed under his banner:

> Ye shall not enter into this our Pilgrimage of Grace for the common wealth but only for the love ye bear to God's faith and church militant and the maintenance thereof, the preservation of the king's person, his issue, and the purifying of the nobility and to expulse all villein blood and evil counsellors against the common wealth of the same. And that ye shall not enter into our said pilgrimage for no peculiar private profit to yourselves not to do no displeasure to no private person but by counsel of the common wealth nor slay nor murder for no envy but in your hearts to put away all fear for the common wealth. And to take before you the cross of Christ and your heart's faith to the restitution of the church and to the suppression of heretics' opinions by the holy contents of this book.[6]

The oath spelled out the agenda of Aske and the other leaders of the rebellion very clearly. For them, the commonwealth and religion were inextricably linked. The spread of new religious ideas – 'heretics' opinions' – and the threat to the monastic way of life – required the 'restitution of the church'. The king was not the pilgrims' enemy; their real opponents were lowly-born 'evil counsellors', men, in other words, like Thomas Cromwell.

It would be easy to view this as simply a clash between the old and the new, to represent the pilgrims as reactionaries trying in vain to stop the tide of reform, conservatives living in the past who wanted to maintain silly superstitions and the elitism of a Church that kept the faithful at one remove from the word of God. The reformers, among whom Cromwell must surely be counted despite more modern interpretations that he was some sort of sixteenth-century totalitarian who did not really believe in anything other than his own power and advancement, were determined to impose the king's authority and to dismantle anything that smacked of devotion to Rome. Aske, forced by circumstances to articulate his beliefs, gave voice to the doubts of many ordinary people (not just in northern England) who believed themselves loyal subjects of Henry VIII. Religion was an integral part of their daily lives. It lay at the root of the very order of things. Now all was beset by uncertainty. The depth and extent of that insecurity lies at the heart of the Pilgrimage of Grace.

During his brief stay in York, Aske, working with other men who shared his views, for he was by no means alone in his determination to be heard, began to coordinate a more wide-spread rebellion. Large numbers of men had risen throughout Yorkshire and the movement spilled over into Lancashire, West-moreland, Durham and Cumberland. The next objective was to take and hold a fortress that would be vital to the outcome. Many of the leading figures of the Church and the local nobility, including Archbishop Lee of York and Lord Darcy, had taken refuge in Pontefract Castle. Soon Lord Latimer would join them. But he was already sworn to the rebels.

There was unrest and armed coercion in Richmondshire before Robert Aske arrived in York. By 11 October it was closing in on Snape. On that day a group of several hundred men, probably fired into action by the proclamation at the Ripon horse fair that the king's army was coming to deliver retribution to the men of Lincolnshire, descended on Jervaulx Abbey. Together with Fountains, Rievaulx and Byland, this was one of the four great Cistercian abbeys of north Yorkshire. Peaceful and prosper-ous in its idyllic setting by the river Ure, Jervaulx was not one of the monastic houses marked for suppression. Its abbot, Adam Sedbar, apparently had no wish to join those who were disaf-fected; initially he seems to have regarded them as more inter-ested in stealing the abbey's horses than doing God's work. For several nights he hid from them until they threatened to burn his abbey to the ground. When he did appear, he claimed to have been physically attacked and forced to take the oath, though other accounts suggested he soon became an enthusiast for the rebels' cause. The oath he took was actually administered by a local gentleman, not an enraged member of the commons. At about this time, though we do not know precisely when or in what circumstances, Lord Latimer and his brother-in-law, Sir Christopher Danby, also took the oath.

Snape lay close to Jervaulx in lower Wensleydale, so it is not surprising that Latimer found himself soon caught up in the wider Richmondshire rising. Lord Darcy told Henry VIII that '[t]hey [the commons] have surprised a great many gentlemen in their own homes', and he specifically mentioned Danby.[7] It is likely, from this report, that Lord Latimer was taken in the same way, forced, by circumstances, to leave his wife and children behind at Snape. A number of ladies in the north were broadly sympathetic to the aims of the Pilgrimage. Katherine's own views at the time may well have been ambiguous: she would have known that her husband was conservative in religious matters, yet she knew, too, that the Parr family were committed to the monarchy and that her brother William was showing an interest in religious reform. No doubt she was nervous for her husband's safety and his future. She would have been as well aware as anyone that siding with rebels, no matter what the circumstances, was a course fraught with danger.

Latimer, like many other gentlemen who became embroiled in the Pilgrimage of Grace, was most probably ambivalent. Men who thought like him were worried about the economic and spiritual implications of the dissolution of the monasteries, fearing the inroads of new ideas in the vacuum that closure would create and also the loss of charity given to the poor. Latimer's position, as the eldest of his branch of the Nevilles, was somewhat unusual. Many of the gentlemen pilgrims were younger sons, who could become involved and take a stand without prejudicing the hereditary rights of their elder brothers. If this sounds surprisingly altruistic, it was an oft-repeated pattern in those days when the survival of the family was so important. The degree of coercion exerted on such men, many of whom were justices of the peace, has recently been questioned. But armed opposition to the king was a highly dangerous path. Latimer and others like him soon took on more prominent roles in the Pilgrimage because they realized, more than Robert Aske, the consequences of failure. It was natural for them to assume leadership of the commons, in any case. Yet they were careful to make sure that it was known that they had not begun this thing, merely sought to bring it to a peaceful and honourable conclusion.

The north Yorkshire rebels, by now 10,000 strong, massed in Richmond on 14 October. Here they elected Robert Bowes, a local gentleman in his forties, like Latimer, as their leader. It is not known where Latimer himself was at this time. Only on 22 October, when he arrived at Pontefract Castle does he emerge again, in the company of Lord Lumley and young Henry Neville, the twelve-year-old son and heir of the earl of Westmoreland. The lad may have been a hostage for his father, but he was carrying the banner of St Cuthbert, a powerful piece of religious symbolism from Durham Cathedral. Used in battle against the Scots, it represented both the piety and the fierce, independent spirit of the north of England. At its centre was a relic, the cloth in which St Cuthbert's body was said to have been buried. 'The banner cloth was a yard broad and five quarters deep . . . made of red velvet, of both sides most sumptuously embroidered and wrought with flowers of green silk and gold . . . in the midst of the said banner was the holy relic and Corporax cloth enclosed . . . covered over with white velvet . . . having a red cross of red velvet on both sides . . .'[8] This and the banner of the Five Wounds of Christ, under which the pilgrims also gathered when they confronted the royal armies, was precisely the sort of symbol hated by the reformers in London.

What did Lord Latimer feel as he sat on horseback beside his old friend and Westmoreland's boy? He had a son himself not many years older, left behind at Snape. Was it elation mixed with apprehension, pride mingled with the cold fear of meeting a traitor's death? He and Lumley, with much experience between them of defending England's northern border for the Tudors, now found themselves at the head of an army estimated to be between 30,000 and 50,000 men, destined for London. It was a sober host, convinced of the justice of its cause and confident that the king would give gracious audience to its demands. But it never got anywhere near the capital.

THE CAPTURE OF Pontefract was a natural goal for Aske and the rebels after their success in the rest of Yorkshire. The Norman motte and bailey castle had been expanded over the centuries and was the greatest fortress in the north. Little of it remains today, but in 1536 it was still the ultimate prize, both for the king who needed to hold it and the rebels who wanted to take it. But the castle had a sinister reputation. Richard II had died there in February 1400, probably starved to death on the orders of Henry IV, the cousin who had usurped his throne. Throughout the Middle Ages Pontefract was used as a prison. It appeared formidable. Yet the sheer size of the castle, covering seven acres, and its commanding position above the town, flattered to deceive. It was not well provided with weapons and was therefore far less easy to defend than might have been supposed.[9] The extent of the anxiety of the lords who had taken refuge within the walls of Pontefract is eloquently expressed in a letter of 15 October to the earls of Shrewsbury, Rutland and Huntingdon, commanding the king's forces at Newark:

> It is true the commons for the most part of Yorkshire be up and today we hear there meet before York above 20,000 men, besides many who have gone to them in Lincolnshire. There is no doubt the commons of this shire and Lincolnshire receive messages from each other. They increase in every parish, the cross goes before them . . . We remain here

according to your advice and indeed know not whither we could depart in surety. I, Darcy, have twice written to the King of the weakness of the castle but have got no answer, and without speedy succour we are in extreme danger, for Tuesday next, at the furthest, the commons will be here as they do affirm, not withstanding your proclamation was sent to York to them to be read. And whereas we hear that the commons of Lincolnshire are on the point of returning home on certain conditions . . . we think it right expedient that the like comfort should be sent hither.[10]

And to this gloomy prognosis was added in a postscript the information that 'news has just come that Lord Latimer and Sir Christopher Danby be taken with the commons and be with them'. So it was known, a week before Latimer arrived at Pontefract, that he had gone over to the rebels, albeit unwillingly.

The letter was signed by the archbishop of York and the other lords waiting uneasily inside Pontefract, but its chief author was Thomas, Lord Darcy, constable of the castle. Darcy was an old soldier who had fallen out of favour with Henry VIII, or perhaps more accurately, with, Henry's former chief minister, Wolsey. He had acquired considerable wealth from his lands but little royal patronage and there are indications that he found the continual obligation to defend England's borders with Scotland irksome, a resentment shared by many northern noblemen. But he was also, like Lord Latimer and Robert Aske, a religious conservative. He did not want to die a heretic and though he never considered himself a traitor, he had talked of rebellion before 1536. Darcy had opposed the king's divorce and was a supporter of Princess Mary's claim to the throne. He and other gentlemen of his persuasion in northern England considered her still to be the true heir of Henry VIII, despite her loss of status. Yet it would be wrong to assume from this that the Pilgrimage of Grace was long planned, or that it was politically inspired and masterminded by a cabal of discontented nobles. The timing of the uprising and the involvement of such large numbers of the common people seems to have genuinely surprised Darcy. In London, it was thought that he protested too much, that he was always in league with Aske. Why else would he have given Pontefract up without a fight and joined the rebels?

The simple answer is that he had little choice. He had been unable to muster men, as the king commanded – they had all gone over to the rebels. Without sufficient manpower to defend it or a ready supply of munitions, Pontefract was merely a hiding place. Certainly no one else seems to have been keen to assume the mantle of leadership. The most senior figure in the castle was the archbishop of York, Edward Lee, but he was not the man to challenge Darcy for this unenviable role.

Lee was in a very difficult position. The second prelate of the realm was no Cromwellian reformer but he did not share the passion of the men of the north. Always careful to stay on the right side of Henry VIII, it was his decision to spend more time in his archbishopric than his predecessor Wolsey had ever done that meant he could not escape the Pilgrimage of Grace. Along with Darcy and his fellow detainees, Lee took the pilgrims' oath at Pontefract after the surrender to Aske's forces. There was little for him to do now but to await the outcome of events.

Once he had made the decision to support Robert Aske, Darcy turned all his experience of soldiering to the rebels' advantage. In Sir Robert Constable, another Yorkshire gentleman sworn by the rebels, he now had someone with whom he could work closely and whom he trusted. The two had fought together twenty-five years earlier against the Moors in Spain, in the service of Ferdinand of Aragon. But they had not taken up arms for the Catholic King just as adventurers; their Christian faith had been central. Now that very faith was under threat in England. There can be no doubt that they subscribed to the articles later drawn up in the name of the Pilgrimage, which called for 'the heretics, bishops and temporal, and their sect, to have condign punishment by fire . . . or else to try the quarrel with us and our partakers in battle'.[11]

Aware that the number of their supporters was growing all the time, but as yet uncertain of the precise tally, Darcy and Aske were confident of fielding an army of 20,000 to 30,000 men by the beginning of the last week of October 1536. Their aim was nothing less than to march on London, nobles, gentry and commons united in their determination to remove the evil counsellors around the king and to make Henry change his mind on the religious direction that had been set. This was, at root, an attempt to turn back the Reformation that had already begun. There were no threats against the person of Henry VIII himself, but belief in the sanctity of kingship, embodied in the coronation rite, had proved an ineffective last resort for four kings of England in the previous two hundred years. Edward II, Richard II, Henry VI and Richard III had all been removed by force from the throne and met miserable ends. Henry could not have taken much comfort in these precedents. Surprised and greatly angered by this huge uprising against him, he had no intention of leading from the front. That task he would leave to others.

The greatest burden of responsibility fell to Thomas Howard, duke of Norfolk, England's premier aristocrat. It was Norfolk who confronted the rebel hosts at Doncaster, as they prepared to journey south. Here, on 27 October, he was met by a group representing the rebels that included Lord Latimer, commander of the Durham and Richmondshire force. The surroundings of this first series of exchanges between Latimer and Norfolk were inauspicious, to say the least. Latimer, however, was a straightforward man and clearly a troubled one, for all the military might displayed behind him. There must have been something in his demeanour that softened Norfolk, a man not given to idle sentimentality; later, he would speak up on Latimer's behalf, against the hostility of both the king and Cromwell. But for now, the duke was merely thankful that he had avoided a battle he knew he could not win.

☙

THOMAS HOWARD, duke of Norfolk, was a small man and his visage was far from heroic. In his portraits he looks more like a vinegary priest than a warrior noble. He had much experience as a soldier but that does not mean he was an especially good one, though he had been present at the great victory of Flodden and had harried the Scots in the brutal summer campaign of 1523. He had also passed two wearying years as lord lieutenant of Ireland, where he became so ill with dysentery that his health seems never to have fully recovered. Yet he was, as his enemies came to know to their cost, a difficult man to gauge. His prime motivation in all things seems to have been to maintain his own power and influence and, by extension, that of his family. He could be devious and hard-hearted but there was in him a strain of almost melancholic realism that predisposed him to eschew confrontation, or at least, to avoid it until he was sure he could emerge victorious. Perhaps this was the result of his years spent as a diplomat, in frequent, fruitless negotiations with the French, whom he seems rather to have favoured as England's international ally. Norfolk knew, better than most, that much of sixteenth-century warfare was about endurance rather than bravery. One poet described him as 'the flower of chivalry', but Norfolk was well aware that chivalry meant mud and diarrhoea and lack of sleep. Undoubtedly, he was proud, though the Howards were not of the old aristocracy, and his second wife Elizabeth, a Stafford, looked down on their pretensions to nobility. Like most English lords, Norfolk had resented Wolsey, and did not mourn his fall. But then he watched as another low-born adviser, Thomas Cromwell, rose in Wolsey's place. And of his monarch's ruthlessness, he could have been in absolutely no doubt. Thomas More, Norfolk's friend, went to the block for his conscience. The duke was not prepared to make such a sacrifice himself, nor did he attempt to defend his niece, Queen Anne. In fact, he presided at her trial. Such responsibilities went with his high office, as well as affording him an opportunity to emerge unscathed from the debacle of the Boleyn marriage. The duke knew when to show restraint, however, and the earlier events of 1536 no doubt heightened a well-developed sense of caution. Besides, he knew that if he could avoid 'an effusion of blood', his own standing would be greatly improved. It has been said that he held the future of the Tudor dynasty in his hands in the autumn of 1536, and this is no exaggeration. In persuading the rebel armies to accept a truce and disband when he met them at Doncaster, he may well have saved Henry VIII's throne.

On 27 October, in relentless autumn rain, Thomas Howard and the earl of Shrewsbury, the ailing commander of the king's force in Nottingham, held two meetings with representatives of the pilgrims at Doncaster. The second of these meetings, on the bridge that spanned the river Don, was attended by Lords Darcy, Latimer and Lumley, as well as Sir Robert Constable. Robert Aske was not there on either occasion, but this does not mean that he had been sidelined. Indeed, it was probably his aim to continue to demonstrate that the pilgrims were led by men of birth and influence. They were, after all, articulating his demands, with the full force of the rebel armies in view. Shrewsbury had always been nervous and Norfolk saw very clearly that the best victory he could hope for would be a truce, leading to the disbanding of the rebel fighters. He put it very simply: 'It was therefore impossible to give battle or to retreat, as we had no horse and they all the flower of the north.'[12] He had assured the rebel leaders that their demands would be heard in London, that they and the Lincolnshire rebels would be pardoned, and that there would be a special sitting of parliament to discuss their grievances. Sir Robert Bowes, who commanded the Richmond-shire contingent, and young Sir Ralph Ellerker, from the East Riding, were to accompany Norfolk back to the king, who would receive the rebels' petition. In return for the duke's assurance that matters would be handled honourably, the rebels agreed to disband and to make no further proclamations until Bowes and Ellerker returned.

Their confidence was utterly misplaced and their loss of momentum disastrous to their cause. Some of the rank and file sensed this; Aske did not. Norfolk had spent long days in the saddle, with nights of broken sleep at best. Part of him was too tired to think beyond the immediate necessity of maintaining the line he had sold to the rebels – be good subjects, avoid bloodshed and all will be well: 'For God's sake,' he wrote in exhausted desperation to the Privy Council, 'help that his Highness cause not my lord of Suffolk to put any man to death unto my coming, nor openly to call the lord Darcy traitor.' But the shrewd politician that he was probably calculated that the worst of the danger was past.

WHAT, THEN, of the rebels? Norfolk's reticence about accusing Darcy publicly was only a ploy. In the same letter he had denounced the old lord in unequivocal terms: 'Fie, fie upon the Lord Darcy, the most arrant traitor that ever was living.' Darcy himself had gone back to his home in south Yorkshire, where he awaited the outcome of Bowes and Ellerker's mission to London, and continued to consult with Robert Aske. Lord Latimer's whereabouts during early November 1536 are unknown, but it seems probable that he returned home for at least a time. Other rebel leaders did the same. If so, it was a brief interlude at Snape with his family, coloured by the knowledge that there was still resentment and unrest among the commons and anxiety about how his own part in the uprising would be viewed by the king.

Latimer's position was unenviable. Compelled to act as spokesman and negotiator for the rebels, he was highly visible. Both sides were suspicious of him all along. From the perspective of Henry VIII and men like Cromwell, he was unreliable. For the rebels, there was always unease that those they had coerced were not fully on their side, despite having taken the oath. Could a man like Latimer be trusted to relay their demands accurately and effectively, to represent them wholeheartedly, without coming to some private arrangement that would save his skin? Personally, Latimer identified with Aske's summation of the ills that beset the realm and what needed to be done to rectify them. Yet he knew the likely consequences of opposing royal authority. Caught in the middle of this great crisis, he could not yet see his way to a comfortable conclusion.

Neither could the king and his advisers, so they decided to play for time. In early November a general pardon was issued 'to the commons dwelling north of Doncaster, who have lately committed open rebellion, tending to the ruin of the country and the advancement of our ancient enemies, the Scots' (a pointed reminder of the vulnerability of the north of England and the international implications of the Pilgrimage). Initially excluded from this pardon was Robert Aske himself, and nine other men. Nothing was said about the nobles involved in the rebellion. The proclamation went on to say that the duke of Norfolk was appointed as lieutenant-general and, as such, would receive the rebels' submission. And it ended on a far from conciliatory note with the threat that further insurrection would be met by the king in person, 'with a main force and army to repress their malice to their utter confusion'.[13] The Privy Council, however, were subsequently able to persuade the reluctant king that the pardon should be without exemptions.

Bowes and Ellerker were gone for almost three weeks. They returned to Yorkshire with only verbal assurances from the king and, in Henry VIII's own words to the duke of Suffolk, 'no certain answer to the petitions of the Northern Men'. In his instructions to the two representatives of the pilgrims, Henry had characterized the articles presented to Norfolk in Doncaster as 'so general, dark and obscure as to be difficult to answer'. This was mere procrastination, mingled with righteous indignation, for Bowes and Ellerker were also to make it clear that 'his Highness taketh it marvellously unkindly that they being his subjects and having long experience of his clemency and his readiness to hear the petitions of all and redress grievances, would attempt a rebellion rather than sue to him'.[14]

These delaying tactics caused divisions among the leaders of

the Pilgrimage and in the third week of November they held a
general council in York, at which Latimer was present, to decide
the way forward. The mood of the York meeting became more
angry as Sir Robert Constable revealed the continued involvement
of Cromwell and his duplicity in trying to split the leadership.
The resolutions from this meeting, which were to form the basis
of the agenda for a much larger gathering at Pontefract in early
December, were sent to the duke of Norfolk. The king chose to
respond himself, on 27 November, in a letter full of venom and
threat, which shows how determined he was to maintain his
authority, even in the face of renewed action. It also reveals his
exasperation with the attitude of the nobility who had been
caught up in the Pilgrimage of Grace and his hatred for Robert
Aske. He told Ellerker and Bowes: 'We have read the letters
addressed by you and others from York to the duke of Norfolk,
and greatly marvel at the ingratitude shown to us in this insurrection, especially by men of nobility and worship, and the great
slackness of you twain that were messengers from the whole
company of that assembly to us, especially that you have not
made us a full answer of your instructions.' There was not much
comfort here for men like Latimer, or, indeed, the archbishop of
York. But worse was to come:

> We are much surprised that, as the commons be now down,
> and perhaps not so ready to rise again as some pretend [this
> was wishful thinking in London] the nobles and you, the
> gentlemen, should have signed such a letter to the duke of
> Norfolk, by which it seems they make themselves a party with
> the commons . . . And now the intent of your pilgrimage with
> the devotion of the pilgrims may appear, for who can reckon
> that foundation good which is contrary to God's command-
> ment, or the executors to be good men which, contrary to
> their allegiance, presume, with force, to order their prince?

He was particularly incensed that the rebels should question
his good faith and the safe-conduct offered. Even the Scots did

not behave this way. The rebels' reaction was a form of insanity. 'What madness has seized them,' he demanded, 'not to see that a small continuance of this will destroy themselves and utterly devast those parts which they inhabit.'

But Henry's full fury was reserved for the rebels' captain:

> We think it no little shame to all you that have been accounted noble to suffer such a villain as Aske, having neither wit nor experience, to subscribe the letters sent to the duke of Norfolk before you all as if he were your ruler. Where is your nobility become to suffer such a villain to be privy to any of your affairs, who was never esteemed in any of our courts but as a common pedlar in the law? We and all the nobles here consider your honour greatly touched by the same. It is only his filed tongue and false surmises that have brought him in this unfitting estimation among you.[15]

The minds of the pilgrim leaders were focused on the discussions at the forthcoming Pontefract meeting and there does not seem to have been much immediate reaction to the king's diatribe, except from Ellerker and Bowes themselves. Chagrined or frightened, both were turned on a path away from the colleagues they had been deputed to represent.

THE ARTICLES drawn up at Pontefract on 2 December, after considerable discussion, represent the most complete rejection of his policies that the king had encountered during his reign. He had been nearly thirty years on the throne, surviving war with France and Scotland, growing economic problems, occasional local uprisings and dissident nobles. Viewed as a schismatic in Europe, in England his authority had grown immeasurably following the split from Rome. But he was not merely driven by the power that came with the Act of Supremacy, or the undoubted attraction of filling his coffers with the proceeds of the sale of Church lands, but a belief, shared with some of his closest

political advisers, that his Church needed to be reformed. He was
no Lutheran, but he looked for an improvement in the spiritual
health of his country. His opponents in the north of England
were similarly concerned about spiritual well-being, while also
being anxious about land enclosures and government interference.
They felt excluded and betrayed. Aske might be 'a common
pedlar of the law' but he had given them voice. His eloquence
can be seen in the Pontefract articles; he still carried most of the
northern gentlemen and clergy with him.

   The views of the archbishop of York, were, however, still
opaque, and this was troubling for the king. Perhaps because of
his rank and a talent for remaining non-committal, Edward Lee
had never before been challenged to reveal his stance. As he
himself put it, when examined in 1537 about his time at Pontefract at the start of the uprising: 'Many lords and gentlemen came
to the castle, but the writer did not join in their counsels or
mingle with them except at dinner and supper.' But by early
December, when he was back in Pontefract (but not staying in
the castle itself) he could no longer hide behind high office and
social niceties. The second day of the conference was a Sunday
and he was asked to preach at the church of All Saints, below the
fortress. This request was conveyed to him by Lord Latimer, who
'came to him the night before and desired him to speak of the
matter, and to be brief, as there was a council at the castle on
Sunday at 9 o'clock'.[16]

   The matter in question was of vital importance to Latimer
and all the other pilgrims. Katherine's husband had himself raised
it towards the end of the previous day's discussions. Lee and the
clergy with him should be asked to 'show their learning whether
subjects might lawfully move war in any case against their prince'.
Here was a dilemma that went to the very heart of the Pilgrimage,
for if the answer was not unequivocally positive, then they were
all committing treason. In articulating this, the most crucial of
the underlying doubts that beset those gathered at Pontefract,
Latimer was brutally exposed. We do not know whether he raised

the matter spontaneously or whether he was deputed to do so, but as a piece of ammunition that might be used against him by an angry monarch, it was powerful. Interestingly, it also presages one of the most fundamental issues raised by Protestant reformers two decades later, though the pilgrims were defending traditional religion, rather than attacking it. In effect, they wanted a theological justification for what they had done and might, perhaps, do in the future if their demands were refused.

Lee, a man not noted for personal courage, was apparently advised by his own entourage not to say anything that would make the situation worse and certainly to do nothing that would provoke his listeners. On 3 December he mounted the pulpit following the early morning Mass on Advent Sunday. We cannot be sure of what he originally intended to say (and possibly neither was he) but his eventual pronouncement, that no man could take up arms without his sovereign's permission, enraged many of his listeners. The arrival of the Lancaster Herald, Thomas Miller, who was carrying the safe-conduct papers for the meeting the next day at Doncaster, either frightened or emboldened Lee into a pro-government stance. There was such an uproar that the archbishop had to be removed speedily for his own safety. But though this episode cast something of a pall over the Pontefract conference, it did nothing to change the content of the twenty-four articles agreed later the same day for presentation to Norfolk, many of which were enthusiastically supported by the array of influential clergy (including Lee's chancellor, vicar-general and chaplain) who were consulted.

This is not surprising, for the Pontefract articles were concerned, above all, with religion. The very first of them, 'touching our faith', was to have the heresies of Luther, Wycliff, Hus and a number of other reformers, destroyed. The next stated flatly that the authority invested in the Royal Supremacy must be restored to Rome, as also the authority to appoint bishops. Mary was to be made legitimate 'and the former statute therein annulled for the danger of the title that might incur to the crown of Scotland'. (If the king could use Scotland as a threat, so could the pilgrims. This fear was one that haunted the Tudor dynasty until the end of its days.) The attack on monasticism was to be halted and the suppressed abbeys 'to be restored to their houses, lands and goods'. The clergy were to be relieved of the heavy burden of taxation thrust upon them by their monarch. There were some economic concerns, notably about enclosures, and attacks on named government officials: 'Lord Cromwell, the Lord Chancellor, and Sir Richard Rich [who was in charge of the newly created Court of Augmentations, set up to oversee the administration of the monastic dissolutions] to have condign punishment, as subverters of the good laws of the realm and maintainers and inventors of heretics.' Cromwell's agents in the north, Legh and Layton, were similarly to be punished 'for their extortions from religious houses and other abominable acts'. Also significant was the request for 'a parliament at Nottingham or York, and that shortly'.[17]

Clear of purpose and with the full expectations of the commons of the north behind them, Aske, Darcy, Latimer and the other Pilgrimage leaders set off for a further meeting with the duke of Norfolk on Doncaster bridge. The king had berated Norfolk and Admiral Fitzwilliam for sounding so desperate about their situation but, finally, his bluster gave way to an acceptance that a military solution was not an option. The duke was told to agree to the demand for a parliament, though at a place of the monarch's choosing and not before the end of September 1537, and to issue a free pardon to everyone involved in the Pilgrimage of Grace. There was considerable discussion, which Norfolk handled with assurance, on each of the twenty-four articles, but much was left to be resolved at this distant parliamentary session. The commons were reluctant to disband but Aske and the lords and gentlemen with him, 300 men on horseback, received the royal pardon gratefully on behalf of the northerners massed behind them. There seems to have been a palpable sense of relief among the leaders that they could now go home. Certainly, they wanted to believe the word of a prince.

Robert Aske went back to Aughton, the place he had set out from some two months before. The king invited him to spend Christmas in London, ostensibly so that he could hear his further advice on how to manage affairs in the north. Henry's capacity for deception must have been extraordinary. This was a man he despised. He would have his vengeance, but there was no need to hurry.

Lord Latimer returned to Snape, to rejoin his wife and children, with the immediate danger past. It was not necessarily the merriest of festive seasons for the Latimer family. Two of his brothers, the volatile Marmaduke and the unpredictable Thomas, had participated in the Pilgrimage, possibly with more enthusiasm than he. If Katherine had not already realized it herself, her husband would have left her in no doubt that he needed to restore his standing with the king as soon as possible. The Parrs had renewed their faithful service to the king during this episode but the Nevilles, though pardoned, were still exposed. Latimer knew that he urgently needed to put his case in London. Early in the New Year he was on the road again. He hoped that the worse was over. Unfortunately, it was yet to come.

LATIMER DID NOT get to London and even if he had, his presence there would not necessarily have worked in his favour. The king ordered him back north, to prepare for military duties on the Scottish border, perhaps as a penance, though Henry and his advisers do seem genuinely to have dreaded the possibility of the Scots taking advantage of the Pilgrimage of Grace to invade. Nor had the unrest in the north gone away. It still rumbled on just beneath the surface, despite the efforts of men like Sir Robert Constable to emphasize the positive outcome of Aske's Christmas at court: 'The King,' he announced in a manifesto on 10 January, 'has declared by mouth to Robert Aske that we shall have our Parliament at York, and also his Convocation for ordering the Faith ... Wherefore, good and loving neighbours, let us stay ourselves and resist those who are disposed to spoil.' And he added, poignantly, 'If it had not been for my disease, by which I can neither go nor ride, I would have come and showed you this myself ... P.S. The Parliament and the Convocation are to be held at York at Whitsuntide, and also the Queen's coronation.'[18]

Aske and Constable were impressed by the king's apparently gracious response. After all, he had brought the date of the meeting of parliament forward and even offered to have Queen Jane crowned there. But there were many others who remained unconvinced by the king's sudden benevolence and who also questioned the good faith of the nobles and gentlemen who had led the Pilgrimage. Latimer's eagerness to be restored to royal favour could easily be misconstrued as betrayal. Such suspicions made men violent. On 20 January, Lord Latimer wrote an anguished letter to Fitzwilliam, in which he described what had happened to Katherine and his family in his absence, although, tellingly, his first concern was for his own reputation:

Thank you for your good report of me in my being among the commons against my will. At Buntingford, on my way towards London, there met me a letter from my Lord Chancellor, my Lord Privy Seal and others of the king's council, signifying that I should tarry in the north, notwithstanding the king's letter to me to come up, because my lord of Norfolk was dispatched. Forthwith I returned homewards, and now, at Stamford, I learn that the commons of Richmondshire, grieved at my coming up [to London], have entered my house at Snape and will destroy it if I come not home shortly. If I do not please them I know not what they will do with my body and goods, my wife and children. I beg to know the king's pleasure and shall follow the same whatsoever come of it ... If it were the king's pleasure that I might live on such small lands as I have in the south, I would little care of my lands in the north. I have but small power, having no rule of men under the king and no house that is strong.[19]

Katherine and the children were being held hostage in their own home, as surety for Lord Latimer's continued commitment to the causes for which the northern men had risen. In Richmondshire, and elsewhere, there was deep suspicion of royal assurances. There is no reason to believe that Katherine was physically assaulted, let alone raped. The invaders were angry but participants in the Pilgrimage had acted under clear codes of conduct which were only very occasionally broken. Yet it must have been a most frightening experience, especially coming after months of uncertainty. Her husband had left her because he urgently needed to clear his name in London, but the mere fact of his going put her in further danger. No letters from Katherine at this time survive, but a glimpse of what she must have felt is provided in a letter from Lady Dorothy Darcy, daughter-in-law of the old rebel leader, to her husband on 13 January 1537. There was, she said, great danger, to herself, her children and their goods, 'the whole country is so fervently set of wilfulness. I beg you to make haste home, which may help to stay the country and put myself and your children in safety. The country hath you in so much jealousy that I know not what I should think or say . . .'[20]

Latimer did return to Snape and the mob dispersed without further destruction to his home and goods. He was unable to stay for long as he was still extremely concerned about clearing his name. The outbreak of new unrest in the East Riding of Yorkshire, led by the maverick knight Sir Francis Bigod (expected, one day, to be Margaret Neville's father-in-law), added further confusion to the tense atmosphere. Bigod was actually an enthusiastic supporter of the new religious ideas and had opposed the Pilgrimage of Grace when it broke out, but he did not approve of Henry VIII's role as Head of the Church and he also feared that the king would use the uprising to come down heavily on the entire north of England, turning it into little more than an occupied territory. Unlike Latimer, Constable and Darcy, Bigod did not believe that Henry would keep his promises. His assessment of the king's good will proved to be accurate, but in taking up arms with John Hallam, one of his tenants, to try to enforce the letter of the Pontefract articles, Bigod sealed the fate of the leading pilgrims. Norfolk was sent once more to the north. There he found widespread unrest throughout the region, but nothing organized on the scale of the preceding October. This allowed him to declare martial law in Cumbria and to proceed with summary executions, which cowed the population. Aske had travelled with him in March 1537, and neither he nor the other pilgrim leaders supported the renewed outbreak of rebellion. Yet this was insufficient to save them. Aske set out one last time for London on 24 March, carrying a letter of commendation from Norfolk. It was not worth the parchment on which it was written. There can scarcely have been a more cynical exercise to lure a marked man to his eventual death. Aske, Darcy and Constable (also summoned to London) were arrested on 7 April for treason and were executed two months later, in June.

The final failure of the Pilgrimage of Grace was a terrible blow for the monasteries. They were seen as centres of opposition and hothouses of dissent, as well, of course, as sources of wealth. Over the next few years they were all dissolved. Plundered and deserted, they could still not quite be destroyed. The ruins of the finest remain in some of the most sublime settings in the English countryside, a monument to a way of life ruthlessly suppressed. It would probably have greatly irritated Cromwell and the king if they had known that, more than 450 years later, these reminders of monasticism are still visited and enjoyed. For it does not take much imagination to close one's eyes amidst the peaceful serenity of Fountains Abbey and see the monks still moving there among the stones, or to catch the chant of plainsong drifting on the wind.

LORD LATIMER was perhaps fortunate to avoid the fate of the eloquent Robert Aske and the elderly lords who had never quite been Henry's men. His brother Marmaduke spent some time in the Tower of London, writing desperate letters to Cromwell, in which he could not refrain from mentioning the involvement of 'my lord, my brother'. Then Latimer's steward, Walter Rawlinson, was accused as a rebel leader in Westmoreland.[21] His own conduct, and that of those close to him, was easily characterized as traitorous. But, in the end, perhaps Latimer was not important enough for his life to be forfeit. He also had influential friends and relatives. Besides Fitzwilliam, he appealed to the brother of his second wife, Elizabeth, writing to Sir Christopher Musgrave on 18 January: 'Recommend me to my Lord Privy Seal [Cromwell], showing him that I was sorry the people spake otherwise than became them of him ... I think his Lordship would not be a hinderer of such of their desires as to be reasonable.' And he went on to reveal, in a few words, the agony he had been through. 'Though I durst not much contrary them, I did my best to reduce them to conformity to the King's pleasure. My being among them was a very painful and dangerous time to me. I pray God I never see such again.'[22] Heartfelt words, if not the bravest, and, as it happened, Musgrave was out of favour himself.

The Parr connection, however, was much better placed to help. William Parr had been at Norfolk's side during the autumn and winter, stout in his defence of the king. But Katherine's brother generally spent little time in the north, preferring to stay close to the court in London. He left the management of the Parr estates to one of his Strickland cousins. His tenants may well have resented his absenteeism and there are indications that he had been enclosing more of his lands. The prospect of rebellious tenants may well have added to his zeal in opposing the Pilgrimage of Grace. Possibly it was her younger brother's rising profile at court and the time he spent in military service with Norfolk that influenced the duke (always a man to watch carefully for who was rising and who was falling) to defend Latimer against accusations of treason. He could find nothing of substance against him, Norfolk told Cromwell in June 1537, and had sent him to London to plead his own cause: 'I cannot discover any evidence other than that he was enforced and no man in more danger of his life . . .'[23]

Katherine's uncle, Sir William Parr of Horton, had also shown unimpeachable loyalty to the Crown during the rebellion. He had been with the duke of Suffolk in Lincolnshire and supervised the executions at Louth and Horncastle in mid-March. Like his nephew, he realized the value of staying in with those at the top. This meant he tried to ingratiate himself with both Norfolk and Cromwell during the summer of 1537 – not the easiest of courses to follow, though the enmity between the two men was less evident at that point. Parr of Horton's presence at the execution in Hull of Sir Robert Constable prompted him to share with Cromwell the following confidence:

> At the execution of Constable, my lord of Norfolk showed me he was as much bound to your lordship as ever noblemen could be to another. I answered that I had heard and partly knew how willing you were to further him and his. He replied: 'Sir William, no man can report more than I know already, for I have found such assured goodness in him to me, that I never proved the like in any friend before; and in myself and all mine shall be, as long as I live, as ready to do his pleasure as any kinsman he hath.'[24]

This gushing manifesto of friendship from a nobleman who could not stand the upstart Cromwell, and was to spend the next three years looking for ways to destroy him, is a telling example of the duplicity that prevailed in Henry VIII's England.

Latimer escaped death, but his life was no longer fully his to direct after the Pilgrimage of Grace. Maybe it never really had been, so unpredictable were the times. Having survived, Katherine Parr's second husband knew he would need to dance to the tune of the king and his ministers for the rest of his days. Keeping on the right side of Thomas Cromwell cost him money and property. He paid small sums in cash every year (he was not especially singled out for this discreet form of blackmail; others paid it, too), and was forced to sell two of his southern manors and the lease of his residence in London. This was more humiliating than financially damaging, especially as even this did not buy peace of mind. But for Katherine, at least, the ordeal of the Pilgrimage of Grace brought one very major benefit. She persuaded her husband that they should move from Snape and distance themselves from the troubles that had such a profound effect on their lives. She had been away from her family for more than seven years, and she no longer wanted to reside permanently in the north of England.

THE LATIMERS moved first to Wyke in Worcestershire, one of the manors that Katherine's husband had been visiting before the troubles of 1536. In late 1537 Wyke was more than a temporary refuge from civil unrest and the fear of death; it was the first stage of a journey that led Katherine to court. Soon, when Lord Latimer acquired Stowe Manor in Northamptonshire in the charming village of Stowe Nine Churches, she was able to live even closer to her Green and Parr relatives. Here, at the heart of England, Katherine could exchange visits with her uncle William Parr, who lived at Horton Manor, near Northampton, and with her Vaux and Lane cousins. For someone who had grown up in a close family atmosphere, and who no doubt wished the same for her two stepchildren, this change to her life must have been a relief and a delight, providing her with companionship while her husband was absent.

For Lord Latimer was often away. He had lost his place on the Council of the North, despite Norfolk recommending that he be retained, but he was often required to do service in northern England. As justice of the peace, on various commissions over the next six years, and also on horseback in further campaigns along the borders, Latimer did the king's bidding. He also needed to manage his affairs at Snape and to keep a residence near York so

that he could have somewhere to stay while on official business
in the north. In 1538 he had purchased lands that once belonged
to the church at Nun Monkton and Kirk Hamerton, just outside
the city. These estates were also intended to provide Margaret
Neville with an income of her own after her father's death, an
indication that Latimer did not believe that young John Neville
would provide adequately for his sister. Katherine joined her husband occasionally over the next four years, perhaps not without
apprehension. The north was still unpredictable and there were
further revolts in 1541, which partly inspired Henry VIII's visit
to York in the company of his new queen, Katherine Howard.[25]

Latimer was also often in London, diligent in his attendance
at the House of Lords. He attended parliament regularly in
1539, though he could not face being present for the session
when Lord Darcy's attainder was made final. It was a small act
of defiance, but a poignant one. The following year saw the
fall of Cromwell, bundled out to the Tower of London from a
meeting of the Privy Council, his badge of St George plucked
off by Norfolk, at last able to demonstrate that the pleasure he
really wanted to do Cromwell was to have him executed.

It has been said that Katherine Parr played an influential role
behind the scenes in Cromwell's downfall, but this is pure
invention.[26] She would not have regretted his demise, but the
idea of her whispering damaging revelations into the ear of Henry
VIII (especially at a time when he was besotted with Katherine
Howard) is simply not supported by any evidence. We do not
even know whether she was at court in the summer of 1540. The
most likely source of this misapprehension is the lengthy doggerel
poem, the 'Ballad of Sir Nicholas Throckmorton', contained in
the Throckmorton Manuscript. Nicholas Throckmorton was a
cousin of Katherine Parr (his mother was a half-sister of Katherine's father) and his very colourful account of his life and times
was almost certainly put into verse by his own nephew, based
on the reminiscences of Sir Nicholas himself. It is entertaining,
if laboured, and though certainly not great poetry, it cannot be

dismissed as an historical source. But there is a need to approach its evidence with extreme caution.

The point at issue concerns Sir George Throckmorton, Katherine's uncle by marriage. Sir George had been in and out of the Tower throughout the 1530s. He was a conservative Catholic gentleman, very like Lord Latimer, but he had overtly opposed the divorce and the religious changes, which Latimer did not. As he had also opposed Cardinal Wolsey much earlier in Henry's the reign, he was clearly unafraid of taking on the very powerful, and equally lucky to have got away with nothing worse than several bouts of incarceration. Cromwell, with an eye to Throckmorton's estate at Coughton in Warwickshire, had hounded him but not actually threatened his life. He must have come to regret his pursuit, for on the very day of his arrest, Cromwell wrote in anguish to Henry VIII denying the accusation that he had been guilty of treasonable conversations with Throckmorton: 'Your Grace', he reminded Henry, 'knows what manner of man Throckmorton has ever been towards you and your proceedings.'[27] The suggestion that he might have been in cahoots with Throckmorton was damaging to Cromwell, but he would have gone to the block if it had never been made. Its source was probably the back-stabbing, venal and unprincipled chancellor, Richard Rich. There is much about the machinations leading to Cromwell's fall that is still not clear, but we should beware of seeing the comely Lady Latimer gliding through Westminster Palace on a mission to erase him.

KATHERINE MUST, though, have become a regular visitor at court once she had moved from Yorkshire. Her brother and sister were both there and it was probably through them, as well as her husband's status as a baron, that she took her place in London society. Anne Parr, in particular, would have been a good source of introduction to the ladies of the court. By about 1538 she was married herself, to William Herbert, a Welsh

soldier of somewhat dubious background and reputation. The
earl of Warwick had put Herbert's paternal grandfather, the earl
of Pembroke, to death during the Wars of the Roses and the
family's influence in Wales waned thereafter. The grandson
owed his place at court to the influence of the earl of Worcester,
a distant relative. 'Black Will Herbert', as he was known to his
contemporaries, had killed a man in 1527 and may have spent
some time in the service of Francis I of France as a result of this
transgression. He was, intermittently, a member of the king's
household during the 1530s and this, no doubt, is how he met
Anne Parr. Given her brother's connections and his good standing with the king, Anne must have seemed a good prospect. She
had been one of Jane Seymour's ladies and retained the role
when Henry eventually married for a fourth time, to Anne of
Cleves. We do not know exactly how Anne's marriage came
about and whether it was a love match, but it is interesting to
note that both Parr sisters seem to have been attracted to dashing men of action who were slightly disreputable. This predilec-
tion was not yet apparent in Katherine but would eventually
have a dramatic effect on her life.

The position of the Parrs seemed to be improving the longer
Henry VIII was on the throne. Katherine's brother was duly
raised to the peerage in 1539, as Baron Parr, and Anne survived
the failure of the Cleves marriage and the disgrace of Katherine
Howard's fall unscathed, still prominent among the ladies of the
court. Lord Latimer, however, continued to be ordered periodi-
cally to the north. His position was eased by Cromwell's overthrow but he was not allowed to rest. He may, though, have been
relieved to stay outside the faction-fighting of the early 1540s in
London, a perilous period at court as the religious conservatives
wrestled with the reformers for influence. During 1542, as the
king moped over Katherine Howard's betrayal of his trust,
Latimer was as much on the move as ever. He attended the first
session of parliament that year but the summer found him on

military service yet again on the Scottish border. Perhaps it was this renewed campaign, as well as the first signs that his health was beginning to fail, that prompted him to make his will in September 1542.

Lord Latimer survived the dangers of warfare and came back down to the capital at some point during the latter part of the year. By then, the decline in his health was much more serious, for he did not attend the first session of the 1543 parliament. He remained at his Charterhouse residence and it was there that he died, probably towards the end of February. In his will, he had left direction that he was to be buried 'on the south side of Well Church in the county of York, where my ancestors lie, if I should die in Yorkshire'. But as he died in London, far away from Snape, his mortal remains were laid to rest in St Paul's Cathedral on 2 March. He made provision for his children, various relatives and, of course, Katherine herself. In addition to the manor at Stowe she was also given the estates near York and the responsibility of bringing up Margaret Neville, and providing support if the girl did not marry in five years. More poignantly, he also bequeathed her his 'best basin and ewer of silver and my two silver flagons'.[28] To his son, John, he left Snape and all its contents and his title. He also set aside sufficient funds to endow a school and pay a schoolmaster to teach 'the sons of the tenements and inhabitants of the lordship of Snape and Well'.

It was a bequest typical of the man. Lord Latimer was a conservative noble who cared for the welfare of his tenants, who preferred to worship God in the traditions of his forefathers, and whose loyalty to the king would have gone unremarked, and probably no more than adequately rewarded, were it not for the Pilgrimage of Grace. He had been fortunate in his third wife, a caring mother to his two children and loyal spouse, and she in him, for his constancy and affection. And now Katherine, Lady Latimer, comfortable if not rich, could contemplate her future once again. At last, the prospect that she might be able to please herself in the choice of a husband seemed to beckon. On the day of her husband's burial in early March 1543, when winter had not quite given way to spring, she had no idea that, four months later, she would be queen of England.

Part Three

'Kateryn the Quene'

1543–1547

CHAPTER SIX

Two Suitors

'God ... through his grace and goodness ... made me to
renounce utterly mine own will.'

Queen Katherine, recalling her dilemma
in the spring of 1543

EASTER SUNDAY fell early in 1543, on 25 March, the official
start of the New Year in the old Julian calendar. For Katherine,
as for the entire population of the country, this herald of a new
beginning could not have come soon enough. The winter had
been hard and long. It set in so early that, in the troubled
northern borders where Lord Latimer had spent his last autumn,
the roads soon became impassable. The news of the birth of
the child, who would very shortly become Mary Queen of Scots,
took four days to travel from Linlithgow in Scotland to Alnwick
in Northumberland, a distance of just over 100 miles. Following
on the poor harvest of the very wet summer of 1542, this was a
time of intense deprivation. Frost and snow sat on the ground
for weeks and the cost of firewood and fish rocketed. The
situation became so bad that a proclamation was issued on
9 February allowing the eating of white meat in Lent. Just before
Easter itself, the mayor and aldermen of London were feeling
the pinch, too, and decided that it would be good to demonstrate some solidarity with their fellow-citizens by announcing

'that [they] . . . should have and be served but with one course at dinner and supper'.[1]

Katherine had much to reflect on as winter began to release its grip. She was thirty years old, widowed for a second time but comfortable financially. Her responsibilities towards her wayward stepson were over, though she did not forget him, as we shall see, which suggests that their relationship remained cordial, if not close. Lord Latimer had particularly required her to look after the welfare of his daughter but her affection for Margaret Neville made this a pleasure rather than a duty. As Lady Latimer, residing at her late husband's residence in the Charterhouse, Katherine was well connected, respected and independent. Once the period of mourning was over, she could consider her future. She was an attractive and intelligent woman with an enquiring mind. Her duty as a loyal spouse fulfilled, Katherine was able, for the first time, to ponder what she might want to do with her life. Two things were obvious to her at once. The first was that she wanted to stay at court; she had done with provincial life. The second was that she wanted to remarry. Both her wishes were granted, but not at all in the way that she had anticipated when she buried Lord Latimer in St Paul's Cathedral. This, at least, was what she came to believe subsequently. But was it really true?

Disentangling the emotions of Katherine Parr in the spring and early summer of 1543 is less straightforward than has been suggested, chiefly because the main source we have to rely on is, of course, the lady herself. But it is worth the effort of unravelling what happened because it illuminates her later attitudes and behaviour. There are, inevitably, gaps in our knowledge (not least of which is the actual date of Lord Latimer's death, which clearly has an important bearing on Katherine's behaviour), but there are strong hints that the decision she eventually made was one that her intellect, if not her heart, had accepted sooner than she subsequently acknowledged. The key to unlocking this mystery lies in the court.

This was evidently a milieu that Katherine enjoyed but whose undercurrents and dangers she perhaps failed to appreciate at a time when she was at last able to put her personal happiness before other considerations. The pattern of her life in the years after her move south from Yorkshire suggests strongly that she liked being in London and close to the centre of events. There is no need to suppose that she had any official position of her own; her husband's status and the contacts of her brother and sister would have given her a sufficient entrée. The belief that she sought a position in the household of Princess Mary early in the winter of 1542–3 is based on a misunderstanding of the documents among her household expenses as queen. We do not need to imagine her forsaking her ailing husband to frequent the princess's splendid residence at Whitehall Palace, busily ordering dresses for the king's elder daughter and gossiping with the other ladies. Apart from the inherent unlikelihood of Katherine making a very calculating and selfish move, abandoning Lord Latimer as he lay dying, Princess Mary was far too interested in fashion to allow someone else to choose her wardrobe. The dresses were in fact ordered by Katherine while still Lady Latimer, for herself and for her 'daughter', in this case, Margaret Neville. Katherine apparently did not pay bills promptly. This tendency may have been endemic among the Tudor aristocracy, but grew worse in Katherine's case with time, an aspect of her character, and the running of her household as queen, that has gone largely unremarked.[2]

Katherine was interested in medicine and herbs and it seems likely, though we cannot know for sure, that she supervised Lord Latimer's treatment during his final illness herself. This does not mean that she spent all her time tending to him, though she is unlikely to have socialized much during the first months of 1543 because of the freezing weather. The same may not have been true in 1542, especially when Latimer was away in the north and she could see more of her family. The court during this year was a strange place, at first in a kind of limbo until after the execution of Katherine Howard in February. Gradually, it began to revive, as Henry VIII emerged from his depression and sense of grievance at his fifth wife's behaviour. Despite the fact that the king was without a consort, the ladies of the queen's household remained at court, including Anne Herbert, who had now to hand back to the Crown the jewels she had supervised for her giddy, doomed mistress. Anne, however, must have realized that she could not expect to rise further without powerful patronage, and though her husband's career had not yet taken off, the Herberts knew enough about the court to survive and hope for better things. So, too, did Katherine's brother, William, who was himself committed to staying in London. His northern lands did not interest him at all and he seldom went there to manage them.

His situation, however, looked far from promising. Cromwell had appropriated the title of earl of Essex on the death of William Parr's father-in-law in 1540. Although he only enjoyed the title briefly before his fall, there was worse to follow for the disappointed Parr. His marriage with Anne Bourchier, on which Maud Parr had staked so much, was by now beyond repair. While many other couples who were incompatible managed somehow to get along, at least with a veneer of success, Anne Bourchier had no interest in observing proprieties. Quite why she hated her husband, who was good-looking and socially adept, is impossible to say. She had always resisted the idea of living with him and disliked court life, which he, of course, embraced wholeheartedly. In 1541, to add insult to injury, she ensured that he would never have her father's title by eloping with a lover of whom little is known but whose child she bore the following year. The blow to Parr's pride (and to the family's as well) was tremendous, and William swiftly took steps to contain the damage. He obtained a legal separation in 1542 and a bill in parliament the following year, in the first month of his sister's widowhood, barring any child of Anne's from inheriting Bourchier or Parr estates. Thus did his great marriage evaporate. Yet he probably already sensed that his future was far from hopeless. As a child, he was close to his sister Katherine. Yet even as he contemplated the collapse of everything he had anticipated since he was thirteen years old, he saw another prospect, more glorious still, beckoning. He could not yet be sure; it all depended on Katherine herself.

Lady Latimer, however, was contemplating her own happiness rather than William's lost earldom. She already sensed the direction her life was likely to take but could not bring herself to acknowledge it because she had fallen in love. The man who had conquered her heart was the only man she ever truly loved for himself, the king's brother-in-law, Sir Thomas Seymour. It is impossible to say when she first became aware of this compelling attraction – perhaps she did not know herself – but, as soon as Lord Latimer was laid to rest, Katherine was more than willing to be wooed. As she told Seymour four years later: 'as truly as God is God, my mind was fully bent the other time I was at liberty to marry you before any man I know'.[3] Nothing could be plainer. And why not? For Tom Seymour was the most desirable man at court.

He was the fourth of six sons of a Wiltshire knight, Sir John Seymour, and he might have remained in obscurity, the younger son of a minor country gentleman, had his sister Jane not replaced Anne Boleyn in the affections of Henry VIII and become the king's third wife.[4] It was a brief marriage but Jane managed to produce the longed-for heir and in so doing justified all the pain that Henry believed he had suffered in his search to ensure the future of his dynasty. Jane's death in October 1537, the result of complications following the birth of Prince Edward, left the king with fond memories and probably ensured the continuing favour of her family. Jane was the closest in age to Thomas but they seem to have been quite unalike in temperament, nor, apparently, did they much resemble each other. Where Jane was fair and calm, Thomas Seymour was tawny and tempestuous. He was a man who bore his good looks dramatically and he played to the hilt his reputation as the most dashing blade at court in the 1540s. William Parr, who had known the Seymour brothers since childhood (he knew Edward Seymour well from their time together in the duke of Richmond's household), was a charming ladies' man, but he could not compete for sheer charisma with the overwhelming presence of Sir Thomas. A versifier and well-travelled sophisticate, with a magnificent speaking and singing voice, Seymour was on good terms with the king. He was also ambitious (perhaps the one trait he shared with his late sister) and though broadly aligned with the religious reformers, not someone to be found deep in study of the Bible. After his death, he was accused of being a non-believer, a serious accusation in an age that found atheism deeply shocking, but this seems to have been part of a deliberate campaign to degrade his memory. Probably he was not especially devout, and in that he may have been more honest than many of his contemporaries. But whatever his personal beliefs, one thing was certain. Although in his mid-thirties, he was still unmarried.[5]

That he should have appealed to Katherine Parr, after nearly fifteen years of dutiful wedlock, is not surprising. Nor is it unreasonable to believe that he was genuinely attracted to her, a slim, elegant and accomplished woman with hair the colour of burnished gold, a warm personality and exemplary private life masking hidden depths of sensuality that a man with his experience of the world might have detected even while she was still married. Katherine had a reasonable income but was not a rich widow. He was aware of this – Seymour was the sort of man who would have found out, however romantic he might appear – so the inference must be that their affection was mutual. His subsequent behaviour strongly suggests that it was. They were close in age, he being about three years older, and she clearly wanted to be his wife. One can conjecture that he might have been content with a less formal relationship, at least to begin with, but whatever his intentions, he clearly pursued them with some alacrity once it was proper to do so. Thomas Seymour liked his roistering persona, but there is absolutely no evidence that he sought to make Katherine his mistress while Lord Latimer was alive. We do not know when they first met but the likelihood is that Katherine's brother was the link. Katherine had probably known Thomas Seymour for some years before she was widowed for the second time.

Seymour's reputation has suffered much over the centuries. Vilified after his death, his image as a shallow, posturing black-guard and womanizer has been meat and drink to historical novelists. Yet there is no evidence that contemporaries thought him unusually dissolute. He may well have enjoyed casual amours with the ladies of the courts he frequented, both in London and overseas, but the names of his mistresses are not known and there is no suggestion that he had illegitimate children.[6] And there were those who admired him during his lifetime, who sought and enjoyed his company, and remained true to him after his death. Nicholas Throckmorton, Katherine's cousin, composing his memoirs years later, wrote: 'He was, at all essays, my perfect friend, and patron too, until his dying end', a generous tribute to someone who is often criticized for reckless selfishness. It is time to look at him again, to try to separate the legend (some of which he might well have enjoyed) from the reality.

Katherine's suitor already had a long career in and around the court, as well as plenty of diplomatic and military experience. This aspect of his life went back well before his sister's time as queen, to when Henry was still married to Katherine of Aragon. In the year 1530 he was in France with one of Henry's favourites, Sir Francis Bryan. Bryan, highly experienced as a diplomat in Rome and France, was known for being outspoken and a man who had pursued his pleasures with brio when he was younger. It may well be that the young Thomas Seymour modelled himself on this clever and energetic man, who had already told the king that the cause of the divorce was completely lost in Rome. But Bryan also knew how to mask his true feelings to good effect in a volatile political climate, a lesson that his protégé forgot in later life.

The life of a diplomat and occasional soldier might have been expected to remain the lot of this junior member of an unremarkable family. He was not cut out for the Church and though his brother Edward showed an early interest in the new learning and religious reform, Thomas seems to have embraced them with less conviction. Though evidently well educated, he liked action, as younger brothers often do. One of his earliest surviving letters finds him at sea with the king's fleet between the Isle of Wight and Portsmouth, on the look-out for French men-of-war infiltrating English waters.[7] He especially loved being at sea and relished a naval scrap. Even his enemies acknowledged his personal bravery. But he was not destined to remain on the fringes, sending dispatches back to London from distant courts. Jane Seymour's bid for the title of queen consort in 1536, as Henry's marriage to Anne Boleyn disintegrated, was very carefully planned: Edward Seymour used his promotion to the position of gentleman of the king's Privy Chamber in early March of that year to get his sister quite literally within reach of the king via a private passage to the Seymours' apartments in Greenwich Palace.

Thomas had to wait a little longer for the same appointment, until early October 1537, less than two weeks before his sister gave birth to her son. It was swiftly followed by a knighthood, and by Jane's death on 24 October. The brief but spectacular rise of the Seymour family now seemed over, yet the Privy Chamber posts meant that the brothers remained close to the king. Their presence reminded Henry that they were his son's uncles and they continued to receive favours from the king. To his knighthood, Thomas Seymour now had added important offices in the Welsh borders, as well as lands in the same area. He also benefited from grants of land taken from dissolved monasteries in Essex, Hampshire and Berkshire at the beginning of 1538.

Perhaps it was this growing portfolio of estates, as well as the continuing goodwill of the king towards his baby son's male

relatives, that prompted the first serious discussion of his marriage –
or certainly the first that is known. The proposal was, at first
sight, a grand one and it was not even instigated by Seymour
himself. Instead, the suggestion was made to Henry VIII by the
duke of Norfolk that his widowed daughter, Mary Howard,
duchess of Richmond, should wed Sir Thomas. Norfolk was
casting around for ways to rehabilitate his family following the
Boleyn affair; he took the view that this would be an advantageous union for the Howards, noting that Seymour was his
choice for Mary because he 'is so honestly advanced by the king's
majesty, as also for his towardness and his other commendable
merits'. But a further comment ascribed to Norfolk is far more
revealing of his outlook: 'there ensueth', he ventured, 'no great
good by conjunction of great bloods together [and] he sought
not . . . nor desired to marry his daughter in any high blood or
degree'. In this superb example of Howard cunning and snobbery
it sounds as though Norfolk was musing on the disaster of his
own marriage to Elizabeth Stafford, as well as delivering a
dismissal of the upstart family with whom he proposed to unite
his daughter. The king apparently found the idea most amusing
and 'answered merrily that if he [Norfolk] were so minded to
bestow his daughter . . . he would be sure to couple her with one
of such lust and youth, as should be able to please her well at all
points'.[8]

Mary had been the wife of the king's illegitimate son, the
duke of Richmond, who died in 1536. She was not yet twenty
and, from what can be seen of the Holbein uncompleted sketch
of her, not displeasing, if perhaps no great beauty. The resemblance to her father is apparent. But, looks aside, Mary Howard
was a high-born lady. She was also an impecunious one, still
fighting her not so devoted father-in-law, the king, for her
jointure as duchess of Richmond. She was not keen to lose it all
together, as she feared would undoubtedly happen if she married
again at this point. In fact, she was far from eager to marry at all,
even someone as attractive as Thomas Seymour.

Seymour's own reaction to the idea was somewhat muted; he never came to seek the lady in person. In fact, his reaction was to let someone else handle further discussion, despite the king's approval. That person was Thomas Cromwell, who, as well as being the chief minister was the father of Sir Thomas's brother-in-law, Gregory.[9] On 14 July 1538 Sir Ralph Sadler, one of Cromwell's most trusted servants, wrote to the minister: 'The king has spoken to Sir Thomas about it [the Howard marriage] and he, considering that your son has married his sister, prefers you to have the maining of the matter.'[10] Sadler himself thought well of Seymour, describing his 'honesty, sadness [which meant seriousness in Tudor England] and other good qualities'. His opinion of Seymour may not have been shared by history, but it is worth noting, for Ralph Sadler was not the sort of man to give praise where it was not due. In the end, nothing came of Norfolk's idea. It does, however, throw a fascinating light on the family politics of Henry VIII's court in the late 1530s. And, as the years went by and both parties remained unmarried, it was not all together forgotten. Eventually it was proposed again, at a crucial point of Katherine Parr's reign as queen consort.[11]

Resuming his diplomatic career, Seymour's lifestyle meant that he was often on the move over the next five years. He had no ties, and no great expectations, so it was the perfect existence for his restless nature. Soon he was back at the French court, going from there to Cambrai, where Mary of Hungary, the imperial regent, was in residence. At this point of his career, it was his monarch's marriage, rather than his own, that he was pursuing. Christina of Denmark, the handsome lady in whom Henry VIII was interested at the time, did not reciprocate, but by the end of the following year Henry's fourth wife, Anne of Cleves, was at Calais on her way to England. Seymour was among the knights who dined with her on 13 December, before her storm-tossed journey across the Channel. His opinion of the German princess's looks is unknown, but the following May Day, when her time as Henry's queen was running out fast (though she did not know it), Thomas Seymour was back in London, enjoying his participation in a major jousting and sporting event at Whitehall. Dressed in white velvet, he must have dazzled Anne and her ladies. But two months later he was on the road again, this time for Vienna and the court of the emperor's brother, Ferdinand of Austria. Henry sent him there to gauge the situation in Hungary and Germany. It was an interesting post, and Seymour learned much. His despatches show that he was a shrewd observer of the military strengths and strategies of Hungary in its battle with the Ottoman Empire. When the siege of Pest failed all together in October 1542, Seymour made his way back through Germany, looking to recruit mercenaries who could be signed to Henry VIII's army. He spent Christmas in Nuremberg and when the king decided not to meet the financial terms demanded by the German soldiers of fortune, Seymour was recalled on 14 January 1543. He would have been back in London at about the time that Lady Latimer knew that her husband was not long for this world. Once he was buried in early March, Seymour could quite properly pay court to her. In age, background and interests, they were well matched, two good-looking people of considerable charm, well connected but not themselves powerful, who liked the court and the life it offered. There was every reason that they should have chosen each other, and Thomas, with his accustomed confidence, set about wooing Katherine in earnest. He seems not to have realized at first that there was a rival suitor. Katherine may not have acknowledged this herself but when she did, it must have made Seymour all the more attractive – and all the more unattainable. For the other man taking a keen interest in Lady Latimer was the king himself.

HENRY VIII had been a widower for just over a year. It was not a state he enjoyed. Like most men of his times, he believed that having a wife was part of the natural order of things. He was not looking for a partner in the modern sense (the idea would have seemed ridiculous to him) but he was undoubtedly an uxorious man. Undeterred by the tally of five previous attempts at wedded bliss, all of which, he firmly believed, had foundered through God's will or man's infamy, he was ready to try again. Lessons had been learned from the disastrous embarrassment of Katherine Howard and he was no longer prey to the attractions of a teenage strumpet dangled in front of him by deeply self-interested factions. He wanted a more mature woman with whom he could hold a conversation, who knew something of the world and possessed the right mixture of intelligence and grace to play effectively the part of queen consort, which, after all, was performed on the international stage. Someone, in other words, in whom he could have trust. It probably also occurred to him that, now he had mended fences with his elder daughter, Mary, after years of tension, it would be a very good thing if he chose a bride who could be a proper companion to her. That would add another note of femininity but also gravity to the court. In fact, his mind was beginning to turn to all of his three children and how he might organize the question of the succession beyond Edward, his immediate heir. Not that he had given up the idea of producing further brothers for the prince. A lady who could produce a duke of York would be exceedingly welcome. Henry knew better than anyone that elder brothers might not always outlive their younger siblings. Above all, one gets the sense that Henry was lonely, that in his heart of hearts he could not quite abandon the notion that he could enjoy a happy, married life with a lady who shared his interests and would never threaten him in any way.

But whatever the mix of his emotions at the time, he was looking, first and foremost, for a wife who would please him. She must meet his standards of attractiveness, or the relationship would founder. And she must have an unimpeachable reputation, to save him from the horrors of Anne Boleyn and Katherine Howard. He was not especially seeking a stepmother for his children – Henry was hardly a family man – but considerations

This striking portrait in Lambeth Palace, the earliest of Katherine, conveys her intelligence and fortitude.

The Great Hall at Gainsborough Old Hall, where Katherine lived during her first marriage to Edward Borough.

Above left Katherine's much-loved younger brother, William Parr, in the late 1530s.

Above right St Mary's Chapel at Snape Castle is one of the few surviving examples of a pre-Reformation private chapel in England. The Latimer family worshipped here.

Below Snape Castle, Bedale, Yorkshire. Katherine's home during her marriage to Lord Latimer and where she was held hostage during the Pilgrimage of Grace.

Above left Cuthbert Tunstall, diplomat and churchman, and kinsman to Katherine's father. He was an important constant in Katherine's life.

Above right Katherine's bedchamber at Sudeley.

Below The grounds of Sudeley Castle, showing the chapel where Katherine is buried.

The Habsburg emperor Charles V, ruler of most of Europe and rival of Henry VIII. He initially viewed Katherine Parr as a useful ally.

A contemporary woodcut showing the martyrdom of the religious reformer, Anne Askew, a gentlewoman uncomfortably close to Katherine Parr.

Right Thomas Howard, third duke of Norfolk, whose cunning helped defeat the Pilgrimage of Grace in 1536.

Below left Stephen Gardiner, bishop of Winchester, who married Henry VIII and Katherine Parr in 1543. An opponent of further religious reform, he became Katherine's enemy.

Below right Thomas Wriothesley, later earl of Southampton, was lord chancellor in the last years of Henry VIII's reign. An able administrator, he is often viewed as a religious conservative, but his major interest was in self-advancement. He was certainly involved in moves to compromise those close to Katherine, including the interrogation and torture of Anne Askew.

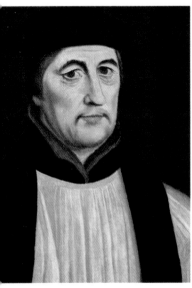

Left Every inch a queen. This full-length portrait shows Katherine Parr at the high point of her time as Henry VIII's consort.

Below The queen's signature. The addition of the initials KP, her family name, was unique among Henry's wives.

Right Katherine painted in about 1545, regal, serene and magnificently dressed.

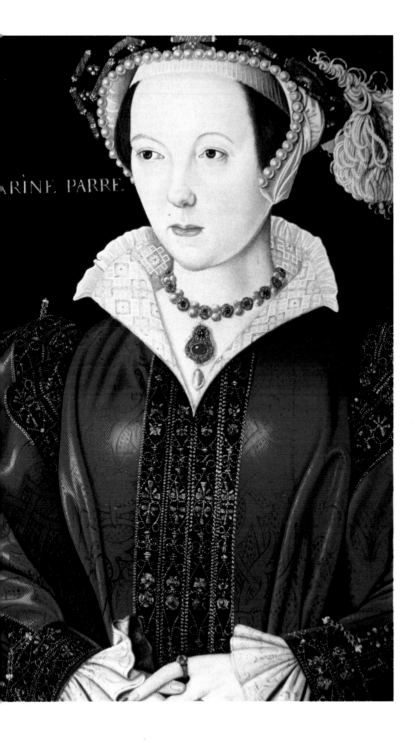

Left Katherine's coat of arms.

Below left Henry VIII in about 1540, magnificent but already overweight.

Below right The ageing Henry VIII as he probably looked at the time of his last marriage.

about their future were beginning to take shape in his mind. Nor, however ill and uncomfortable he might be from time to time, was he looking for a nurse. He wanted a wife for his bed and a worthy queen for his kingdom. In June 1543 he would be fifty-two years old. He was undisputed master of the kingdom he had ruled for thirty-four years but he still yearned for one more chance at connubial bliss. Perhaps he sensed that a good marriage would revive more than just his flagging spirits and ailing body. It might improve England's standing as a European power. He was not, though, looking to find a high-profile foreign bride. The negotiations would be endless and the outcome might just be another Anne of Cleves. Always a shrewd observer of what was going on around him and ever-charming to the ladies of the court, an idea began to form in his mind. Lady Latimer had all the qualities he desired. 'For beside the virtues of her mind,' wrote John Foxe, 'she was endued with rare gifts of nature, as singular beauty, favour and a comely personage; things wherein the king was greatly delighted.'[12] She was an ideal choice for his sixth wife. Once the decision had been taken, it seemed such an obvious course that he was quite prepared to be patient and wait for the lady's formal acceptance of his marriage proposal. He could also watch his brother-in-law's discomfiture with some amusement.

What was Henry VIII actually like in 1543, both as man and king? We think we know him – he is surely the most instantly recognizable English monarch – yet he was not an easy man to know and it was an important part of his office to preserve that aura of being different from ordinary men. There are portraits of him from every decade of his life. Once he became king, they were all intended to capture his authority and magnificence. Yet they tell a sad story. Physically, he was by the 1540s a far cry from the golden youth (albeit with a rather girlish face) who captivated European observers when he came to the throne back in 1509. The clean-shaven young man with bobbed hair had been replaced by the more severe, bearded image of the mature king, his hair cropped close to his head beneath the jewelled caps he always wore in public. And the taut, athletic body of the sportsman and jouster was long gone. In 1515, the year before the birth of Princess Mary, when he was twenty-four years old, his waistline measured $35^{1}/_{2}$ inches. By 1540 it had expanded to 49 inches and was still increasing. Two years later, even as he was contemplating marrying for the sixth time, it was noted that he was 'already very stout and daily growing heavier, he seems very old and grey . . . three of the biggest men to be found could get inside his doublet'.[13] Hardly, then, an enticing prospect as a husband. Of course, he dressed superbly, ever-conscious of his image as a monarch, yet the bulky layers of Tudor clothing only added to his girth. The impression must have been over-whelming.

Given his massive size, it is hardly surprising that Henry's health had suffered. In this respect his athletic past caught up with him and actually contributed to his difficulties. By the late 1530s he was suffering from problems with his legs, caused, it is now thought, by old injuries that had never healed properly and led to bone disease. When this flared up, the pain was intense. Over the years, the king became less and less active and the vicious circle of pain, immobility and weight-gain continued. In March 1543, the king's secretary, Sir William Paget, wrote to Edward Seymour: 'the king's majesty is now well again, who hath two or three days been troubled with a humour descending to his leg'.[14] This was nothing new, and it would only get worse. One revealing detail of this is the increase in the king's orders for hose. This had averaged a little over 100 pairs a year between 1535 and 1539; in the years 1543–5, 322 pairs were supplied for the increasingly diseased royal legs.[15] Henry was already walking with the aid of a stick but he did not yet need the contraption of a chair on pulleys that moved him from one part of Whitehall Palace to another at the end of his reign.

Failing eyesight was also bothering him, as it had his paternal grandmother, Lady Margaret Beaufort, and would, eventually, his daughter, Mary. Henry sometimes used a reading glass, set in wood with a handle, and he also wore spectacles, which were kept in a golden case engraved with the arms of England. These fitted onto the nose and could be held in place with ties – not very dignified, perhaps, but useful in helping him to read, and probably seen only by those very close to him, since reading was something he still did in the privacy of his bedchamber. There is a wonderful illustration in one of the Royal Manuscripts in the British Library that shows a younger king reading his psalter in a chair beside his bed. Although the figure of the king himself is out of proportion, with a large head atop an impossibly small body, making him look rather like a bookish gnome, the surroundings are superbly rendered. On the tiled floor, at his feet, are two more beautifully bound books. Henry collected such fine things, with more taste and less trouble than he collected wives.

The glasses speak of the king's determination to deal with his problems and make the necessary adjustments that come with age. Despite the agonizing bouts with his legs and the traumas of his personal life, Henry VIII had most definitely not given up on life or the business of being a king. He could no longer joust or play tennis but his cultural interests remained of great importance to him. His library of books and manuscripts had been growing throughout his reign and though the majority of them were, by the 1540s, kept in his three principal residences (Greenwich, Hampton Court and Whitehall), some also travelled with him as he visited his lesser houses in the country. During the course of his lifetime, the collection moved increasingly from manuscripts, many of which had been inherited from his father and more distant royal ancestors, to bound and printed books.

In the absence of accurate figures for the number of volumes possessed by Henry VIII, an indication of the importance he attached to them lies in the care taken of the collection. There is no surviving catalogue of the contents of the Greenwich library at the time of the king's death, but we do know that it was housed on one of the upper floors of the palace (to safeguard it from flooding), that it had seven desks for the reading and storing of books and a large table, under which more volumes were kept. There were 329 volumes in all at Greenwich, mostly arranged by colour rather than topic. The larger and more precious books, including 'two great bibles in Latin' and 'a great book called an herbal', were listed separately.[16] By 1542, when Henry was more often at Whitehall than Greenwich, the privy councillor Sir Anthony Denny, who grew ever closer to Henry in the monarch's final years, made an inventory of the 910 books in the upper library. By this time, a more sophisticated system of cataloguing had been developed for what was very much a working library. It contained 'one table covered with green cloth with sundry cupboards in it to set books in with four old curtains of buckram fringed with green silk to hang afore the books'.[17]

Henry's collection was wide-ranging, covering romances, music, medical books, volumes on the conduct of warfare, gen-ealogies showing the Tudor descent from Adam and Eve, and many French manuscripts. There were items connected with personal faith, Bibles, psalters, ordinals and many works of theology. The theological works reflected the king's intense interest in the great debates of the Reformation and his own developing ideas as the divorce from Katherine of Aragon slowly progressed. The contents of the libraries came from different sources; some were gifts, others commissions, or dedications from writers wanting to make a name for themselves. Many more came from the dissolved monasteries. As a younger man, Henry had been an avid note-taker (always in Latin) and underliner, but in later years he tended to skim the contents, send the book out to various learned parties (often with opposing viewpoints) and then summon the readers in for discussions. His mind was still very active, even if his body was not. He enjoyed disputation, providing, of course, that his view prevailed. An educated spouse must have seemed appealing. No doubt he did not dwell on the fact that the last wife who could talk on something like equal terms with him was Anne Boleyn.

The development of his library bears witness to the progression of his own views during his reign but it still took second place to his main cultural interest, music. Henry was more than just a competent musician. He could perform on the lute and virginals, and he studied the organ. At his death, he possessed over 300 musical instruments, a collection that rivals his library in its different way. Music was an important part of Henry's daily life and he had, certainly when younger, been no mere listener but a keen participant, playing the recorder and singing with his courtiers. More than thirty pieces written by him survive. Many were arrangements of continental compositions but he was clearly proficient enough to undertake such work and he also wrote several Masses, though these have subsequently been lost. He employed sixty professional musicians, a number of whom performed regularly in his Privy Chamber. As the reign went on, he tended to follow the fashion for Italian musicians, among whom were the Bassano brothers, Venetian singers who lived in the Charterhouse, near Katherine Parr. As queen, she would become an enthusiastic patron of the brothers. It is even possible that they were a link between Katherine and Henry VIII before she married the king.

He was less devoted to the fine arts. Of course, he collected many fine things but there was no one area of concentration. He expected to have his portrait painted and for the result to send out inescapable messages about his earthly power, but his patronage of painters was rather half-hearted. It had been Anne Boleyn who introduced Hans Holbein the Younger to Henry's court and the king himself does not seem to have viewed Holbein with any great enthusiasm. Perhaps the famously controversial portrait of Anne of Cleves did not help Holbein's cause. By the 1540s, Henry was patronizing the Flemish artists Scrots and Master John as well as the miniaturists the Horenbouts. Holbein never, so far as we know, painted Katherine Parr.

The king was a complex man. In any consideration of Henry at this stage of his life, it is easy to concentrate on his gigantic frame and reduce the man inside to a series of well-worn clichés. In this way the king becomes a cruel, fat, much-married tyrant, who, as the old saying goes, spared no man in his anger and no woman in his lust. This cut-out Henry has become an historical legend, the stuff of blockbuster television series. Like all legends, it contains elements of truth. But there was more to him than this enduring reputation suggests. As he looked at the condition of his kingdom in 1543 and weighed the threats to it, both internal and external, he was determined to maintain his power and authority in the face of a storm that he, as much as anyone else, had unleashed more than a decade earlier.

His personal beliefs were firmly fixed on a 'middle way' in religion. This had been made clear in a letter written to the ambassador in France in 1540. The occasion was the fall of Cromwell (who had been accused of fomenting heresy) but the message was clear: 'the king's majesty hath of long season travailed, and yet most godly travaileth, to establish such an order in matters of religion, as, neither declining on the right hand nor on the left hand'.[18] To underline this approach, three religious radicals and three Catholics were executed at the same time. One of the Catholics was Richard Featherstone, tutor to Princess Mary since she was nine years old. The following year, the princess's former Lady Governess, the countess of Salisbury, was beheaded in the Tower, as the king made sure that all those who had supported his elder daughter, and the Catholic opposition she represented, were eliminated. Politics and religion were inextricable, for above all else, the king wanted unity and the maintenance of an orthodoxy that was unique to Henrician England. His was 'a middle way neither Lutheran nor tradition- ally Catholic'. The king had fully endorsed the destruction of shrines, removal of images, cessation of pilgrimages and the assault on superstition that characterized the first phase of the Reformation in England. He had dissolved the monasteries and, through the wholescale distribution of their lands, set in motion a major change to English society.

Yet Henry could not be reconciled to the teaching of Martin Luther. The distaste he had felt as a young man for the German reformer never faded. The king maintained the straightforward piety in religious observance that was so important to his daughter Mary – a vital link between the two of them that has often been overlooked. Henry heard Mass regularly. It was an important part of his daily life and he could not be shaken in his belief in transubstantiation. This belief in the Real Presence of the body and blood of Christ in the bread and wine of the Mass was a fundamental point of difference between Henry and the reformers. But it was not the only one. Justification by faith alone did not convince him, either. He believed there must be more to salvation and would not accept that good works and charity did not play their part in the redemption of the soul.

These convictions were incorporated into new instructions for the clergy of England issued in spring 1543. Known as *The King's Book*, they had been commissioned in 1540 as a replacement to *The Bishop's Book* of 1538. Often seen as a setback for the cause of reform, *The King's Book* (or *A Necessary Doctrine and Erudition for any Christian Man*, to give the work its proper name), was, in fact, the result of lengthy discussions among all Henry's bishops. The work did not diverge so far from its predecessor as has been supposed but there were those, including Archbishop Cranmer, who wanted further reform and hoped that the process started in the 1530s would be an evolving one. The king saw things differently in 1543 and was committed to safeguarding the equilibrium in religious matters that he had striven so hard, and so bloodily, to effect. This was made clear in the preface to *The King's Book*, which begins:

> Like as in the time of darkness and ignorance, finding our people seduced and drawn from the truth by hypocrisy and superstition, we by the help of God and his word have travailed to purge and cleanse our realm from the apparent enormities of the same; wherein, by opening of God's truth,

with setting forth and publishing of the scriptures, our labours (thanks be to God) have not been void and frustrate; so now, perceiving that in the time of knowledge the Devil (who ceaseth not at all times to vex the world) hath attempted to return again ... into the house purged and cleansed ... *we find entered into our people's hearts an inclination to sinister understanding of scripture, presumption, arrogancy, carnal liberty and contention;* we be therefore constrained, for the reformation of them in time, and for avoiding of such diversity in opinions as by the said evil spirits as might be engendered, to set forth, with the advice of our clergy, such a doctrine ... with the principal articles of our religion, as whereby all men may uniformly be led and taught the true understanding of that which is necessary for every Christian man to know ...'[19]

He did not mention that Christian women could be similarly contaminated by a 'sinister understanding' of the scriptures but the italicized phrases are eerily prescient of his alleged reaction to Katherine Parr's religious interests three years later. Katherine's personal beliefs in 1543 were still developing and there was nothing about this aspect of her life that troubled the king.

Henry knew that the issue of further reform divided his churchmen and the shifting groupings of those around him at court. Perhaps that did not displease him; and if the conservatives wanted to think they were in the ascendant, he would humour them, for a while. But while the year of his marriage to Katherine Parr was for a long time viewed as the nadir of the evangelicals, recent scholarship has shown that this is too simplistic an interpretation.[20] It amused Henry to keep people in check, and possibly the choice of his new wife figured in these considerations. She was the widow of a staunch supporter of the old faith but her brother was aligned with the reformers. It was not obvious where Katherine herself stood, but her character, unostentatious piety and virtue were unassailable.

English religious policy remained fluid throughout the 1540s and it should be remembered that the overwhelming majority of the king's subjects were content to follow his lead and to acknowledge him as Supreme Head of the Church. And in 1543 religion was far from being the king's only preoccupation. He still kept a very close eye on international developments. The Reformation had long since become a major factor in European affairs, complicating traditional rivalries. Henry (a heretic, but at least a Christian one, unlike the Turks with whom France had sided against Emperor Charles V) sat on the sidelines for much of his reign, courted from time to time by both sides but trusted by neither. He liked to think of himself as an important player in Europe, but in truth he was not. England had not been involved in a war on the Continent for many years, though there were scares of an invasion in the late 1530s, when it was feared that France and the Holy Roman Empire might unite to impose the old Catholic order on England. This threat receded, but relations with France remained uneasy, in part because of the situation in Scotland. The northern border was a constant headache for Henry. His dealings with his nephew, the flamboyant, promiscuous but still very Catholic King James V, were always difficult. He may have physically borne a strong similarity to the young Henry VIII but James was keen to govern Scotland well after the inevitable difficulties of his long minority and he meant to do so without interference from his relatives. The Scottish king resented English bullying and his uncle's ill-disguised aim of imposing his will on the Stuart monarchy. He would not agree to become a client of the Tudors, despite the fact that his mother, Margaret, was Henry VIII's elder sister. But she died in 1541 and James was not, in any case, on good terms with her.

By the autumn of 1542, James V's determination to push the English away from his borders led to the campaign that had called Lord Latimer back to the north. It was to prove a disaster for the Scots. On 24 November a raiding party of Scots, consisting of many of the nobility who had joined James's 18,000-strong army, found itself cut off amid the salt marshes and rising tide of the river Esk, in the aptly named 'debatable lands' of the border. Facing them was a force of experienced English lancers under Sir Thomas Wharton.[21] Though Wharton's force was much smaller, amounting to no more than 3,000 men in total, it wreaked havoc on those involved in an ill-considered advance. At the ensuing battle of Solway Moss many Scots were captured and their army put to flight. James V, who was not actually at the battle, retired to Edinburgh, with a view to re-grouping. He had certainly not given up and was hopeful that his French queen would produce an heir. At the beginning of December, his wife, Mary of Guise, gave birth to a daughter. James never saw the child. By that time he was already unwell with a disease that progressed at shocking speed. Following swiftly on the news of Wharton's success against the Scots, Henry VIII soon learned, presumably without much real sorrow, of the death of his nephew.

The story that James, on his deathbed, had observed of the state of Scotland and his baby daughter's arrival, 'It began with a lass and it will end with a lass' is probably apocryphal. But, for Henry VIII, the birth of Mary Queen of Scots, in a mourning and deeply divided kingdom, was an unlooked-for opportunity and one he meant to use to good effect. His plan, to marry the little girl to his own son, Prince Edward, amounted to an annexation of Scotland. As a ploy, it was ahead of its time. Though uniting the two crowns was an obvious solution to centuries of low-level but wearingly destructive combat along the border, the French were not yet ready to lose their influence in Scotland. Mary of Guise was from a powerful faction at the French court and though many Scottish nobles disliked her, there was insufficient support for Henry VIII among the Scottish aristocracy for the king to be able to gain control immediately of the infant Queen of Scots. He knew that he needed to consolidate and extend his influence in Scotland before his policy could be brought to successful fruition. A massive military invasion and occupation was simply out of the question.

As the frigid weather lifted, Henry had much to keep him

occupied. He was accustomed to upheaval, opposition, foreign threat, obloquy, failed marriages and unreliable nobles. He knew that, for all his efforts, he had only one male heir, who was still a child. The likelihood of a lengthy minority, such as the Scots now faced, was impossible to ignore. The question of the succession had to be addressed, and his personal life stabilized. He wanted to marry again. At some point unknown, but probably not later than April, he asked Lady Latimer to be his wife. She did not give him an immediate reply and so he waited, while she grappled with her emotions, though it is unlikely that he ever gave any serious consideration to the thought that she might refuse him.

Katherine was faced with a truth that must have seemed overwhelming at first. Thomas Seymour was exciting and promised a personal happiness quite different from her previous husbands. But the king was the king. He offered Katherine and her family power and wealth undreamed of when the Parrs of Kendal set out on their tortuous road to advancement eighty years before. Ultimately, he could not be denied. In fact, he was so convinced that he had made the right choice that he allowed Katherine a lengthy period to respond to his proposal of marriage. During that time, probably spent at her home in the Charterhouse, she had ample opportunity to contemplate what she would lose and also what she would gain. Subsequently, she acknowledged her anguish, but at the time she was prudent enough to keep it well within the circle of her immediate family.

Thomas Seymour, whose attentions to Katherine may have heightened the king's own interest, was wise enough to know that he should leave the field clear. Katherine would not be his, or, at least, not yet. If he had to give her up, losing her to Henry was less of a disappointment than if she had chosen anyone else. Perhaps Seymour looked to the future. The king was elderly, in progressively bad health and his wife would probably survive him, unless unexpected illness or death in childbirth intervened. If the king should pass away first, she would not be merely Lady Latimer, the widow of a provincial lord who had displeased his monarch, but Queen Katherine, and would retain her royal status. His disappointment may well have been leavened somewhat by the realization that Katherine was worth waiting for, in more ways than one.

Plans were already afoot for Seymour to resume his diplomatic career. As early as 10 March, Chapuys, the imperial ambassador, noted that he was to be sent back to the Netherlands as Henry's representative there. In fact, he did not leave until early May, which suggests that the king did not view him as a serious rival. He may, if we attribute more devious motives to Henry, have wished to dangle Seymour under Katherine's nose while she debated his proposal, as a test of her judgement and Seymour's self-control. More likely, the delay was caused by quite extraneous factors such as the overall diplomatic situation and the inevitable slowness of decision-making. Seymour had accepted that he must do as he was bid. There were no histrionics. But Katherine had yet to agree that she would be the king's sixth wife.

It cannot have been easy for her, since it was so far removed from what she really wanted. Neither can it have been a complete surprise. Henry had not picked her name from a list and it is inconceivable that she did not know of his interest. Later, she wrote that reflection and prayer had caused her, eventually, to see that it was God's will that she became queen: 'Howbeit,' she wrote in 1547 to Thomas Seymour, 'God withstood my will therein most vehemently for a time, and through his grace and goodness made that possible which seemeth to me most impossible; that was, made me to renounce utterly mine own will, and to follow his will most willingly.' It had been, she acknowledged, a long struggle. 'It were too long to write all the process of this matter. If I live, I shall declare it to you myself.'[22]

How much of this was intended to convince herself, as justification for the path she had taken, is open to question. But it does speak of a passionate nature eventually reaching an accommodation with reality through what Katherine perceived to be God's will. It does not necessarily mean, as has often been thought, that Katherine was already being influenced by religious reformers who had persuaded her that she was the vessel through which the changes to religion in England could be safeguarded, and even progressed still farther. Far more likely is that, at the time, she had followed the encouragement of her family and recognized the privileges and riches (as well as the dangers) that came with being Henry's consort. Her quandary was a serious one, and, being a woman of her times, she wished to assign the final decision to God's will, rather than earthly considerations.

It is possible, though, to detect something of the timing of her journey to the throne that spring. At the end of April, even as his friend, Thomas Seymour, was preparing to leave for his new diplomatic posting, William Parr began to receive favours from the king. His career, already blighted by his unfaithful and intransigent wife, seemed to have stalled and he lacked the drive to improve himself through his own efforts. Yet on 23 April he was appointed Knight of the Garter and shortly afterwards awarded the office of Lord Warden and Keeper of the Western Marches towards Scotland. William Parr had never shown much interest in the north, despite his family links, but he was granted both the Garter and this prestigious post on the borders, probably in anticipation of his sister's marriage to the king rather than his own merits.

The following month, William Herbert, husband of Katherine's sister Anne, received favours of his own, this time in Wales. But while the Herberts remained at court and Anne prepared herself to support her sister as queen, William Parr was in Darlington, keen to prove himself as administrator and soldier but having little opportunity to excel in either role. Thomas Seymour's brother, Edward, earl of Hertford, did the fighting and the duke of Suffolk, as lord lieutenant, was the chief contact of the Privy Council. Parr's desire to make his mark was understandable but Suffolk did not appreciate it and Cuthbert Tunstall attempted to smooth troubled waters, not entirely successfully.

Yet if William was a worry to his elderly cousin, Tunstall, who had watched over the Parr siblings for years, must have been delighted when he learned that Katherine had finally agreed to accept Henry. After much reflection, the realization of the immense benefits that would accrue and the acceptance that it was her duty (and God's will) that she become queen, prevailed over Katherine's fears and doubts, and her regret at having to give up Thomas Seymour. By the middle of June her decision was evidently made. Lord Lisle wrote to his friend William Parr on 20 June from Greenwich: 'my Lady Latimer, your sister, and Mrs Herbert be both here at Court with my Lady Mary's Grace and my Lady Elizabeth'.[23] The fact that the king's daughters, who had not been together earlier in the spring, were noted as being at court with Katherine and her sister is surely significant. The king himself had only arrived the previous day, having spent some time inspecting the port at Harwich – a further indication that he had not been pressing his suit with Katherine importunately during this period. But there may well have been other considerations of propriety in observing a period of mourning for Lord Latimer. It is certainly possible that Katherine had, in fact, made up her mind to accept the king before June, and that a decision had been made to postpone the actual wedding, so that it did not seem indecorously close to the burial of her second husband. So it may be that her agitation was intense, but of shorter duration than she herself wanted to acknowledge in retrospect. A longer period between acceptance and ceremony would also have given her time to contemplate her approach to the role of queen consort and to begin to put certain elements of this in place. A good relationship with Mary and Elizabeth was fundamental to her strategy. Once married, and confident in being queen, she could develop it further.

This was not to be an ostentatious wedding. Nowadays we

might describe it as a quiet affair for family and close friends. But even in its organization, Henry VIII cleverly sent mixed messages to his watching courtiers and clergy. The licence was issued on 10 July, by the reformer Archbishop Cranmer, 'for the marriage of his sovereign lord, king Henry, with Katherine Latymer, late the wife of lord de Latymer, deceased, in whatever church, chapel or oratory he may please, without publication of banns, dispensing with all ordinances to the contrary for reasons concerning the honour and advancement of the whole realm'. The ceremony itself, however, was conducted by Stephen Gardiner, bishop of Winchester, a Catholic who had supported the divorce but who had strong reservations about many of the changes of the English Reformation. And, as a further sign of the balanced approach that Henry wanted in religious matters, the ceremony was conducted in English with the oration, given by Gardiner, in Latin. What he said has not survived.

Just two days passed between the licence and the wedding. Katherine and Henry were married on 12 July at Hampton Court, in the Queen's Closet, a private chapel close to the king's, above the Chapel Royal. The time of day is not recorded, nor is any description of Katherine's dress, but the names of all of those present are known. William Herbert and the earl of Hertford (Thomas Seymour's brother) were among the gentlemen of the king's party, as was Sir Thomas Darcy, son of the man whose participation in the Pilgrimage of Grace had cost him his life. Katherine was supported by her sister, by John Dudley's wife, Jane, by Katherine Brandon, the duchess of Suffolk, and Hertford's wife, Anne, who, as would become apparent after Henry VIII's death, was probably far from enthusiastic about Katherine's elevation. The royal ladies, Margaret Douglas (the king's niece), Mary and Elizabeth, also witnessed Henry and Katherine take their vows. Twenty people crowded into the small room, which measured about 10 by 14 metres, for the brief ceremony.

Henry VIII commanded his pronotary to make an official record of the marriage, which records the precise vows taken by the king and Katherine Parr. Virtually unchanged by the Reformation or the passing of centuries, they are the words still spoken at Anglican weddings:

> then the king taking her right hand, repeated after the bishop the words, 'I, Henry, take thee, Katherine, to my wedded wife, to have and to hold from this day forward, for better for worse, for richer for poorer, in sickness and in health, till death us do part, and thereto I plight thee my troth.' Then releasing and again clasping hands, the lady Katherine likewise said, 'I, Katherine, take thee Henry to my wedded husband, to have and to hold from this day forward, for better for worse, for richer for poorer, in sickness and in health, to be bonaire and buxom in bed and at board, till death us do part, and thereto I plight unto thee my troth.'[24]

Richard Watkins, the king's lawyer, further observed that 'the putting on of the wedding ring and proffer of gold and silver followed; and the bishop, after prayer, pronounced a benediction'.

Celebrations afterwards must have been restrained, for no account of them survives. It had been noted that Henry spoke his vows with enthusiasm. Katherine was perhaps more nervous. Later that same day, she was proclaimed queen of England, but there was no great entry into London planned and nothing was ever mentioned of a coronation. If Katherine was less exuberant than Henry on their wedding day, it does not necessarily mean that she harboured any last-minute doubts about what she was doing. A discreet image was what she wanted to project at the beginning, while she was still so new to the business of being queen. In her own mind, she was perfectly calm. Romance was in the past. A great and wholly unexpected opportunity had come her way. Now she was determined to enjoy, rather than endure, the fact that she was the sixth consort of Henry VIII.

CHAPTER SEVEN

The Queen and Her Court

'*She was dressed in a robe of cloth of gold and a petticoat
of brocade with sleeves lined with crimson satin ... her
train was more than two yards long.*'

The secretary to the duke of Najera,
reporting in February 1544

AT HOME AND ABROAD, the marriage met with a warm response.
Thomas Wriothesley, the king's secretary, wrote to the duke of
Suffolk on 16 July: 'I doubt not of your grace knowing ... that
the king's majesty was married on Thursday last to my lady
Latimer, a woman, in my judgement, for virtue, wisdom and
gentleness most meet for his highness; and sure I am his majesty
had never a wife more agreeable to his heart than she is. Our
Lord send them long life and much joy together.'[1] Wriothesley's
wife, Jane, became one of Katherine's ladies-in-waiting, though
the relationship between the ambitious politician and the queen
apparently deteriorated over time. But in July 1543 his charming,
rather understated praise typified what seems to have been a
general reaction to the king's sixth wife. It was certainly echoed
by Edmond Harvel, the English ambassador to Venice, who
wrote flatteringly of the new queen's beauty and favourable
comments he had received from prominent Venetians. Sir Ralph
Sadler, who had survived Cromwell's downfall and now laboured

145

with the poisoned chalice of being ambassador to Scotland, wrote
to William Parr that Katherine's marriage had 'revived my troubled spirits and turned all my cares to rejoicing. And, my lord, I
do not only rejoice for your lordship's sake ... but also for the
real and inestimable benefit and comfort which thereby shall
ensure to the whole realm.'[2]

The diplomatic community in London, caught by surprise
when the marriage was announced, do not seem, at first, to have
known quite how to react. The long-serving imperial ambassador,
Eustace Chapuys, failed to mention it until 27 July, when he
informed Granvelle, the bishop of Arras and one of Charles V's
closest advisers in the Netherlands, that 'the king espoused the
queen privately and without ceremony'. The same day, he referred
almost obliquely to the event, in a despatch that mostly had to
do with international affairs in Scotland and in Germany, which
were, no doubt, his prime concern at the time. It is possible that
Chapuys was somewhat piqued at not having picked up rumours
of the wedding before it happened. He had, months earlier,
commented on the king's attentiveness to ladies of the court in a
general way, but does not seem to have spotted Lady Latimer as
a likely choice. Since Chapuys liked to present himself to his
master as being *au courant* with all the latest gossip (even though
he was not) he may have chosen to play down the significance of
yet another wife for this much-married king. In truth, because
the licence was issued so close to the actual ceremony, it is hardly
surprising that Chapuys was in the dark. Yet soon he became an
admirer of Katherine's, noting her graciousness and kindness,
particularly to Mary, the princess he had worked so indefatigably
to support for a decade. Initially, though, he reported rather slyly
that there was at least one person who was completely confounded by the step Henry had taken. That person was the king's
fourth wife, Anne of Cleves. She had, so Chapuys claimed to
have heard, 'taken great grief and despair at the king's espousal
of this last wife, who is not nearly so beautiful as she, besides

that there is no hope of issue, seeing that she had none with her two former husbands'.[3]

There may well have been more than a grain of truth in this description of the chagrin of Anne of Cleves. Despite the well-known rhyme about the six wives of Henry VIII, Katherine Parr was not, of course, the only one to survive. Anne was still very much alive in 1543. She would outlive both Henry and Katherine Parr, but her situation at the time of Henry's sixth marriage was not one that she evidently found comfortable. That she should have harboured hopes of once again becoming queen may seem extraordinary in retrospect, but we should not suppose that she was unusually thick-skinned or naive. Though the king had treated her with kindness since their divorce her prospects were limited. She had observed the debacle of his marriage to Katherine Howard and must have hoped that he would reconsider, especially since he had got to know her better. Clearly, she had never understood (or never accepted) that the king found her physically repellent. In January 1540, the French ambassador had described her as being of 'medium beauty' – not a ringing endorsement, perhaps, but clearly she retained some confidence in her appearance. It is also probable that she had never been as ignorant about the procreative side of marriage as had been claimed by her ladies in 1540. Three years later, still aged only twenty-eight, she may well have believed that she was a better child-bearing prospect than the twice-widowed and childless Katherine Parr. As it was, the king took some pains to reconcile her to his new wife, inviting her to court in 1543 and again in 1546. There can be no doubt that Katherine would have done her best to be welcoming to this German princess, a rather wistful figure trapped in a foreign land.

Whatever onlookers may think, a marriage is generally successful only if there is genuine affection between husband and wife. Henry VIII was, when Katherine married him, the most absolute monarch England had known. There was about him a palpable air of menace. He was also old by Tudor standards, frequently irascible, and beset by ill-health. Yet the depth of his love for Katherine Parr has often been overlooked. He showered her with jewels and dower manors, showed marked favouritism to her family and was delighted to show her off whenever he could. Her company seems to have been a real source of pleasure to him, perhaps because of her personality but also because they shared many interests. No one has ever seriously considered that she might have loved him, too; her feelings are most often characterized as a ruthless suppression of love for Thomas Seymour, finding its outlet in religious study and writing, coupled with a not all together attractive opportunism in taking the benefits of queenship. But Katherine was a complex woman emotionally, and if she was not in love with Henry when they married, she came to have real affection for him, through getting to know him, and through her attentions to his children.

Circumstances certainly played a large part in the development of a strong bond between the king and his sixth wife. The plague, that scourge of summer in the cities, had just hit London when Katherine and Henry were married. 'This summer', recorded the chronicle, 'was great death in the city of London and suburbs of the same, wherefore the king made proclamation . . . that no Londoner should come within 7 miles where the king lay.'[4] This was a particularly virulent outbreak of the plague. It lingered well into the autumn and the court stayed away from the capital. This meant that the newly-weds were almost continuously together for the first six months of their marriage, as Henry avoided contagion and his wife got to know the manors and hunting-lodges that he possessed in Surrey, Bedfordshire, Oxfordshire and Buckinghamshire.[5] Ampthill in Bedfordshire was a particular favourite. Henry rarely hunted on horseback any more, so he had new standings built in the park from which he could shoot game. His wife, a keen huntswoman and archer of some prowess could enjoy the pastime at his side. They spent most of October and November 1543 at Ampthill, while the plague continued to be so devastating in London that the sessions of the Law Courts were moved out to St Albans in Hertfordshire.

Henry returned briefly to Whitehall just before Christmas. Life was not all pleasure for the king, and the business of government never stood still. Meetings of the Privy Council took place regularly wherever he was. Despite the conclusion of a treaty with the Scots for the marriage of their infant queen to Prince Edward, affairs north of the border remained high on the English government's agenda. And the Emperor Charles V was pleased to note that the king of England seemed more inclined to join with him against the French than had been the case for some years. At home, Henry continued to pursue his middle way in religion; three evangelicals were burnt at Windsor two weeks after the royal wedding. Yet the king resisted attempts to bring down Archbishop Cranmer. Perhaps he was 'the greatest heretic in Kent', but he was still Henry's heretic and the monarch had no intention of replacing him, though with his typical capacity for keeping people guessing, he did not publicly commit himself to Cranmer for several weeks. Instead, Henry went back to Hampton Court to join his wife and children for the festive season. It was the first family Christmas he had known for a good many years.

KATHERINE WAS NOW well established as consort, bedmate and stepmother, greatly helped by the unbroken time she had spent in the king's company. Her confidence had come gradually, but she was so naturally gracious and intelligent that it was not a difficult transition from being a minor noblewoman to being a queen. The court was in her blood. The only one of Henry's wives who had been prepared in any way for queenship was Katherine of Aragon, and even she had been the youngest child of a royal family. Anne Boleyn and Jane Seymour had both been ladies-in-waiting with an eye to the main chance, Anne of Cleves was the sister of a German princeling and Katherine Howard had grown up unloved, ill-educated and undisciplined, sexually pre-cocious but completely unfit to occupy a throne. Katherine Parr brought no such baggage with her and was the stronger for not having sought the role of queen or been craftily dangled in front of Henry VIII. It gave her an independence that the other wives had lacked.

Two crucial facets of the way she approached her role can be discerned from the start. The very day after her wedding, she requested 'fine perfumes' for her bedchamber at Hampton Court. A month later she ordered a large quantity of sweet-smelling herbs in pouches, specifically for her bed. Katherine was evidently concerned to make her boudoir enticing for the king and, given his sensitivity to Anne of Cleves (about which Katherine might well have heard from her sister and other women of the court) this was a clever move. The queen's apartments at that time were located over the kitchens, and though this kept them warm in winter it must have been very unpleasant in the heat of the summer. Cooking odours are hardly conducive to lovemaking, and Katherine knew, literally from her wedding-night, that she must do something about this if she was to ensure frequent visits from her husband. This is not to suggest that she was over-whelmed by his attractions. Henry lumbering into view in his nightshirt and the servants all hastily taking their leave must have been a daunting prospect, but Katherine was equal to it. More alarming by far was the possibility that he would lose interest or stay away. Katherine Parr was a sensual woman herself and she understood Henry very well in this respect. In order to make sure her skin stayed soft and touchable, she took milk baths. Physical contact would be vital to the success of their marriage.

And on that success hinged the fortunes of her family, the second of her priorities in the summer of 1543. On 20 July she sent her brother, William, a letter, informing him that it had 'pleased God to incline the king to take me as his wife, which is the greatest joy and comfort that could happen to me'. She went on to tell her brother that he was 'the person who has the most cause to rejoice thereat', and requested him to 'let me sometimes hear of your health as friendly as if I had not been called to this honour'.[6] This touching letter underlines her strong affection for her brother and exhibits almost a slight hesitancy about her new status. It has been suggested that her comments show bitterness towards William, but they are surely a straightforward statement of family affection, and more than a little celebratory.

Katherine Parr's devotion to family typifies the major social preoccupation of sixteenth-century England. As queen, she chose the Parr family badge, a maiden's head, as her own. And, unique among all queen consorts of Henry, she incorporated her family name in her signature, signing herself 'Kateryn the Quene KP'. She might have been Lady Latimer when she married Henry VIII, but in her own mind she was always a Parr. By the end of the year, she saw her commitment fully rewarded when, two days before Christmas, the king created her brother earl of Essex and her uncle Baron Parr of Horton, in the Presence Chamber at Hampton Court. William Parr had waited seventeen years for the title that his mother hoped would be his when she limited her two daughters' prospects by purchasing his marriage to Anne Bourchier. It had taken another, all together greater match by his elder sister to grant him the elusive earldom that his wife's behaviour denied him. Katherine loved him dearly, as she did her uncle, and she must have felt immense satisfaction in witnessing the ceremony that raised them both high. But she, of course, was higher still.

KATHERINE WAS NOW the greatest lady in the land and also one of the richest. When she married Henry VIII she received the dower lands that traditionally formed part of the queen consort's income. These were widely scattered over the south and midlands of England, ranging from Dorset in the west to Suffolk in the east and also encompassing substantial estates in Herefordshire and Worcestershire, on the Welsh borders. Baynard's Castle was the official residence of all Henry's queens in London, though Katherine did not spend much time there. It was used as storage for much of her wardrobe, especially winter items, like furs, and as the London residence of Anne and William Herbert. The manors, like most of her jewels, the chapel goods and even some books, had previously belonged to Katherine Howard. They went with the office and not the person. The 1542 inventory of Whitehall listed all the chapel stuff of the late queen; subsequently, it passed to Katherine Parr. The jewels that Anne Herbert looked after for her sister had previously adorned the shapely form of Henry's fifth wife. Some had even belonged to Jane Seymour. Katherine seems to have enjoyed wearing them. Presumably she did not allow herself to dwell too much on their past. And the king bought her many new pieces as well as providing her with manors of her own, that would remain hers if he died. In mid-1544, she was granted Hanworth, Chelsea and Mortlake in south-west London. Of these, her favourite became Hanworth, where she was to establish her dowager household in 1547.[7]

The trappings of royalty were easily acquired, but what is especially interesting about Katherine Parr is how she set about developing her image and the implementation of her approach to being a queen. This is not to suggest some feminist subtext; Katherine appreciated the limits as well as the possibilities of the queen consort's role, but she was astute at turning opportunity into advantage. The prolonged honeymoon with Henry VIII gave her unrivalled access to a man who few people knew really well and she learned quickly how to please him. And one effective way to do this was to be, in appearance and demeanour, precisely the kind of wife he wanted. She was to be an ornament, as well as a companion. What she definitely had no intention of being was a nurse. The Victorian view of Katherine Parr as a matronly lady who spent most of her time on her knees changing the bandages on Henry's damaged legs is not someone that the queen herself would have recognized. Nor, indeed, would the king have wanted such a wife.

Instead, he took pleasure in a woman who adapted with style and enthusiasm to the role of being queen. In every aspect of her new life, Katherine was determined to leave her mark. She loved clothes and soon possessed a wardrobe stuffed with beautiful and expensive items: gowns, sleeves, kirtles, petticoats, partlets and placards in an array of colours, though the most common were crimson, purple and black. Crimson was always the queen's favourite colour. She dressed her footmen and pages in crimson doublets and hose and she chose to wear crimson at one of her earliest and most important public functions, the reception in February 1544 for the Spanish duke of Najera.

The textiles she chose throughout her reign were a luxurious mix of costly fabrics: cloth of gold and silver (she was particularly fond of the latter), damasks, taffetas, silks, satins and velvets. During the three and a half years she was Henry's wife, she ordered 315 yards of black velvet and 95 yards of black satin, as well as 34 yards of orange damask. The black satin was often used to make night gowns, the informal wear of high-born ladies in the evenings and not to be confused with apparel for sleeping.[8] Katherine also loved shoes and had a collection that could compete with any modern lady occupying such a high-profile position. In the first year she was queen 117 pairs of shoes were delivered, though the number fell to a more moderate 47 for the following seven months.[9]

Even in intensely personal matters, the crimson theme was repeated. The queen's lavatory must have been one of the most opulent privies in the whole of Tudor England at the time. It had a crimson velvet canopy, cushions covered in cloth of gold and a seat of crimson velvet for the royal posterior. A removable commode was covered with red silk and ribbons, attached with gilt nails. Seldom can bodily functions have been performed in such splendour.[10]

A queen must be magnificent but also a trend-setter, and

Katherine balanced her support of contemporary jewellery design-
ers like the Dutchman Peter Richardson with continued patronage of John Skut, the tailor to all Henry's previous queens and to
Princess Mary. Apart from the fact he began his royal service for
Katherine of Aragon in 1519, nothing is known of his background. Clearly, he was good enough to be in demand over a
very long period. The garments Skut made for Katherine reflected
the latest fashions, the same type of French, Dutch, Italian
and Venetian styles that she had ordered for her stepdaughter,
Margaret Neville, before becoming queen.[11] The queen was also
a great admirer of embroidery, which suggests that she, like her
stepdaughter Mary, was highly proficient with a needle. Katherine patronized the embroiderer Guillaume Brellant, who was
already working for the Crown when she married Henry VIII.
The young Elizabeth, with her already well-developed eye for
what would please, gave her stepmother New Year's gifts in the
years 1544 and 1545 featuring beautiful covers that she had
worked herself.[12]

The earliest portrait of Katherine as queen tells us a great deal
about the image she sought to present. It is an impressive full-
length portrait (the first of an English queen) painted probably
in 1544 by the Flemish court painter known as Master John.
Katherine's exalted rank and grandeur are emphasized by the
sumptuousness of her French fashions and her jewels. She wears
'a gown of cloth of silver tissue woven with a very large repeat
pomegranate design. The tight-fitting bodice has a square neck-
line and a low-pointed waistline, while the conical shape of the
skirt is created by her farthingale.'[13] The sleeves also have a rich
fur lining, indicating that the portrait was painted in winter. The
queen is adorned with a pendant and necklace and an unusual
girdle made of cameos. The girdle seems to have been a favourite,
though it and the other pieces of jewellery had once belonged to
Katherine Howard. The crown-headed brooch, however, seems
to have been her own, possibly a gift from Henry. The pomegran-
ates are an interesting decoration for the gown, since they were

the badge of Katherine of Aragon, who was also credited with introducing the farthingale to England.[14] Whether this was conscious homage to the woman who was, in all likelihood, Katherine's own godmother as well as Henry's first wife we shall never know. No doubt Henry would have said something if he found the reminder irritating.

A year or so later, Queen Katherine was painted by William Scrots in more informal dress but still exhibiting the demeanour and style of a king's wife. She appears, if anything, rather more serious and her brown eyes are looking slightly to the right. Her jaunty black velvet cap sports a white ostrich feather and gold tassels and is bordered with white satin and pearls, neatly offsetting its otherwise rather mannish character, and her auburn hair. The rest of Katherine's attire that is visible is richly embellished, with four bands of metal thread embroidery (which the queen loved) down the front of the beautifully shaped bodice and double bands of the same work on the full sleeves. The embroidery is of Tudor roses and lovers pinks. But it is the collar, V-necked and in the very latest Italian whitework, that shows how closely Katherine followed continental fashion. The pendant worn in the slightly earlier, full-length portrait, has been attached in this painting to a ruby, pearl and diamond necklace also worn by Katherine Howard. The contrast between the more plainly dressed young minor aristocrat of the early 1530s portrait in Lambeth Palace and the jewelled, burnished queen of the mid-1540s could not be more marked.

Katherine chose her clothes and jewels for these portraits to underline her rank and to present herself to the world as queen of England. Yet she was also presenting herself to Henry in a way she thought he would want and establishing herself strongly as a regal figure in her own right. He does not appear to have commissioned the portraits of Katherine himself; they were undertaken on her initiative, and were very much about image-building. There were more portraits of Henry VIII's sixth wife than any other sixteenth-century queen of England, except for

Elizabeth. And they formed part of Katherine's wider development of her role as queen, since they also demonstrate her patronage of the arts.

As queen, Katherine was able to pursue her existing cultural interests and to develop new ones. She was a patron of as many as half a dozen artists and miniaturists working at the court, less well known to history than Hans Holbein but popular with the English aristocracy at the time. They included Scrots, Giles Gering, John Bettes and possibly Levina Teerlinc, the female miniaturist who worked at the courts of all three of Henry VIII's children. Teerlinc was given an annuity of £40 per annum in 1546, the start of a long and prestigious career that saw her rise to be one of the women of Queen Elizabeth's Privy Chamber. They would have met when Elizabeth was a girl at her stepmother's court. Holbein himself died at the end of 1543, but not before Katherine had commissioned from him two covered cups and a brooch.

If painting was Katherine's first love among the arts, she was also a keen supporter of the Bassanos, the court musicians, and a great lover of dancing. As was common at the time, some of her household staff were more than competent musicians. John Cooch, the steward of the queen's wine-cellar, was later described by Bishop Parkhurst, her chaplain at the time, as 'well-skilled in music'. The combination of good music, and, presumably, a good choice of wines by Cooch, again paints a picture of a woman who was highly convivial and at home in her environment.

Books were another pleasure, harking back to the education she had received as a child. Katherine clearly loved them for their beauty as well as their contents and, like the king, she built up a collection. Perhaps the most magnificent of all Katherine's books was one described as 'a book of gold, enamelled black, garnished with twenty-eight small table rubies and one rock ruby upon the clasp and on each side of the book a table diamond'. The contents of this gorgeously bound volume are not given. At the time of her death, among the books she possessed were a Book of Psalms covered with crimson velvet and garnished with gold, a little book covered with green velvet with stories and letters finely cut, two books of the New Testament, both covered with purple velvet and garnished with silver and gilt, one in English and one in French, and a dozen or so other books, covered in blue, black and crimson velvet, or with leather. The queen's copy of the 1542 English translation of *A Sermon of St Chrysostome* by the Oxford scholar John Lupset can still be seen at Sudeley Castle, bearing her signature, 'Kateryn the Quene, KP' on the title page. And to lighten the otherwise serious and reflective tone of the queen's library, there was also an Italian printed copy of Petrarch's *Canzoniere e Trionfi*.

During her time as queen of England, Katherine would not merely collect and read books, but also write them herself.[15] As an author, she was keen to order and distribute copies for her ladies and friends and her accounts show how she patronized the royal printer, Thomas Berthelet, in this respect: 'Delivered to my lord of Chichester [George Day, the bishop of Chichester and the queen's almoner by 1545], for the queen's grace, the first day of May, 6 books of the psalms prayers, gorgeously bound and gilt on the leather, at 16 shillings the piece.'[16] This is about £250 a copy in today's money. Copies of Katherine's books of prayers can still be seen at Stonor House at Oxfordshire and in the Mayor's Parlour at Kendal in Cumbria.

The possession of books was only one aspect of the queen's intellectual interests. In order to read and understand, as well as to keep her mind sharp and ensure that she was properly fitted for her place at Henry's side, Katherine decided to improve her own skills, particularly in the area of Latin. French appears to have been a language she could handle with ease, no doubt as a result of her own mother's proficiency in the language, but her Latin was rusty. There could not have been much call for it in Yorkshire and her sister Anne, by her own admission, needed to brush up her Latin when she became a patron of the scholar Roger Ascham. Writing from Cambridge in 1545, Ascham told the queen's sister: 'At last, I send you your Cicero, most noble lady; since you are delighted so much by his books, you do wisely to study them. You will study most diligently and not need any exhortation.'[17] The same approach to her studies of Latin and its great writers was no doubt followed by the queen herself, though there is debate about how much of the language Katherine actually knew before she married Henry. However, if, by 1545, Anne (then countess of Pembroke) was an admirer of Cicero she must have started from at least a base of familiarity and there is no reason to believe that Katherine's knowledge would have been inferior. Katherine was evidently a good linguist and a quick learner in all she did. The opportunity for improving her Latin was one she eagerly embraced. She had, of course, secretaries at her disposal who could help her in Latin composition, and the evidence points to the fact that her main interest was in translation of well-known texts from the original Latin into English vernacular. Significantly, she chose the Eton schoolmaster and playwright Nicholas Udall to work with her on one of the major literary endeavours of her time as queen, the translation of the *Paraphrases of Erasmus*. Udall had a louche reputation (he had been accused of sadistic corporal punishment and buggery while at Eton, though evidently this was no impediment to employment at court) but he had also produced, in the 1530s, a textbook called *Flowers for Latin Speaking*. It may be that Katherine's Latin bloomed again with his help and the opportunity for mutual study with her stepdaughter, Mary, who had continued her own Latin tuition into adulthood.

KATHERINE HAD showed from the outset of her reign that she was dynamic, full of ideas and able to handle the process of becoming queen with aplomb. One fascinating insight into this sophisticated transition is in the report of the visit of the duke of Najera in the mid-winter of 1544 – for it is easy to overlook that Katherine had to perform on an international stage as well as an

English one. And on this particular occasion she had a starring role.

The duke had been serving Charles V at the court in Brussels and decided, for reasons that are not clear, to return home via England at the beginning of 1544. His visit was therefore private rather than official, in the sense that he did not have a diplomatic mandate, but since it was undertaken at a time of improved relations between the emperor and Henry VIII, when there was talk of an alliance against France, it may well have had an ulterior motive. Certainly, Charles V had no objection to one of his aristocrats stopping off in England and being received by the king and queen. No doubt Henry did not attach to it the same importance as did the duke's secretary, Pedro de Gante, but we should be grateful to de Gante, nevertheless, for the description he has left us of how his master was received by Queen Katherine.

Najera had first been granted an audience with Henry, it being customary for the king and his consort to receive such dignitaries separately. After a few apposite comments about the king, such as the observation that 'for many centuries there has never been a Christian Prince nor infidel who has ordered so many executions, as well of his immediate relations, as of gentlemen, clergy and other persons, for having spoken against his proceedings', the secretary passed on to more pleasant matters. Accompanied by Katherine's brother, William, earl of Essex, and the earl of Surrey, Najera went 'to the chamber of the Queen, who was accompanied by the Princess Mary . . . Many ladies attended the Queen, amongst them a daughter of the Queen of Scotland [this was Lady Margaret Douglas] . . .' The duke had then kissed Katherine's hand and she received him 'in an animated manner. From thence they conducted the duke to another apartment, where stood another canopy of brocade, with a chair of the same. The Queen entered with the Princesses and having seated herself, she commanded the Duke to sit down, and musicians with violins were introduced. The Queen danced first with her brother, very gracefully; then the Princess Mary and the

Princess of Scotland danced with other gentlemen, and many
other ladies did the same.' But de Gante was especially impressed
by a Venetian gentleman of the king's household who danced so
lightly that he appeared to have wings on his feet. He went on:
'After the dancing was finished (which lasted several hours) the
Queen entered again into her chamber, having previously called
one of the noblemen who spoke Spanish, to offer in her name
some presents to the Duke, who again kissed her hand; and on
his requesting the same of the Princess Mary, she would by no
means permit it, but offered him her lips . . .' This does not mean
that Mary was especially forward in her behaviour; it was noted
in the fifteenth century that English women kissed on the lips.
But it does provide a glimpse of the princess completely at odds
with her historical reputation as a gloomy hysteric.

The secretary went on to give a full description of Katherine's
demeanour and clothes. She had, he said, 'a lively and pleasing
appearance and is praised as a virtuous woman. She was dressed
in a robe of cloth of gold and a petticoat of brocade with sleeves
lined with crimson satin and trimmed with three-piled crimson
velvet: her train was more than two yards long. Suspended from
her neck were two crosses, and a jewel of very rich diamonds and
in her head-dress were many and beautiful ones. Her girdle was
of gold with large pendants.'[18]

It is a superb description of a woman who relished such
occasions, knew instinctively how to put people at their ease and
was not afraid to behave with the right mixture of elegance and
restraint. In short, it was a triumphant performance, perhaps all
the more remarkable for the fact that, as Ambassador Chapuys
himself recorded, Katherine was 'slightly indisposed' at the time.
Whatever her ailment, the queen had not allowed it to get in the
way of the occasion. And she had 'particularly inquired after Your
Imperial Majesty', Chapuys reported to Charles V.[19] No wonder
that, at this point, the ambassador clearly considered Katherine
to be an imperialist at heart. He may have been riddled with

gout, as was the emperor himself, but he and the rather formal duke of Najera were delighted with the queen.

PERSONAL APPEARANCES at state occasions were an expected part of a queen's life but there were many other areas in which she could leave her mark, and although Katherine relished visibility, she also valued her own comforts and the ability to decide how these could be shaped. Her attitude to property, both those she lived in and owned, is a further indication of the kind of queen she wished to be. Katherine recognized the importance of the queen's role as landowner and, with typical thoroughness, set about ordering a complete survey of her properties. She was especially keen to preserve her forests and parks and was not at all impressed by the conditions reported in a number of them, notably the forest at Gillingham in Dorset, which had suffered decay and neglect. The new queen demanded in no uncertain terms that it receive attention: 'We ... are not willing such unlawful demeanour be used in any our said forest nor parks and especially not within our said forest and park', she wrote sternly.[20] This attention to detail may in part be explained by Katherine's background; she had, after all, helped run Lord Latimer's household and so she had a good knowledge of what was involved in running estates efficiently.

We do not know whether Katherine actually visited Gillingham. Its distance from London, as with several of her other properties, meant that she was reliant on her employees to manage them well. But there were others that she could influence directly, particularly where her own comfort was concerned. At Hampton Court, where she had become queen of England and where she spent a considerable amount of time in the first year of her marriage, Katherine undertook a major architectural project, consisting of extensive alterations to the queen's apartments. These were originally ranged along the east side of the inner court and formed part of the royal family's private lodging. The rooms had been altered and extended for Jane Seymour, who had spent only the weeks of her confinement in them and died less than two weeks after giving birth to Prince Edward. Their connotations were sad and an air of what might have been hung over them, as well as the more earthy odours coming up from the kitchen directly below the queen's Privy Chamber. Warmth in winter was all very well, but Katherine Parr had married Henry at the height of summer and her olfactory senses were not pleased by the location of her bedchamber. She may also have wished to avoid competing with the ghost of Jane, the one queen who had provided Henry with a son and whose memory he probably held dearer than he had the living woman. Katherine's solution was to move, and to do so quickly. Less than six months after her marriage, she occupied a completely new set of apartments around the south-east corner of the outer court, incorporating some of Wolsey's original building of 1526.

There must have been a great deal of noise and activity (presumably much of it undertaken in the autumn months when the king and queen were on progress in the Home Counties) as major structural alterations were made. Ceilings were raised, walls built up, partitions installed and stairs built so that the new apartments could be reached directly from the courtyard below. Katherine accepted that accessibility was important and that the public part of her role was vital, but she wanted a greater sense of space and some privacy, which had become increasingly difficult in the old arrangement. Katherine was not accustomed to the press of people seeking audiences, the demands of a lifestyle that had to be regimented in order to make the court run smoothly, the constant travelling from one manor or palace to another. During the first six months of 1544, Katherine lived in fifteen different manors. As queen, she was almost always on view, even if only to her female staff. Small wonder she sought to establish a place that was distinctly hers at Hampton Court.[21] The new lodgings also had a tranquil southern aspect, looking out over the sunken fishponds and flowerbeds. But at Hampton Court, as elsewhere, she was never alone, except perhaps in her own thoughts and in prayer. Her household, whether in full complement or a smaller, travelling staff, was always with her.

THE COMPOSITION of this household was one of Katherine's immediate preoccupations after her marriage. As with previous queens, it combined personal appointments, a kind of inner sanctum, with professional civil servants, many of whom had served court for many years. However, the death of the long-serving lord chamberlain of the queen consort's household, the earl of Rutland, only two months after Katherine's wedding, opened the door immediately for the new queen's relations. The countess of Rutland, so influential over female appointments, retired from court after her husband's death. Her role passed effectively to the queen's sister, Anne, who became chief gentle-woman of her chamber. Lord Parr of Horton, the queen's elderly uncle, replaced Rutland. Ill-health meant that he was not often at court, but his niece was determined he should have the post and that his advice and support should be available if needed. Parr's daughter, Lady Maud Lane, became one of the queen's ladies and a close confidante. The Latimer connection was also represented, with both Margaret Neville and Lucy Somerset, Katherine's stepdaughter-in-law, included among her attendants.

These four ladies probably had the most intimate relationship with Katherine when she first became queen. Lady Margaret Douglas, the charming and lively survivor of two failed love affairs and her uncle the king's associated wrath, was also a close confi-dante, as were Lady Mary Parr, the queen's aunt by marriage, Jane, Viscountess Lisle, Lady Joan Denny and Lady Elizabeth Tyrwhit. Katherine Brandon, the duchess of Suffolk, became a friend, but though she was present at the marriage ceremony her influence seems not to have been significant until 1545.

The composition of the Privy Chamber changed over time as

new ladies took the place of those who died or retired. Margaret Neville, for example, died in 1545. It has been pointed out that a significant number of the ladies were the wives of men who themselves held office at court and that the ladies probably owed their own positions as much to their marital circumstances as anything else.[22] Yet the king does not seem to have considered some of the complement a sufficient ornament to his wife, or the office of queen. He wrote to her from France in the autumn of 1544 that 'Where she asks his pleasure as to accepting certain ladies into her chamber in lieu of some that are sick, he remits their acceptance to her own choice; and although some that she names are too weak to serve, they may pass the time with her at play.'[23] This singularly patronizing comment suggests that Henry had scant idea of how his wife and her circle actually passed their time. In due course, he would find out.

To be at court with Queen Katherine, to serve in her household and share in the wealth and influence that she now possessed was a fine opportunity for her relatives, and also for the northern families who had been clients of the Parrs since the fifteenth century, as Sir Nicholas Throckmorton (a half-cousin) remembered very well:

> Lo, then my brethren Clement, George and I
> Did seek, as youth do still in court to be
> Each other state, as base, we did defy
> Compared with court, this nurse of dignity
> Tis truly said, no fishing to the seas
> No serving to a king's, if you can please . . .[24]

The rise of the Parrs was not so overtly political as that of the Boleyns, nor was it mired in controversy; though some may have sneered at it, most kept quiet.[25] Places were found for servants from Snape and from the extended family of Maud Parr's northern relatives. Their most notable representative was Mary Odell, a chamberer who sometimes actually shared the queen's bed.

Among the more interesting peripheral appointments was that of Henry Seymour, brother of Sir Thomas, as Katherine's carver. How frequently he performed this role, which was largely ceremonial, we do not know. Probably not too much should be read into the appointment. The Seymours were keen to preserve their place in public service and Katherine would have had a much more frequent reminder of her erstwhile suitor in the person of Edward Seymour's wife, Anne, who was a lady-in-waiting.

The professional civil servants dealt primarily with the day-to-day running of the queen's household. Sir Thomas Arundell, her chancellor and auditor, was a very experienced courtier, originally from Cornwall, who had married Katherine Howard's sister, Margaret. This connection apparently did him no harm. Sir Edmund Walsingham, former lieutenant of the Tower of London, became the queen's vice-chamberlain in 1544. He had done well out of his time in the Tower and had guarded many famous prisoners, including Anne Boleyn, Thomas More and Katherine Howard, though he was not greatly liked, perhaps because of his former office. Sir Philip Hoby, the receiver for foreign receipts, has been described as 'the quintessential lay Tudor diplomatic representative'; his extensive European travels and knowledge of languages provided a useful background. His office in Katherine's household was an important stepping-stone for him in a career that peaked under Edward VI. Wymond Carew, a Cornishman like Arundell, was brother-in-law of Sir Anthony Denny and served as Katherine's treasurer. The queen's eventual comptroller was Sir Robert Tyrwhit, a distant northern relative and husband of Lady Elizabeth Tyrwhit, who first served Katherine as her master of the horse.[26]

The efficiency of these gentlemen is, however, open to question. At the end of her first six months as Henry's consort Katherine signed off her accounts, but thereafter this was evidently deemed to be inappropriate for a queen. Thereafter, her auditor did it for her. Perhaps this was unfortunate, since the financial officers seem to have been very slow and Katherine apparently did not ask enough questions about this aspect of her household. Stephen Vaughan, an English diplomat in Antwerp, struggled long and desperately to get payment owed to his wife, who had served in Katherine's chamber. She had died of the plague, leaving him with several small children to bring up alone. At the end of 1544 he was writing to William Paget, the king's secretary, asking him not merely to help him find another wife but, more urgently, to get the queen to pay what she owed him: 'about £360 for labour and stuff of my wife's, wherein she spent her life, and has owed it since her first being Queen'. He begged Paget to 'remind Mr Arundell, her grace's chancellor, and Mr Bucler, her secretary, of it'.[27] Neither responded with any alacrity, but then Katherine herself was not quick to settle bills.

Walter Bucler, Katherine's secretary, spent considerable amounts of his time abroad. Henry VIII used him on diplomatic missions to the Protestant princes of Germany and he was a known supporter of religious reform, as was Hoby. So, increasingly, were many members of the queen's household, both male and female. Yet it would be wrong to see Katherine's establishment as being comprehensively 'evangelical', as those who espoused the furtherance of religious change are now normally described. The bishop of Chichester, the queen's almoner, was a moderate traditionalist who was deprived of office under Edward VI and restored by Queen Mary, at whose coronation he preached. And William Harper, the clerk of the queen's closet, was a religious conservative from the west of England. His duties involved a great deal of day-to-day contact with the queen, as he did most of her secretarial work and even ordered flowers on her behalf. Nor did all Katherine's ladies veer towards what would become Protestantism, though those probably closest to her were all well-educated women for whom religious study was to become a serious preoccupation.

❧

KATHERINE'S inner life and her personal beliefs when she married Henry VIII have been the topic of much debate. The precise nature of her beliefs in July 1543 is unclear. She has been characterized as 'a woman with a mission', her zeal for religious reform already in place, underpinning her acceptance of Henry and her entire approach to being queen of England.[28] But is this really the case? In fact, we know nothing of Katherine's beliefs at the time of her marriage. It is easy to look back and see a direction that fits in with subsequent events. In this interpretation, Katherine is a clever, committed reformer at the point when she becomes queen. Indeed, the opportunity to do God's work, to be His agent, is the rationale for accepting Henry in the first place. She is already a believer in religious change but now sees, through a process of gradual revelation, the opportunity to achieve much more: to uphold the reformers against the conservatives and to take the process, which might otherwise have stalled, to a further level.

It is unlikely the truth is so straightforward. Katherine's family (who were probably her prime consideration when she agreed to marry the king) were associated with reform but not ostentatiously so. We can certainly wonder what impact Lord Borough's more vehement support for new ideas might have had on his daughter-in-law back in the early 1530s but it seems unlikely to have been entirely positive. Presumably Katherine did socialize with Sir Francis Bigod, another outspoken partisan of reform, while she was married to Lord Latimer, but we simply do not know how close their acquaintance was or what she thought of him. He was a prospective father-in-law to young Margaret Neville, rather than a mentor to Katherine. On the other hand, Lord Latimer is generally viewed as a religious conservative, yet it was his New Testament in English that Katherine still had in her possession when she died, which must surely mean that Latimer approved of reading the Bible in the vernacular.

It seems safe to say that when she married Henry there was nothing about Katherine that set alarm bells ringing with him or with conservatives like Stephen Gardiner. But she may, of course, have been good at concealing her hand, a trait that would present her as a conniving woman and not an entirely appealing one. She was certainly seen as pious but that was entirely proper in a woman of her class and background. The more serious tone of her court, in contrast with the levity associated with Katherine Howard, brought forth favourable comments. One of her legal advisers, Francis Goldsmith, wrote to her on his appointment that she had 'made every day like Sunday, a thing hitherto unheard of, especially in a royal palace ... God has so formed her mind for pious studies, that she considers everything of small value compared to Christ ... Her piety cherishes the religion long since introduced not without great labour to the palace.'[29] This fulsome praise, originally written in Latin, probably tells us more about Goldsmith than it does about Katherine and, in addition, there is debate about its precise dating. In the first eighteen months of her marriage, Katherine was so busy balancing a number of priorities that it is hard to believe that making every day like Sunday was really one of them. Her ideas, like her grasp of queenship, were developing throughout this time but that does not mean she came to the marriage with religious reform as her main objective. She lived in complicated and fast-moving times and her initial aims were surely to secure the king's love and confidence.

Religious study, was, in any case, fashionable among aristocratic women, and not just in England. Marguerite of Navarre, sister of the king of France, had written a widely admired work, *The Mirror of the Sinful Soul*, more than a decade earlier. Katherine was evidently a keen reader and it was natural for her Privy Chamber to become, over time, the centre for discussion of devotional works. But, without belittling the pursuits of Katherine and her ladies unduly, their activities began as something more akin to the meetings of a modern book group. In the climate of the 1540s, however, such interests inevitably attracted attention and the ladies may have encouraged each other down more radical paths. Katherine's own ideas seem to have developed quite rapidly after the first year of her marriage, but it is more likely that the process was one of evolution rather than fixed intent before she became queen.

Her spare time, such as she had, was not solely focused on self-improvement. There was a pleasure-loving side to Katherine – and she clearly loved her life as queen. Her household ate and drank heartily, danced and sang and enjoyed sports. The queen kept hounds and hawks for her hunting, parrots to amuse her and dogs as much-loved companions. Her spaniel, Rig, must have looked splendid in his 'collar of crimson velvet embroidered with damask gold' and its rings of silver gilt for attaching his lead.

These details paint a picture of an energetic, determined but also vivacious woman who very consciously set about establishing an image and a role for herself. The apparent contradiction between the lover of finery and the student of scripture is easily explained by the complexity of Katherine's character and the preoccupations of the times in which she lived. The respect in which she was clearly held from the early days of her marriage is a testament to her good sense and the dignity which she brought to being Henry's queen. Even more impressive was how she made a success of her relationship with the royal children, providing them, for the first time, with a family life. For Katherine realized, from the outset of her marriage, that she could influence not just the present but the future if she could give them the visibility that she also sought for herself.

CHAPTER EIGHT

The Royal Children

> 'I affectionately and thoughtfully consider with what great
> love you attend both me, your mother, and scholarship at
> the same time . . .'

Queen Katherine's encouragement to Prince Edward, 1545

IT WAS AGNES STRICKLAND, the celebrated Victorian biographer of England's queens, who first highlighted the importance of Katherine Parr's relationship with the children of Henry VIII: 'How well the sound sense and endearing manners of Katherine Parr fitted her to reconcile the rival interests, and to render herself a bond of union between the disjointed links of the royal family, is proved by the affection and respect of her stepchildren, and also by their letters after Henry's death.'[1] Miss Strickland was less convinced that Henry himself was owed any credit for recognizing that Katherine might play a positive role in the lives of his offspring, but in this she was, perhaps, uncharitable, though it is easy to see why she reached the conclusion that the king had 'glaringly violated the duties of a father to his daughters'. Henry, as has been noted before, was primarily looking for a wife for himself when he married Katherine. At the same time his mind was already turning to the future, and particularly the succession, and in this respect he had realized that he needed to consider all three of his children. In fact, he dined with both Mary and

Elizabeth in September 1542, the first time, so far as is known, that such an event had taken place. Shortly afterwards, Mary returned to court permanently. Elizabeth was, of course, too young to reside there, but it is significant that both sisters were summoned to meet Katherine Parr in June 1543, before her marriage to the king was announced. We do not know whether this was at Katherine's suggestion or Henry's, but he obviously approved. And it is easy to believe that his bride-to-be, an experienced stepmother who had, after all, brought up Margaret Neville, would have wanted to establish a good rapport with the king's daughters before the wedding took place. Henry was a selfish man but no longer a foolish one where marriage was concerned. A wife who pleased him and who also got on well with his family was the ideal choice.

The role that she would play with all three children was clearly something that had occupied Katherine's thoughts as she considered her response to the king's proposal of marriage. In this there was more than just a genuine desire to contribute to their happiness, and that of their father. Katherine realized that her position as Henry's queen would be strengthened if she could fulfil the role of mother to the two younger children and become a friend and supporter of Mary. Perhaps she suspected that she was unlikely to have children with Henry herself, though she must have hoped to become pregnant. Meanwhile, maintaining an interest in the existing family was vital. Her priorities would perhaps have changed had she produced a child of her own, but being a parent to other women's children was a responsibility that Katherine assumed with grace and dedication. There was, no doubt, an element of calculation, however subconscious, in her approach to becoming a royal stepmother, but she brought a genuine enjoyment to the part she had to play. Her personality was well suited to the demands of the task. She was, after all, a woman who liked people and whose natural inclination was to make them welcome in her life. Her own childhood had been happy, despite the loss of her father when she was very small.

She was determined that her third husband's younger children should come to know that childhood did not have to be an affliction that meant isolation from the world. Instead, it could be a rewarding period of preparation for the challenges that lay ahead.

Henry himself had known this, in the distant past. As a second son, he grew up with his sisters in the household of his mother, Elizabeth of York, secure and loved yet with none of the pressures that weighed on an heir. But the death of his brother, Prince Arthur, so soon after his marriage to Katherine of Aragon, altered Henry's existence profoundly. His childhood idyll was transformed into a life of study and serious application for what lay ahead. Perhaps he always resented this loss of freedom. The ten-year-old who danced with such abandon at his elder brother's nuptial celebrations was, only five months later, a king-in-waiting. The sudden ending of his own childhood must have been an ordeal; yet this does not seem to have made him any more sensitive to what his own children might feel.

History may not have viewed Henry as an attentive parent but he cannot be judged by the standards of our time. The royal children were brought up in accordance with accepted practice, where a separate household for the Prince of Wales and smaller establishments for princesses, often living together, were the norm. Courts were no places for small children and Mary had always had a household of her own until her parents' divorce, when she went (extremely unwillingly at first) to live with Elizabeth. Thereafter, Henry's two daughters had mostly shared a household, at least until the early 1540s, though Mary sometimes stayed with Prince Edward and there were also occasions when the royal children were all together, especially at Christmas. So Henry's family were, in reality, considerably closer to one another (if not to him) than the prevailing image of dysfunctionality suggests. On the other hand, the king was an infrequent visitor to his children's establishments, though he claimed to love them all.

Katherine knew this and set about turning his affection, buried by the legacy of failed marriages and the sheer business of kingship and politics, to the children's advantage. She was convinced that they should be included more in Henry's life and thoughts, not just paraded as marriage fodder in the case of the girls or left in splendid isolation, as Edward had been. Important as her encouragement was, however, it must be acknowledged that her success was largely because her approach chimed well with considerations that Henry was already developing about the future of England, and his children's roles. Perhaps she did not materially alter their prospects, but she helped provide a climate in which their lives were relieved of uncertainty, at least so long as Henry remained alive and she was his consort. The early months of her marriage, when she was almost continuously with the king, provided Katherine with an ideal opportunity to influence him and to establish a bond with his children. Where this could not be done directly (Katherine's first duty was to the king and she could not often visit the younger children in person) the new queen used intermediaries, such as Margaret Neville, to visit Elizabeth, and she began a correspondence with her stepson that was to give great pleasure to both of them. Circumstances made it inevitable that she could not often be in sight, but Katherine was determined that she should not be out of mind. But what were her stepchildren like in 1543, and how did they react to her efforts on their behalf?

PRINCE EDWARD was three months short of his sixth birthday when Katherine married his father. Victorian historians and numerous historical novelists have depicted him as a lonely and sickly little boy, overwhelmed by the responsibilities that would be his on Henry's death, and frequently unwell. A greater contrast to the obstreperous but hardy Yorkshire lad John Neville, who had been Katherine's first stepson, could scarcely be imagined. Yet in reality, 'my lord prince', as he was known, was far from being a child weighed down with cares, and his health, despite the occasional scare that went with his age, did not give rise to any great concern. Childhood death stalked Tudor England and there must always have been the realization that he might not attain his majority. The prince's life was, however, carefully organized to protect him as much as possible from the threat of disease. His household moved among the king's manors, hunting-lodges and smaller palaces on the fringes of London, well scattered in pleasant countryside with healthy air. Access to him was restricted, to minimize risk and protect him from the perils of the plague and other evils that bred in the cities, particularly in the summer. No food was offered to him that had not been meticulously tasted beforehand and even his laundry and clothing was subject to rigorous standards of hygiene and preparation before any apparel came near the royal body. Nothing, it was hoped, was left to chance where Edward's well-being was concerned. A devoted staff, composed mostly of women, looked after him day and night. His household was still under the charge of Lady Bryan, a highly experienced lady mistress who had been responsible, at various times, for both his sisters. The king trusted her and she was not afraid to speak her mind when it came to the children's welfare. Edward's early years in her care, with his rockers and his nurse, were mainly passed in the pleasant surroundings of Hunsdon, Havering, Hertford and Ashridge, with all the toys, playmates and attention that he could possibly want. He was a happy, active child, as Lady Bryan enthusiastically reported to Thomas Cromwell very shortly before that minister's fall in 1540: 'My Lord Prince's grace is in good health and merry . . . his grace danced and played so wantonly that he could not stand still, and was as full of pretty toys as ever I saw a child in my life.'[2] Among his companions was the young Jane Dormer, later the favourite lady-in-waiting of his sister Mary. Their early games of cards together sound charming, but religious differences separated them later. The Dormers were adherents of the old religion and Jane's marriage to a Spanish nobleman in 1558 took her out of England for the rest of her life. But by then the little prince she had helped entertain was five years in his grave.

Edward's privileged and pampered lifestyle was only occasionally interrupted by glimpses of the outside world where, on his father's death, he would suddenly take centre-stage. Foreign diplomats sometimes came to call, offering compliments but also reminders that Edward was a public personage. He was not always the most welcoming of hosts and did not like being inspected. So unused was he to male company as a very small boy that he found the long beards of two emissaries from the German Protestant princes alarming and sobbed bitterly into his nurse's shoulder. When his father married Katherine Parr, Edward himself was newly promised in marriage to the baby Queen of Scots. His thoughts on this development are unknown but he already knew that he was not like other people, so perhaps the idea of marrying a queen was perfectly natural to him, despite his tender years.

Family life, however, in the sense of having two parents close at hand, was not something he had ever experienced. This was partly a product of his position as heir to the throne but it was also brought about by circumstances. His mother had died less than two weeks after his birth and his father spent very little time with him. That much, at least, he had in common with Katherine's first stepson. But he had not been neglected by other members of his kindred. His half-sister, Mary, was old enough to be his mother and effectively filled that role for him until Katherine Parr came along. Mary visited him often and showered him with presents. Their close relationship would eventually sour during his reign, the victim of court intrigues and genuine religious differences, though it foundered also on Mary's inability to acknowledge that he was no longer a child. But that she loved him dearly is beyond doubt and he was fortunate to have her attention when he was so young. He also spent time with his other sister, Elizabeth, who was only four years older than him, but whose prospects appeared much less glorious. They too had a strong bond of affection, forged in living arrangements that were sometimes shared, as was their schoolroom, and deepened by their desire to please their father the king and, increasingly, his sixth wife, Katherine, the woman they both called their mother.

Katherine Parr came into Edward's life in the last year of what might be termed his unfettered childhood, when plans were about to be made for his education and training as a future king. Her influence, if not direction, of the choice of tutors and study for her stepson is evident in his correspondence with her. There was also a marked closeness of outlook between her own ideas and those of key members of Edward's household staff. But her importance to Edward personally went even beyond this, for she was the link between the prince and the person he wanted to please more than anyone else in the world – his magnificent, but distant, father.

The prince seems to have been rather frightened of Henry and for this he could hardly be blamed. His father's visits, though few and far between, were stressful for everyone in Edward's household and required the boy himself to put on a performance that clearly made him nervous. Such meetings were not intended as opportunities for idle chit-chat but for Edward to prove that he was equal to the role of being Henry's heir. They were about progress and attainment, rather than paternal love, and Edward was carefully prepared by his tutors for these visits. He must also have received help with the first surviving letter to his father, in May 1544:

> Therefore, as often as I recall my mind to that unbounded goodness of yours towards a little manikin like myself, and as often as I inwardly reflect upon my various duties and obligations, my mind shudders – yea, it shudders, so that while shuddering, it also leaps with a marvellous delight: your majesty and the sweetest open-heartedness together carry me away. Hence it is forever before my eyes, the idea

that I am worthy to be tortured with stripes of ignominy, if through negligence I should omit even the smallest particle of my duty.[3]

The reaction of the reader to this cloying combination of exaggerated flattery and self-abasement is to shudder even more than the prince himself, but to do so overlooks the intention behind this abject missive, which goes on for another page or so, with liberal references to Cicero and Plato. Edward was demonstrating that he fully appreciated the sublime benefits of his father's kingship, for did not Plato teach 'that, after all, is the happiest government in which the kings are philosophers or the philosophers are kings. But our happiness I never can sufficiently admire, over whom bears sway the most philosophic of kings and the most kingly of philosophers.' And in the brilliance of his father was Edward's own glorious future reflected. Of course, the 'little manikin' was not the originator of this letter himself, though he may well have participated in its composition. The words were almost certainly those of Edward's tutor, Richard Cox, and they were written at a time when John Cheke, the distinguished Regius Professor of Greek at St John's College, Cambridge, was appointed to join Cox, as the prince's education started in earnest.

Katherine's part in these appointments was probably indirect. Henry is unlikely to have left the selection of those who were to train his son for kingship entirely to his wife, much as he loved her. But by the spring of 1544 her influence was considerable and the king was preparing to nominate her as regent during his absence on the battlefield in France. She certainly took a keen interest in Edward's education and it is reasonable to suppose that she knew and approved of the choices that were being made. Katherine was in the process of developing her own ideas and establishing herself as a patron of learning, as queen consorts before her had done. Her own position would be further strengthened by supporting the prince's team of tutors, who were among the greatest academic figures of their day.

Richard Cox, then in his early forties, had been educated at Eton and King's College, Cambridge. For a time he was headmaster at his old school and had been chaplain to both Archbishop Cranmer and the king himself. He was also close to William Butts, the king's chief physician, Sir Anthony Denny, keeper of the privy purse and later first gentleman of the Privy Chamber, and William Paget, the king's secretary. With powerful friends like these he scarcely needed the queen's approval, though he was, no doubt, glad of it and of her devotion to Prince Edward. What is significant, both from the perspective of Edward's upbringing and Katherine's own interests, is that this was a close-knit coterie of intellectually outstanding men, committed to the English Reformation. Most wished to see religious reform go further, though they were not so outspoken in the latter years of Henry's reign as they became under his son.

By the summer of 1544, as Edward approached his seventh birthday, his letter to his father served notice that the prince himself realized that his early childhood was soon to be left behind. His household would now become predominantly male, as befitted his position as heir. It was time to start his preparation for the throne in earnest, with the most ambitious syllabus and the finest minds that England could offer. Combining the best of the humanist approach to the classics with a study of Christianity, an approach that distilled the ideas of European reformers and presented them in the light of English experience, the education Edward received was the most excellent that could be offered in the 1540s. And, despite the impression that might have been given by his correspondence with his father, the prince was not a lonely swot. His schoolroom was shared with a group of privileged boys of noble birth, who would be his courtiers and advisers when he ruled. Healthy physical activity was also part of their daily regimen, as were music and modern languages. It was a well-balanced syllabus but also a disciplined one. Cox, who was later described by one of his pupils as the greatest teacher but also the greatest beater, used the cane to reinforce his authority.

Even Edward was not exempt, though the thrashing he received when his stubbornness became too much for Cox to bear seems to have been sufficient to ensure that he knuckled down to his Latin grammar thereafter. There was no residual animosity on Edward's part towards Cox, whom he addressed in 1546 as 'my most loving and kind preceptor'.

The appointment of John Cheke as Cox's deputy in the summer of 1544 was significant for both Edward and his step-mother. At just thirty years old, Cheke was the greatest Greek scholar of the Tudor age. His pioneering work on Greek pronunciation had caused division at Cambridge and earned him the disapproval of Stephen Gardiner, bishop of Winchester and the university's chancellor. The controversy that ensued fuelled Cambridge politics for some years but did nothing to diminish Cheke's reputation. He was soon to develop a major influence over Edward, whose studies flourished under his direction. The child loved the world that his new tutor opened up for him and responded eagerly to a curriculum that in 1544 included memorizing passages from Erasmus and the Bible and at the beginning of 1545 moved on to Latin composition. If this sounds dry, Cheke knew how to leaven the drearier aspects of learning, by arranging visits from other scholars to share their ideas with the prince and even getting John Leland, the antiquary who had travelled throughout England, to come to talk about the country Edward was born to rule. Cheke also used his Cambridge contemporary Roger Ascham, who later taught Elizabeth, to help with day-to-day instruction in the classroom and to teach calligraphy.

It has been said that Cheke owed his appointment to Katherine Parr. He was certainly a protégé of her almoner, George Day, and he remained close to the queen for the rest of her life. Both he and Ascham were ever-conscious of the need to have patronage at court. It was all well and good to be part of the prince's household and to travel with him to the tranquil royal houses of southern England, but the need for royal patronage above and beyond the association was important, and Katherine's was increasingly sought. Cheke was an important contact with Prince Edward and knew of the boy's increasing affection for his stepmother. Her encouragement of his studies worked to everyone's advantage.

For, unlike with his father, Edward could write to Katherine whenever he desired. There was no need for the formality of his correspondence with Henry, the waiting for the appropriate occasion or the artificiality of tone. If Henry responded to his son's letters the answers have not survived, but Katherine was not too remote to reply. She was a natural recipient of the prince's efforts at composition, the mother who was always there to give praise and show an interest in his efforts. Edward seems to have kept mementos of Jane Seymour, the mother he had never known, but it was Katherine's love that helped to shape him and provided the maternal constant that was lacking in his life.

'Most honourable and entirely beloved mother,' his earliest known letter to her began:

> I have me most humbly recommended to your grace with like thanks, both that your grace did accept so gently my simple and rude letters, and also that it pleased your grace so gently to vouchsafe to direct unto me your loving and tender letters, which do give me much comfort and encouragement to go forward in such things wherein your grace beareth me on hand, that I am already entered. I pray God I may be able in part to satisfy the good expectation of the king's majesty, my father, and of your grace, whom God have ever in his most blessed keeping.

The letter was signed 'Your loving son, E. Prince'.[4]

Since Katherine herself was embarking on studies to improve her written Latin and her general understanding of the classics, she was able to demonstrate to the prince, by example, that they were both working towards a similar goal. As his letter shows, he was greatly appreciative of her encouragement. And Katherine knew that praise is a great motivator: 'with what diligence you have cultivated the Muses, the letters you sent me can already be very ample witnesses – epistles which seem to me to shine both with the elegance of Latin discourse and more polished structure far surpassing all the others you sent me'. Though there has been debate about Katherine's actual proficiency in Latin, this letter indicates that she certainly felt able to comment knowledgeably about her stepson's style and to compliment him on his growing fluency of form and expression. She would be delighted, she said, to hear from him daily but fully appreciated that he was occupied with his studies and she would not believe him dilatory, since she knew that he was balancing his love of her with his love of learning 'so that love toward your mother on the one hand and desire of learning on the other entirely free you from any suspicion of negligence even without a hearing'.[5]

The dictates of Edward's education and the duties of a queen consort meant that Katherine did not see the prince as often as he would have liked. Her first visit to him seems to have been during the royal honeymoon in the autumn of 1543, when she and Henry saw both Edward and Elizabeth at Ashridge. The queen did, however, make sure that he was with her during his father's absence in France, when she brought all the children together during the period of her regency. Subsequently, their paths crossed on occasions of state, at Christmas and at other times that her schedule permitted. The boy's love of his stepmother grew over the years, though the tone of his letters was sometimes characterized by a degree of condescension and even priggishness. Katherine seems to have taken this in good part and did not reprove him for his comments on her Latin: 'I perceive that you have given your attention to the Roman characters, so that my preceptor [Cox] could not be persuaded but that your secretary wrote them, till he observed your name written equally well.' In what was, perhaps, an excess of honesty, he continued: 'I also was much surprised. I hear, too, that your highness is progressing in the Latin tongue and in the *belles lettres*. Wherefore

I feel no little joy, for letters are lasting; but other things that seem so perish. Literature also conduces to virtuous conduct, but ignorance thereof leads to vice ... Everything that comes from God is good; learning comes from God, therefore learning is good.'

Katherine would have said amen to that. Perhaps she realized that the patronizing tone of this letter was as much a product of Cox's pen as her stepson's; there are marked similarities between it and the earlier epistle to Henry.

Edward does not ever seem to have commented specifically on Katherine's own religious writings, though just after he became king he praised her 'godliness and knowledge, and learning in the Scriptures'. But whatever he felt about her literary skills, whether in English or in Latin, his love for her did not end with his father's death. She was always, to him, his 'dearest mother' whom 'I do love and admire with my whole heart'. This is a fitting testimony to Katherine's skills as a parent.

MARY, THE KING's elder daughter, does not seem to have been at all jealous of Katherine's success with her young brother. Her own affection for the queen was as great, in its way, as the earnest love of the little prince. Katherine's marriage to Henry VIII gave Mary the longest period of unbroken happiness she had known since childhood. It was a much-needed interlude of peace in a life that had known extreme contrasts of light and darkness, affording Mary the opportunity to recover from a decade of turmoil in the company of a woman she liked and respected.

She was twenty-seven years old at the time of her father's sixth marriage, petite and still attractive, with a sad smile that gave evidence, if any were needed, of what she had endured. Until the age of seventeen she had been a princess and her father's heir, the only surviving child of the many pregnancies of her Spanish mother, Henry's first wife, Katherine of Aragon. As one of the queen's ladies, Maud Parr probably knew the infant

Mary, though tales of the princess and Maud's elder daughter playing together as children are almost certainly fanciful. Mary always had her own household and it is unlikely that Maud brought Katherine to court with her, as her primary duty was to the queen and neither she nor the other ladies could cope with caring for their own children at the same time. As a small girl, Katherine may well have heard talk of Princess Mary and her progress, and while it is not impossible that they met as children, there is no firm evidence to suggest that they did.

Mary's childhood was a happy one. She was loved by both parents and Henry spent more time with her than he did subsequently with either of his two younger children. Talented, intelligent and pretty, she was the perfect English princess. The king was very proud of her musical ability, her grace and her beautiful auburn hair. He was also quite without compunction in using her at an early age and often as a diplomatic pawn. Mary was engaged at different times to the dauphin of France, her cousin the Emperor Charles V and spoken of as a bride for James V of Scotland, not to mention numerous other more distant prospects. Nothing came of any of these marriage possibilities. Beneath the displays of parental affection, Henry was concerned at the implications of marrying his only legitimate heir outside the kingdom, envisaging a time when other European countries might have undue influence on English affairs. Katherine of Aragon did not share his doubts. Mary had been as well educated, by the standards of her day, as Prince Edward would be twenty years later. Her mother was convinced that Mary was able to rule, as her formidable grandmother, Isabella of Castile, had done in Spain at the end of the fifteenth century.

Henry, however, was not so minded. He believed that women were inferior and he was not prepared to seek a solution to his dynastic weakness by wedding Mary to any of his rivals, real or potential, in the hope that she would provide grandsons. He wanted a male heir of his own body, not hers. And he was also tiring of Katherine of Aragon, a woman six years his senior who, by the late 1520s, was well past childbearing age. The idea of seeking a new wife may well have been in his mind before Anne Boleyn caught his eye. The course which he followed in his determination to be rid legally of Katherine, combined with her obduracy and Anne's fierce ambition, changed English history. Many would suffer as a result, but none more so than Mary, the princess whose life was shattered by her parents' divorce.

Even after the divorce was pronounced, it seemed that Mary might weather the storm. She was careful not to criticize directly her father's new marriage. But the birth of Elizabeth in September 1533 meant that Henry could no longer procrastinate about the situation of his elder daughter. His decision was unequivocal. Mary was declared illegitimate, told that she must expect her household to be reduced, and deprived of the title of princess. This she could not accept, refusing to comply with her father's demands and exhibiting a disdain that bordered on haughtiness. She was a proud young woman and the destruction of her expectations so completely gave her, she thought, no choice. Compromise was not possible. Encouraged by Katherine of Aragon, and supported by the imperial ambassador, Eustace Chapuys, Mary embarked on a battle of wills with her father and with Anne Boleyn, the hated 'concubine' who had replaced her mother. It was not a combat that she could ultimately win.

For almost three years she remained defiant, resisting all attempts to break her spirit. Just before Christmas 1533, she was packed off to join the baby Elizabeth at Hatfield House, an unwilling appendage to the establishment run by Elizabeth's lady governess, Anne Shelton, a member of the Boleyn family. Though not entirely friendless at court, Mary's own household shrunk to half a dozen loyal servants. Henry reduced her allowance, so that she was forced to mend her own clothing, and he demanded the return of the jewels that she loved and the plate that had graced her table as a princess. The countess of Salisbury, her beloved governess, was removed. Throughout this period, she only saw her father once, and then she was not able to speak to him. Her encounters with Anne Boleyn, who came to see her daughter on several occasions, invariably ended with a cold rejection of Anne's attempts at reconciliation and Henry's second wife departing in renewed fury at Mary's absolute refusal to acknowledge her as queen, or to accept that Elizabeth took precedence over her. When it came to calculated insults, Mary Tudor was an accomplished practitioner. In March 1534, Chapuys reported to Charles V:

> When the king's 'amie' went lately to visit her daughter, she urgently solicited the princess [Mary] to visit her and honour her as queen, saying that it would be a means of reconciliation with the king, and she herself would intercede with him for her, and she would be as well or better treated than ever. The princess replied that she knew no queen in England except her mother and if the said 'amie' (whom she called madame Anne Boleyn) would do her that favour with her father she would be much obliged. The Lady repeated her remonstrances and offers and in the end threatened her but could not move the princess.[6]

There was, though, a price being paid for this contemptuous rejection of peace overtures: Mary's health was permanently affected. Unhappy and fearful, she found it hard to sleep and lost her appetite. The stress exacerbated gynaecological difficulties she had apparently experienced since the onset of puberty. Her 'illnesses' were probably connected with menstruation and it seems that heavy, painful periods frequently confined her to bed. One episode was so severe that Henry sent his own doctor, William Butts. The royal physician's diagnosis was illuminating – he thought Mary was suffering from stress and sorrow but nothing really life-threatening. His suggestion that Mary would recover if allowed to see her mother was humane but quite impermissible from Henry's perspective. He did not want the two women together, reinforcing each other's opposition to him and possibly plotting with Katherine's nephew, Emperor Charles V, who had thus far failed to take any direct action on her behalf. So Mary remained cut off from the court, at loggerheads with her father and often unwell. Given Henry's determination to brook no opposition to his marriage or his reforms (he had, by this time, pronounced Royal Supremacy over the Church in England) it is remarkable that he allowed Mary as much leeway as he did. More and Fisher were put to death in 1535 for their refusal to take the oath to the new Act of Succession. The king's feelings towards his daughter were more ambivalent. She was banished and subjected to harassment and threats of physical abuse, but Henry's remarks to Chapuys indicate that he was genuinely troubled by the breakdown of their relationship. Her stubbornness, however, could not be allowed to go on indefinitely.

The breaking point came in the tumultuous year of 1536. Mary's mother died at the beginning of January, still in love with the man she had married twenty-seven years earlier. But Anne Boleyn was far from invulnerable. She miscarried (historical tradition has it that the foetus was male, but we cannot be sure) on the day of Katherine of Aragon's funeral, since when her position was never the same again. In truth, her marriage to Henry had been troubled for some time. Anne was clever but fiery and Henry had wearied of her rages and her strong will. She had made many enemies and not been afraid to take the fight to them. Quite what part Henry played in her downfall, one of the greatest travesties of justice in English history, we shall probably never know, but Mary, watching from a distance, was informed that Anne's days were numbered. The false confidence this gave her, especially after Anne's execution, is evident in the flurry of letters seeking restoration of parental favour that she wrote to her father and to Thomas Cromwell, his chief minister and architect of Anne's demise.

Nature and judicial murder had removed both Henry's wives in the space of five months. Only one major obstacle remained to the complete authority that he was determined to exercise – Mary herself. In the space of three terrible weeks Mary was browbeaten into submission. She was told that the lives of her supporters were endangered and that she might also go the way of Anne Boleyn if she did not acknowledge the invalidity of her parents' marriage, her own illegitimacy and her father's position as Head of the English Church. Distraught and isolated, Mary was compelled to face up to the reality of what the king might do. On 22 June 1536 she signed the statement Cromwell had drafted for her. Utterly weary in body and spirit, her capitulation cost her dearly and she never forgave herself for what must have seemed like a pact with the devil.[7]

In the years that followed, Mary's relations with her father were smoothed over, but there remained a current of unease that afflicted them both. Henry wanted, indeed required, her love but he knew that she had met his demands under duress. The past could not be rewritten and her affection must always be qualified. She would never love him as she had done in childhood; he had hurt her too much. But could he even trust her? That remained the unspoken question. To love him was Mary's duty as a daughter and that is probably how she saw it, while he lived. By the end of 1536, Mary already had a moderate-sized household again and an increased allowance, though it was adequate rather than generous. Relations with Jane Seymour were good and she derived brief comfort from that until Jane died, after giving birth to Prince Edward. The arrival of a male heir at last clarified her position in England, though not necessarily outside it. At home she was no more than the king's elder daughter, the Lady Mary, a privileged royal bastard with no role in England's future and entirely dependent on the king. But duty did not equal affection and Mary's thoughts turned to her Habsburg relatives, to Charles V, her cousin, who became a kind of surrogate father. He never gave her more than fair words but it was to him she looked for succour. And to Charles she was still a princess and rightful heir to the throne of England, since Henry had been excommunicated when Edward was born.

Mary knew, once the lessons of 1536 sunk in, that her security and peace of mind, such as she had, rested on unswerving obedience. The defiant young woman disappeared, to be replaced by one ever-willing to do her father's bidding. Marriage proposals came and went with a regularity she viewed almost cynically, for she understood that Henry could not let her go. Ironically, her one serious chance of becoming a wife was when duke Philip of Bavaria came to court her in person in 1539. Though he was a Protestant whom she may well have accepted in order to establish a life of her own, terms could not be agreed and Henry was too preoccupied with the forthcoming Cleves marriage (and, later, how he could be extricated from it) to bother much about Mary. Once, in a rare moment of self-awareness, he told diplomats from France who were trying to negotiate a marriage between Mary and the duke of Orléans that he 'loved his daughter well, but himself and his own honour more'. So she remained outside his orbit, often with Edward and Elizabeth, an occasional visitor to the court in London, but well informed of what was going on there. She became a political survivor out of necessity. Being unremarked was preferable to celebrity and, besides, she enjoyed leading a quiet life, indulging her passion for gambling with her ladies and returning to the educational studies interrupted in 1533. If there were any doubts lingering about her father's intentions for those who had supported her cause, his execution of leading courtiers of the so-called 'Aragonese' party in the late 1530s and the appallingly brutal beheading of the elderly countess of Salisbury in 1541 served as reminders of what those who had upheld her rights might still suffer if she did not exercise supreme care.

Nor was it just those once close to her. Cromwell, whom she had regarded as a mentor, was cast aside and put to death in 1540, while Henry's fifth wife, Katherine Howard, went to the block for adultery at the beginning of 1542. Mary did not get on with Henry's very young bride at first, but their relationship had improved, if they were never close. The teenage queen's tragedy, however, must have brought home to Mary how near she had come to sharing a similar fate six years earlier, though for very different reasons. And yet Katherine's demise also, though not immediately, signalled a change in her own fortunes.

As the summer gave way to autumn, the king's spirits revived and he decided that he wanted Mary back at court permanently. Her retinue would lift the atmosphere as well as his own spirits. She was a young woman who liked finery and fashion and the court would be less subdued and more glamorous when her household was established there. Considerable work was undertaken on her apartments at Hampton Court in time for Christmas 1542 and Mary duly arrived to spend much more time in her father's company. Her presence attracted the court ladies and certainly made the festive season much more lively than it had been the previous year, when Henry was sunk in gloom. In London itself, Mary's comfort was also suddenly a priority and expense no problem. So construction began on a new residence at Whitehall, completed in 1543. It was a separate courtyard house built right on the river wall. The first floor was almost entirely glass on the east side, affording magnificent views of the Thames and was far more splendid than anything Mary had known during the years since her fall from favour.[8] Yet this gesture was more than a token of her father's desire for her company. Henry was ageing and in poor health. He knew he must think again about the succession and the situation of his daughters. Bringing Mary back into the public eye was part of a strategy he had begun to consider before his marriage to Katherine Parr. His new queen, however, became a staunch champion of the princess, and her regard for Mary, which was clearly demonstrated, certainly improved Mary's prospects, as well as enriching her life.

Soon after the wedding, Katherine gave Mary a present of a pair of beautiful gold bracelets, set with rubies, emeralds and diamonds. The gift showed her generosity (and her new-found access to the sort of riches that would have been well beyond the reach of Lady Latimer), as did the presents of purses containing

money, which were often exchanged as tokens of female friendship among the aristocracy. The choice of jewellery, though,
exhibited a keen appreciation of her stepdaughter's character.
This does not mean that Katherine was trying to buy Mary's
affection; it is clear from her actions that the princess approved,
from the outset, of her father's latest wife. Rather, it shows an
instinctive understanding of shared enjoyment in lovely things.
Clothes and jewels mattered very much to both women, as did
entertainment, the cultural life of the court and the joys of the
outdoors. Music was another passion that brought them together,
as Katherine noted when she sent one of her favourite musicians
as a messenger to Mary, praising his 'skill in music, in which you,
I am well aware, take as much delight as myself'. The life at court
suited the queen and the princess. Their relationship thrived on
conversation and diversion and being part of other people's lives
(Mary was a godmother to numerous children) as well as the
more serious pursuits of high-born ladies, study and religion.

The perceptions that have come down to us of Katherine Parr
and Mary Tudor are those of a Protestant bluestocking and a
Catholic bigot respectively. This depiction would make it seem
impossible that they had much in common, let alone a predilec-
tion for the trappings of wealth and privilege. But this characteri-
zation is an invention of a much later age. Neither woman was so
firmly set in her ways that their relationship suffered. Mary had
accepted her father's religious changes, perhaps with some reservations but these do not seem to have bothered her unduly, and her
humanist education meant that she was not clinging to a stultified
concept of the religion in which she had been brought up. The
Mass was important to her, as it was to her father, and while he
lived, Katherine was herself in regular attendance at this central
ceremony of religious observance in Henrician England. It is true
that, while she was queen, Katherine's faith developed along
different lines from Mary's, and that Mary banned Katherine's
best-known publication, *The Lamentation of a Sinner*, when she
ascended the throne, but much had changed in Mary's life during

the intervening years. In the mid-1540s, Mary was happy to encourage her stepmother's study of Latin and to participate in Katherine's major literary project as queen, the translation of Erasmus's *Paraphrases of the New Testament*, undertaking the translation of St John' Gospel herself. Illness made it impossible for Mary to finish her contribution; Francis Mallet, who was Katherine's chaplain but moved to Mary's household, completed the work.

There is no reason to suppose that Mary's illness was convenient and that she had reservations about what she was doing. She later expressed concern for being credited with something that was not entirely her own work but Katherine reassured her:

> Now since, as I have heard, the finishing touch (as far as the translation is concerned) is given by Mallet to Erasmus's work upon St John, and nought now remains but that proper care and vigilance should be taken in revising, I entreat you to send over to me this very excellent and useful work ... that it may be committed to the press in due time; and farther, to signify whether you wish it to go forth to the world (most auspiciously) under your name, or as the production of an unknown writer. To which work you will, in my opinion, do a real injury, if you refuse to let it go down to posterity under the auspices of your own name, since you have undertaken so much labour in accurately translating it for the great good of the public, and would have undertaken still greater (as is well known) if the health of your body had permitted. And since all the world knows that you have toiled and laboured much in this business, I do not see why you should repudiate that praise which all men justly confer on you. However, I leave this whole matter to your discretion and, whatever resolution you may adopt, that will meet my fullest approbation ... Most devotedly and lovingly yours, Katherine the Queen.[9]

Mary did not refuse this appeal. How could she? The letter, with its combination of praise and gentle encouragement, is very much a companion to the one that Katherine had earlier written to Prince Edward. It is composed in a different style, as one adult to another, but shows a similar mastery of persuasion. There can be no doubt, though, that Katherine was genuinely impressed by what Mary had produced. And so Mary, the first Tudor queen, became a published author, like her stepmother, though she is scarcely remembered for having translated Erasmus's paraphrase of what is sometimes described as the most beautiful of the Gospels into the English language.

But in 1543 all this lay in the future. Katherine's immediate priority in her relationship with Mary was to ensure that Henry remained steadfast in his intentions towards the young woman. She appreciated that Mary's position was of international, not merely domestic, importance. Fences were being mended with Charles V as Henry contemplated the likelihood of war with both France and Scotland, and the revival of Mary's prospects would be well received at the imperial court in Brussels. The new queen's kindness towards the princess was noted by the imperial ambassador within weeks of her marriage. He told the emperor: 'The king continues his good treatment of the princess, whom he has retained with the queen, who shows her all affection.' Chapuys went on to add, rather smugly, that Elizabeth, whom he referred to as 'the daughter of Anne Boleyn', had been sent off to join her brother.[10] The ambassador got to know Katherine well over the next two years and he was charmed by her grace and her consideration towards him, as well as her evident love for Mary, the princess he had supported through perilous times. Charles V was also pleased that the king of England had at last married a sensible woman who seemed well intentioned towards his cousin and the Habsburg cause in general. Katherine was definitely to be cultivated, he told his ambassador.

Mary might have spent longer with her father and stepmother during the autumn progress, but she fell ill towards the end of September and was not permanently reunited with them until they returned to Hampton Court for Christmas. This separation did her no harm, however. Her father's sixth marriage had given him new purpose and, as he prepared to go to war with France, he also forged ahead with his intention of clarifying the succession. The act that was passed in parliament in February 1544 was a landmark in English history, the first time that the right of females to succeed to the throne was spelt out in statute law. It also made clear that Henry still hoped to have children with 'the most virtuous and gracious lady Katherine, now queen of England, late wife of John Neville, knight, Lord Latimer deceased, by whom as yet his majesty hath none issue, but may have full well when it shall please God'. The occasion of the act, its text went on to say, was that the king

> most prudently and wisely considering and calling to his remembrance how this realm standeth at this present time in the case of the succession ... recognizing and acknowledging also that it is in the only pleasure and will of Almighty God how long his highness or his entirely beloved son, Prince Edward, shall live ... his majesty therefore thinketh convenient afore his departure beyond the seas, that it be enacted ... that in case it shall happen the king's majesty and the said excellent prince his yet only son Prince Edward and heir apparent, to decease without heir of either of their bodies lawfully begotten ... then the said imperial crown and other the premises shall be to the Lady Mary, the king's highness' daughter, and to the heirs of the body of the same Lady Mary ... and for default of such issue the said imperial crown and other the premises shall be to the Lady Elizabeth, the king's second daughter ...[11]

England had no Salic Law barring women from the throne, as did France, but there had never before been an explicit piece of legislation giving them the right to succeed. The act was also remarkable for omitting the mention of all save Henry's direct heirs. Neither of his sisters' children were included, though Margaret Douglas, daughter of the Queen of Scots, Henry's elder sister, was at court in attendance on Katherine Parr, and his younger sister's two daughters both had girls of their own. In time, this would give rise to serious problems, but, for now, the king considered that he had done his duty for his country and for his family. Mary had not legally regained her title of princess and she was still regarded as illegitimate. But she and her younger sister could take comfort in the knowledge that, after their brother, they were Henry's official heirs. The Act of Succession signified an improvement in their fortunes which their step-mother, Katherine, welcomed wholeheartedly.

THE 'KING'S second daughter', as the Act of Succession called her, was nearly ten when Katherine became her father's wife. Elizabeth was a highly intelligent child (Henry had reason to be proud of all his children in this respect, though he does not appear to have made much of it), watchful and suitably grave in her rare public utterances. Her reaction to her mother's downfall, and its effect on her, is one of the great mysteries of the Tudor period. She had clearly been schooled never to speak of her mother in public and she carried this habit with her throughout her life. It must have taken a great effort of will. She is said to have remarked on the change in the way her servants addressed her when she, like Mary before her, was declared illegitimate and denied the title of princess, but her household staff were deter-mined that she should not be forgotten. Lady Bryan famously wrote in high dudgeon to Thomas Cromwell about the state of Elizabeth's wardrobe in August 1536: 'I beg you to be good lord to her and hers, and that she may have raiment, for she has neither gown, nor kirtle nor petticoat, nor linen for smocks, nor kerchiefs . . .'[12] The list went on, giving the impression of a little girl literally denuded by her mother's disgrace. Anne Boleyn had spent £40 a month (£14,000 today) on herself and her daughter and now, having presumably grown out of everything in recent months, Elizabeth had nothing. Lady Bryan's request was evi-dently met, for it was not repeated, and the problems were temporary. There was never any question of Henry repudiating Elizabeth, despite lurid tales from Europe that Anne had confessed at the last that Elizabeth was the product of her incestuous union with her own brother, George Boleyn. Henry knew that Elizabeth, who bore a strong resemblance to him (and to her siblings), was his.

By the time Lady Bryan was despatched to run Prince Edward's nursery, Elizabeth and Mary were sharing a household. Mary became very fond of her younger sister, reporting her progress to the king and buying her toys and clothes. Elizabeth continued, like Mary, to be well served. Her own staff was headed by Lady Blanche Herbert and Katherine Ashley became her chief gentlewoman, probably as early as the end of 1536. Kat Ashley was the daughter of a Devon family with reformist religious leanings. She was probably still in her teens when she entered Elizabeth's service and helped shape her early education. Elizabeth loved her dearly but her influence on the princess was at its greatest after the death of Henry VIII.

Elizabeth did not see much of her father, but then nor did Edward, the heir to the throne. Despite the shadow that hung over her mother, there is no reason to suppose that she was neglected or unhappy as a child, though precise details of her day-to-day existence at this time are scant. Anne Boleyn's ambitious plans for Elizabeth's education were largely followed, even though Elizabeth was no longer being trained to rule. Those who met her were struck by her powers of expression, her self-possession and her desire to do the right thing. Thomas Wriothesley, then Clerk of the Signet, reported to Henry VIII that the six-year-old Elizabeth talked to him with all the gravity of a woman of forty when he had visited her and Mary at Hertford Castle in 1539. Elizabeth herself was also keen to have her father's approval – and that of Katherine Parr. For the one thing missing in her life, which she had perhaps not realized until Katherine came along, was a mother.

It appears to have been quite a revelation. Elizabeth's earliest surviving letter, dated 31 July 1544, is to Katherine Parr. Written in Italian, in the fine italic hand that Elizabeth was to embellish so superbly in coming years, this missive tells us much about the girl who wrote it and also about Katherine, too:

> Inimical Fortune, envious of all good, she who revolves things human, has deprived me for a whole year of your most illustrious presence, and still not being content with that, has robbed me once again of the same good; the which would be intolerable to me if I did not think to enjoy it soon. And in this my exile I know surely that your highness' clemency has had as much care and solicitude for my health as the king's majesty would have had. For which I am not only bound to serve you but also to revere you with daughterly love, since I understand that your most illustrious highness has not forgotten me every time that you have written to the king's majesty, which would have been for me to do. However, heretofore I have not dared to write to him, for which at present I must humbly entreat your most excellent highness that in writing to his majesty you will deign to recommend me to him, entreating ever his sweet benediction and likewise entreating Lord God to send him best success in gaining victory over his enemies so that your highness, and I together with you, may rejoice the sooner at his happy return. I entreat nothing else from God but that He may preserve your most illustrious highness, to whose grace, humbly kissing your hands, I offer and commend myself. From St James on the thirty-first of July, Your most obedient daughter and most faithful servant, Elizabeth.[13]

At first glance, this seems a curiously stilted effort. It is, nevertheless, very revealing, once the allowances for etiquette, formality of address and Elizabeth's still imperfect grasp of the Italian language have been appreciated. And the choice of that language is surely significant. Elizabeth was, of course, eager to demonstrate her skills in a tongue that was neither Latin nor

English, but her own proficiency at the age of eleven in both was clearly taken as given. She shared language tutors with Edward and was an outstanding pupil. She must also have known that her stepmother would understand what she wrote. Perhaps she had discussed her progress in modern languages with Katherine at earlier meetings, and she might also have seen the copy of Petrarch that we know the queen possessed.

The letter also demonstrates Elizabeth's tendency to hyperbole, an aspect of her character that developed even more with time and infuriated her sister when Mary became queen. She had, for example, definitely seen Katherine during the previous twelve months, at Ashridge during the royal honeymoon progress, and kept in touch with her through Margaret Neville's visits. The queen's generosity towards her younger stepdaughter was also obvious in the gifts of clothes shown in the accounts, including a beautiful gown of purple cloth of gold.[14] And her 'exile', which has often been misinterpreted as some sort of banishment for having offended her father, referred merely to the fact that Edward and Mary had already gone to join Katherine at Hampton Court in the summer of 1544 while Elizabeth remained behind, temporarily, in London.[15] She had, in fact, dined with her father, brother and sister on 26 June, not long before Henry VIII set sail for France. It is unclear why Katherine was left out of this family occasion but one possible explanation is that she was spending time with Margaret Douglas, Henry's niece, who was about to be married to the Scottish nobleman Matthew Lennox. Finally, the reason that Elizabeth had not dared write to her father was a straightforward one of propriety; one did not normally address the king directly, but it was permissible to do so through his wife, the queen. Elizabeth does not say how she knew that Katherine was mentioning her in letters to the king, but it was certainly true. Possibly the queen had already told her stepdaughter this in another letter that has not survived, or through other contacts between their households.

Elizabeth, like Edward and Mary, shared with Katherine a

love of study. She was keenly aware of her stepmother's growing interest in religious ideas and at the end of 1544, when she was back at Ashridge, she sent a New Year's gift which she believed would allow her to highlight her continuing educational progress while also pleasing the queen. It was a translation of a literary work by another royal lady, Marguerite of Navarre, called *Le Miroir de l'Âme Pécheresse*. The young princess called it *The Mirror or Glass of the Sinful Soul*. Elizabeth was self-effacing about her efforts, but believed that Katherine would appreciate them because of the 'affectuous [ardent] will and fervent zeal which your highness hath towards all godly learning ... Which things considered have moved so small a portion as God hath lent me to prove what I could do. And therefore have I ... translated this little book out of French rhyme into English prose, joining the sentences together as well as the capacity of my simple wit and small learning could extend themselves.' In this work by the sister of Francis I of France, Elizabeth had perceived that the writer 'can do nothing that good is or prevaileth for her salvation, unless it be through the grace of God'. It is the earliest statement of her own religious views and one that she knew would appeal to the queen. But she begged Katherine not to judge her translation too severely or to show it to anyone else, an indication of how close she was to her stepmother by this time. She added:

> I trust also that, howbeit it is like a work which is but new begun and shapen, that the file of your excellent wit and godly learning in the reading of it ... shall rub out, polish and mend (or else cause to mend) the words ... the which I know in many places to be rude and nothing as it should be. But I hope that after to have been in your grace's hands, there shall be nothing in it worthy of reprehension, and that in the meanwhile no other but your highness only shall read it, lest my faults be known to many.[16]

The bond of affection and respect, the delight in the interest of the queen of England in her upbringing, is clear from the presentation of this gift. Here is an exceptional child blooming, encouraged and loved by an exceptional woman. For her exile was soon over. Elizabeth spent the period of her father's French campaign with Katherine, as part of a family unit. She joined her brother and sister at Hampton Court, at the queen's command, and stayed with them as the court moved south of London, avoiding the inevitable summer contagion.[17] They hunted together in various royal parks, while the younger children's education continued and Mary acted as her stepmother's companion. And Katherine did not neglect, as Elizabeth had appreciated, to remind Henry in all her letters to her absent husband that 'my lord prince and the rest of your children are in good health'.[18]

Elizabeth, gratified to be included, would not have objected to this rather curt and impersonal reference to herself and Mary. Like her sister, her status was clarified by the legislation that confirmed the order of succession earlier in the year. She had not suffered Mary's emotional traumas and was eager to expand her educational attainments. But the period she spent with Katherine in the summer and early autumn of 1544 provided her with an experience that was much more formative than the schoolroom. It gave her the unique opportunity to observe a woman ruler in action. For, as queen regent, Katherine's time was taken up with much more than maternal obligations and sporting pastimes. While Elizabeth watched, Katherine governed England. This practical lesson was far more valuable than anything her tutors could have devised, and it left an indelible impression.

CHAPTER NINE

Regent of England

*'The King's Majesty hath resolved that the Queen's High-
ness shall be Regent in his absence . . .'*

Minutes of the meeting of the King's Council,
Whitehall, 7 July 1544

ONE WEEK AFTER the council recorded that Henry VIII had
made his wife of barely a year regent of England, the king set sail
for France. He had not crossed the Channel since the end of
1532. On that occasion Anne Boleyn, confident, magnificent but
not yet queen, had accompanied him to a meeting with Francis I
at Calais. Anne's star at the time was in the ascendant (she
married Henry secretly within a couple of months) but she was
never required to govern in his name. Before Katherine Parr, only
his first queen, Katherine of Aragon, had performed such a role.
Then, as in the summer of 1544, Henry was an ally of the Holy
Roman Emperor and at war with France and Scotland. And on
both occasions Henry was fortunate to have a capable and intelligent wife who proved herself not merely equal to the task, but
who relished the responsibility.

This was an age when it was believed that women were
inferior to men in all matters of judgement; yet Katherine did not
have far to look for examples of women rulers who were effective.
In Scotland, Mary of Guise, the French mother of the infant

Queen of Scots, was, like Katherine Parr, twice-widowed, hand-some, red-headed and charming. Mary needed all her wits and allure to protect her daughter amid the treachery and violence of Scottish politics. And across the North Sea, in the Netherlands, Mary of Hungary, the Habsburg princess who was the younger sister of Emperor Charles V, had been his regent since 1531. As austere and Flemish in appearance as Mary of Guise was Gallic and captivating, Mary of Hungary daily confronted a task that was more complex than anything Katherine would know. Squeezed dry by years of war, increasingly troubled by religious and social divisions, the Low Countries were in constant upheaval and exceptionally difficult for anyone to govern, let alone a woman. Mary of Hungary's demanding life was not entirely lacking in pleasure (in 1544 she had a beautiful palace built at Binche in what is now Belgium), but her frustration at the responsibilities of government, which she took very seriously, occasionally spilled over in her letters to her brother. Doing business with 'these people', as she referred to the Estates or parliament of the Netherlands, was enough to drive one mad, she lamented.

Whatever the merits of these two ladies, there were very few men in the sixteenth century who welcomed government by a female. 'To promote a woman to bear rule, superiority, dominion or empire above any realm, nation or city', proclaimed the Scottish religious reformer John Knox, 'is repugnant to nature, contumely to God, a thing most contrarious to his revealed will and approved ordinance, and finally it is the subversion of good order, of all equity and justice.'[1] By the time of writing this uncompromisingly shrill assessment of women rulers in his polemical tract *The First Blast of the Trumpet against the Monstrous Regiment of Women*, Knox had seen enough of female power, above all, power wielded by Catholic women, that he could no longer hold back his disgust. Yet the mere fact of his being compelled to write could be viewed as an indirect acknowledge-ment of the achievements of Mary of Guise and Mary of Hungary and, later, Mary Tudor as well.

Like the two Marys, Katherine was not, of course, acting alone. Henry had ensured that her council was composed of an effective mix of churchmen, soldiers and administrators. So when she sat down to discuss the business of the day she was supported by Thomas Cranmer, archbishop of Canterbury, and Thomas Thirlby, bishop of Westminster, who were both seasoned politicians. Edward Seymour, earl of Hertford, an experienced soldier and diplomat who led the English armies on the Scottish borders, provided military expertise, while Thomas Wriothesley, recently appointed lord chancellor, was responsible for the financing of the war. Sir William Petre, clerk to the council, supervised its administration and day-to-day running. Katherine also added an appointment of her own, her uncle, Lord Parr of Horton. He seems to have been too ill to attend actual meetings but the fact that she nominated him betrays perhaps a hint of nervousness, despite the public face of quiet confidence that Katherine presented. Her brother was with the king's army in France, excited by the prospect of action and hoping for glory. He was not available for consultation and it may be that the queen felt more comfortable with the knowledge that she could at least contact her uncle and bring his views into decision-making should the necessity arise.

If there were differences of opinion that emerged during Katherine's nearly three months as regent they could not have been material; no evidence of dissension survives. Moreover her councillors had some things in common. None was of the old nobility. Their immediate forbears were royal servants, not aristocrats with long family trees. All had prospered as a result of Henry VIII's changes in government and the redistribution of wealth and power brought about by the Reformation in England. The duke of Norfolk was the premier noble, but his family (as his estranged duchess liked to remind him) was not an old one and the king, who viewed Norfolk with displeasure after the fall of Katherine Howard, wanted him as a military commander in France. Henry believed that he could count on the men he had appointed to advise his wife, who were professionals rather than rivals in a power struggle. Yet the men who supported Katherine Parr were very different in personality and did not by any means have the same personal goals. For in the regency council of 1544 can be detected some early pointers to the divisions that would characterize English politics after Henry's death.

Hertford was less flamboyant than his brother, Thomas Seymour, Katherine's former suitor, but he was ambitious and could already see his way to a much more powerful role. Although no one dared speak of it, the likelihood that Henry VIII would survive many more years seemed remote. As the elder uncle of Prince Edward, Hertford could expect much more, in the not so distant future, than heading a force of marauders laying waste to southern Scotland. Wriothesley, on the other hand, was a career civil servant who controlled the purse strings and contemplated a successful future in which he, too, would play a central role in English government. Their religious differences in 1544 were less obvious than they would become a few years later, but Hertford tended to the new ideas and Wriothesley to a more conservative set of beliefs. Probably there was not much love lost between these two ambitious men, whose wives both served in the queen's household. Anne Hertford and Jane Wriothesley each had their own reasons for resenting Katherine Parr, Anne because she viewed the queen as an upstart and Jane because Katherine had written her an unsentimental letter about the death of an infant son. But in the summer of 1544 these negative feelings did not intrude on their husbands' ability to work with the queen regent.

The churchmen also held different views. Cranmer, having survived the dangerous struggle for power between religious conservatives and reformers in 1543, was known to have the king's support and, if not entirely unassailable, was in a stronger position than he had been for some years. He was convinced of the need for further reform, and in these crucial weeks of war, when he was frequently in the queen's company and acted as her personal confessor, it may be that he influenced her own developing ideas on religion.[2] His Litany in English was published in May 1544, and much of it survived in the later *Book of Common Prayer*. But Cranmer believed there was still work to be done to move forward the Reformation in England. Thirlby, however, was not so convinced, and his closeness to the conservative Stephen Gardiner demonstrates, once again, Henry VIII's desire for balance among his advisers. An able diplomat, Thirlby had already conducted missions to Charles V and became resident ambassador at the imperial court in 1545. His religious reservations, though, had not alienated Cranmer on a personal level and it was said that 'there was no man living could more friendly esteem any man of himself' than Cranmer did of Thirlby.[3]

William Petre was a Devon man, of wealthy but certainly not high-born background. His father was a successful cattle farmer and tanner, with sufficient money and standing to send his son, one of several brothers, to study law at Oxford. He had risen quietly with Thomas Cromwell, being actively involved in the great work of the dissolution of the monasteries and on a number of diplomatic missions. His skill as an administrator meant that he continued to prosper after Cromwell's fall and, as secretary to Katherine's regency council, he found himself responsible for running the entire bureaucracy of the country while his superior, the new royal secretary, William Paget, was away with the king in France. Capable and confident when it came to dealing with the demands of extensive paperwork, Petre was a safe pair of hands.

Katherine's first year as queen had given her time to get to know this small group appointed to stay with her in England, and she worked well with them. Her actions and letters show that she was a practical and energetic ruler with a good grasp of the essentials of her situation. It was her role to maintain peace and stability at home while the king was on campaign, to aid the military effort with supplies of money and materiel and to communicate the king's success when it came. She was also responsible for the welfare of the heir to the throne, an important consideration should Henry die suddenly. As regent, she possessed considerable powers. Five proclamations were issued during her tenure of office, covering a range of issues, such as the price of armour, the arrest and trial of deserters and the prohibition from appearing at court of anyone exposed to the plague. Where financial matters were concerned, Katherine was granted the right to disburse monies from the Treasury, though this had to be countersigned by two other members of the council. Her frequent letters to Henry VIII kept him informed of what she was doing, exhibiting a nice balance of wifely concern for his welfare and queenly command of the government he had entrusted to her direction. On 25 July she wrote: 'Letters from the Council . . . at Calais . . . informed me of your good health and the prosperous beginning of your affairs, for which I thank God. The Council here have ordered £40,000 to be on Monday next conveyed to you . . . Here they will be diligent to advance . . . against the beginning of next month, as much money as possible.' Nor was it just money that she was sending: '4,000 men are to be put ready at one hour's warning, the Lords of the Council here, who have already ordered the general musters throughout the realm, have eftsoons written to the commissioners in parts near the sea most meet to have men transported from . . .' And a postscript in her own hand added: 'I feel bound to advertise your Grace of the diligence of your councillors here.'[4] This sounded just the right note of cooperation while reinforcing her own position, and is typical of Katherine's skill in such matters.

All this gives the impression of activity, efficiency and optimism. But it is not the real story of the war of 1544. Katherine was ably fulfilling her husband's expectations but the reality of the situation was influenced by wider international considerations over which Henry had no direct control. And what, in any case, was he doing leading an army of over 40,000 men into northern France when he was old by the standards of his day and in poor health?

THE ANSWER to this question lies in the long-standing rivalry for supremacy in western Europe that dominated the first half of the sixteenth century. The Emperor Charles V ruled, with the help of his family, a huge swathe of lands, from the Netherlands, through Germany to Austria and central Europe in the north of the Continent, and the Iberian peninsula and much of Italy in the south. The Holy Roman Empire dated from the days of Charlemagne and if, as has famously been said, it was neither holy nor Roman, in the year 1544 it remained a formidable territorial mass. The only major power that stood against it was France, whose king was so determined to counter imperial influence that he had given support to the rising swell of religious rebellion in Germany and actually allied with the Turks, who were harassing the eastern borders of Charles V's empire. Such a move would seem, on the face of it, much more scandalous than Henry VIII's schism with the pope, but Francis I escaped excommunication, in part because the papacy never forgave Charles V for the sack of Rome in 1526.

Henry liked to think of himself as a power-broker in European politics, the strong king of England whose support could tip the balance in favour of either the empire or France. But, in truth, he was largely an observer of events. The high standard of English diplomats sent to the European courts spoke well for his interest but the course of his own reign made it difficult for him to translate intelligence into action. There was, however, one underlying theme. Although centuries of warfare with France made the emperor the more natural ally for England, Henry resented the power of Charles V. The king also had to consider, as he weighed up his foreign policy aims, that France menaced him on two fronts – across the Channel, in Calais, but also in Scotland, where the pro-French party would try to establish control and thwart his plans for bringing the two crowns together.

The king's goal in his dealings with his northern neighbour was a simple one. It was to fulfil his own father's desire to unite the Scottish and English crowns, a quest begun in 1503 with the with the marriage of Margaret Tudor, Henry's elder sister, to James IV. But several bloody battles and interminable skirmishes and raids during the first half of the century produced no clear result. This endemic warfare, punctuated by intense diplomatic efforts involving much mutual suspicion and threat, had not, in fact, allowed Henry to realize his aim. Margaret Tudor died in 1541 a disappointed woman, without either her son, James V, or her daughter, Lady Margaret Douglas, at her side, her father's schemes apparently in tatters. But her brother had not given up and the death of James V the following year appeared greatly to strengthen his hand. For how could a small country, ruled by a baby girl who was at the mercy of brutish nobles, hope to survive without his direction? The treaty of Greenwich, betrothing Edward to Mary Queen of Scots, encapsulated his dreams not just for his heir, Edward, but for the British Isles as a whole.

Treaties, however, can be easily broken. And Henry's heavy-handedness, coupled with his inability to occupy Scotland, meant that there would always be a third player in Scottish affairs. Mary Queen of Scots was half French, which made the appeal to the 'auld alliance' with France stronger than ever. Scotland may have been remote but it was by no means isolated on the international stage. James V's widow was a member of one of the most politically adroit families in Europe. Her handling of a perilous, unstable situation was masterly. In her first year as Dowager Queen, Mary of Guise had given fair words (but no more) to the English ambassador, Sir Ralph Sadler, about allowing the little Scottish queen to be brought up in England with her fiancé, Prince Edward. But Mary Queen of Scots' only move at the time was to the safety of Stirling Castle, where her mother continued to play off the pro-English interests against one another, with the help of Scotland's premier churchman, Cardinal Beaton, an opponent of Henry VIII. The greedy and untrustworthy earl of Arran was fobbed off with the title of Governor to the infant Mary, and his rival, the earl of Lennox, was fooled by the twenty-eight-year-old dowager into thinking that she might seriously consider him as a prospective husband. All this was impressive enough, but Mary of Guise's most important success in the year 1543 was to get her child crowned as queen at the age of nine months. As the adult Mary Queen of Scots would find out, not even an anointed queen was safe in Scotland, but for the time being her coronation bound the nobility to her, greatly strengthening her position and buying much needed time for Mary of Guise to shore up French support. It was a remarkable triumph and a blow to the ambitions of Henry VIII, who resorted to military means to force the Scots to honour the treaty of Greenwich. This torch-and-burn campaign along the Scottish border, known as the Rough Wooings, was led by the earl of Hertford. It began in May 1544 and was still continuing when Katherine Parr became regent.

Henry VIII had promised, with the kind of threat reminiscent of his fury at the rebels of the Pilgrimage of Grace, that he would raze Edinburgh and slaughter its inhabitants 'to the third and fourth generations'. He was never able to make good on this bloodthirsty notion, but in one respect he could claim a victory that certainly meant he was still a player in Scottish politics. By late March, the earl of Lennox realized that Mary of Guise was never going to marry him. He took himself and his allegiance south and, on 29 June, he married Lady Margaret Douglas, the niece of Henry VIII and one of Katherine Parr's chief ladies. This magnificent wedding at St James's Palace, with both the king and queen in prominent attendance, was Katherine's most important public event since her own marriage. The match was intended to send a message to the Scots that Henry would continue to take an active role in their affairs, by promoting the ambitions of one of their leading aristocrats and giving him lands and honours in England. Margaret's chequered romantic past, which involved two *amours* with members of the Howard family and brief imprisonment in the Tower, not to mention reproofs from Cranmer for her continued giddy behaviour, was swiftly and completely put behind her. This lively and attractive woman of twenty-nine, who had been a companion of Katherine's step-daughter Mary since they were both girls, fell in love with the husband her uncle had chosen for her, and theirs was a very successful match. The new countess of Lennox, who was, by Tudor standards, well past the first flush of youth, counted herself lucky that she had finally found a handsome and politically ambitious husband and she wholeheartedly devoted herself to his interests. From the perspective of her uncle, Lennox was much more than just a suitable match for a prominent member of his family. He had a substantial number of men at his command and, having spent time at the court of Francis I, he had first-hand knowledge of French political and military affairs. And it was in France that Henry intended to achieve a victory that would set the seal on his reign.

KATHERINE'S APPOINTMENT as regent marked the end of a long period of preparation for the French campaign. Henry had declared war against France in the summer of 1543 and was engaged by the terms of his agreement with Charles V, made at the end of the year, to take up arms in France by 20 June 1544. He missed this deadline by a few weeks; the press of business, the continuing problems with Scotland, the settlement of the succession, as well as the need to organize and prepare a large force, all took time. Then there was an unwelcome return of the old trouble with his legs in the early spring. Chapuys reported to Mary of Hungary on 30 March: 'For the last eight days the king has been ill of a sore in one of his legs, which during 48 hours has brought on a slight fever. He is now, thank God, free from it and yet he is still indisposed and keeps his room.'[5] This development must have given Katherine cause for concern. Although it is impossible to say precisely how well briefed she was on international affairs, we know that Henry did talk to her about such matters and that he continued to do so for at least another year.[6] Charles V himself was convinced that her influence was significant: 'You are doing the right thing', he told his ambassador in March 1544, 'in keeping on good terms with the Queen; do not fail, whenever opportunity offers, to address her Our most cordial commendations.'[7] Katherine's continued warmth towards imperial visitors was noted once again when the Spanish duke of Albuquerque arrived and it was remarked that the queen's reception of him had been even greater than the king's. There had not been an English queen so supportive of Charles V or his representatives for twenty years.

Welcome as Katherine's stance was, it could not disguise the fact that there was tension between Henry VIII and Charles V that did not bode well for the outcome of their cooperation. The two monarchs had different goals and an entirely contrasting attitude to the conduct of the war. For Charles, it was a chance to settle, once and for all, the relationship with France. He would do this through military defeat if he could, but he wanted the English army to be the main agent of such an outcome. Unwilling (and unable) to contemplate a march by his own armies as far as Paris, he nevertheless hoped that Henry might be induced to commit English forces in such an enterprise. But though a decisive outcome such as the burning of the French capital would be thrilling, Charles was wise enough to know that there was more than one approach to getting his way. A few losses here and there, indeed, even the mere fact of English involvement, might induce the king of France to sue for peace. And if he should follow such a course, then Charles, ever pragmatic, would engage in diplomacy that suited himself first and foremost. Perhaps he did not enter the war with the deliberate intent of double-crossing Henry VIII, but he was perfectly prepared to do so if he felt circumstances warranted it. Henry had known Charles for most of his life – they had met personally, years before – but he does not ever seem to have had the measure of this astute, complex and fundamentally untrustworthy man. He should, perhaps, have seen what was coming when, well before any English soldier had set foot in France, and though he had hoped for an imperial declaration of war against the Scots, Charles refused to support him in Scotland. The emperor knew that trade in the Low Countries would suffer and so, he reasoned, 'it would seem strange, inconvenient and almost dishonest for us to declare war to the Scots'. He went on to point out that Henry VIII had declined, for his part, to declare war on the German duke of Holstein. This kind of tit for tat, accompanied by any amount of specious excuses (Mary of Hungary excelled at the art of pettifogging justification), was a canker at the heart of the Anglo-imperial alliance.

Henry may not have cared about Holstein but he was determined to attack France. His dislike of Francis I, now riddled with disease himself, ran very deep. He must privately have scoffed at the letter belatedly addressed to him by the man he had wrestled with for his entire reign (quite literally, at the Field of Cloth of Gold more than two decades earlier), offering to 'pay the arrears of pension due'. With superb disingenuousness, Francis I went on to appeal to old ties of amity: 'I cannot persuade myself', he wrote, 'that, on your part, the friendship and brotherhood, in which we have always lived, has suffered any diminution, for I can assure you that, so far as myself am concerned, it has not been impaired in the least.'[8]

Yet though Henry had always viewed Francis I as a rival, and undoubtedly wished to strike a telling blow against him, his motives were not entirely egotistical. It is easy to depict the king as a foolish old man, hell-bent on one last glorious military venture, but there was a rationale behind the course he took. The French king did, indeed, owe him a great deal of money in the form of reparations from earlier conflicts and it was quite clear that diplomacy alone would not bring about its repayment. There was no reason to trust the offer Francis made. Tellingly, it did not arrive until after the English forces crossed to northern France. Henry had seen the collapse of the treaty of Greenwich and the rise of French influence in Scotland. And Calais itself, England's lone outpost on French soil, was under threat from the great French fortress at nearby Ardres. In Henry's mind, the best way to defend English interests at Calais and the territory surrounding it (known as the Calais Pale) was to launch a two-pronged attack. A force commanded by the duke of Norfolk would besiege Montreuil, a hilltop town girt with huge walls some twenty-five miles inland from Calais, while another army would attack Boulogne. This second assault Henry intended to lead himself. At the back of his mind there was also the memory that Wolsey and Charles V had dissuaded him from attacking Boulogne in 1523. He had been younger then, but in his mind it was not too late to take the town now. When it fell, he was determined to be there to receive its capitulation.[9]

This decision caused a huge collective intake of breath. Henry's imperial ally, who had spent large parts of his life in the saddle at the head of his armies, was dismayed. Surely it was not necessary for the king, at his age, to wage war in person? The suggestion that he was too decrepit for the fight caused Henry great offence. His response was withering:

The reasons, moreover, which your majesty alleged for himself to remain at home, and not attend the expedition in person – such as his illness and so forth – were not sufficiently strong, and might, on the contrary, be brought to bear against your majesty, inasmuch as his [the king's] present indisposition was accidental and transitory, whereas gout, from which your majesty had been suffering lately, was an awful disease, a return of which at the approaching autumn season would be extremely dangerous.

As the king went on to explain, he had no intention of making the heroic gesture that was hoped for by his gout-ridden ally: 'It would be far better to lay siege to two or three large towns on the road to Paris, than to go on to the capital of France and burn it down. As to counting upon the rebellion and consequent assistance of the French people against their king, that was pure vanity, for never before had the French risen in rebellion against their king.'[10]

This was an astute and realistic assessment, demonstrating not just the contrast in personalities between Charles V (who, incidentally, never had the slightest intention of leading his troops personally into northern France) and Henry VIII, but also their expectations of what could be achieved. However, the misgivings about the king's direct participation in the campaign were by no means all on the imperial side. There clearly was concern in London, as Chapuys reported during Henry's spring illness:

> the reason why many of those who are about the king's person do not wish him to cross the Channel on this occasion is, among others, that they are afraid of his suddenly failing in health, and also that, if they have to take care of his person, all military operations will necessarily be delayed and the march of their army slackened through it; besides which the king's chronic disease and great obesity require particular care lest his life should be endangered.[11]

Katherine, however, does not seem to have been one of those who tried to dissuade Henry from his purpose. She already knew her husband well enough to appreciate how important this was to him and, indeed, to her. He was ready to assign her the responsibilities of the regency and the safeguarding of his heir. Henry made a will in 1544 before he left England; although it has not survived, the assumption is that he nominated his wife to remain as regent in the event of his death. Probably he did not regard this as a serious possibility, despite the fears of his advisers described by Chapuys. In fact, the king's health returned and actually improved as he busied himself for the departure. Margaret Douglas's grand nuptials were a fitting statement of his power and confidence in the final days before he left. On 8 July he bade farewell to Katherine and travelled, via several of his Kentish manors, to Dover. Nearly a week later, he crossed the Channel, and, on Monday 14 July, as was reported by a steward who kept a diary of the campaign, 'the king's majesty came to Calais about the hour of seven of the clock at night, where he was royally received with a great number of horsemen and archers'.

Katherine made her own unique contribution to the war effort by writing a prayer for men to say entering into battle. It is one of the earliest of her religious writings and remained one of the most popular. Brief but elegantly expressed, the prayer is notably lacking in bloodthirsty sentiments:

> O Almighty God and lord of hosts, which by thy angels thereunto appointed, dost minister both war and peace, and which didst give unto David both courage and strength, being but a little one, unarmed and unexpert in feats of war, with his sling to set upon and overthrow the great huge Goliath. Our cause now being just, and being enforced to enter into war and battle, we most humbly beseech thee, O Lord God of hosts, so to turn the hearts of our enemies to the desire of peace, that no Christian blood be spilt, or else grant, O Lord, that with small effusion of blood, and to the little hurt and damage of innocents, we may to thy glory, obtain victory. And that the wars being soon ended, we may all with one heart and mind, knit together in concord and unity, laud and praise thee, which livest and reignest world without end. Amen.[12]

It is not known whether Henry VIII took a copy of his wife's prayer with him. His attention, in any case, was firmly on what needed to be done to move things forward in France. Once across the water, he reviewed plans and was briefed by the duke of Suffolk, commander of the army that would attack Boulogne. The king does not seem to have been greatly impressed by what he found out and decided that he would have to become more personally involved. Henry discovered there was a great deal that required his attention: 'we be so occupied,' he wrote, 'and have so much to do in foreseeing and caring for everything ourself, as we have almost no manner of rest or leisure to do any other thing'.[13]

But he was in no hurry to move and did not come himself to
Boulogne until 26 July. The main assault on the town with big
guns began on 3 August. It seemed that all was proceeding
broadly to plan.

But on the same day that Henry left his palace at Greenwich, Mary of Hungary wrote a long missive to Chapuys, in
which she was at great pains to deny responsibility for any delay
or dereliction in the supply of provisions for Norfolk's army outside Montreuil. 'If the English campaign happens to be in want
of provisions, it will certainly not be the fault of the queen,' she
asserted, 'who has not failed to give all possible attention to the
matter ... In fact, the queen has hitherto acted in this affair in
such a manner that the English ought to be perfectly satisfied.'
This despatch has mistakenly been assigned to Katherine herself
(she and Mary were both known as 'Queen Regent') and cited
as evidence of her ability to defend her handling of important
military aspects of her regency; but it is nothing of the kind.
Rather, it is further proof of the difficulties in the Anglo-
imperial alliance that would only get worse with the passing
weeks.[14]

KATHERINE AND the regency council moved to Hampton Court
in late July, to escape the threat of plague. All three of Henry's
children soon joined her. Their company was welcome and it was
during this period that Elizabeth observed her stepmother as a
ruler, absorbing the realization that a queen could handle the
mass of papers, participate in discussions with advisers and take
decisions as well as any man. It must have been obvious to her
that the pressure of work was inescapable for the queen and that
Katherine was coping with it admirably. There were many letters
and despatches to be read and answered daily, for Henry had his
own council of advisers with him in France and the Council of
the North was also actively involved in monitoring the Scottish
situation. Initially, Scotland took up more of Katherine's time

than the war in France. One of her earliest interventions was in
connection with the large number of Scottish prisoners in northern
England, many of whom could not afford to pay for their own
food in jail. What was to be done with these people, the queen
and her council were asked, and would the king meet the costs of
feeding them? Katherine's reply was level-headed and humane.
She commanded that 'taking order for the bestowing of such as
be able to bear their own charges', the poorer prisoners, who
were 'stout, busy or otherwise like to do any hurt being at
liberty' were to be committed to several different prisons and 'if
extreme necessity shall so require' be given some small relief until
the king's pleasure was otherwise known. The rest were to be
released upon bond.[15]

It was a major part of Katherine's role to ensure that England
was quiet, calm and information was carefully controlled by the
government. Her attention to morale on the home front can be
seen in her response to the almost inevitable rumours of a French
invasion in early August 1544. She wrote to reassure her husband
that she had dealt promptly and effectively with this potential
threat to stability. As soon as she had established, through local
justices of the peace, that the invasion scare was without foundation, 'we thought good to advertise you of the same, lest any
other vain report passing over might have caused the king's
majesty to have conceived other opinion of the state of things
here than, thanks be unto God [they are] . . . all things here are
in very good quiet and order'. A similar rumour in the south-
west of the country was also investigated and found to be without
foundation. As Katherine remarked in a despatch to the council
with the king in France, 'a landing of Frenchmen about Gloucester was unlikely'. She was told by the justices of the peace that
'all was well and the rumour supposed to arise by the despatch of
the navy from Bristol for the conveyance of [the earl of] Lennox'.[16] But scaremongering was not the only source of possible
social disorder. A considerable number of 'aged and impotent'
French citizens had been resident in London for years and were

alarmed about their situation now that France and England were at war. Fearing deportation and threatened with violence if they set foot outside their homes, they petitioned for tolerance, which the queen was inclined to grant. Henry agreed with her decision and a proclamation was issued on the last day of September allowing them to stay.[17]

As well as her frequent reassurance that all was well in England and her equally constant references to the health of Henry's children, Katherine was keen, also, to place her personal relationship with the king squarely in his thoughts. She wanted him to know how much she missed him. She wrote, while still at Greenwich:

> The want of your presence, so much beloved and desired by me, makes me that I cannot quietly enjoy anything until I hear from your majesty . . . The time, therefore, seemeth to me very long with a great desire to know how your highness hath done since departing hence . . . whereas I know your majesty's absence is never without great respect of things most convenient and necessary, yet love and affection compelleth me to desire your presence . . . Love makes me in all things to set apart my own commodity and pleasure and to embrace most joyfully his will and pleasure whom I love.
>
> God, the knower of secrets, can judge these words not to be only written with ink, but most truly impressed in the heart . . . And even such confidence I have in your majesty's gentleness, knowing myself never to have done my duty as were requisite and meet to such a noble prince, at whose hands I have received so much love and goodness that with words I cannot express it.
>
> Lest I should be too tedious unto your majesty, I finish this, my scribbled letter, committing you into the governance of the Lord, with long life and prosperous felicity here, and after this to enjoy the kingdom of His elect.
>
> By your majesty's most humble, obedient loving wife and servant, Kateryn the Queen, K. P.[18]

No doubt the king was pleased to receive this charmingly worded avowal of Katherine's devotion, but he was no great correspondent himself. Travel, the press of things that needed to be done and perhaps, also, the desire to write only when he had something positive to say meant that Henry VIII did not reply directly to the queen for more than a month. His response, however, is interesting, because of the detail he gives her about the state of the siege of Boulogne and the political situation with Charles V and Francis I. The main part of his letter does not contain pleasantries; it suggests, rather, that the king had a high regard for his wife's intelligence and grasp of what was going on, and that they had discussed the conduct of the war and its associated diplomacy at length before he left England.

Katherine's letters to Henry had been delivered by one of her personal servants, and the man remained longer than anticipated in France because the king wanted to send him back with the good news that Boulogne had fallen. Unfortunately, the taking of the town was being delayed because of a lengthy wait for the necessary gunpowder to arrive from Flanders. He felt sure that it would be there in a matter of days now and went on to tell the queen: 'But meanwhile, without loss of men, we have won the strongest part of the town ... and can keep it with 400 men against 4,000 enemies.' He also acknowledged the bravery of the castle's defenders, saying that the Burgundians and the Flemings supplied to him by Charles V 'are no good where any danger is'. Yet his confidence that Boulogne would soon be in English hands was not matched by any similar confidence about the diplomatic reality of his position. He already knew that Francis I was suing for peace and expressed his uneasiness over what Charles V might do, but he did not yet fully grasp that his ally would proceed without him. The emperor's demands of the French seemed to him extreme. Well, if that were so, he would take a similar stance: 'viz, arrears of pension, damages suffered by the war, the realm of France and the duchies of Normandy, Aquitaine and Guienne. Either the emperor mindeth no peace', he went on to remark, 'or would pluck the honour of compounding it, although the French king says that he never made means to the emperor for peace. Pray communicate this to the Council.' Finally, he added a postscript in his own hand, updating her on the very latest military situation in Boulogne: 'this day, 8 September, we begin three batteries and have three mines going, besides one which has shaken and torn one of the greatest bulwarks. I am too busy to write more but send blessings to all my children and recommendations to my cousin Margaret [his niece, the new countess of Lennox] and the rest of the ladies and gentlewomen and to my Council.'[19]

Three days later, following the arrival of the powder, a final assault was made on Boulogne and the castle's last defences crumbled. The town surrendered on 14 September. It had been energetically defended by the Sieur de Vervins, a young French nobleman, who was later arrested by the French and beheaded. But after two months that had seen the loss of hundreds of lives and the near exhaustion of the English artillery, the town belonged to Henry VIII. He entered it like a medieval monarch vanquishing the opposing host: 'The king's highness, having the sword borne before him by the Lord Marquess of Dorset, like a noble and valiant conqueror, rode into Boulogne, and the trumpeters standing on the walls of the town sounded their trumpets at the time of his entering, to the great comfort of all the king's true subjects . . . And in the entering there met him the Duke of Suffolk, and delivered unto him the keys of the town . . .' The chronicler omitted to add that Henry had sat, in full armour, astride his warhorse in the pelting rain watching the 2,000 civilians turned out of Boulogne trudge towards the French lines at Abbeville. Many died of disease, hypothermia (it was a very cold and wet autumn) and starvation, the forgotten victims of a nasty war.

The glorious entry was, of course, a propaganda exercise. Katherine lost no time in capitalizing on it when the news of Henry's success was brought to her by her brother-in-law, Sir

William Herbert, on 19 September. It would be especially important to have the news of the king's success made known throughout the country but nowhere more so than the north, where the Scottish borders remained uneasy. So the queen immediately sent to the earl of Shrewsbury and the Council of the North the order that: 'The queen having this night advertisement by Sir William Herbert of the Privy Chamber, that Boulogne is in the king's hands without effusion of blood, Shrewsbury shall cause thanks to be given to God, by devout and general processions in all the towns and villages of the North, and also signify to the Wardens of the Marches this great benefit which God has heaped on us.'[20]

Katherine was at Woking in Surrey with the council when she issued orders for her husband's success to be extensively communicated. She was keeping well clear of central London because of the plague and had just issued a proclamation forbidding anyone who had contact with the disease to come to court. The capture of Boulogne seems to have given her sufficient confidence to believe that she did not have to attend council meetings daily. For the remainder of the month she and the royal children hunted in the south-east, in what was perhaps a deliberate effort to encourage family spirit and let off some steam. It cannot have been entirely enjoyable, for the wet weather that was wreaking havoc on northern France was equally prevalent across the Channel. In fact, it was so cold that Katherine had to send for some of her furred winter garments from the store at Baynard's Castle. But the rain was not the only dampener of celebrations in England. For, on the very day that Henry entered his new territory in France, Emperor Charles V made a separate peace with Francis I, leaving the English high but not at all dry outside Montreuil, and still at war with France.

HENRY'S INITIAL reaction to this betrayal was surprisingly phlegmatic. It was an unwelcome development, but by no means unforeseen. He had indirectly alluded to the possibility in his letter of 8 September to his wife. Francis I always believed that he could drive a wedge between the two mistrustful allies and the loss of Boulogne, though distressing, was a price he was willing to pay if he could bring the wider threat to a halt and sow diplomatic discord at the same time. In fact, by the terms of the treaty of Crépy, he did very well for a king whose country had been invaded by two of his enemies at the same time. But Charles V's campaign had really ended after his army's abandonment of the siege of St Dizier in mid-August 1544. Unwilling to fight long into the autumn and fearing, perhaps not without justification, that Henry might make his own peace with the French, he simply decided to get in there first. Nor was he willing to accept Henry VIII's offer to mediate on his behalf with Francis. His own pride and suspicion of his ally were too strong. Nevertheless, it looked as though he had paid a high price for his peace. Henry remarked subsequently that one would have thought Francis I the victor and Charles V the vanquished. The emperor agreed that a marriage would take place between Charles, duke of Orléans, the second son of the French king, and a Habsburg princess, either his own daughter, Maria, or his brother Ferdinand's daughter. This new-found friendship, and the sense of French entitlement that Henry had noted, seemed to be reinforced by the entry into Brussels of Queen Eléonore of France (the emperor's sister), accompanied by Orléans, her unappealing stepson, and the festivities that followed. The bride's dower lands were, however, to remain Habsburg territories, thus containing the ability of the French to do further damage to Charles's European domains. Above all, the arrangement bought the emperor time to deal with the continued rise of Protestantism in Germany. He wanted no further distractions in northern France for the time being and so he abandoned Henry VIII to pursue his own aims.

The most significant consequence for the English was the decision, made barely a week after the treaty of Crépy, to pull its army back from the siege of Montreuil. The town had not been an unreasonable target for a force better supplied and commanded than that led by the duke of Norfolk and Lord Russell but circumstances made it completely unattainable in 1544. The attempt to take it was hampered by the very long supply lines and the inability of Mary of Hungary and her council to meet what they soon came to believe were the unreasonable demands of the English force. The town had never been completely encircled and this put the besiegers under a very great disadvantage. But far worse than this military weakness was the inescapable reality that Norfolk's troops were starving. In total, the English force invading France consumed 15 million pounds of food and drink every month, but this was not sufficient to feed Norfolk's troops. By mid-September, a loaf of bread cost six times its real value and, if made locally from unground grain from diseased crops, it could be poisonous. When meat did arrive eventually from England, it was almost always rancid. Even beer was in short supply. Dysentery ran wild through a camp made all the more vile by the incessant rain and deplorable hygiene. Eventually, there was no forage even for the horses. Many of Norfolk's soldiers were German mercenaries who remained unpaid. It is hardly surprising that they became fractious. So when the order to fall back to Boulogne was given, the duke was mightily relieved.

Yet he was partly the architect of what nearly became his undoing. Time had not changed the habits of Thomas Howard. An anti-imperialist all his life, he was never keen to leave Calais and sit around outside Montreuil, uncertain of his orders and perhaps realizing that the town was going to be extremely difficult, if not impossible, to take. An accomplished whiner, as well as an arch-manipulator, the duke had delayed his departure from Calais for a month, awaiting Russell's arrival. He wanted to be sure that Russell could share any blame that might be laid if, as Norfolk suspected, things did not go well. Russell immediately obliged him by entering into the spirit of rivalry. He wrote to the king in mid-July complaining of Norfolk's attitude, saying it was likely to damage Anglo-imperial relations. And he made the interesting suggestion that either Thomas Seymour or Richard Cromwell, nephew of the king's executed chief minister, should be sent as an independent adviser to assess the situation. There was no response to this proposal and both Russell and Norfolk realized that they must attempt to capture Montreuil, even though neither probably thought it feasible. Their departure from the town was, by late September, itself a risky enterprise. The French armies were not far away and Norfolk's troops were unlikely to survive an all-out battle, but they managed to get back to Boulogne unscathed. Henry was beside himself with fury when, shortly after his return to England, he learned that the dukes of Norfolk and Suffolk had decided to fall back still further, to Calais, leaving Boulogne dangerously exposed.

The king's overall mood, however, was one of personal satisfaction. The capture of Boulogne had always been his priority and the prize was now his. Never mind that a fortune would have to be spent to rebuild its fortifications and defend the town or that the war would drag on for another eighteen months, leading to deep-seated resentment in France and a determination not merely to regain Boulogne but to take Calais, too. Henry showed no concern that his own country was bankrupt as a result of the excessive demands put upon its exchequer and Wriothesley's inadequate financial skills. The chancellor had reckoned in March 1544 that the campaign would cost £250,000, of which sum the king already had £134,000. The deficit was to be made up by speeding the sale of monastic lands and a further debasement of the coinage. But the final cost of the war was eight times higher than Wriothesley's initial calculation. In Antwerp Stephen Vaughan raised as much as he could through loans, and the Privy Council attempted to help by sending lead stripped from monastery roofs; but all this did was flood the market, reducing its value. To the king, none of this mattered. In his own mind, Henry VIII had got what he wanted. He would return to England a successful war leader. Boulogne was his Agincourt and he had made sure that the Tudor dynasty could take its place in the history of valour alongside its Plantagenet forebears. On the last day of September he took ship from Calais, bound for England and a joyful reunion with his queen.

Katherine, who had been concerned that French ships might try to intercept her husband as he returned home, was at Eltham Palace when she heard the news that Henry had landed in Kent. It is possible that her sharp mind had already grasped some of the difficulties that lay ahead, but she knew that she would no longer play a direct part in decision-making. Her influence, though, was riding high and she would make the most of that. Katherine had written a prayer for the king, too, in which she asked Jesus to 'indue him plentifully with heavenly gifts. Grant him in health and wealth long to live. Heap glory and honour upon him. Glad him with the joy of thy countenance. So strength him that he may vanquish and overcome all his and our foes, and be dread and feared of all the enemies of his realm.'[21]

But, for the moment, to reinforce her position as a dutiful and desirable wife, Katherine took her leave of the royal children and went without them to Otford Palace in Kent, where she and Henry VIII met again in early October. They spent some time together at Leeds Castle near Maidstone and eventually made their way back to London. It was something of a second honeymoon. The king had every reason to be satisfied with the way Katherine had handled affairs in his absence and she, in her turn, seems to have derived great satisfaction from what she had achieved. Their joint perception of success, Henry's in France and Katherine's in England, strengthened their relationship. Her life as queen of England had become much more fulfilling than she could ever have dared to hope when she married Henry fifteen months before. There was every reason to believe it would continue. And now she had the time and opportunity to develop her own ideas, to give them shape and utterance, and to bring them to a wider audience. She could be so much more than just another wife of Henry VIII.

CHAPTER TEN

The Queen's Gambit

> *'I never knew mine own wickedness, neither lamented for my sins truly, until the time God inspired me with his grace, that I looked in this book; then I began to see perfectly, that mine own power and strength could not help me, and that I was in the Lord's hand, even as the clay is in the potter's hand.'*

> Katherine Parr, *The Lamentation of a Sinner*,
> November 1547

KATHERINE CONTINUED in good spirits and high in the king's favour as the New Year dawned in 1545. Her interest in foreign affairs was undiminished and her graciousness much appreciated in diplomatic circles. Nowhere was this more apparent than in her leave-taking of the veteran imperial ambassador Eustace Chapuys, who reported in detail his final interview with the queen in May 1545. Chapuys had been in England, with occasional breaks, for sixteen years. He had lived through the interminable agony of the divorce from Katherine of Aragon, and was a staunch supporter of Princess Mary when she was virtually friendless. During his time in a country he did not admire, whose ruling class he regarded as self-seeking and untrustworthy, he had faithfully performed his duty to Charles V. He knew Henry VIII well – or, at least, the public face that

Henry presented to ambassadors – and the two men developed a grudging regard for each other. They were of an age and time that had not been kind to either of them. Half paralysed by gout, Chapuys was finally being allowed to depart, but he first needed to bid the king an official farewell. On his way to the royal apartments, the ambassador was flattered to discover that the queen meant to waylay him:

> having traversed the garden facing the queen's lodging, and arrived nearly at the other end close to the entrance of the king's apartments, my own people informed me that the queen and princess were following us quickly. I hardly had time to rise from the chair in which I was being carried before she approached quite near, and seemed from the small suite she had with her, and the haste with which she came, as if her purpose in coming was specially to speak to me. She was only accompanied by four or five women of the chamber . . . and opened the conversation by saying that the king had told her the previous evening that I was coming that morning to take my leave of him. While on the one hand she was very sorry for my departure, as she had been told that I had always acted well in my offices, and the king had confidence in me, on the other hand she doubted not that my health would be better on the other side of the water. I could, however, she said, do as much on the other side as here, for the preservation of the amity between your majesty and the king, of which I had been one of the chief promoters.

The queen continued in this vein, emphasizing how important was the continued friendship of Henry VIII and Charles V and asked Chapuys to 'use [his] best influence in favour of the maintenance and increase of the existing friendship'. Nor did she forget to enquire in more detail about the ailing emperor himself: 'She asked me very minutely and most graciously, after your majesty's health and expressed great joy to learn of your majesty's

amelioration . . . I then asked to be allowed to salute the princess
[Mary], which was at once accorded, she, the queen, being
anxious, as it seemed to me, that I should not suffer from having
to stand too long.' Katherine withdrew tactfully, so as not to
eavesdrop on what passed between the ambassador and her
stepdaughter, but Mary, perhaps concerned by protocol, as well
as remembrance of unhappier times, did not converse for long
with Chapuys and before he went up to the king, Katherine
returned to her own, highly effective brand of personal diplomacy,
enquiring of the health of Mary of Hungary: 'She said that the
king was under great obligation to her majesty for having on all
occasions shown so much good will towards him, and she
continued with a thousand compliments on the queen-dowager's
virtue, prudence and diligence. After some other conversation,
the queen returned to her lodgings without allowing me to stir
from where I was.'[1]

It is hard to imagine any of Henry's other wives, with the
exception of Katherine of Aragon, who was born to the role of
royal diplomat, holding such a conversation. Nor did Mary of
Hungary, about whom she was so pleasant, have anything like
Katherine Parr's easy manner in such matters. But though Henry's
sixth wife continued, even in difficult times, to try to soothe
Anglo-imperial relations, it should not be supposed that her
interest in foreign affairs was exclusively on the Habsburg side.
For by the spring of 1545 the queen's secretary, Walter Bucler,
had been in Europe for some months, on a secret mission. He
was trying, with his colleague, Dr Christopher Mont, a former
ambassador to the court of Saxony, to forge a league between the
German princes and the kings of England and Denmark. This
diplomatic initiative was not, in itself, new; Henry VIII had been
sporadically involved since the late 1530s in attempts to gain an
initiative in his relations with Charles V by allying with the
emperor's troublesome German subjects. This was a major incen-
tive in the disastrous match with Anne of Cleves. But in 1545
nothing of substance emerged, despite a flurry of despatches.

Henry VIII eventually grew impatient with the vacillating Germans and, in December 1545, Bucler was finally called home. But the fact that Katherine could have been so effusive to Eustace Chapuys when a senior member of her own household was attempting to undermine Charles V in his German domains suggests a deviousness of which Henry himself would have been proud. Chapuys's replacement, François Van der Delft, did pick up information about Bucler's mission after he took up his new post in the summer. Thereafter, the emperor and his servants were much less convinced of Katherine's benign influence, despite her fair words.

If the queen's hopes for a German alliance were not realized, it was a setback she seems to have taken with equanimity. She remained close to Henry and his children and her personal life was beginning to take a shape that would find her fulfilled intellectually and spiritually. Yet there was sadness as well as pleasure for Katherine in 1545 because sometime during that year her beloved stepdaughter, Margaret Neville, died, leaving the queen without the support and love of someone whose life she had shaped for more than a decade.

The precise date of Margaret Neville's death is unknown, as is the cause of her demise. She made her will at the end of March 1545 and probate was not granted until almost exactly a year later. The supposition must then be that she knew she was seriously ill when the will was written, but that she did not die immediately. Her will is remarkable for the devotion displayed to Katherine, her 'only and sole executor' and for its strong faith in reformed religious ideas. Written at a time when the term 'Protestant' was still not in general use in England, it is, nevertheless, unmistakably Protestant in its conviction. Margaret begins by stating:

> first, I bequeath, yield up and commit to the hands of my
> most merciful father my soul, yet all my whole substance, as
> well spiritual as corporeal, most steadfastly trusting unto his

mercy that he through the mercies of my saviour and only mediator Jesus Christ will now perform his promise unto me that death may have no power over me but that through his grace I may boldly say, 'O death where is thy victory? O hell where is thy sting?', being above all other things most certain that trust in him shall not be confounded.

Reiterating her faith in God's mercy, asking forgiveness for all her sins, Margaret went on to address the arrangements for her possessions:

And now as I have mercy of my merciful father, diverse and sundry talents which it hath pleased him to commit into my hands, that I may not be counted like unto the unprofitable servant which hid the talents of his lord in the earth, I shall most humbly beseech my dear sovereign mistress, the Queen's highness, to take all and singular my said talents unto her hands to be disposed of to the glory of God as her highness shall think most best . . . and knowing furthermore that her grace is of such perfect godliness and wisdom that she can much better dispose them to the honour of and discharge of my duty than I can myself devise, I shall most humbly desire her grace to take the ordering of the same.

After bequests to several friends and servants, Margaret left her lands at Hammerton 'as well as the 1,000 marks which my father gave unto me to my marriage' to her 'dear sovereign mistress, the lady Katheryne Parr, Queen of England, France and Ireland'.[2]

Her pride in her stepmother as well as her abiding affection shines through this moving avowal of personal faith and belief in redemption. She was twenty years old and unmarried, despite her father's provision for her and her childhood betrothal to the executed traitor, Bigod's, son. Katherine had transformed her life, providing her with maternal love, companionship and an entrée into the highest circles of the land that she could only have dreamed of as a little girl. No portrait of her survives, but in her will she has left us a picture of a young woman of grace, deep affections and simple but firm religious faith. In fact, she strongly mirrors the queen herself.

Margaret's loss must have affected Katherine deeply, but the queen was not a woman given to maudlin sentimentality. Indeed, she had already demonstrated this, and the view of death shared by her stepdaughter, in a letter to Lady Jane Wriothesley, wife of the lord chancellor (and one of her own ladies-in-waiting), written following the death of Lady Jane's baby son. Even at a time when infant death was common, Katherine's words seem unfeeling – almost lacking in basic humanity. Her commiserations begin with the far from compassionate observation that she understands 'it hath pleased God of late to disinherit your son of this world, of intent he should become partner and chosen heir of the everlasting inheritance, which calling and happy vocation ye may rejoice'. It is perfectly apparent, however, that Lady Wriothesley was not rejoicing at all and reproof for the extent of her maternal grief soon followed. 'For what is excessive sorrow but a plain evidence against you that your inward mind doth repine against God's sayings, and a declaration that you are not contented that God hath put your son by nature, by his adoption, in possession of the heavenly kingdom?' Only those who have doubted the message of everlasting life allow themselves to rail against death, says Katherine: 'but those that be persuaded that to die here is life again, do rather long for death, and count it a solace than to bewail it as an utter destruction . . . if you lament your son's death, you do him great wrong and show yourself to sorrow for the happiest thing there ever came to him.' And, after all, she concluded, there was always the possibility of future offspring, particularly if the disconsolate mother calmed down and accepted 'God's will, for then he 'can at his pleasure repay your loss with such a like jewel, if gladly and quietly ye submit and refer all to his pleasure'.[3]

We can make allowances for a profound difference in outlook between the mid-sixteenth century and our own times where reactions to infant mortality are concerned. Nor are the religious sentiments expressed in any way heretical. But the uncompromising tone of Katherine's letter to a bereaved mother still jars. She had never known such a loss herself, but this did not stop her from lecturing someone who was still trying to come to terms with a very painful experience. Perhaps she felt it was her regal duty to provide very clear and definite guidance, in the hope it would speed Lady Wriothesley's recovery. Katherine was a woman who had learned well, by this time, to keep her emotions in check. She may also have reasoned that she had made sacrifices herself and that dwelling on the past was unhealthy. There is a further possibility that she did not much like Jane Wriothesley. It is certainly a very chilly letter. The recipient's reactions are unknown, but it is hard to imagine that she took a great deal of comfort in what her royal mistress had written. It is quite possible, however, that Thomas Wriothesley took umbrage at Katherine's reproof of his wife. He would wait a while, until the right circumstances presented themselves, before he moved to take revenge.

Margaret Neville's will and her own thoughts on death give us a flavour of Katherine's developing views on religion. So, too, does Princess Elizabeth's New Year's gift at the end of 1544, her translation of *The Mirror of the Sinful Soul*,[4] which describes the author's journey from acute awareness of her own sinfulness to acceptance of God's love and justification by faith. 'Trusting also,' as Elizabeth wrote in her prefatory letter to her stepmother, 'through His incomprehensible love, grace and mercy, she (being called from sin to repentance) doth faithfully hope to be saved.' For Katherine herself was undergoing such an epiphany, one which, driven on by a formidable determination, an intelligent mind and ability to use her own position as queen to maximum effect, would make her among the most successful writers of the sixteenth century, and an important influence on the history of England.

❧

WE DO NOT KNOW precisely when Katherine first decided to turn her study of scripture and her growing interest in religious ideas into published works of her own. The process was probably more the result of a combination of deepening faith, and the opportunity that her position gave her to express that faith publicly, than any sudden revelation. The queen's first work appeared in June 1545. Produced by the royal printer, Thomas Berthelet, it was entitled *Prayers Stirring the Mind unto Heavenly Meditations* and was so successful that an enlarged version was brought out as early as November the same year. By 1548, this book, its contents 'Collected out of holy works by the most virtuous and gracious Princess KATHERINE, Queen of England, France and Ireland', so its title page proclaimed, was in its fifth edition. As an author, Katherine was an overnight success. But what were the influences on her and what was she trying to achieve, beyond the satisfaction of seeing her name in print?

Katherine lived in a world that can seem very similar to our own, peopled by power-hungry, greedy men and women who lived for the moment. People at court were highly competitive, displaying conspicuous consumption, in the form of jewels, clothes, property and entertainment. It was a time of economic uncertainty and rising debt, warfare and strange new diseases that could have catastrophic impact. But appearances are deceptive, and life in mid-sixteenth-century England was also fundamentally different from that of today. The view of family as the root of a stable and thriving system was deeply ingrained, as was the accepted order of social division, with the king as its head. The citizens of England in the 1540s knew their place because they wanted the assurance of stability that came with such knowledge. And they lived in a country where belief in God pervaded daily life. Secularism would have horrified them. Yet this was a world also riven by increasing doubt, as the abstractions of Martin Luther's initial arguments with the authority of the Church took on much more painful immediacy. Katherine's husband had removed his country from the centuries-old allegiance it owed to the pope in Rome and had begun, with the help of politicians and churchmen who favoured reform, to forge his own Church of England. At the time Katherine Parr became the king's sixth wife, the struggle for what would constitute the essential content of that Church's beliefs, and its form of worship, was still continuing. Katherine, as queen of England, found herself in contact with a ferment of ideas. She was exposed to the great debates, the key questions that occupied the minds of the literate governing class of England. That she decided to make her own contribution is entirely in keeping with her background and character. She realized the unique opportunity her position afforded. The possible disadvantages, even dangers, did not, apparently, occur to her.

As queen, Katherine had wholeheartedly embraced the conviction of the aristocracy in Tudor England that study was a lifelong process. It was no mere pastime, pleasurable though it might be, but part of becoming a more rounded and complete person. In fact, it was almost a duty. To sit down with her ladies to read the scriptures was as natural as returning to the study of Latin, indeed, perhaps more so. For there was one huge difference between the Bible Katherine had read as a child at Rye House and the passages she now studied in her privy chamber. The Bible was now available in English – at least, to noblemen and their wives.

There had been various versions of the Bible, or, at least, parts of it, in English for some years. The concept of an English Bible was originally a humanist project rather than an overtly Protestant one, and this is an important point to remember in respect of the climate in which Katherine Parr began her literary career.[5] The bold lines between 'Catholic' and 'Protestant' characterized by many historians are a product of hindsight. They were not so readily visible to those who were alive at the time. In fact, William Tyndale's English New Testament had first appeared as long ago as 1526. Thereafter, further translation was slow (Cranmer himself believed at one point during the 1530s that it would not be completed before Doomsday) and often controversial. The king's views remained equivocal. But in 1538 Miles Coverdale, who became Katherine Parr's almoner ten years later, was asked by Cromwell to produce a further revision. Coming just a year after the final suppression of the Pilgrimage of Grace and with the threat of a Franco-imperial crusade against the excommunicated Henry VIII, the timing is highly significant. The work was printed in Paris and appeared in England as the Great Bible in April 1540. The following year a new edition appeared, with a preface by Cranmer. Coverdale's text omitted some of the more obvious Lutheranism of Tyndale's earlier version, probably in order to make it more acceptable to the king.

We should not underestimate how marvellous the Great Bible must have seemed to Katherine Parr and the women of her court. Here was the word of God in the vernacular, at last, strong and direct, without the need for interpretation by priests, speaking to them as individuals. Its impact was profound. And Katherine, seized with the wonder of it, was certain that the richness of understanding and self-awareness engendered by religious study should be brought before a wider audience, in the English tongue. The intellectual stimulation, the literal soul-searching, the acknowledgement of man's sinfulness and God's salvation, all informed her desire to be part of the great discussions of her day. She was an expressive writer, as her letters show, and her literary projects would demonstrate her competence as an editor and patroness of learning. There was also another aim: wherever possible, she would reiterate the great achievements of Henry VIII, her husband, who had freed England from the tyranny and superstition of Rome. He was a new Moses leading his people to deliverance. In an ordered society, Henry was still the father of his country. All hope for the future sprang from the king.

Though Henry and Katherine were increasingly to discuss (and sometimes to dispute) religion, the influences on the queen came from a number of different people. Chief among these was probably Archbishop Cranmer. It is difficult to be specific about the extent of their contact or the effect it had on Katherine directly, but this very vagueness is, as Diarmaid MacCulloch points out, revealing: 'the relationship between the archbishop and Henry VIII's last queen ... is so obscure as to suggest deliberate discretion'.[6] Cranmer was particularly skilled at this kind of political nuance. The early 1540s were a very difficult time for him and he would have been acutely aware of the benefits that could accrue from closeness to the queen as well as the pitfalls. Indeed, he may have been more aware of the latter than Katherine was herself. He had been an ally of Anne Boleyn and was stunned at her fall. Few men at the time knew the king's unpredictability better than Cranmer. His own ideas on matters such as the eucharist were still taking shape. There might have been much that he hoped Katherine could achieve, but his connection with her must not be obvious. It would do neither of them any good in those trying times.

Nevertheless, she saw him almost daily while she was regent and his influence, while not flaunted, was pervasive. The queen's commitment to promoting English as the language of worship mirrored Cranmer's current preoccupations. As we have seen, his Litany in English appeared in May 1544, an important element in the propaganda effort to support Henry VIII's war with France. The king's subjects could attend services that were partly in English and remember him in their prayers in their native tongue.[7] But this does not mean that the Mass in Latin was abandoned, and, in fact, some elements of the service had been conducted in English for a very long time. But the English Litany was highly significant. Its essence survived in the Book of Common Prayer and was a major element in the subsequent form of worship under Edward VI and Elizabeth. The Litany was reprinted in October 1544 when it appeared in a volume also containing a translation of a work originally attributed to the executed Bishop Fisher of Rochester, who had so bravely supported Katherine of Aragon. This was a slim volume entitled *Psalms or Prayers*, which first appeared in English in April 1544.

It has been suggested that the English version of Fisher's work, which is more a statement of Catholic rather than reformist faith, may be Katherine Parr's first, anonymous publication.[8] It is true that Katherine ordered copies of the combined work and that the following year Thomas Berthelet published Katherine's *Prayers or Meditations* in one edition with the Litany and the *Psalms or Prayers*. This is not conclusive proof of collaboration between the queen and the archbishop but it certainly indicates that their efforts were tending in the same direction.

Yet if Katherine had worked on translating the *Psalms or Prayers* in the first year of her marriage to the king, then this points to an influence on her thoughts earlier than her contact with Thomas Cranmer. And it also introduces more complexity in charting her spiritual journey. The connection between the martyred Fisher and Katherine Parr is George Day, bishop of Chichester, her almoner. Day had been Fisher's chaplain, though he had avoided the bishop's fate. He had embraced religious reform in the 1530s but now was pulling back from more extreme evangelical views. His moderation, carefully balanced, eventually meant that he could not support the sweeping changes of Edward VI. Perhaps, as his relationship with the queen blossomed, he saw an opportunity to encourage her desire to improve her Latin with a manageable project, a translation of his deceased master's book of prayers. It was not, however, an entirely innocent choice, nor one without risk. Fisher's name could hardly have been welcome to the king's ears and so it was better for the whole endeavour to remain anonymous. The extent to which Day might have helped Katherine can never be known, but the association of the *Psalms or Prayers* with an executed traitor and the possibility that the translation was a joint effort may explain why Katherine's name was never directly associated with it. Without this explanation, its anonymity is rather odd. Katherine was not shy about seeing her name in print or in encouraging others (like Princess Mary) to acknowledge their own work.

Day's influence on Katherine was not confined to this one

project. A great admirer of Erasmus himself, he probably encouraged the queen to read more of the works of this giant of the
humanist movement. There were others, too, who helped develop
her enthusiasm for making the writings of great men available in
English. Her most ambitious undertaking, the organization of
the translation of Erasmus's *Paraphrases upon the New Testament*,
was put under the overall editorial direction not of Day but of
Nicholas Udall. Quite how Udall was chosen for this task by the
queen remains a mystery, but he and Day could hardly have had
more contrasting personalities or backgrounds.

Udall had enjoyed, to say the least, a chequered career, and
one in which religion had played little part. An Oxford graduate,
he had divided his time between writing plays, publishing a
textbook on conversational Latin and involvement in education.
Between 1534 and 1541 he was headmaster at Eton, a post that
was poorly paid, though it was prestigious. As we have seen, he
acquired there a reputation for flogging that one of his pupils
remembered with a shudder as late as 1575. But it was not for
the brutality of his regime at Eton that he was most notorious.
Several robberies at the school were investigated by the Privy
Council and one of the scholars who confessed to having stolen
silver and plate implicated Udall in activities that were all together
more unacceptable to the mores of sixteenth-century England
than the mere theft of precious objects. Hauled in to answer these
accusations, Udall confessed to numerous offences of buggery,
a crime punishable by death. Somehow he managed to avoid
the extreme penalty, perhaps through the intervention of an influential patron. Thomas Wriothesley and Richard Cox, Prince
Edward's tutor, have both been suggested as possibilities, and
either could also have suggested him to Katherine as the person
to take on the *Paraphrases* project. The queen evidently did not
hold his dubious past against him, nor, given the way gossip
circulated at court, does it seem likely that she would have been
completely ignorant of it.

Udall assumed direction of the work with commendable

diligence and an effusive enthusiasm which sounds almost flowery to modern readers. He was especially keen to acknowledge the role of the queen as his patron and to emphasize the devotional piety of the young aristocratic women of England. Writing in the preface to the *Paraphrases*, which were finally published after three years of work in 1548, Udall fell over himself to praise Katherine, describing how

> all these your unceasing pains and travails do finally redound. Leaving in the prosecution of so large a matter as neither my slender wit can well contrive, nor my rude pen is able to wield. I shall in this present only thank God in you, and you in God, for causing the Paraphrases of Desiderius Erasmus of Rotterdam upon the New Testament to be translated into English for the use and commodity of such people, as with an earnest zeal and with devout study do hunger and thirst for the simple and plain knowledge of God's word; not for contentious babbling but for innocent living; not to be curious searchers of the high mysteries, but to be faithful executioners and doers of God's bidding; not to be troublous talkers of the Bible, but sincere followers of God's precepts therein contained; not to be irreverent reasoners in Holy Scripture . . . but to be humble and lowly workers of God's glory.

He went on to pay tribute to Katherine's strong guidance of the project: 'And that in your Highness, for the most speedy expedition of your most godly purpose to bring God's word to the more light and the more clear understanding, distributed this work by portions, to sundry translators, to the intent it might all at once be finished . . . ye have therein, most gracious Lady, right well declared both how much ye tender God's honour and also how earnestly ye mind the benefit of your country.'[9]

Flattery aside, Udall was right to single out Katherine's skilful approach to the translation of so massive a work. It was not, of course, unusual to divide responsibilities in this way; the work on the Great Bible, the King's Book and other religious projects was undertaken by a team of clerics. Apart from Udall himself, who translated the Gospel according to St Luke and possibly also St Matthew and the Acts of the Apostles, the other accredited translators were Thomas Key, who was encouraged to participate by George Owen, one of Henry VIII's doctors, and who tackled St Mark, and Princess Mary, who undertook perhaps the most challenging of all, St John, at her stepmother's urging. They were an interesting and diverse team: the disgraced but resilient schoolmaster, the long-suffering and bastardized eldest child of the king and the lesser-known preacher in the queen's household. Lending a keen supervisory interest, and possibly also involving herself in the translation of St Matthew, which remained unattributed, was Katherine herself. In its scope and impact, this English translation of Erasmus's work represents the queen's greatest literary achievement. How much she directly contributed is open to conjecture. Stephen Gardiner, who disliked the entire concept of the work, later decried both the inadequate Latin and the selective editing of the anonymous translator of St Matthew. This has been interpreted as an indirect attack on Katherine, on the assumption that Gardiner knew very well the identity of the person concerned, and was, by 1547, an inveterate enemy of the queen. It is not clear how he obtained a copy of the *Paraphrases* before publication, nor is his critique conclusive proof that Katherine Parr took an active role in translation. What is certain is that the *Paraphrases* was given a great deal of publicity by the Edwardian government (20,000 copies were in circulation between 1548 and 1551) and that they established Katherine as the leading patron of vernacular religious writing in England.

Until the end of 1545, Katherine Parr's individual religious writings had been sparse, confined to a few prayers. She was becoming experienced as a collector and editor of existing material (the *Prayers or Meditations* was based on writings of St Thomas à Kempis), but her influences were varied and largely emanated from the European continent, the origin of all the new ideas. She studied both Catholic humanist writers and Lutheran reformers, and attended Mass regularly. Discussions with her husband on the various strands of religious beliefs and current trends seem to have formed a major element of their social relationship – perhaps almost too much so for Henry's liking, as the months went by. But if his patience was becoming tried, Katherine was ever more eager to express herself. In this she no doubt received encouragement from her religious advisers and her closest companions in her Privy Chamber, her sister Lady Herbert and cousin, Lady Lane, as well as Lady Joan Denny, wife of Sir Anthony Denny, keeper of the privy purse, moderate reformer and a growing influence in the king's Privy Chamber. Then there was also the more zealously reforming Katherine Brandon, duchess of Suffolk, whose friendship with the queen seems to have intensified in 1545. Attractive, outspoken and opinionated, the duchess was widowed in August of that year at the age of twenty-six and it may be that her loss brought her closer to the queen, who later referred affectionately to 'my lady of Suffolk' in one of her letters to Thomas Seymour.

Against this backdrop of intellectual stimulation and support, Katherine embarked on the writing of a book that was entirely hers, not a compilation or a translation of existing material. It must encapsulate her own beliefs and experience and present them in a manner that would strike a chord with her readers. So was the *Lamentation of a Sinner* conceived, the first work of its kind in English written by a woman. The fact that the woman was a queen added immeasurably to its importance, and its success.[10]

The *Lamentation* begins on a sombre note, acknowledging the writer's sinfulness and her 'obstinate, strong and intractable heart'. She is well aware of the task she has set herself:

> Truly, I have taken no little small thing upon me, first to set forth my whole stubbornness and contempt in words the which is incomprehensible in thought . . . next this to declare the excellent beneficence, mercy and goodness of God, which

Above Edward VI, the stepson who adored Katherine Parr, shortly before his accession to the throne in 1547.

Right An older Edward as king, with no evidence of the illness that was to take his life in the summer of 1553.

A recently discovered portrait thought to be Lady Jane Grey, Katherine's ward and chief mourner at her funeral.

ANNO DNI   1 5 4 4

LADI MARI   DOVGHTER TO
THE MOST   VERTVOVS PRINC
KINGE HENRI   THE EIGHT

THE AGE OF   XXVIII YERES

Mary Tudor, eldest child of Henry VIII, in 1544, the year she was
restored to the succession. She was close to Katherine, whose friendship
brought her much happiness in an otherwise difficult life.
Mary's youthful attractiveness is still evident here.

Princess Elizabeth in the last year of her father's reign, shortly before she joined Katherine Parr's household and began her dangerous flirtation with Sir Thomas Seymour.

Mary Tudor as queen, in an unflattering portrait commissioned by her husband, Philip II of Spain. A decade of stress and uncertainty had taken its toll.

Right The coronation portrait of the twenty-five-year-old Elizabeth I.

Below Elizabeth's signature as queen.

The cover of Elizabeth's translation of *The Mirror of the Sinful Soul*, given to Katherine as a New Year's gift in 1544/45. The queen's initials, KP, are in the centre.

Elizabeth's gift to her father on 20 December 1545 was this sumptuously embroidered trilingual translation of her stepmother's *Prayers or Meditations*.

Mary Howard, duchess of Richmond, Norfolk's daughter and widow of Henry Fitzroy, Henry VIII's illegitimate son. She was twice considered as a wife for Sir Thomas Seymour, Katherine Parr's last husband.

Edward Seymour, duke of Somerset. The elder brother of Jane Seymour and uncle of Edward VI, he took over the government of England after Henry VIII's death. His relationship with Katherine, both as dowager queen and wife of his younger brother, Thomas, was uneasy.

Anne Stanhope, duchess of Somerset, was the duke's second wife. Fecund and feisty, she had been one of Katherine's ladies-in-waiting, but despite their shared religious views, the queen disliked her intensely.

A miniature of Sir Thomas Seymour from the time he first wooed Katherine, prior to her marriage to Henry VIII.

Sir Thomas Seymour, Katherine's fourth husband, is shown with the full beard fashionable in the late 1540s. The poem in the background, praising his attributes, is by his loyal servant, John Harington.

Left Katherine's tomb in St Mary's Chapel at Sudeley Castle, rebuilt by Victorian architect George Gilbert Scott.

Below left The inscription on Katherine's coffin.

Below Katherine Brandon, duchess of Suffolk. A close friend of Katherine's, she was the reluctant guardian of the queen's orphaned daughter, Lady Mary Seymour.

is infinite, unmeasurable: neither can all the words of angels, and men, make relation thereof . . . Who is he that is not forced to confess the same, if he consider what he hath received of God, and doth daily receive? Yea, if men would not acknowledge and confess the same, the stones would cry it out.

This early passage shows the queen at her best; the language is strong and direct, her intention clearly shown. She will hold her personal experience up for public scrutiny, describing the strong sense of unworthiness she believes that she shares with her readers. This is, however, balanced with the joyful acknowledgement of God's goodness. But, by the end (118 pages later), she has returned to the darker theme of the judgement that awaits those who do not live by God's word: 'Truly, if we do not redress and amend our living according to the doctrine of the gospel, we shall receive a terrible sentence of Christ the son of God . . .' In-between is an outpouring of views on death, salvation, the evils of the papacy and the debt that England owes to Henry VIII, good preaching, marriage of priests, the upbringing of children and the belief that scripture should be read by all. It is an amalgam of reforming religious ideas, based on a set of convictions that were characterized by the term 'evangelical' at the time. A few passages are closer to Calvinism than Lutheranism.

Yet though Katherine intended her work to set an example of how a queen could make public her private thoughts on religion, and despite its undoubted popularity as Protestantism grew in England, the *Lamentation* has not stood the test of time well. It is neither great literature nor compelling religious writing. No one but a specialist in the period would sit down to read it today. By turns rambling, repetitive and derivative, it is heavily based on St Paul's teachings and epistles. Though written as prose, not poetry, the work owes a good deal to Marguerite of Navarre's already famous personal statement of belief. There may even have been an element of competition. When Elizabeth began her translation of *The Mirror of the Sinful Soul* (perhaps at her stepmother's prompting) it may also have occurred to Katherine that she might attempt a similar piece of literature. Could not an English queen rival a French one in this way? The 'celebrity memoir' is not a recent phenomenon, and both Marguerite and Katherine knew that there was a market for queens who went public with an account of their religious passions.

And yet the authentic voice of Katherine Parr comes strongly through in the *Lamentation*, despite its weaknesses. Above all, there is left the indelible impression of a woman for whom the reading of the Gospel in English has been a profound and revelatory experience:

> Truly, it may be most justly verified that to behold Christ crucified, in spirit, is the best meditation that can be. I certainly never knew mine own miseries and wretchedness so well by book, admonition, or learning, as I have done by looking into the spiritual book of the crucifix. I lament much I have passed so many years not regarding this divine book, but I judged and thought myself to be well instructed in the same: whereas now I am of this opinion, that if God would suffer men to live her a thousand year, and should study continually is the same divine book, I should not be filled with the contemplation thereof.

Katherine was no theologian, nor did she claim to be. The split in Christianity clearly distressed and troubled her: 'It is much to be lamented', she wrote, 'the schisms, varieties, contentions and disputacions, that have been and are in the world about Christian religion.' She may have hoped that, in setting forth for public scrutiny her growing spiritual awareness, she could help unite the disparate elements of religious reform behind the changes her husband had brought about in England. Her desire is to glorify Henry VIII who 'hath taken away the veils, and mists of errors, and brought us to the knowledge of the truth, by the

light of God's word'. He is likened to the great deliverer of the
Jews in the Old Testament: 'our Moses, a most godly wise
governor and king hath delivered us out of captivity and bondage
of Pharoah. I mean by this Moses king Henry VIII my most
sovereign honourable lord and husband . . . and I mean by this
Pharoah the bishop of Rome, who hath been and is a greater
persecutor of all true Christians, than ever was Pharoah of the
children of Israel.' For Katherine the queen of England, sturdily
anti-papal, is very much also the dutiful wife, as she is keen to
emphasize: 'If they be women married, they learn of St Paul to
be obedient to their husbands, and to keep silence in the
congregation, and to learn of their husbands, at home.'[11] Henry
VIII would have been delighted by such sentiments, but he did
not live to see them in print. The *Lamentation* was published in
the autumn of 1547, some nine months after his death. The
reason for the gap between Katherine's completion of the draft
and its publication lay in the difficult last year of the royal
marriage. Henry VIII would have expected the sentiments of
praise and deference contained in the *Lamentation*. Unfortunately,
they were increasingly ones he did not himself recognize in his
sixth wife as the New Year dawned in 1546.

NOBODY CAN SAY with absolute certainty what happened to the
relationship between the king and the queen in the final twelve
months of Henry's reign. The highly coloured accounts of plots,
hysterics and reconciliations described by the martyrologist John
Foxe are not precisely contemporary, though they may have been
partly based on recollections of people close to Queen Katherine
at the time. For centuries they were taken as a true historical
record, but there is nothing to give them direct corroboration, at
least in the level of detail they relay. There is, however, a great
deal of indirect evidence that the queen's views and associations
were public enough for those around her to become targets in a
renewed battle between conservative forces and those that sought

further religious reform. And there is also the testimony of the diplomatic community that all was not well between Henry and Katherine. It is likely that these threads were interwoven and that the key to understanding them lies in the state of England and, more fundamentally, in the capricious personality and deteriorating health of the king.

At the beginning of 1546, Katherine had no immediate reason to doubt the king's continuing devotion to her. His New Year's gift of £66 13s 14d (about £20,000 today) was in keeping with the generosity he had always shown her, especially as it came at a time when the English economy was in tatters following the war with France. To add to the overall impression of family harmony, Elizabeth decided to continue with the theme of translation of religious works as New Year's gifts which she had begun a year earlier. This time, however, the recipient was not Katherine, but the king himself. And the book she had chosen to translate, into French, Latin and Italian, in a virtuoso demonstration of her burgeoning linguistic skills, was none other than the queen's own version of the *Prayers or Meditations*, an expanded version of which had just been published in November 1545.

The Latin preface to this trilingual translation begins with a fulsome tribute to her father's importance and benevolence and describes how she came to choose the subject of her gift: 'so I gladly asked (which it was my duty to do) by what means I might offer to your greatness the most excellent tribute that my capacity and diligence could discover. In the which I only fear lest slight and unfinished studies and childish ripeness of mind diminish the praise of this undertaking ... for nothing ought to be more acceptable to a king, whom philosophers regard as a god on earth, than this labour of the soul.'

Continuing in this vein, she waxed lyrical about the merits of her stepmother's achievements, describing the 'pious exertion and great diligence of a most illustrious queen', who had composed the work in English, 'and on that account may be more desirable to all and held in greater value by your majesty'.[12]

It may well have been his daughter's gift, so earnestly addressed, that first brought home to Henry VIII the extent of Katherine's involvement in religious writing.[13] It is hard to believe that he knew nothing at all about it, since the queen does not appear to have deliberately concealed her interests from her husband. Despite the fact that they had separate households, there was much commonality of outlook between the two establishments, and many of the queen's ladies were married to men who were close to the king, either as members of the Privy Council or in his Privy Chamber. A considerable number of people were aware of Katherine's projects, and gossip was the lifeblood of the court. Henry was always occupied by the business of government yet he still saw his wife frequently. It is true that his increasing immobility meant that she more often came to him by this time. At the beginning of their marriage it had been his custom to visit the queen in her apartments, but by early 1546 the situation was largely reversed. Perhaps this did give her a degree of autonomy she had not previously experienced – and this may not have ultimately worked in her favour.

It does, though, seem highly plausible, that the king had paid scant attention to Katherine's developing literary career. With all the difficulties he faced at home and abroad (he had still not made peace with France), his priorities lay elsewhere. In so far as he gave Katherine's religious interests any thought at all, he probably dismissed her activities as a worthy hobby, rather like the study of Latin. But the realization of Katherine's success as an author, and the influence she undoubtedly exercised over his children, must have been forcibly brought home to him when Elizabeth's gift was perused. Henry had amply displayed his affection for his wife. She was no mere adornment but a helpmate, intelligent and committed. But the king had a monstrous ego and he did not appreciate being upstaged. Determined as he was to tread the path of moderation in his reformation of the Church, he was also concerned about the spread of books and study in the vernacular, fearing that too much discussion spread dissension, especially among the unlearned and the ill-intentioned. Elizabeth, pouring over her copy of the *Prayers or Meditations* at Hertford Castle, may not have been aware of this, but Katherine must surely have been familiar with the great speech that Henry VIII made to parliament at its prorogation on Christmas Eve 1545.

This was to be his last appearance before the lords and representatives of the realm of England. He had dominated them throughout his reign and they helped him, in the previous decade, impose a new religious order on the country. But now, despite age, despite declining health, he was so out of patience with the splits disfiguring the Church he had created, that he decided to appear in person to answer the Speaker's loyal address. Normally this was done, on the monarch's behalf, by the lord chancellor, but Thomas Wriothesley had been the subject of a hate campaign by those who opposed his efforts to search out forbidden books and the king probably realized that Wriothesley's unpopularity would undermine the message that needed to be put across. Besides, he wanted to deliver it himself. Heartfelt, direct and eloquent, there is no reason to suppose that anyone else wrote it for him. Like his children, Henry was a splendid orator when he chose to be. His 1545 speech is one of the greatest of the Tudor era.

He did not start by berating his audience. Instead, he thanked them for their support in the war against France, describing the necessity of taking Boulogne and acknowledging the subsidy they had voted him. He also praised them for passing the recent Chantries Act, a piece of legislation that completed the suppression of religious houses begun a decade earlier, saying 'firmly trusting that I will order them to the glory of God and the profit of our commonwealth ... doubt not, I pray you, that your expectation shall be served'. On this matter, he and his parliament were at one. But there were other matters that troubled him mightily: 'Yet,' he continued, 'although I with you, and you with me, be in this perfect love and concord, this friendly amity cannot continue, except you, my lords temporal, and you my lords spiritual, and you my loving subjects, study and take pains to amend one thing, which is surely amiss, and far out of order, to the which I most heartily require you; which is that charity and concord is not among you, but discord and dissension beareth rule, in every place.' St Paul's epistle to the Corinthians emphasized the importance of charity and love. So what was the reality in England, as Christmas time drew near? 'Behold, what love and charity is amongst you, when the one calleth the other heretic and anabaptist, and he calleth him again, papist, hypocrite, and pharisee? Be these tokens of charity amongst you? Are these the signs of fraternal love between you?' The blame he laid clearly at the door of 'the fathers and preachers of the spirituality . . . Alas, how can the poor souls live in concord, when you, preachers, sow amongst them, in your sermons, debate and discord?' Warming to his theme, the king did not mince words: 'Amend these crimes, I exhort you, and set forth God's word, both by true preaching and example-giving, or else I, whom God hath appointed his vicar, and high minister here, will see these divisions extinct and these enormities corrected.' He went on to highlight one area that troubled him exceedingly – the misuse, as he saw it, of the scripture in English. This had opened up contention that he had never anticipated and his anger against it was magnificently expressed:

> And though you be permitted to read holy scripture, and to have the word of God in your mother tongue, you must understand, that it is licensed you so to do, only to inform your own conscience, and to instruct your children and family, and not to dispute, and make scripture a railing and a taunting stock against priests and preachers, as many light persons do. I am very sorry to know and hear how unreverently that most precious jewel, the word of God, is disputed, rhymed, sung and jangled in every alehouse and tavern . . .[14]

It was an uncompromising message, delivered by a king on whom the ravages of time were all too evident. His audience must have known, though they would not have dared to give it voice, that he was unlikely to appear before them again. Many were moved to tears by his words. This was Henry VIII's last public statement on the Reformation in England, a Reformation to which he, personally, was deeply committed. Did he regret the introduction of the Bible and the litany in English? These had been, after all, a major part of his evolving religious policy in the 1540s. But if he still believed, as seems probable, that the premise of what he had authorized was sound, he was deeply troubled and offended by the liberties that had been taken with it, by the cacophony of raised voices stirring up controversy and hatred. Henry wanted unity and obedience. The old autocrat, weak in body but still firm of purpose, could not tolerate dissension. It was impious and dangerous. The line between a heated discussion in a tavern and sedition against the state was a very thin one. Although not a man given to self-doubt, he must have wondered whether he had opened a veritable Pandora's box. But of one thing he was certain. The spread of scripture in the vernacular had gone farther than he intended. Those who persisted in the sort of ostentatious displays he had so witheringly criticized would feel his wrath.

Given this context, Elizabeth's New Year's gift to him may well have been mistimed. And there was also further cause for alarm. We do not know whether the king and queen compared the presents they were given by his children, but Katherine had received from her stepdaughter a further literary effort that would probably have given the king pause for thought. One has to admire the child's output, if not her originality. This time, it was a translation of the first chapter of John Calvin's *Institutes of the Christian Religion*, first published in Geneva in 1541. Henry VIII had never admired Luther, but the more extreme Calvin must have been even more distasteful to him. Nor can we be certain that the king was entirely unaware, as has often been presumed, that his wife had commenced writing the *Lamentation of a Sinner*. The revelation that Katherine was now involved in an original composition of her own would certainly have aroused his interest, if not his benediction.

He was not, though, a man who liked confrontation on the domestic front, any more than he condoned it in his kingdom. When relationships had become difficult with his former wives, he tended to keep his irritation within himself, until it burst forth in deadly earnest. For two and a half years he had doted on Katherine Parr. Her confidence was high and the satisfaction she evidently derived from her religious projects only added to her sense of fulfilment. She had made herself into an exemplary consort for a great monarch, and this gave her the boldness to proceed with her writing and her commitment to learning. In important matters, she was still viewed as a channel to the king. When the authorities at Cambridge University wrote to her at the beginning of 1546 asking for her intercession on the university's future, she responded with a further indication of her beliefs, arguing again the inestimable merits of Christian education in English as the truest road to academic attainment.

The queen began by taking the chancellor to task for writing to her in Latin when

> you could have uttered your desires and opinions familiarly in the vulgar tongue, aptest for my intelligence: albeit you seem to have conceived rather partially than truly a favourable estimation both of my going forward and dedication to learning . . . showing how agreeable it is to me . . . not only for mine own part to be studious, but also a maintainer and cherisher of the learned state, by bearing me in hand that I am endued and perfected with those qualities and respects which ought to be in a person of my vocation.

She politely thanked them for their flattery but went on to admonish them on their curriculum:

> And for as much (as I do hear) that all kind of learning doth flourish amongst you in this age, as it did amongst the Greeks at Athens long ago, I desire you all not so to hunger

for the exquisite knowledge of profane learning, that it may be thought the Greeks' university was but transposed, or now in England again renewed, forgetting our Christianity, since their excellency only did attain to moral or natural things: but rather I gently exhort you to study and apply these doctrines as means and apt degrees to the attaining and setting forth the better Christ's reverent and most sacred doctrine: that it may not be laid against you in evidence, at the tribunal seat of God, how you were ashamed of Christ's doctrine . . . and that Cambridge may be accounted rather as an university of divine philosophy than of natural or moral, as Athens was . . .

What had happened to the Katherine Parr who had studied hard to improve her Latin when she first married Henry VIII, that she should now reprove the scholars of Cambridge for their use of classical languages and a classical curriculum? Her stepson was, after all, being instructed and prepared for kingship by John Cheke, one of the foremost classical scholars of his day, an appointment which, in all probability, she had influenced. Perhaps she thought this approach would sit well with her husband, despite his reservations about the spread of the vernacular in religion. Or maybe they are very much her own views, reflecting the enthusiasms for English that she describes in the *Lamentation of a Sinner*. Whatever the explanation, she was able to tell the university, terrified that it would lose financing and independence as a result of the Chantries Act of 1545, that she had succeeded in pleading their case to the king. 'His highness,' she wrote, 'being such a patron to good learning, doth tender you so much, that he will rather advance learning and erect new occasion thereof, than to confound those your ancient and godly institutions.' The letter finished with the words: 'Scribbled with the hand of her that prayeth to the Lord and immortal God, to send you all prosperous success in godly learning and knowledge. From my Lord the King's Majesty's manor of Greenwich, the 26th of February.'[15]

This may have been the last time that Katherine was directly involved in matters of national importance, or, for some months at least, that she had the king's ear. The very next day the imperial ambassador, Van der Delft, a Fleming who had replaced Chapuys in Charles V's service, wrote in his despatch to the emperor: 'I hesitate to report that there are rumours of a new queen. Some attribute it to the sterility of the present queen while others say there will be no change during the present war. Madame Suffolk is much talked about and in great favour; but the king shows no alteration in his demeanour to the queen, although she is said to be annoyed at the rumour.'[16]

As well she might have been, for although Van der Delft was probably wrong about the likelihood of Katherine Brandon as a replacement (her religious leanings would surely have upset Henry VIII more than Katherine's) there were tensions in the royal marriage. The queen was slowly becoming aware of them, and their implications. First and foremost, the king's health was deteriorating, and the constant pain in his legs, coupled with an immobility that meant he had to be moved around his palaces on a kind of mechanical chair, affected his entire outlook. And the imperial ambassador might have hit upon a sensitive point when he referred to Katherine's childlessness. For as Henry became more ill, so the consciousness of his wife's failure to provide him with brothers for Prince Edward must have been more acute. Then there was the king's noticeable capacity for boredom with his wives after the first few years of marriage. So Katherine entered the most difficult and perilous time of her marriage to Henry VIII, in a country where the king's speech of the previous Christmas Eve had produced no effect. Religious dissension was stronger than ever, as the forces of religious reform and conservatism mingled with the naked ambition of the king's advisers to produce a poisonous brew. The spring and summer of 1546 were deeply anxious and unpleasant months, when Katherine was to discover just how much she had lost her hold on her husband. Into this already unpredictable situation, there intruded the presence of another woman – not the duchess of Suffolk, nor even one who looked to supplant Katherine in the king's affections. This woman's motives were entirely different, but her outspoken beliefs and publicity-seeking threatened the queen's security and perhaps her survival.

Her name was Anne Askew.

ANNE WAS the daughter of a Lincolnshire landowner and Member of Parliament, well-born and well educated. Her father was a prominent member of his local community and there has been speculation that she knew Katherine Parr during the queen's first marriage. But that was nearly twenty years previously, when Anne would have been about ten years old, so any kind of closeness between them, even supposing that they had met at this time, seems far-fetched. As a young bride, Katherine Borough, as she then was, would have paid no more than polite attention to the children of neighbouring worthies. Much, though, had happened to Anne Askew since her apparently uneventful childhood. The process of her 'conversion' to evangelical religious ideas is scantily documented, even in what she herself said about her past. The trigger may well have been an unhappy marriage to Thomas Kyme, into which she was propelled by her father when her elder sister, Kyme's intended wife, died suddenly. She had two children with her husband, but family life evidently became increasingly unrewarding. So she turned to study of the Bible, becoming ever more convinced that the 'old superstitions of papistry' must be overturned. In the Bible, Anne seems to have found a satisfaction lacking in her marriage, and she did not hold back in airing her views. This brought her into conflict with the local Church authorities and she became notorious in Lincolnshire for her extremism. The complete breakdown of her marriage soon followed, though there are varying accounts of where the blame lay. Anne's apologists later claimed that she was thrown out of the house by her exasperated husband and left to fend for herself, but

Catholic commentators claimed that she initiated the split so that she could 'gad up and down the country a gospelling and gossiping where she might and ought not. And this for divers years before her imprisonment; but especially she delighted to be in London near the court.'[17]

This censorious description of a selfish and obsessive young woman overlooks the fact that Anne may well have come to London desperate to seek a legal separation from her husband and that she was, through family connections, very close to the court already. One of her brothers was the king's cupbearer and a half-brother, recently deceased, a gentleman of the king's Privy Chamber. Her sister was married to a lawyer in the duchess of Suffolk's household. One of Anne's chief religious advisers was John Lascelles, whose testimony against Katherine Howard had helped bring down Henry VIII's fifth wife. So Anne was no crazed outsider or opportunist, but a woman close to the levers of power and influence. It was that very proximity that perhaps propelled her but which also made her dangerous. For Anne was increasingly ostentatious in her religious beliefs and behaviour, and although she was released after her first examination by Bishop Bonner of London in the summer of 1545, when she may or may not have recanted what were perceived as heretical views on the sacrament, she did not choose then to retire quietly. One year later, in the festering climate of religious dispute and political enmity that characterized a debt-ridden, impoverished England, where spying and betrayal were commonplace, Anne Askew again took centre stage. This time, it was her connections, as much as her beliefs, that prompted the actions taken against her. Like it or not, she had become a pawn in a deadly game. The stakes could not have been higher or simpler, for the intention of Anne's enemies was to strike, through her, at the very centre of power and to compromise Queen Katherine, perhaps fatally.

Bishop Stephen Gardiner, who had married Katherine Parr to Henry VIII at Hampton Court, has often been cast as the architect of this final struggle between the forces of religious conservatism and further reform, and represented as the arch-enemy of Katherine Parr. This interpretation is based more on John Foxe's account of the 'plot' against the queen in 1546, described with such colour and detail in the *Acts and Monuments*, than on specific evidence. Gardiner's beliefs were well known; he never attempted to hide them and was eloquent in their enunciation. His character tended to the confrontational – John Dudley, Viscount Lisle, once slapped him in the face at a meeting of the Privy Council, and there were others who would happily have done the same – but he was still a highly experienced politician and diplomat. The king disliked him but recognized his abilities, as well as his capacity to cause trouble. This latter propensity did not much bother Henry, who could happily sit back and witness dissension among his advisers. But by the summer of 1546, the king's infirmity meant that he was unpredictable and his reactions to what was going on around him were slower. There seemed to be much to play for and Gardiner took up once again the cause of combating religious innovation and heresy. He had returned to England after a prolonged and difficult period of diplomatic negotiation, which resulted in an official ending to hostilities with France and the signing of a new treaty with Emperor Charles V. Neither of these could, in reality, have been viewed as a great triumph for England, but Gardiner, who was greatly concerned about his country's international weakness, had, at last, been able to conclude matters successfully. Now he turned his attention once more to domestic affairs, determined to regain the momentum that he had lost while in Europe and to challenge the 'new men', Lisle and Hertford, Paget and Denny, for influence over Henry VIII. And always, at the back of his mind, must have been the fate of his much-loved nephew and secretary, Germain Gardiner, executed for treason early in 1544. For though religious differences have often been cited as the driving force behind the struggles of the last summer of Henry VIII's reign, this fight was as much about power politics as about belief. The queen's position was bound to be affected, because breaking her hold over her husband was a crucial step in gaining the king's ear. Many of those in key positions, including some Katherine would have counted as friends, stood to gain by limiting her role. Stephen Gardiner and his supporters were not the only ones. Foxe's dramatic narrative of Katherine's perils paints too simple a picture.

His account was, of course, written after the events it describes, and for a particular purpose, which was to glorify the Protestant changes that were so speedily introduced under Edward VI and to reinforce the Elizabethan religious settlement of 1559, still far from secure when the first edition of Foxe's work came out in 1562. The tale that Foxe tells so well reveals a world of cunning, duplicity and danger in which Katherine is the heroine and Gardiner and Wriothesley, his henchman, the villains. Foxe is quite clear on this point: 'The conspirers and practisers of her death were Gardiner, bishop of Winchester, Wriothesley, then Lord Chancellor, and others. These men, for the furtherance of their ungodly purpose, sought to revive, stir up and kindle evil and pernicious humours in their prince and sovereign lord, to the intent to deprive her of the great favour which she then stood in with the king.'

According to this account, it is Katherine herself who supplied the ammunition for her enemies. She had become bold enough 'to debate with the king touching religion'. Henry, who always had a very high opinion of his own views on such matters, bore Katherine's disputations quietly, despite the pain from his legs: 'in cases of religion as occasion served, she would not confine herself to reverent terms and humble talk, entering with him into discourse, with sound reasons of scripture'. This had evidently gone on for some while, without Katherine realizing that she might be over-stepping the mark. For ill-health, as well as his own imperious character, was shortening Henry's tolerance for these frequent sessions of religious study: 'The sharpness of the disease had increased the king's accustomed impatience, so that he began to show some tokens of dislike; and contrary to his manner, one day breaking off the conversation, he took occasion to enter into other talk, which somewhat amazed the queen.' But not sufficiently, it would seem, for her to pick up the warning signals and, besides, Henry continued outwardly all the signs of affection to which she was accustomed. It was only once the queen had left, that, behind her back, the irritated Henry gave vent to his true feelings, saying: 'A good hearing it is when women become such clerks, and a thing much to my comfort, to come in mine old days to be taught by my wife.'

As Foxe tells it, Gardiner's presence at this encounter between Katherine and Henry was fortuitous, but the wily politician and diplomat was not going to miss the opportunity presented to him by the king's displeasure with his too-clever wife. Stoking Henry's pride and ego, he went on to draw a sinister parallel between the ideas Katherine had espoused and sedition: 'the religion so stiffly maintained by the queen did not only disallow and dissolve the policy and government of princes, but also taught the people that all things ought to be in common ... he durst be bold to affirm that the greatest subject in this land, speaking those words that she did speak, and defending likewise those arguments that she did defend, had with justice by law deserved death.'

But he could not say more, without Henry's permission, about the queen and those around her, as she and 'her faction' would be 'the utter destruction of him', unless the king agreed to protect him. 'Which if he would do,' the bishop is said to have added, 'he with other faithful counsellors, would disclose such treason, cloaked with this cloak of heresy, that his majesty should perceive how perilous a matter it is to cherish a serpent in his own bosom.'

The imagery was strong and effective. While keeping up a pretence of love and interest, Henry let the unsuspecting Katherine talk herself further and further into difficulty, while Gardiner and his creatures moved to find evidence against the queen by examining her reading material and preparing to strike at her through the ladies who served her. This considered approach, would, it was thought, bring better results than a sudden onslaught. So they sought 'to ascertain what books forbidden by law she had in her closet . . . they thought it best at first to begin with some of those ladies, whom they knew to be intimate with her, and of her blood'. The three specifically mentioned at this stage were Lady Herbert, Katherine's sister, Lady Lane, her cousin and Lady Tyrwhit. Foxe goes on to say that 'it was devised that these three should first of all have been accused and brought to answer to the six articles [the act passed in 1539] and upon their apprehension in the court, their closets and coffers should have been searched, that somewhat might have been found by which the queen might be charged; which being found, the queen herself presently should have been taken, and likewise carried by night by barge to the Tower'. This scheme, says Foxe, was close to being implemented when fate intervened. The king revealed what was intended to one of his physicians, Dr Wendy, and the bill of articles against Katherine, signed by Henry himself, was dropped by an unnamed councillor, found by 'some godly person and brought immediately to the queen'.

Thus forewarned in the nick of time, Katherine became hysterical. She 'fell immediately into a great agony, bewailing and talking on in such sort, as was lamentable to hear and see, as certain of her ladies and gentlewomen being yet alive, who were then present about her, can testify'. Dr Wendy, summoned to attend her, advised her that the best course of action was to 'shew her humble submission to the king'. If she did this, Wendy was convinced that she would find her husband 'gracious and favourable to her'. Meanwhile Henry, hearing that Katherine was suddenly taken very ill, came himself to see her. Seizing her opportunity, she lamented that she had displeased the king and that he 'had utterly forsaken her'. Moved by this spectacle of distress, Henry offered words of reassurance and after about an hour, in which her fears began to alleviate, the king returned to his own quarters in the palace of Whitehall.

The rest of the story has been told often enough. Katherine

realized that she had, at least, bought some time and that she must move urgently to regain the king's good opinion. 'And so first commanding her ladies to convey away their books which were against the law, the next night after supper she, waited upon only by the lady Herbert, her sister, and the lady Lane, who carried the candle before her, went to the king's bedchamber, where she found him sitting and talking with several gentlemen of his chamber.'[18] After a courteous greeting, Henry turned the talk to religion, appearing to desire the queen's opinion. But Katherine was well prepared. The set-piece speech reported verbatim by Foxe is reminiscent of the volte-face of another Katherine, in Shakespeare's *Taming of the Shrew*. Gone is the fervent, argumentative queen who had tried the king's patience once too often. She told him:

> Since therefore, God has appointed such a natural difference between man and woman, and your majesty being so excellent in gifts and ornaments of wisdom, and I a silly poor woman, so much inferior in all respects of nature to you, how then comes it now to pass that your majesty, in such causes of religion, will seem to require my judgement? Which when I have uttered and said what I can, yet must I, and will I, refer my judgement in this, and in all other cases, to your majesty's wisdom, as my only anchor, supreme head and governor here in earth, next under God, to lean to.

In her place is a loving, submissive wife, who had never wanted anything more than to distract her husband from the suffering and discomfort that plagued him. In response to Henry's challenge, 'Not so, by St Mary, you are become a doctor, Kate, to instruct us, as we take it, and not to be instructed or directed by us', the queen assured him he was much mistaken. It would be preposterous, she said, for a woman to try to teach her husband:

> And where I have, with your majesty's leave, heretofore been bold to hold talk with your majesty, wherein sometimes in

opinions there has seemed some difference, I have not done it so much to maintain opinion, as I did it rather to minister talk, not only to the end that your majesty might with less grief pass over this painful time of your infirmity, being attentive to our talk, and hoping that your majesty shall reap some ease by it; but also that I hearing your majesty's learned discourse might receive to myself some profit.

Foxe records the old king's relief and delight with these modest, dutiful and loving sentiments: 'And is it even so, sweetheart? And tended your arguments to no worse end? Then perfect friends we are now again, as ever at any time heretofore.' Sitting on his lap, Katherine received Henry's embraces and was restored to favour. But the last act of this little drama was not quite played out. No one had told Lord Chancellor Wriothesley about the king's change of heart. So when he turned up with an armed guard of forty men to arrest the queen, he found her in the gardens down by the river, taking the air and full of mirth, in her husband's company. He was sent away with Henry's reprimands ringing in his ears. 'Knave, arrant knave,' the king cried, 'beast and fool.' Thus, according to Foxe, was Katherine Parr saved from the fate that had befallen two of Henry VIII's other wives, escaping 'the dangerous snares of her bloody and cruel enemies for the gospel's sake'.[19] She emerges triumphant from a heinous plot that is entirely aimed at her religious beliefs, to become, though Foxe does not say so explicitly, England's first Protestant queen. Foxe claims that he obtained his information from an unnamed person who 'heard it from archbishop Cranmer's own mouth'. But by the time Foxe was writing, Cranmer himself was dead, as were Katherine herself, her sister, Lady Herbert and her cousin, Lady Lane.[20] So how much of this emotional story is really true?

There most certainly was a concerted move against the more extreme reformers in the summer of 1546, but Anne Askew, the most famous sufferer of this period, is not mentioned at all in Foxe's narrative of the threat to Queen Katherine. This may well be because he did not want to complicate his story. Nor was Foxe writing narrative history as we would understand it nowadays. His work, as it relates to the Reformation in England, is more like the recording of an oral history, centred on people rather than unfolding events. Elsewhere in the *Acts and Monuments* he gives a full account of Anne's examination, torture and martyrdom. Her fate is central to our understanding of the threat faced by Katherine and how it eventually receded.

The campaign against the reformers started in April 1546. It is probably no coincidence that this was so soon after Gardiner's return from Europe. The bishop and his supporters did not have to wait long for a reason to take up the attack for in April Dr Edward Crome, a reformer who had long courted controversy, preached an outspoken sermon attacking the Mass and the idea of the real presence of Christ in the bread and the wine. Crome was arrested, accused of heresy, and recanted. But, when required to deliver his recantation in public, he repeated his heretical ideas with renewed force.[21] The government, faced with the threat of public disorder caused by high taxes and rocketing food prices, could not allow this public defiance of the regime to go unchallenged. Heresy was a crime against the state and those who espoused Crome's views needed to be unmasked. A number of evangelicals, including Hugh Latimer, a favourite of the duchess of Suffolk, and Rowland Taylor, who was close to Cranmer, were arrested. So, in June, was Anne Askew. And Anne's detention made many of those in positions of influence very nervous indeed. Her beliefs were well known and it was clear from the outset that she was fully prepared to die rather than abjure them. But Anne was well connected and might, it was hoped, implicate others. However much they might personally have found Anne's religious views distasteful, politically ambitious men like Gardiner and Wriothesley, jockeying for position with their reform-minded rivals, were interested first and foremost in using Anne to effect a political coup. This would have been 'a conservative victory comparable with the toppling of Cromwell.

Perhaps it would have been greater, since those who were left standing would take charge of the minority government that was plainly approaching.'[22]

Anne appeared first before the Privy Council with her husband, Thomas Kyme. There were, of course, those among the councillors who were ill at ease in the presence of this feisty gentlewoman, attractive and articulate, who started as she meant to continue by denying that she was Kyme's wife. Some of them must have wondered how close their own wives were to this formidable woman. It is unlikely, incidentally, that Anne intended to protect Kyme, but her disavowal of him at least meant that he was allowed to return home to Lincolnshire, while Anne was detained for examination by the Privy Council. Over two days she was questioned at length, irritating Gardiner with her pert answers, which show her to have been a witty and effective speaker, as well as possessing an impressive knowledge of scripture. When Wriothesley directly sought her views on the Eucharist, Anne replied: 'I believe that as often as I in a christian congregation do receive the bread in remembrance of Christ's death, and with thanksgiving, according to his holy institutions, I received therewith the fruits also of his glorious passion.' This opaque response did not sit well with Gardiner, who, she said, 'bade me make a direct answer. I said I would not sing a new song of the Lord in a strange land. Then the bishop said I spoke in parables. I answered, "it is best for you, for if I show you the open truth you will not accept it." Then he said I was a parrot.'[23]

Yet while Gardiner may have detested Anne's presumption, there were other councillors who had very different reasons to be fearful for her – and for themselves. The next day she was again brought before the Council at Greenwich and attempts were made to clarify her views of the sacrament. She told them 'that I already had said what I could say. Then after many words they bade me go aside. Then came my lord Lisle, my lord of Essex [the queen's brother, William Parr] and the bishop of

Winchester, requiring me earnestly that I should confess the sacrament to be flesh, blood and bone. Then I said to my lord Parr and my lord Lisle, that it was a great shame for them to give counsel contrary to their knowledge.'

Spoken in the presence of Gardiner, these words must have made William Parr uncomfortable. He and Lisle clearly hoped to influence Anne Askew to recant, and, in so doing, save her life. But they must have feared what would happen if she could not be persuaded. Gardiner and the conservatives on the Council, they knew, would use this woman's intransigence for their own ends. Could Anne be relied upon to keep silent, or would she drag down with her, to ruin, if not to the stake, all those close connections she had at court? William Parr must surely have felt apprehensive for both his sisters at this time, and for those close to him who did not share Anne's taste for martyrdom. Their beliefs, as she herself pointed out, were not new, but their futures depended on weathering this storm. And Anne could not be persuaded to compromise her faith, roundly rejecting Gardiner's attempts at personal persuasion. When he asked to speak with her 'familiarly' she told him: 'So did Judas, when he betrayed Christ.' Infuriated, Gardiner then told her that she would be burnt. 'I answered that I had searched all the scriptures, yet I never find that either Christ or his apostles put any creature to death.' In an age of hatred, uncertainty and intolerance, it was an unanswerable rebuke. But it did not save her.

In fact, for this determined and immensely courageous woman, the worse was yet to come. Though she had not given William Parr the reassurance that she would quietly simmer down, thus removing the threat to those who knew her and shared her beliefs, with herself she made a pact to reveal nothing that would compromise others. How she kept this silent faith is one of the great horror stories of the Tudor period. Removed first to Newgate prison, Anne became very ill. She would not, however, be deflected, even by Nicholas Shaxton, a reformer who had recanted and came to her in the prison to urge her to follow the same course. She told him that it would have been good for him never to have been born. Thus obdurate, she was sent by Richard Rich, a conservative member of the Privy Council and one of the sixteenth century's most famous time-servers, to the Tower of London. She could hardly have expected much mercy from the man who had betrayed both Thomas More and Thomas Cromwell, but what happened next was unusual even for a brutal age.

Anne's death was of no real importance to the enemies of religious reform. There had been martyrs before, and would, no doubt, be others in the future. But in the power struggle that was being played out over the diseased body of the king, it was the living woman that still mattered. Now, at last, was made clear the true motive behind her incarceration. When Richard Rich came to the Tower to interview the prisoner, accompanied by Wriothesley, he did not waste time with theological niceties. Instead, wrote Anne, he 'charged me upon my obedience to show if I knew any man or woman of my sect. My answer was that I knew none. Then they asked me of my lady of Suffolk, my lady of Sussex, my lady of Hertford, my lady Denny and my lady Fitzwilliam.' Anne denied any knowledge of the religious convictions of the ladies mentioned. Neither would she name gentlewomen who, Rich contended, had given her money while in prison, though she did eventually acknowledge that she had received support from two men claiming to be acting on behalf of Lady Denny and Lady Hertford. This was the closest her interrogators came to the queen's Privy Chamber.

Impatient with her refusal to name names, Rich and Wriothesley decided to resort to torture. The enormity of what they did Anne remembered in her clear, spare prose:

> Then they put me on the rack, because I confessed no ladies or gentlewomen to be of my opinion; and there they kept me a long time, and because I lay still and did not cry, my lord chancellor and Master Rich took pains to rack me with their own hands till I was nigh dead.

Then the lieutenant [of the Tower] caused me to be loosed from the rack. Immediately, I swooned away, and then they recovered me again. After that I sat two long hours reasoning with my lord chancellor upon the bare floor. But my Lord God, I thank his everlasting goodness, gave me grace to persevere, and will do, I hope, to the very end.[24]

The image of this young woman of, perhaps, twenty-five years, her body broken and her eyes half-blinded by the racking, sitting on the floor of a dungeon in the Tower, continuing to argue with Thomas Wriothesley after his hideous personal involvement in her torture, comes powerfully across to us over the centuries. The lord chancellor's own wife had been devastated by the loss of a baby son a few years earlier. Did he hope, as he turned the rack, to extract some revenge on Katherine Parr and her pompous dismissal of his wife's grief, by getting this defenceless woman to blurt out the names of the ladies around the queen, even to declare that the queen herself shared her extreme views on the sacrament of the Eucharist? Or was it merely the opportunity to bring down those who threatened his survival in the new order that would come after Henry VIII's death that propelled him to such barbarity? The torture of a gently-born woman was shocking even to his contemporaries. Fearful that he would be held to account for permitting Anne Askew's agony, the lieutenant of the Tower, Sir Anthony Knevet, took himself off at great speed to lay his account before the king, who, it was reported, 'seemed not very well to like their extreme handling'. Soon the news of what had been done leaked out, causing revulsion that damaged the government. But mistress Askew had glossed over the fact that Knevet had allowed the torture to proceed in the first place. For this, he must have had a high-level mandate. His alarm that things were going too far may equally have been prompted by resentment that members of the Privy Council were impinging on his area of responsibility. Chillingly, it is certainly possible that the king himself had authorized the violence meted out to Anne.

She was, in truth, a difficult woman who had never shirked from promoting herself, or from courting trouble. Her supporters apparently encouraged her to write down the process of her examination by the Privy Council and the terrible suffering she endured so patiently afterwards. It is unusual to have such a complete account of this battle with authority from a sixteenth-century woman. But Anne needed little encouragement; she was quite evidently a very confident person, keen to relay her side of the story. She had never sought to hide her beliefs and her failed marriage, which cut her adrift from society, gave her independence as well as vulnerability. She is the antithesis of the submissive wife in Foxe's account of the queen's conciliatory exchanges with Henry VIII; the martyrologist, who probably fabricated this part of his story, may well have wanted to underline the differences between the two women. Reforming zeal was admirable, but a strident female who refused authority was not the ideal standard-bearer for a new religion. Later Protestant commentators were more comfortable with Anne's martyrdom and her exhortations to prayer than with her uncompromising self-awareness.

Anne was given further opportunities to recant, but she remained steadfast. On 26 July 1546 she was burnt at the stake in Smithfield with three male companions, including John Lascelles. Unable to stand because of her injuries, she was conveyed in a chair and held upright at the stake by a chain bound around her waist. The duke of Norfolk and her tormentor, Wriothesley, watched as she died. But also present, in a singular act of public support, was Nicholas Throckmorton, the queen's cousin and a member of Katherine Parr's household. It may have been not only sympathy that Throckmorton conveyed, and gratitude for Anne's silence, but an underlying message that Katherine herself was out of danger. The attempt to compromise her had failed.

✎

KATHERINE HERSELF had nothing directly to say about the events of the summer of 1546. Yet, even if we discount the veracity of Foxe's verbatim account of how her downfall was planned and averted, Anne Askew's fate definitely points to a concerted attempt to incriminate some of the ladies who were closest to Katherine. Furthermore, her own behaviour during these months is indicative of an anxious queen. As early as February, at about the time that the rumours concerning her position were beginning to circulate in the diplomatic community, she ordered new coffers and locks for her chamber. This may, of course, have been simply the result of existing wear and tear, but it does suggest that she felt the need to ensure greater security for her possessions. Early in spring, her uncle, Lord Parr of Horton, who had rarely been at court since she became Henry's consort, was summoned back to fulfil his role as Katherine's chamberlain, despite his age and ill-health.[25] The queen gave into his safe-keeping a number of books which would, no doubt, have been of great interest to the authorities, since book burnings intensified after a royal proclamation against heretical writings issued on 8 July. These were only reclaimed, by one of her most trusted servants, three months after the death of Henry VIII.[26]

Her chagrin may not have been wholly confined to the knowledge that she was a quarry for the bishop of Winchester and his allies. In June 1546, even as she struggled to safeguard her position, negotiations were resumed by the duke of Norfolk for a marriage between Thomas Seymour and Mary Howard, duchess of Richmond. Naturally, the queen did not comment on this development, though it is hard to believe that it improved her emotional well-being. But, as in the 1530s, nothing came of the discussions. The duchess's brother, the earl of Surrey, despite being sympathetic to reform (one of his gentlemen was Anne Askew's cousin), was not keen on this resurrected alliance and seems to have knocked it on the head. So his sister once more failed to become Lady Seymour, and Katherine's former suitor remained free.

And what of the king in all this? The interweaving of fact and fiction in this story of plot and persecution leaves his part in proceedings, and, indeed, his attitude towards his wife, far from clear. The most likely explanation seems to be the one that lies just below the surface of Foxe's hyperbole. Henry was well known for his capriciousness, a characteristic that was intensified by his physical decline. All the evidence points to the fact that his wife had begun to irritate him, not so much by her beliefs as by her frequent contending with him in public. Over-confidence in her hold on the king mingled with unbridled enthusiasm about her religious studies caused her to presume too much on his goodwill. One lesson Katherine seems to have forgotten from the experience of her predecessors was how swiftly that goodwill could disappear. She was still charming, attractive and healthy, but she was childless and increasingly opinionated. These last two weaknesses rankled with the king. It may well be that he took the opportunity offered to him by the conservatives, whispering in his ear, to put his wife in her place. When he perceived that this game might go too far, he drew back from it by making sure that the queen was alerted to the threat and giving her an opportunity to remove compromising literature from her chamber. For Henry knew that the attempt to incriminate the queen's ladies was an attack on their husbands, as much as the queen herself, and he was not minded to give Gardiner and his allies the upper hand. In fact, the conservative campaign had even targeted his own servants and he was furious when one of his favourites, George Blagge, whom he called his 'pig', was imprisoned in Newgate and sentenced to be burnt. Blagge was pardoned, but the king did not forgive Wriothesley for, as he put it, 'coming so near to him, even to his Privy Chamber'.[27] Henry, though ailing, was still no fool. The attack on his queen was also, indirectly, an attack on him.

In the end, Katherine had been saved because this old man, so often represented as a monster in his last days, loved his sixth wife. He had grown tired of marital failure and he appreciated what Katherine had brought to his life and his family. So she survived. Yet the queen's position had been weakened by the efforts to bring her down and she was unable to recover it fully. This, though she did not know it at the time, was to be a benefit for both her enemies and for those ambitious men whose wives continued in her service.

From late summer to early winter in 1546, the royal marriage returned to the harmony that had been such an important feature of its first six months. Katherine became again the adored stepmother and indulged wife. Prince Edward, who was at court in August, wrote frequently to her. Beneath his characteristic tone of obsequious stiffness, there are still the glimpses of genuine affection. Her countenance, he said, 'excites my love'. 'When at court with the king,' he wrote, 'I received so many benefits from your majesty that I can hardly grasp them.' He could not repay them but he rejoiced to hear of her progress in virtue and goodness and he wanted her to know that he wrote 'both for love and duty'.[28] Katherine, keen to ensure that her hold over her stepson was not diminishing and to reinforce her regal status as queen of England, sent the prince a twin portrait of herself and Henry VIII as a New Year's gift at the beginning of 1547. Acknowledging his letter of thanks, the queen said she was 'gratified by your appreciation of my little New Year's gift, hoping that you will meditate upon the distinguished deeds of your father, whose portrait you are so pleased to have, and his many virtues'.[29]

The queen's life focused once more on family and occasions of state. Henry was glad to parade her when the French admiral Claude d'Annebaut arrived in England in August for the official signing of the treaty hammered out by Gardiner early in the year. This was no Field of Cloth of Gold, but it was still a magnificent affair and Henry was determined that both Katherine and his daughter Mary should look their very best. Nor was Katherine's family forgotten. Her brother received the admiral and his entourage, which numbered nearly 1,000 men, at Greenwich

Palace and Cuthbert Tunstall would have lodged him at his London residence, Durham House, but it had recently been damaged by fire. Instead, d'Annebaut lodged with the bishop of London, Edmund Bonner, until he and his party were conveyed downriver to Hampton Court where the king, queen and royal children awaited them.

Flashing jewels that the king had supplied from the extensive royal collection, Katherine was every inch the Tudor consort. Henry VIII had called a halt to her literary career but he seems to have taken great pleasure in acknowledging her importance to him as wife and queen. He showered her with precious stones and clothes and luxurious accessories. The royal accounts show that she ordered, at this time, numerous pairs of Spanish gloves from 'Mark Milliner', including two pairs of 'perfumed gloves of crimson velvet and purple, trimmed with buttons of diamonds and rubies'. There was also a 'collar of crimson velvet trimmed with lace of gold' and numerous pairs of golden aglets (which were used to fasten clothing) beribboned and bejewelled. And shortly after Anne Askew's death, the king gave orders that

> John Lange, jeweller of Paris, and Giles Lange, his son, [have] licence to bring or sell into the king's dominions . . . all manner jewels and precious stones, as well set in gold and embroidered in garments as unset, all manner goldsmiths work or gold and silver, all manner sorts of skins and furs of sables . . . new gentlesses of what fashion or value the same be . . . in gold or otherwise as he . . . shall think best for the pleasure of us, our dearest wife, the queen, our nobles, gentlemen and other.[30]

Once more, Katherine accompanied the king on an autumn tour of southern England, which involved hunting and feasting. In a sign that she was still in need of intellectual stimulation, she began to learn Spanish. But she did not leave Henry's side until early December, and then the parting was his choice, not hers. The king had passed a golden few months with his wife, but as the chill of winter began to bite, Henry's intimations of his own mortality grew stronger. His failing health must have been apparent to Katherine, but she could not gainsay his will. For most of December, throughout Christmas and into the New Year, the king closeted himself with a small circle of advisers at Whitehall. Outwardly, the prospect of his imminent death was not openly conceded, least of all by Henry himself. But he knew that time was running out. He must make arrangements for his son's minority, without distractions. So Katherine and Mary passed Christmas without him. 'The queen and court', reported Van der Delft, the imperial ambassador, 'have gone to Greenwich, although she has never before left him on a solemn occasion.'[31] Small wonder, then, that Katherine had sent a double portrait of the king and herself to his heir. She did not want to be forgotten and was trying to put down a marker for her own place in any future regime. But, as the French ambassadors told Francis I, she was kept away from her husband. Writing on the same day that Edward thanked his stepmother for her New Year's gift, they noted that they had learned

> from several good quarters that this king's health is much better than for more than 15 days past. He seems to have been very ill and in great danger owing to his legs, which have had to be cauterized. During that time he let himself be seen by very few persons. Neither the queen nor the Lady Mary could see him, nor do we know that they will now do so. We have great reason to conjecture that, whatever his health, it can only be bad and will not last long.[32]

It was not so bad, however, that the king had ceased to rule. In the last days of his reign he moved decisively, some would say vindictively against the forces of conservatism, refusing to remember Bishop Gardiner in his will or to give him a role as his son's adviser when Edward became king. And, irritated by the pretensions of the Howard family, he imprisoned both the earl of Surrey and his father, the duke of Norfolk, in the Tower, on charges of treason. Surrey was executed a matter of days before the king's demise but the old duke, a major figure in English politics in the first half of the sixteenth century, was saved by the king's death. It must have given him a grim satisfaction to know that he had bested his monarch at last.

We do not know whether Katherine saw Henry again after the beginning of December, 1546. Her apartments at Whitehall were prepared for her return there on 11 January and though it has often been assumed that she did not, in fact, take up residence there again, her letter to her stepson quoted earlier is signed from Westminster, not Greenwich.[33] However, no evidence survives that she was allowed to see her husband in his final days. Henry was not a man who liked scenes and he was working hard, against the clock, with Hertford, Paget and Denny, to assure the future shape of English government. These men had their own reasons for keeping the queen away. In his physical weakness, mindful as they were of his affection for Katherine, there was always the possibility that she might persuade him to a course of action that did not sit well with their own ambitions. A death-bed parting between husband and wife therefore seems extremely unlikely.

In fact, it fell to Anthony Denny on Thursday 27 January 1547 to tell the king that 'in man's judgement, you are not like to live'. Faced with this reality, Henry's thoughts turned to his immortal soul. He believed, he said, 'the mercy of Christ is able to pardon me all my sins, yes, though they were greater than they be'. But he did not ask for his wife, and prevaricated even on whether he would see a priest, saying that if it were to be any, it should be Dr Cranmer. He would, however, sleep for a while before he made up his mind.[34]

By the time Cranmer, summoned from Croydon on a bitter night, arrived in the royal bedchamber, Henry could no longer speak. All he apparently could do, when the archbishop exhorted him to show some sign that he died in the faith of Christ, was to squeeze Cranmer's hand. In this simple gesture the king demonstrated, at the last, his commitment to the religious changes in

England that he had guided, sometimes in seemingly contradictory fashion, over the previous twenty years. Shortly after, in the small hours of 28 January 1547, he died.

Katherine's third husband had been a giant of a man. To this day, whatever one thinks of him, he dominates the history of England. The queen must have known, when they broke the news of his death to her, that her life without him would be profoundly different.

Part Four

The Last Husband

1547–1548

CHAPTER ELEVEN

The Secrets of Spring

'Set doubts aside
And to some sporting fall'

From a poem written by Sir Thomas Seymour for Katherine Parr

DRESSED IN BLUE VELVET and wearing a widow's ring of gold with a death's head on it, Katherine watched the obsequies for Henry VIII from her private chapel, the Queen's Closet, in St George's Chapel, Windsor. Henry's interment beside Jane Seymour, on 16 February 1547, marked the end of a magnificent and costly funeral. Vast amounts of black cloth had been ordered for the mourners, for Henry's household servants, his wife's ladies, and the households of Mary and Elizabeth, as well as black velvet for his two daughters themselves.[1] The procession conveying the king's coffin from Westminster to Windsor was made up of more than 1,000 horsemen and hundreds of mourners on foot. It was four miles long and attracted crowds of onlookers. Stopping overnight at the former convent at Syon in Middlesex, the cortège arrived at Windsor in the early afternoon of the 15th. Masses and dirges for the king's soul had been said along the route but the main service, the Requiem Mass, did not start until the following day. Bishop Gardiner officiated, assisted by the bishops of Ely and London.[2] Although Henry VIII had died holding Archbishop Cranmer's hand, the man who had helped the king split with Rome took no part in his funeral. For the good of his soul, Henry wanted the familiar Latin forms of the old religion, not the simplified English rites of the reformers.

It is interesting to speculate on what must have been passing through Katherine's mind as she witnessed these events. Dislike of Gardiner and distaste that the form of the ceremony did not sit well with her own beliefs was probably tempered by a natural grief for her husband's passing. And there must have been other, more earthly and immediate concerns: questions about her own interests now she was dowager queen and, most crucial of all, the future of her relationship with the nine-year-old boy who would be crowned king of England in four days' time. She had pinned her hopes on continuing to be a strong presence in Edward's life, maintaining her influence over his development and acting as his regent, with the advice and support of a Privy Council. But now, after only two and a half weeks of widowhood, she was a deeply frustrated woman.

To her dismay, she had learned that the clock would not be turned back to 1544. Henry VIII had spoken of her with affection in the will that had been drawn up a month before his death. Katherine was, he said, his 'entirely beloved wife' and he had left her very comfortably, if not exactly generously, supported from a monetary point of view. 'The queen shall have', he commanded, '£3,000 in plate, jewels and stuff, beside what she shall please to take of what she has already, and further receive in money £1,000 besides the enjoyment of her jointure.' She would always be served and waited on as befitted a queen, with a large household and all her dower properties.[3] Her manors at Hanworth and Chelsea were fine houses set in beautiful grounds, both big enough to support a household that numbered well over a hundred people. She could still exercise patronage, continue her writing, live a life of privilege and comfort. In the government of the realm and in the upbringing of her stepson she would, however, play no further part. Power would not be hers. It had passed elsewhere.

We do not know exactly when Katherine learned of her exclusion, or by what means. Nor is it possible to say when she was told of Henry's death. The information may have been imparted all at once, but it seems more likely that the full realization of her situation did not dawn on her immediately. Henry VIII's death was not made public until three days after his demise. During that time, Denny, Paget and Edward Seymour, working closely together, contrived to maintain the appearance that the king was still alive. Denny's position in the Privy Chamber meant that he controlled physical access to the inner sanctum, where Henry's body lay stiffening in the great bed where he had breathed his last in the early hours of 28 January. The normal rhythms of the royal day continued, as food was taken in and ceremony observed. But behind the scenes, as this brilliant deception was enacted, there was a great deal of activity. The politicians to whom the dead king had entrusted the direction of England were determined to ensure a smooth, unchallenged passage to the new regime, and this involved careful planning. Two things were of paramount importance: possession of Henry's will and control of the new king's person. Katherine had neither of these. But Edward Seymour, earl of Hertford and the elder of Edward VI's two uncles, did.

Henry had given his will to Seymour for safe-keeping not long before he died. The king and his closest advisers worked on it over Christmas 1546, laying out precise and detailed instructions for the type of government that would rule during Edward's minority. This was based on a Privy Council of sixteen (the executors of the will) who were appointed for life. The arrangement has been described as being 'hermetically sealed' – there was no way in and the only way out was death. A further twelve assistants to the councillors were named, though they were not to be privy councillors themselves. It was a system designed to negate, as far as possible, the possibility of faction and to provide continuity, as well as good counsel, for the young king as he grew towards manhood.[4] In addition to keeping the machinery of government going, the councillors were expected to devote themselves to Edward's development and training for the day that he would assume direct control himself. This was a grave responsibility and it is something that was taken very seriously by the politicians who served Edward, whatever their personal disagreements. There is no doubt that very careful consideration was given by Henry VIII to how the regime that succeeded him could be made to function. Yet in giving the will into Seymour's hands he demonstrated, even before its provisions could be put into practice, that his brother-in-law was likely to emerge as the key player in the new government.

As Henry's life was drawing to a close, the corridors and antechambers of Whitehall were scenes of whispering and activity, in preparation for what was to come. In the three days following the king's death, while the charade that he still lived was faultlessly executed, Paget and John Dudley stayed in London to ensure that all was in place when the announcement was made on 31 January. It was delivered to a sombre House of Lords by Wriothesley, the lord chancellor, who wept as he made his statement. Seymour, meanwhile, had set off to break the news of Henry's death to Edward. The boy was living with his sister Elizabeth at the time in Hertford Castle. The two children heard the news together and were greatly distressed. Their sorrow is not hard to understand. Edward could hardly have been expected to welcome the crown soon to be placed on his young head, and Elizabeth faced an uncertain future. She may have been considerably reassured later when she learned that her father's will had left her a wealthy and independent young woman. The terms of that will regarding the succession were read to the Privy Council on 31 January. Nothing else was disclosed, which was only prudent, as monetary sweeteners had been written in by the canny Paget, to ensure the acceptance of the role now publicly sought by Edward Seymour. The following day, with his uncle at his side, Edward VI returned to London, taking up residence in the Tower prior to his coronation. The earl of Hertford completed his assumption of power by appropriating jewels and plate from the royal jewel-house and by securing the agreement of his colleagues that he should be named Lord Protector of the realm and Governor of the king's person. The day after Henry VIII's funeral he was given the title of duke of Somerset, on the interesting grounds that the late king had wished to strengthen the nobility, an explanation that Henry, who had worked throughout his reign to weaken that institution, would have found rather rich.[5] Thus were the terms of the will, on which the old king had laboured in his last weeks, disregarded before the new king was even crowned.

Edward Seymour's promotion was cleverly executed but apparently widely endorsed by members of the Privy Council. A collective form of government of the sort laid down in Henry's will might, in any case, have been unworkable in the longer term and it is not surprising that the decision was taken early to amend it. The hierarchical nature of Tudor society meant that citizens, at all levels, felt more comfortable with a single, identifiable leader. There were some caveats, the most important of which was the notion that the Lord Protector would 'take counsel' from his colleagues. The new duke of Somerset progressively dispensed with this dictum and time would show that, despite his diplomatic and military experience, he was not equal to the great office he had so assiduously sought. For the time being, he had the goodwill of most of the key personnel of the last years of Henry's reign. But by no means everyone close to the old king or the new was happy with the arrangements struck behind closed doors. Katherine Parr, for one, had anticipated a quite different outcome.

A TRIO OF DOCUMENTS, two no more than barely legible fragments, provide the clues to what the queen had desired. They reveal that, for a while, she refused to accept how Henry VIII and his erstwhile advisers, who suddenly wielded power in England (and whose wives, only days before, were her own ladies-in-waiting) had simply cut her out of political life. Though there has been much discussion about the authenticity of Henry's will and the machinations of his councillors, little attention has been paid to Katherine Parr's expectations of the regency and her attempts to clarify her position. All the emphasis has been on her personal life, her impetuosity in following the dictates of her own heart at last, the apparent abandonment of her dignity as she swiftly succumbed to a former suitor's charms. Yet Katherine's behaviour may well have been prompted by more than a combination of petulance and romantic love. It could, also, have had a considerable degree of self-interest.

As Katherine whiled away the Christmas season at Greenwich with Mary, she undoubtedly had time to ponder her husband's absence and to grow uneasy about what was happening at Whitehall. Her security depended on being close to the king. She knew he was very ill – the deterioration in his condition was evident to all who saw him – but he had survived other, serious bouts in the past, and though his death seemed imminent, neither the queen nor anyone else could be certain of when it would come. Her return to Whitehall in the second week of January may have given her the hope that she would be able to see the king again, but there is no evidence that she did. Whether or not she requested and was denied access we cannot know, but the likelihood is that if Henry had expressed a desire to see her, he would not have been disobeyed. His behaviour in cutting himself off from both Katherine and Mary in the last two months of his life points to the firm conviction on Henry's part that he did not want emotional partings and that neither woman would have any future role in government. At the end of his life, Henry was as consistent in his dismissal of female competence in such matters as he had always been. A temporary regency, in time of war, when he was absent for a short period, was perfectly acceptable. But he saw no need for a female regency once he was gone, especially as Katherine Parr was not the natural mother of his heir.

Isolated and anxious, Katherine did not know that Henry had made a new will, dry-stamped with his signature on 30 December 1546. Her hopes seem to have been pinned on the 1544 will, which has not survived, but evidently made her think that she would be appointed regent for her stepson. The evidence suggests that she clung to this belief even after she was told of Henry's death, since there are two documents among her accounts for the year 1547 which are signed 'Kateryn the Quene Regente KP'.[6] Neither has a legible date. So when could they have been written? Might it be that Katherine was informed of the king's death when the official announcement was made (or even earlier) but that the shape of the new regime, and the fact that she had no role in it, were not divulged to her at the same time? If so, Edward Seymour and his colleagues were risking a confusion that could have been dangerous, though they may have believed that the dowager queen was in no position to mount a challenge to their authority, however it had been acquired. They would have been right in the sense that Katherine had no army or supporters to call upon to uphold her. The weakening of the queen's position in the last half of 1546 had increased the power of those who shared her religious interests. Yet now they were determined to abandon her and keep her well away from any exercise of power. They knew her too well. Her strength of character, her place in the new king's affections, her energy and drive were an alarming combination in their eyes. Such a woman must not be allowed to preside over their deliberations.

It seemed that there was little Katherine could do and no one to whom she could turn. Archbishop Cranmer had admired the queen as a person, and he and other reformers applauded her patronage of new ideas. As the consort of Henry VIII, she had been a highly effective conduit, but as his widow she could deliver little. Cranmer was Edward VI's godfather and now fully embraced the opportunity offered by the 'new Josiah', as the little king was called, to push forward a much more radical agenda than would have been permitted by his late master. Edward

Seymour and most of the council agreed with Cranmer; he no longer needed the much-reduced influence a dowager could wield. Nor was there any help forthcoming from members of her own family. Katherine's brother, William, had known Edward Seymour since childhood. He was inextricably tied to the new order and sided with his friend in his successful bid for the Protectorship in the days after Henry's death. His reward was to be created marquess of Northampton on the day of the royal funeral; and the price was the abandonment of his sister's ambitions. Looked at objectively (and William Parr was not actually a cold man) Katherine had served her purpose. Anne and William Herbert enjoyed good relations with Edward Seymour too and were not in a position to help with Katherine's political aspirations, though they were to provide her with clandestine support of a rather different sort as the months progressed.

Then there was, still, Cuthbert Tunstall. Now aged seventy-three and suffering from spasmodic ill-health, Katherine's elderly cousin never considered retirement. Mostly, he was away in the north, ensuring good government and overseeing the defence of the borders with Scotland. Despite his personal reservations about the progress of religious reform, he enjoyed a good working relationship with the new regime and took part in the coronation of Edward VI. He was also one of the executors of Henry's will, and given Katherine's evident concerns about her role and her rights, it is quite possible that she discussed her situation with him during his time in London in February 1547. Tunstall had watched over Katherine since her early childhood, helped arrange her marriage to Lord Latimer and received gifts from her when she became queen. He and her uncle, Lord Parr of Horton, were the abiding parental influences in her life and she clearly valued them both greatly. Tunstall may have been a man of God but he had a politician's instincts. However much he cared for Katherine and sympathized with her point of view, he would, surely, have counselled that she was best to accept her fate. Certainly, he would have wished her happiness in the new-found freedom that she did not necessarily want. Perhaps he advised her to put the past behind her and take her life in a new direction. Now, after all, she could please herself.

Yet even with all the odds stacked against her, Katherine did not give up easily. She clearly believed that she had a legal case to make and so she took expert advice. In the manuscripts of the marquess of Salisbury at Hatfield House there is a note from the lawyer Roger Cholmeley 'and others' addressed to Queen Katherine. It is endorsed 'Minutes noting the Queen's estate and some [of] her Grace's affairs depending upon the same.' Its contents are, understandably oblique, framed in the cautious legal language of men who were well aware of the sensitivity of the topic on which they had been asked to give counsel. 'Whereas her Grace asked to be advised of them', they wrote, 'whether a certain oath taken by the King's servants, and sent for their consideration, is invalidated by his Majesty's decease, they reply that they think not. Touching certain other questions submitted to them, they have delivered their opinions to Sir Anthony Cope, her Grace's vice-chamberlain.' The document is signed by Cholmeley and three other lawyers.[7]

Historians do not know what the 'certain oath' taken by the king's servants was. Clearly, Katherine had in her possession evidence that she believed bolstered her contention that she should not have been left out of Edward VI's government. The term 'the queen's estate' does not, in Tudor times, refer solely to Katherine's lands and possessions but to her place in national affairs. But if Cholmeley's carefully worded response gives only the most teasing of clues to Katherine's struggle for power, and apparently offers some encouragement, the queen did not use it as the basis for furthering her cause. It has always been assumed that she gave up, lured by other distractions. Heady romance, many have thought, deprived Katherine of her judgement, emphasizing the fact that she had accepted defeat in her quest for power. That, however, is not the only possible interpretation of the relationship that she rekindled after Henry VIII's death.

For the queen's lover was every bit as frustrated as she and together they could hope to achieve much more effectively what had been denied to them separately.

THE PRECISE DETAILS and timings of Thomas Seymour's secret courtship of Katherine Parr are unknown. It has been suggested that she became his mistress only a matter of weeks into her widowhood, but that would have been a speedy conquest even for one who enjoyed the reputation of sweeping ladies off their feet. In the immediate aftermath of Henry's death, Katherine had to observe strict mourning. Prior to the royal funeral, access to her must have been very limited. And she was quite evidently involved in a covert struggle with the new regime. Her priority at this time seems to have been her relationship with her stepson. On 7 February, Edward wrote thanking her for a letter she had sent 'which is a token of your singular and daily love to me'. He commiserated with her on their joint loss, observing: 'And now, as it hath seemed good to God, the greatest and best of beings, that my father and your husband, our most illustrious sovereign, should end this life, it is a common grief to both. This however consoles us, that he hath gone out of this miserable world into happy and everlasting blessedness.'[8] The child had called her 'dearest mother' and she must have derived comfort from his continued affection. Even though there was only a slim chance of her bid for the regency succeeding, surely she would not have compromised her chances, or divided her attention, by indulging so soon in a sexual liaison.

Thomas Seymour, too, had much to occupy his mind during February 1547. The prospects of Katherine (and possibly Mary and Elizabeth also) may well have figured in his considerations, but he was primarily concerned with improving his own situation. It was, in those days, frequently the lot of younger brothers to believe themselves hard done by, and Thomas felt particularly keenly the disparity between himself and Edward Seymour. By a mere accident of birth, his brother seemed to have gleaned all the spoils. Henry VIII had named Thomas as one of the assistant councillors in his will and left him £200, but this was small beer in comparison to the power and wealth his elder brother now enjoyed. Thomas wanted more and the Protector obliged. On 16 February, as Katherine Parr watched the body of Henry VIII being laid to rest at Windsor, Thomas Seymour was created Baron Seymour of Sudeley in Gloucestershire and given additional lands worth £500 per annum. The next day he was also appointed to the office of Lord High Admiral, and named a Knight of the Garter. And he was awarded a full place on the Privy Council.

Still, he did not consider these adequate rewards. Although he has been depicted as a greedy chancer, his disgruntlement was not entirely unfounded. He had served his king well during the last four years of Henry's reign, accepting the loss of Katherine Parr with surprising equanimity for a man who sometimes found it hard to contain his emotions. Instead, he devoted himself wholeheartedly to diplomacy and his military career. He was with the king in the French war of 1544 and participated in the capture of Boulogne. By October, when Henry and Katherine were enjoying a tender reunion in Kent, Thomas was both master of the ordnance and an admiral of the English fleet. The sea was a genuine love and he revelled in his new appointment, breasting the waves in his flagship, the *Peter Pomegranate*, and producing plans for making the English navy a more effective tactical fighting force.[9] At home, he became a Member of Parliament for Wiltshire, though he does not seem to have attended often. It was not really his milieu. More gratifying was the possession of Hampton Place, outside Temple Bar in London, which was granted to him late in 1545. With an enthusiasm bordering on pretentiousness, he renamed his new property Seymour Place.

So he was neither overlooked nor forgotten, but he was not one of the great men. There was no leading role for him in national affairs. He was well off but aspired to be rich. Above all, he was not accorded the respect he believed should be his as the king's uncle. His brother had taken it all for himself. Thomas believed that the roles of Protector and Governor of the King's person should never have been vested in one man. Looking for historical precedent to support his views, he found encouragement in the arrangements made for the minority of Henry VI. Yet he overlooked the fact that this was not the most promising of history lessons, for Henry VI's reign produced civil war and vicious faction-fighting, but it was true that Henry V's brothers had divided responsibilities for their nephew between them. Seymour convinced himself of the seriousness of his argument. And he knew, once Henry VIII was in his grave and Katherine Parr began to emerge from her seclusion, where he could find a sympathetic ear – and perhaps much more. There was still a strong spark of desire, and, indeed, of deeper affection, between them. A permanent union would bring them personal happiness and political opportunity, if they could continue to manage their relationships with the royal children successfully. The extension of Somerset's authority on 12 March, which allowed him to bypass the advice of the Privy Council if he saw fit, must also have brought home to both Thomas and Katherine the realization that their individual options were disappearing. It was against this backdrop of unpalatable political reality that the new Lord Seymour of Sudeley and the dowager queen renewed their inter-rupted romance during the lengthening spring days.

The course of their liaison is revealed in the love-letters they exchanged at this time. This correspondence, preserved in various collections in England, provides us with a compelling picture, rare for the Tudor period, of the private passions of two high-profile individuals. Their emotions are powerfully on display, unsullied by the passage of four and a half centuries. The language is uncomplicated and direct: 'I would not have you think', wrote Katherine, in the earliest of the letters in the sequence, 'that this mine honest goodwill towards you to proceed of any sudden motion or passion . . .'[10] Thomas soon put her mind at ease: 'I beseech your highness to put all fancies out of your head that might bring you in any one thought that I do think that the goodness you have showed me is of any sudden motion, as at leisure your highness shall know to both our contentions ... From the body of him whose heart ye have, T. Seymour.'[11] And he ended with the amusingly revealing postscript that 'I never overread it after it was written, wherefore if any faults be I pray you hold me excused.'

As no doubt she did. Katherine was a woman of thirty-four, widowed three times. He was three years older and had never been married. This was not a young couple discovering love for the first time. Yet we can still feel their excitement, their hopes and fears, the rising tide of resentment against the elder Seymour and his wife felt by Katherine, and Thomas's attempts to counsel and calm her. In this written testimony of a love reborn, Thomas Seymour is measured in his advice on how to deal with the situation. He realizes that work will have to be done to make their relationship acceptable to those in power, but he does not come across as a self-serving braggart propelling a gullible woman towards the altar, but as a gentleman in love. Of course, there were advantages in marrying Katherine; she was quite a different proposition from the Lady Latimer he had first courted. She would for ever be 'Kateryn the Quene KP', even when she became his 'most loving, obedient and humble wife', and he always addressed her as 'your highness'. But his feeling for her appears genuine.

Only one of the letters around the probable time of their marriage is dated, so we cannot say with certainty when the relationship resumed or exactly how this came about. The earliest opportunities for public meetings must have been after the coronation of Edward VI. Seymour had played a prominent ceremonial role in proceedings but there is no record of the queen, or either of her stepdaughters, attending. Yet Katherine was evidently allowed to see Edward and it may have been one of these 'official' appearances at court that provided the impetus for the renewal of their love. The courtship was, however, pursued well away from the glare of prying eyes, in Katherine's dower manors at Chelsea and Hanworth. In this respect, the new regime's concern to control the queen's access to her stepson allowed her to conduct her private life without great risk of unwanted scrutiny. Somerset was to discover that marginalizing the queen led to unforeseen complications. For Katherine and Thomas took full advantage of their freedom.

In the beginning, there was caution mingled with evident delight. She had stipulated that they should exchange letters only once a fortnight, but broke this rule herself almost immediately. They began secret trysts at Chelsea, where Seymour would stay overnight, though Katherine warned him: 'When it shall be your pleasure to repair hither, ye must take some pain to come early in the morning, that ye may be gone again by seven o'clock.' She did not want to be discovered in bed with him at the time the house was rising. Discretion was still important to her, though only up to a point. 'And so, I suppose, ye may come without suspect. I pray you let me have knowledge overnight at what hour ye will come, that your portress may wait at the gate to the fields for you.'[12] This was all well and good, but such comings and goings, as Katherine's instructions acknowledged, inevitably involved other people. Servants might be trusted, but word got out. Their affair had not long been consummated when it appears to have been known in the household of Katherine's brother, William Parr. 'I met with a man of my lord marquess as I came to Chelsea', reported Seymour, 'whom I knew not, who told Nicholas Throckmorton that I was in Chelsea fields with other circumstances which I defer till at more leisure.' He was, he said, remembering to burn her letters. This prudence, however, could not conceal his midnight visits to the pleasant manor of Chelsea.[13]

Soon the gossip about the comings and goings was known in the Herbert household as well. On 16 May, Seymour dined with Katherine's sister and brother-in-law, and Anne Herbert, who was apparently being used as a post-box for messages between the queen and Seymour, decided it was time to probe more deeply. 'She waded further with me', reported the bashful lover, 'touching my lodgings with your highness at Chelsea.' His first reaction was to deny the charge, saying that he merely happened to be passing en route to the bishop of London's house. He maintained this defence for some time, 'till, at last, she told me further tokens, which made me change my colours, which, like a false wench, took me with the manner'. His lame story thus demolished, Seymour decided that he could trust the woman he now referred to as 'my sister'. She was not quite that, yet, but he would now happily take her into his confidence, knowing that Anne could report back to Katherine 'how I do proceed in my matter'. By this, he meant preparing the ground for acceptance of their marriage. Meanwhile, he hoped that Katherine would write to him every three days and he begged her to send him one of the miniatures of herself that she had commissioned when she was married to Henry VIII: 'Also, I shall humbly desire your highness to give me one of your small pictures, if ye have any left, who with his silence, shall give me occasion to think on the friendly cheer that I shall receive when my suit shall be at an end.'

Katherine responded by saying that she had 'sent in haste to the painters for one of my little pictures which is very perfect by the judgement of as many as have seen the same; the last I had myself I bestowed it upon my Lady of Suffolk'. She also reassured him about the Herberts, saying that she had decided to take her sister completely into her confidence: 'It seemed convenient unto me,' she wrote, 'at her being here ... to open the matter unto her concerning you (which I never before did) at the which unfeignedly she did not a little rejoice, wherefore I pray you at your next meeting with her to give thanks for the same, taking the knowledge thereof at my hand.'

She had said, in the same letter, that if Somerset mentioned the prospect of her marrying again, she would be ready with an answer, 'so that he might well and manifestly perceive my fantasy to be more towards you for marriage than any other'. But she went on to say that she was 'determined to add thereto a full determination never to marry, and break it when I have done, if I live two years'. Meanwhile, though she expected to see the king later the same week, and knew Seymour might be there, as well, she would continue to behave in public with all due restraint. Thomas was alarmed by her sudden hesitancy about marriage itself. 'Ye shall not think of the two years ye wrote of in your last letter before this', he responded. And, to drive the point home, he told her how pleased he was that she was seeking his advice on how to handle disputes with his brother about her lands.[14] Clearly, by this point, he did not want her to waver.

Any hesitation she might have very fleetingly felt was soon overcome. She was genuinely in love and, as he had reminded her, marriage was to their mutual advantage. The passage of time was only exposing her still more to the perils and uncertain status of being merely a dowager queen. So, probably some time in the last two weeks of May 1547, Katherine Parr took as her fourth husband Lord Thomas Seymour of Sudeley. The marriage may have taken place earlier in the month (Seymour's letter of 17 May lends credence to this possibility) but as the correspondence he and the queen exchanged is carefully phrased, we cannot be sure. No information about the priest who performed the ceremony, the location in which it took place or those who witnessed it, has ever been found. This conspiracy of silence was necessary to protect the newly-weds, who could not yet live together publicly. First, they had to embark on an urgent campaign to get the possibility of their union accepted by the young king and his advisers. Katherine was especially concerned about this aspect, writing, 'I would desire you to obtain the king's letters in your favour, and also the aid and furtherance of the most notable of the Council, such as ye shall think convenient.' Her political sense had not entirely left her, despite her emotional commitment to Thomas. Once they had succeeded in gaining official approval, they could then make the delicate admission that, in fact, their marriage had already taken place. Neither of them could be sure how this acknowledgement of their deceit would be received.

MARRY IN HASTE, repent in leisure, so the saying goes. Once the deed was done, the back-tracking was far less pleasant than the anticipation of Seymour's stealthy midnight creeping through the spring blossoms of Katherine's Chelsea garden. It was all very well for the Herberts to condone the marriage. Others, whose friendship Katherine had enjoyed, or whose support Seymour needed, reacted with a mixture of cool disapproval and warm anger. One of the earliest casualties, before the marriage had even taken place, was the queen's relationship with her elder step-daughter. Mary continued to live with Katherine for several months after the death of Henry VIII, but she moved out of the dowager queen's household in April. This was partly because she was now a substantial woman of property in her own right, under the terms of her father's will. It was natural that she wished to establish her own household, to be independent, and to spend some time inspecting her new estates. Yet Katherine had been her closest companion for what would prove to be the happiest four years of her adult life and their parting should have been a matter of regret to both women. Instead, it may have come as a relief to the queen, distracted by her affair with Seymour and unwilling to recognize Mary's disapproval of her behaviour. But disapprove Mary most certainly did. The extent of her distaste can be judged from the clinical detachment of her response to Seymour, when he tried to involve her in his quest for Katherine's hand: 'I have received your letter,' she wrote, 'wherein, as me thinketh, I perceive strange news, concerning a suit you have in hand to the Queen for marriage, the sooner obtaining whereof, you seem to think that my letters might do you pleasure.' Apart from the carefully implied reprimand, she was determined to

remind him – and Katherine herself – of the indelicacy of their
actions:

> it standeth least with my poor honour to be a meddler in
> this matter, considering whose wife her grace was of late,
> and besides that if she be minded to grant your suit, my
> letters shall do you but small pleasure. On the other side, if
> the remembrance of the King's majesty my father (whose
> soul God pardon) will not suffer her to grant your suit, I am
> nothing able to persuade her to forget the loss of him who
> is as yet very ripe in mine own remembrance.

She asked him not to think unkindly of her and she would
be glad to help him in other ways, 'wooing matters set apart,
wherein I being a maid am nothing cunning' (a strong hint
that she was aware of what had been going on at Chelsea), 'both
for his blood's sake that ye be of, and also for the gentleness
which I have always found in you'.[15] By the end, her tone had
softened a little, but the overall message, that she wanted
nothing to do with the personal life of her father's last wife, is
very clear. Her letter was dated 4 June, revealing that Seymour
moved very quickly to get influential support for his marriage to
Katherine.

If Katherine was dismayed by Mary's answer, she wisely
refrained from any further personal involvement. She may have
calculated that her stepdaughter would not stay offended for long,
and in this she was correct. Mary's *froideur* was a setback, but not
a major one. And Katherine had made her own first move, even
earlier than Thomas's, to give their union the ultimate respect-
ability. The queen and her husband knew that it was the little
king's approval that mattered, and they had reason to believe that
Edward's unreserved benediction could be obtained if he was
approached the right way. Opportunity soon presented itself. At
the end of May, possibly within days of her actual marriage,
Katherine was at court with the king. While there, she wrote him
quite an extraordinary letter. This Latin epistle has not survived,

but its gist can be easily discerned from Edward's reply, written on 30 May:

> Since I was not far from you, and in hopes every day to see you, I thought it best to write no letter at all to you. For letters are tokens of remembrance and kindness between such as are at a great distance. But being at length moved by your request, I could not forebear to send you a letter: – first, to do somewhat that may be acceptable to you, and then to answer the letter, full of kindness, which you sent me from St James's. In which, first, you set before mine eyes your love toward my father the king, of most noble memory; then your goodwill towards me; and lastly your godliness, your knowledge and learning in the Scriptures.

Her words had clearly pleased him greatly, combining the three things he valued most at that point in his young life. The boy went on to reassure her that 'I do love and admire you with my whole heart. Wherefore if there be anything wherein I may do you a kindness, either in deed or work, I shall do it willingly.'[16]

His trust was, of course, deceived. The clue is in the last line of his reply, which strongly implies that Katherine had, in general terms, asked for his support and favour. He could not have known that his beloved stepmother, while professing her continuing love for Henry VIII, was actually softening him up so that she could obtain his agreement for her marriage to his uncle.

Edward was also very fond of Thomas Seymour. The dashing sea-dog appealed just as much to his nephew as he did to Katherine Parr. Again, this affection provided an opportunity for manipulation, but the king lived in a tightly controlled environment and Seymour realized very early after the death of Henry VIII that he would need to buy his way into it if he was to have any real hope of influence. He was prepared to be liberal, and was soon bribing John Fowler, a gentleman of the Privy Chamber. Fowler was to be his conduit to Edward when he could not see him personally, or when he wanted ideas put in the

king's mind. Chief of these was his own marital status. Fowler
was to prepare the ground for acquiescence to the choice of bride.
This he duly did, but Edward's response was not what his uncle
and stepmother would have wanted. On consideration, he first
suggested Anne of Cleves, still very much alive and occasionally
in attendance at court. The reply suggests that Edward rather
liked her. But then, on mulling it over, he decided he had the
perfect solution. His uncle should marry 'my sister Mary, to
change her opinions'. Apparently Thomas was amused by his
nephew's matchmaking schemes; marriage to Mary would have
required the permission of the entire Privy Council and he was
not going down that road. Edward needed to be steered to give
the right answer. 'I pray you, Mr Fowler,' Thomas said, 'if you
may soon, ask his Grace if he should be contented I should marry
the Queen.' Katherine had not occurred to Edward as a likely
wife for his uncle, which is hardly surprising, given her protestations of undying love for Henry VIII. Yet by 25 June the
king was writing to Katherine to thank her for marrying Thomas.

It has been claimed that Edward's letter was dictated by
Seymour himself. There is no firm evidence to support this
contention but it seems probable that there was a discussion
about the content of the king's missive to his stepmother. Edward
was accustomed to composing even personal letters after consultation with his tutors so it is unlikely that he would have resisted
advice over the wording of something that affected so closely
someone that he loved. The expression of his sentiments, however, is in keeping with other letters he wrote to Katherine. He
began:

> We thank you heartily not only for your gentle acceptance
> of our suit moved unto you, but also for your loving
> accomplishing of the same, wherein you have declared not
> only a desire to gratify us, but also moved us to declare the
> goodwill likewise that we bear to you in all your requests.
> Wherefore, ye shall not need to fear any grief to come, or to

suspect lack of aid in need; seeing that he, being mine uncle
[here he refers to the duke of Somerset], is of so good a
nature that he will not be troublesome by any means unto
you; and I of that mind that of divers just causes I must
favour you. But even as without cause you merely require
help against him whom you have put in trust with the
carriage of these letters, so may I merely return the same
request unto you, to provide that he may live with you also
without grief, which hath given him wholly unto you. And
I will so provide for you both that hereafter, if any grief
befall, I shall be a sufficient succour in your godly or praisable
enterprises. Fare ye well, with much increase of honour and
virtue in Christ.[17]

This cynical play on a child's emotions does Katherine Parr
and her fourth husband little credit. She had evidently acted the
reluctant bride to good effect. It also reinforces the historical
view of her impetuosity and poor judgement in becoming Seymour's wife in unseemly haste. That is certainly one possible
explanation, but the couple may have believed that their interests
were not served by waiting. Katherine was already involved in
what would turn out to be a protracted dispute with Somerset
over her lands and jewels. She needed a protector of her own
and the fact that he was the duke's brother perhaps seemed, to
her, an advantage. Love and self-interest are powerful incentives,
sufficient, in this case, for an affectionate stepmother to turn a
child who greatly admired her into a pawn. But her relationships
with the royal children had always been built on an element of
strategic devotion, as, indeed, was her marriage to Thomas
Seymour.

EDWARD'S LETTER to Katherine shows how sensitive were the
relationships within the Seymour family, for it was here, more
than any other source, that rancour was felt. The duke of
Somerset and his brother are recorded in history as very different

men, representing the good and bad sides of the Tudor aristocracy. For hundreds of years, Somerset was 'the good duke',
someone who had favoured the ordinary man, a Protestant
reformer and benevolent ruler whose good intentions were
thwarted by unscrupulous, power-hungry political foes. Thomas,
by contrast, was a loud-mouthed, swaggering intriguer, an atheist
struggling by all possible means for his own advancement, with
no fraternal feelings or loyalties. They could not have been more
different.

And yet, in reality, they were much more alike, as siblings
often are. Their physical closeness is striking. Their portraits
show that they shared the same features, particularly the same
nose, and the same colouring. Thomas looks more directly at the
viewer, his gaze almost challenging, as befits his reputation.
Edward's eyes veer to the side and he appears paler and more
effete, an impression heightened by the double stranded, rather
feminine, necklace he is wearing. Not too much, though, should
be read into these slight distinctions. Both were hugely ambitious
and opportunistic. Somerset is now seen as a man of autocratic
tendencies who disdained to rule with advice, damaged the
economy, pursued an unrealistic foreign policy and sowed the
seeds of his own destruction. Thomas was the infuriating younger
brother with pretensions above his rank and competence. The
reality, however, was that neither man was capable of the great
responsibilities the elder brother had taken upon himself and the
younger one so avidly sought. They had served Henry VIII well
enough, but, thrust into the limelight by the accession of their
nephew, they were both found lacking.

Their relationship is a complicated one. Looking back, it is
easy to discern an inevitable outcome; such vision was not, of
course, available to them at the time. Thomas was an irritant, but
he was still the Protector's kin, and they saw each other frequently. Exasperation and resentment were felt on both sides,
but the ties of blood were strong. If anyone was to marry the
queen dowager, Somerset preferred it to be his brother. He may

have disliked the deception, the way Thomas had presented him with a *fait accompli*, but, as his sister-in-law, Katherine could be controlled more readily (or so Somerset hoped) than if she remained independent, or even married someone else. His greed and lack of tact were already causing the queen much aggravation, as he gave away the leases on her dower lands without consulting her and deprived her of her personal jewellery collection. Her fury against him mounted by the day: 'my lord, your brother, hath this afternoon a little made me warm', she told her new husband. 'It was fortunate we were so much distant, for I suppose else I should have bitten him.'[18] This was not a happy introduction to the Seymour family circle. But if Katherine disliked Somerset, it was nothing to the detestation she felt for his wife.

The duchess and her husband had attended Katherine's wedding to Henry VIII and she had subsequently been one of the ladies of the queen's Privy Chamber. The only child and heiress of her father, she had been born Anne Stanhope and was a couple of years older than Katherine Parr. On her mother's side, she could trace her lineage back to Edward III. Already the mother of seven children by Edward Seymour, she was, in fact, his second wife, having married him shortly after the death of his first wife, Katherine Fillol, probably in 1535. There were persistent rumours that Edward's first marriage was unhappy and stories circulated about Katherine Fillol's supposed infidelity with her own father-in-law. Whatever the truth about his first wife, with whom he had two sons, Edward Seymour's marriage to Anne Stanhope was a solid and apparently happy union. It is possible that the knowledge of something murky in her husband's past made Anne especially protective and fuelled her determination to support his political ambitions. She was no shrinking violet herself and she was well versed in court intrigue, having played the dutiful sister-in-law and chaperone to Jane Seymour at the time of Anne Boleyn's downfall. Well known for her interest in the new learning, her association with Anne Askew in the last year of Henry VIII's reign placed her in some danger, as it did her husband and, indeed, Katherine Parr. By 1547, the duchess was an established patron of evangelical writers and would become even more active in this respect during Edward VI's reign. She was a woman of considerable intellect and strong personality, utterly dedicated to her husband's career. But she seems not to have had many female friends. One of the most constant was, however improbably, Mary Tudor, who never forsook her, despite the growing disparity in their religious ideas. Their friendship is further proof of the fluidity of relationships at court in the mid-Tudor period and the fact that people did not take firm sides or fit neatly into the labels of Protestant and Catholic that historians have applied to them. Moreover, although she shared Katherine Parr's religious interests, the duchess and the queen could not abide one another.

Their personal animosity has been characterized as a rivalry for precedence at court, fuelled by the tensions between their husbands. There is no direct proof that Katherine demanded that Anne carry her train on a visit to court, or that Anne refused, saying subsequently: 'Did not Henry VIII marry Katherine Parr in his doting days, when he had brought himself so low by his lust and cruelty that no lady that stood on her honour would venture on him? And shall I now give place to her who in her former estate was but Latimer's widow, and is now fain to cast herself for support on a younger brother. If master admiral teach his wife no better manners, I am she that will.'[19]

The sentiments may well have been harboured by the duchess of Somerset – they have the ring of truth about them – but there is no contemporary corroboration of such a quarrel and Anne must have known what court etiquette was, even if she did not like it. Katherine's feelings about her erstwhile attendant and new sister-in-law are clear and only served to intensify the difficulties in the relationship between Thomas Seymour and his elder brother. For Katherine assigned all the blame in her dealings with the Lord Protector to his shrill, pushy and downright deceitful wife.

Her dislike of the duchess of Somerset was evidently of long standing. Henry VIII's death and Katherine's changed circumstances, her disappointment and feeling of grievance, may all have combined to exacerbate it, but the ill-will was already there. In the first of her love-letters to Thomas Seymour, the queen complained that his brother had promised on more than one occasion to come to see her so that they could discuss 'such requests as I made to him'. Somerset kept putting her off and she was becoming impatient. But she knew who was really to blame for this casual treatment: 'I think my lady hath taught him that lesson; for it is her custom to promise many comings to her friends and to perform none. I trust', she continued, somewhat acidly, 'in greater things she is more circumspect.'[20]

It soon became obvious that she was not. It is all very well to play down the rivalry between the two women, as modern writers have done, and assert that Anne Somerset was merely an intelligent, committed and strong-minded woman traduced by male historians. She may have been all these things, but the fact that Katherine hated her is inescapable. And matters between them, at least for a time, would only get worse. In the same letter in which she had threatened to bite the duke, Katherine was not just venomous against the duchess, she actually stooped to obscenities. 'What cause have they to fear having such a wife?' she ranted. 'It is requisite for them continually to pray for a short despatch of that hell.' The word hell was used as slang for female genitalia in sixteenth-century England and it was not the language of well-born ladies. The earnest religious commentator had temporarily forgotten herself in this dispute with her fourth husband's family. Nor can there be any doubt that the marriage of Katherine and Thomas added further fuel to what was already a combustible fraternal relationship.

Katherine might let off steam by calling the duchess of Somerset names, but she soon discovered that her own image had been badly dented by her speedy alliance with Thomas. Her stepson could not protect her from the reaction of public opinion,

and saucy comment began to circulate about the queen's intemperate behaviour, her virtue compromised by more base desires.
Thomas, in typically direct fashion, threatened that 'whosoever
shall go about to speak evil of the queen, I will take my fist from
the first ears to the last'.[21] Many people questioned the common
sense of the couple in conducting an affair that, if Katherine had
quickly become pregnant, would have raised questions about
whether the child was Henry VIII's or Thomas Seymour's.
Thomas was furious and talked about bringing in legislation to
protect Katherine's good name. It was, of course, much too late
for that. The queen herself tried to revive her reputation by
ordering dozens of copies of the *Psalms or Prayers* and the *Prayers
or Meditations* from the printer Thomas Berthelet, one of which,
printed on vellum, was probably a gift for the king.[22] This may
well have pleased him and for several months he continued to
exchange affectionate letters with his stepmother. But she had
used him and, as time went by, he realized that he had been
manipulated. His life ever more stringently organized and access
to him increasingly difficult, it was in this climate of criticism
of his uncle Thomas that Edward's childish regard towards
Katherine Parr became one of the most serious victims of his
stepmother's remarriage.

FAMILY FEUDS and ribald public comment added to the difficulties of Katherine as she embarked on her fourth marriage, but in
other respects she and Thomas had reason to be pleased that they
had brought off a mutually advantageous match. Living as they
did in fast-changing times, there was no reason to suppose that
Somerset's position was unassailable. Besides, they believed they
had an effective counter-strategy. It was not a precise balance for
the duke's power and his hold over the king, but it promised
continuing influence and an attractive flexibility. For if neither
Katherine nor her husband had given up on the idea of separating
the function of Governor of the king's person from the Protec-

torship itself, they believed they had alternative options. These centred on the young female heirs to Edward's throne.

The immediate successor, Mary, had left Katherine's roof, offended by her conduct and eager to establish a household of her own. But Elizabeth, provided for equally, but still only thirteen years old, came to live with the queen at Chelsea in the spring of 1547, before Katherine was married to Thomas Seymour.[23] Not long after, Lady Jane Grey, the daughter of the marquess of Dorset, came to live at Seymour Place. Thomas bought her wardship for £2,000 (more than £600,000 today) and thereby secured control of another girl with a claim to the throne. His loyal servant, John Harington, who handled the negotiations, told Dorset that the lord admiral thought very highly of Jane: 'she was as handsome as any lady in England'. This was a generous tribute to a child of ten, whom he had probably seen from time to time at court but did not know well. Thomas was, however, well aware that Henry Grey and his wife, Frances, the niece of Henry VIII, were unhappy at the marquess's exclusion from Somerset's inner circle. Dorset was just the kind of ally Thomas needed and, as well as flattering comments about young Jane's beauty, he held out a much more glittering possibility. She might, he said, be wife to any prince in Christendom, and 'if the king's majesty, when he came to age, would marry within the realm, it was as likely he would be there, as in any other place'.[24] Buoyed up with this expectation for their eldest daughter, the Dorsets were happy to give her to Seymour's wardship. This arrangement may seem heartless and calculating today, but at the time such provisions for aristocratic children were commonplace and thought to be highly advantageous.

So, in the summer of 1547, Thomas Seymour effectively controlled the destiny of three royal ladies and had good grounds for believing that his quest for greater power could progress still farther. Soon, though, he was to find that maintaining a queen was an expensive undertaking and that sheltering a king's daughter would tempt him down the path of scandal and ruin.

'This frail life'

> 'Those that be about me careth nothing for me, but standeth
> laughing at my grief.'
>
> Katherine Parr's deathbed denunciation of her husband

AS THE FURORE concerning Katherine's fourth marriage began
to die down, the queen was able to pick up again, with some
relief, the work on her religious publications which she had put
aside in the latter part of 1546. These had not been abandoned;
they were waiting for a more propitious moment to reach their
conclusion, to be made available to the small but powerful literate
class of England whom Katherine hoped would be the vehicle for
their eventual wider dissemination. She was especially keen to
finish the work on the *Paraphrases of Erasmus*, and it was in
September 1547 that she wrote to her stepdaughter Mary,
encouraging her to take the credit for her translation of St John.
There remained a considerable amount to be done on the overall
project, and the *Paraphrases* did not appear in print until the last
day of January 1548, three years after the work was begun.
Meanwhile, Katherine's own friends, including the duchess of
Suffolk, encouraged her to press ahead with the publication of
The Lamentation of a Sinner. This came out in November 1547,
with a preface of more than ten pages by William Cecil, who
would later become Elizabeth I's chief minister. He was, at that

time, a key member of the household of the duke of Somerset, and if it seems odd that someone close to Katherine's brother-in-law should produce an adulatory introduction to this very personal exposition of religious faith, it serves to remind us that the community of shared belief among the reformers was sometimes stronger than family frictions.

Cecil was keen to emphasize Katherine's regal status, her virtue and her acknowledgement of sinfulness. She was a 'woman of high estate, by birth made noble, by marriage most noble, by wisdom godly, by a mighty king and excellent queen, by a famous Henry a renowned Katherine, a wife to him that was a king to realms: refusing the world wherein she was lost, to obtain heaven wherein she may be saved'.[1] No mention here, then, of her fourth marriage, or the comment it had provoked. Katherine is rehabilitated by Cecil's praise and by the fact that she had been the wife of Henry VIII. His preface struck just the tone the queen must have wanted and exhorted a wider audience to explore its revelations, for their own spiritual profit. The queen's writings no longer needed to be concealed. They added support to the programme of religious change to which the government, now freed from the constrictions of Henry VIII's determination to keep a middle way, was committed. By the time of the publication of the *Lamentation*, the imperial ambassador was lamenting that Mass was no longer heard in the house of the Lord Protector. And no more was it celebrated in the queen's dower manors or at Seymour Place. So, while the dispute between the Lord Protector and his brother was by no means resolved, Katherine could concentrate on the more positive aspects of her life. As well as her publications, she also needed to focus on the upbringing and education of Jane Grey and Elizabeth Tudor.

Jane was based at Seymour Place, where her life seems to have been happy and straightforward. She was just ten years old, small and slight, but with the Tudor colouring of reddish hair and pale skin. The tradition that she was a priggish, serious little girl ill-treated by her parents and cast out into the care of

Katherine Parr is part of the centuries-old Protestant hagiography of Jane. A recent biography of Jane and her sisters paints a more balanced picture.[2] Certainly clever and committed to her studies, she was to grow into a strong-minded young woman of considerable intellect, whose reformist ideas were fully in keeping with those of her parents, especially her father, Henry Grey, who was viewed as a radical in his time. Katherine Parr nurtured Jane's belief through her own example, but she did not create the Protestant martyr of history; the groundwork for Jane's developing personality had been laid at home, in Bradgate, her father's country seat in Leicestershire.

Life at the lord admiral's impressive London dwelling brought Jane closer to the most influential people in England, but, though no doubt aware of her status, she was probably too young to realize that opportunity can also breed danger. We actually know very little about the daily pattern of her existence, or the details of her schooling at this time. She seems to have adapted well to the separation from her friends and sisters and to have been genuinely fond of her guardian and his wife. Whether she held any warm feelings for the Lady Elizabeth, four years her senior, and closer to the throne, is another matter.

The difference in their age, coupled with the fact that Elizabeth spent most of her time with the queen at Chelsea and Hanworth, suggests that the cousins were not close. They do not appear to have shared lessons. No record of their opinions of each other, no letters exchanged or conversations held, have survived. This silence can, perhaps, be attributed to the inevitable loss of evidence with the passage of time. But it may also indicate something more. Elizabeth was very conscious of who she was, the daughter of Henry VIII and second in line to the throne. Her childhood had been more insecure than Jane's and, though she was a wealthy young woman, she was still illegitimate in the eyes of the law. Katherine Parr had been her stepmother for four years and, though they had not lived together for all that time, they had formed a close bond. Elizabeth may not have relished sharing her attention with a distant relative whom she hardly knew. Whether she heard talk of Thomas Seymour's scheme to marry Jane to Edward VI when they were both of a suitable age must remain a matter of speculation, but had she been aware of the plan it would surely not have endeared Jane to her.

Elizabeth had arrived to take up residence with Katherine, bringing her own servants and household, many of whom had been with her for years. Hers was an establishment within that of the queen and Seymour. Closest of all were Elizabeth's governess, Katherine (Kat) Ashley, Ashley's husband, John, and Thomas Parry, the cofferer, who was responsible for managing Elizabeth's finances. None of these was a stranger to the queen or, indeed, her husband, and the intention was that Elizabeth's personal life would be more secure and dependable under the protection of Katherine Parr. Her business affairs (for, like her half-sister, Mary, Elizabeth was essentially a business in her own right) would continue to be managed separately. The terms of the settlement on both sisters in Henry VIII's will were clear and the Privy Council was entrusted to carry them out carefully. Domestic arrangements were another matter, and Katherine seemed the ideal person to direct the young lady's continuing education and preparation, presumably, for the marriage market.

Katherine Parr already knew that Elizabeth was receiving a first-class education. Her tutor in the spring of 1547 was William Grindal, a Greek scholar from St John's College, Cambridge, and protégé of Roger Ascham. He also knew John Cheke and may have helped tutor Edward VI before he became king. As the troubled year of 1546 drew to a close, Grindal took up a full-time position with Elizabeth. He was an immediate success with his very able thirteen-year-old pupil, to the delight of Ascham, who paid the new tutor the great compliment of saying that he did not know 'to what degree of skill in Latin and Greek she [Elizabeth] might arrive, if she shall proceed in that course of study wherein she hath begun by the guidance of Grindal'.

But, to the great sorrow of all who knew him, Grindal's

promising career was tragically cut short when he died of the plague in January 1548. Elizabeth was devastated. She did not, however, bow to her stepmother's wishes when a replacement was discussed. Katherine wanted Francis Goldsmith, who had long been a faithful supporter of hers, but Elizabeth had other ideas. Her choice was Roger Ascham. She had lost the young man he had trained and now she wanted the older scholar himself. A considerable battle of wills ensued, with Elizabeth involving Cheke in the discussion. Ascham, uneasy at being the cause of disagreement between the queen and her stepdaughter on such an important matter, actually counselled Elizabeth to accept Goldsmith. He reported to Cheke that the princess had told him 'how much the queen and my lord admiral were labouring in favour of Goldsmith. I advised her to comply with their recommendations . . . and entreated her to set aside all her favour towards me and to consider before all else, how she could bring to maturity that singular hope in her awakened by Grindal's teaching.'[3]

Ascham's tactful approach did not prevail. Elizabeth had her way. The outcome shows a remarkable spirit and determination in a girl who was grappling, as was Katherine, with quite different emotions in her life at the time. For the much-missed William Grindal was not the only man to have awakened something in Elizabeth. Thomas Seymour had unleashed a flood of quite different desires. In so doing, he caused Katherine much anguish and nearly compromised Elizabeth fatally.

ALTHOUGH THE TAUNTS aimed at his wife had died down, Thomas Seymour's discontent continued to simmer throughout the autumn of 1547. He did not accompany Somerset on the military campaign against the Scots in September and was furious when the Lord Protector did not even appoint him in a temporary capacity as Governor of the king's person during his absence. The man put in charge of Edward at the time, Sir Richard Page, was,

Thomas claimed, a useless drunkard. He did not mince words when anger took him. And his frustration began to creep into his feelings for Katherine, now the period of secret wooing was replaced by the day-to-day reality of living with a queen of England. There was no escaping the fact that she had a high profile (his feelings about her literary career may not have been so different from those of Henry VIII) and that her household was costly. As Sir Nicholas Throckmorton remembered:

> Her house was term'd a second court of right,
> Because there flocked still nobility
> He spared no cost his lady to delight
> Or to maintain her princely royalty.[4]

All this, and his underlying resentment at his junior role in government combined to make Tom Seymour a volatile spouse. He was also a very emotional man, not uncommon in Tudor England, but his trademark loud oaths – much of his displeasure was preceded by the exclamation 'By God's precious soul!' – were often followed by outbursts of intemperate anger. These may have been short-lived, but Katherine, now bound to obey him by her marriage vows, even if she was a queen, found them frightening. Her status was a source both of pride and jealousy. It was said that he did not like her being alone with other men, even members of her household. Thomas Parry, Elizabeth's cofferer, recalled Kat Ashley relating an incident of what seems like quite unreasonable sensitivity on Seymour's part: 'And as for the jealousy of my lord admiral, I will tell you: As he came upon a time up a stair to see the queen, he met with a groom of the chamber upon the stair with a coal basket, coming out of the chamber, and because the door was shut, and my lord without, he was angry and pretended that he was jealous.'[5] This sounds extraordinarily petty, and Mrs Ashley dismissed it as being of little importance, perhaps no more than a joke. But if Katherine did hold private conversations with other, more senior members of her household, especially on financial matters, it is not entirely surprising that her husband might want to be included. If, on the other hand, his attitude was driven by sexual jealousy, then it says a good deal for Katherine's continued attractions at the age of thirty-five. And Katherine, of course, had a considerable temper of her own. Their relationship was certainly not a placid one. The coal basket incident is not dated, but presumably took place in the colder months of the year. By then, the queen had ample reason for jealousy of her own. Her husband's behaviour towards Elizabeth was giving rise to gossip and threatening her own peace of mind at a time when Katherine herself had just become pregnant. What should have been a happy period of her life, the fulfilment of all her hopes when she married for the fourth time, turned progressively into a time of bewilderment and distress.

The origins of Seymour's increasingly dangerous flirtation with Elizabeth seem to go back to the very beginning of his marriage, or, at least, the time that he and the queen were officially living together as man and wife. Katherine Ashley, not, admittedly, the most reliable of sources, when questioned on 'what familiarity she hath known betwixt the Lord Admiral and the Lady Elizabeth's Grace', claimed that these goings-on had started at Chelsea, 'incontinent [immediately] after he was married to the queen'. Her further revelations have enlivened the pages of many an historical novel and several films. There have been assertions that Seymour was a sexual predator preying on a young girl, of three-in-a-bed romps, of passion-filled trysts and an unwanted pregnancy. The reputations of Thomas, Katherine and Elizabeth were dragged through the mire by contemporaries and what took place during the space of barely a year, when Elizabeth lived with the queen and her last husband, has provided titillation ever since. The story that Elizabeth had a son by Seymour makes good television drama but is poor history. Yet, even allowing for exaggeration and the fearful circumstances in which Kat Ashley and Thomas Parry poured out their tales under interrogation, it is clear that Seymour's relationship with his wife's stepdaughter did raise eyebrows at the time and that it troubled Katherine. But what did, in fact, take place, and what should we make of it now, more than 450 years after these events took place?

Had there been merely a couple of isolated incidents, it is likely that Seymour's behaviour with Elizabeth might never have been known, or, at worst, dismissed with some tongue-clucking as overly boisterous. Kat Ashley, however, relates a pattern of contact between her young charge and the master of the house that seems to have begun as horseplay but soon turned into something less innocent. She reported:

> He would come many mornings into the said Lady Eliza-
> beth's chamber, before she were ready, and sometime before
> she did rise. And if she were up, he would bid her good
> morrow, and ask how she did, and strike her upon the back
> or on the buttocks familiarly, and so go forth through his
> lodgings; and sometime go through to the maidens [Eliza-
> beth's ladies], and play with them, and go forth: and if she
> were in her bed, he would put open the curtains, and . . .
> make as though he would come at her: And she would go
> further into the bed, so that he could not come at her.

Further revelations poured forth from Elizabeth's governess. One morning 'he strave to have kissed her in her bed', but mistress Ashley 'bade him go away for shame'. At Hanworth, Katherine, perhaps by now alerted to what was going on and having reasons of her own for not wishing her husband to spend too much time by himself with her stepdaughter, joined in as well. At Hanworth, 'they tickled my lady Elizabeth in her bed, the Queen and my Lord Admiral'. By now, Katherine was an accomplice in more than tickling. In the garden at Hanworth, Seymour pretended to take exception to a black gown that Elizabeth was wearing. He 'cut her gown into one hundred pieces, being black cloth'. Ashley reproved Elizabeth for permitting such behaviour, but the girl told her 'she could not do with all [she was unable to resist] for the Queen held her, while the Lord Admiral cut it'.

Katherine Ashley was eventually concerned enough about what lay behind all this to broach her misgivings with Thomas Seymour himself, though apparently she did not raise anything with Katherine. She 'told my lord the things that were complained of, and that my lady was evil spoken of', following another morning when Elizabeth had run to her ladies when she heard Seymour trying to come into her chamber. The source of this particular complaint seems to have been the gentlewomen, rather than Elizabeth. Thomas, however, showed no contrition. 'The Lord Admiral swore, God's precious soul! – he would tell my Lord Protector how it slandered him, and he would not leave it, for he meant no evil.'

And, so it appears, he was true to his word. His morning visits continued in his own house. 'At Seymour Place, when the Queen lay there, he did use a while to come up every morning in his night-gown, barelegged in his slippers, where he found the Lady Elizabeth commonly at her book: and then he would look in at the gallery door, and bid my Lady Elizabeth good morrow, and so go his way.' Again, said Kat Ashley, she complained. She told him 'it was an unseemly sight to come so bare-legged to a maiden's chamber; with which he was angry, but he left it'. Perhaps, at last, he began to feel the weight of Katherine Ashley's concern for her mistress. But by then, he might also have sensed his wife's dismay. Ashley recounted a strange incident in which Katherine reproved her, claiming that Seymour had seen Elizabeth 'cast her arms about a man's neck'. This accusation the girl tearfully denied, and, as her governess pointed out, 'there came no man but Grindal, the Lady Elizabeth's schoolmaster'. There was, thought Ashley, an all together different slant. She suspected 'that the Queen was jealous betwixt them, and did but feign this, to the intent that . . . [I] should take more heed, and be, as it were, in watch between her and my Lord Admiral'.[6]

The most obvious explanation for these events, as remembered by Elizabeth's governess, is that there was an underlying attraction between Thomas Seymour and the princess that neither openly acknowledged nor, on the other hand, wished to curtail, or even conceal. Seymour's behaviour cannot be explained away as that of a surrogate parent who lacked experience in judging what was appropriate behaviour towards a teenage girl. The concept of adolescence did not exist in Tudor England. Elizabeth was a young woman of marriageable age and, as the famous portrait of her painted probably in the last year of her father's reign shows, she was regal but attractive. Lady Browne, the Irish beauty admired by both the earl of Surrey and Thomas Seymour, had joined Elizabeth's entourage at the age of about eleven. By the time she was fifteen, she was married to Sir Anthony Browne, a man nearly thirty years her senior. The age gap of twenty-four years between Elizabeth and Thomas Seymour was rather less than that. Elizabeth was a strong-willed and sometimes imperious young lady, very conscious that she was a king's daughter, who passed her fourteenth birthday in September 1547. Though secure in the affection of her household and her stepmother, she had never encountered the kind of attention she received from Seymour. Perhaps she was a little intimidated, but the excitement of it seems to have outweighed any real fear. At any point, she could have made it very plain that his approaches were repugnant to her, complained to Katherine, the Privy Council, her sister Mary, even the Lord Protector himself, if she had chosen. She was young but not defenceless. No doubt she was confused and later she seems to have been genuinely contrite, but at the time it was probably the most thrilling encounter of her life.

Thomas, for his part, could not desist. His behaviour was not connected with his wife's pregnancy, or part of some devious, sinister plan to provide himself with marital insurance for the future; it was merely a feature of who he was. He liked the admiration and the company of women. Elizabeth and her giggling maids were the perfect audience for his exuberance and his ego. Still smarting at his relative political insignificance, this half-play, half-serious pursuit of Henry VIII's younger daughter was an amusing diversion. Her reactions, and the occasional scolding of Katherine Ashley (who was more than a little sweet on him herself) doubtless encouraged him still more. He might swear his great oaths, but he knew that what he was doing might cause tittle-tattle. Quite simply, he did not care. But in indulging himself with Elizabeth Tudor he risked ruining her reputation and greatly hurting his wife. Yet these considerations were pushed aside, as was the even more serious possibility that all this might yet come back to haunt him if his quarrel with his brother escalated. But between June 1547 and May 1548, when Elizabeth left Katherine Parr's household, though there may have been rumour and innuendo, there was no public scandal. Katherine Ashley was herself partly to blame for indulging her charge too freely. In the summer of 1547 it was not the fact that Elizabeth was tickled in bed by Thomas Seymour that amazed the duchess of Somerset (who had daughters of her own) but that she was allowed unchaperoned on a barge on the Thames in the evening. And nothing improper reached the ears of Henry and Frances Dorset, the parents of Lady Jane Grey. Thomas Seymour's plans for their daughter were extremely ambitious, but he seems to have been a kind and responsible guardian to her.

So there remain questions unanswered and unknowable about the 'romance' of Thomas and Elizabeth. Its long-term impact on the princess at an impressionable time of her life can only be guessed. In the short term, however, matters reached a point where Katherine Parr felt it necessary to send Elizabeth away. Thomas Parry, while under arrest at the beginning of 1549, gave his version of what had happened. His account was, admittedly, second-hand and based on a confidence from Katherine Ashley. Parry had been questioned on Seymour's intentions towards Elizabeth in the autumn of 1548, and recalled Mrs Ashley saying 'that the Admiral loved her [Elizabeth] but too well, and had done so a good while; and that the Queen was jealous of her and him, in so much that, one time the Queen, suspecting the often access of the Admiral to the Lady Elizabeth, came suddenly upon them, where they were all alone [he having her in his arms]: wherefor the Queen fell out, both with the Lord Admiral and with her Grace also'. Shaken and angry, though perhaps not entirely surprised by what she had witnessed, Katherine sent for Elizabeth's governess 'and told her fancy in that matter; and of this was much displeasure. And it was not long, before they parted asunder their families [households]; and, as I remember, this was the cause why she was sent from the Queen; or else that her Grace parted from the Queen: I do not perfectly remember ... whether she went of herself, or was sent away.'[7]

Perhaps Parry was being disingenuous here, to try to salvage something of Elizabeth's reputation, torn to shreds by the admissions of himself and Katherine Ashley. The truth is that Katherine, six months into an uncomfortable pregnancy, could no longer condone the relationship between her stepdaughter and husband. Her physical and mental well-being was too fragile to endure further stress and she knew, much more than Thomas or Elizabeth's servants, or even the princess herself, how the world would view this behaviour if word spread. So, in May 1548, Elizabeth moved into Hertfordshire to take up residence with Sir Anthony Denny and his wife, Joan, who was Katherine Ashley's sister. There, after some time for reflection, she wrote to the queen, expressing concern for her health and alluding to the interview that had taken place between them before she left:

Although I could not be plentiful in giving thanks for the manifold kindness received at your highness' hand at my departure, yet I am something to be borne withal, for truly I was replete with sorrow to depart from your highness, especially leaving you undoubtful of health. And albeit I answered little, I weighed it more deeper when you said you would warn me of all evils that you should hear of me; for if your grace had not a good opinion of me, you would not have offered friendship to me that way that all men judge the contrary. But what may I more say than thank God for providing such friends to me, desiring God to enrich me with their long life and give me grace to be in heart no less thankful to receive it than I now am glad in writing to show it. And although I have plenty of matter, here will I stay, for I know you are not quiet to read. From Cheshunt, this present Saturday.

Your highness' humble daughter, Elizabeth.[8]

Elizabeth had evidently heard Katherine out in chastened silence, unable, at that point, to defend herself or give much of an explanation of her behaviour. The queen was the only mother she had ever known, a figure of enormous influence in her young life. And now she realized that she had parted from her with scarcely a word.

Yet she remained in contact with Thomas, apparently with his wife's knowledge. She held no grudge against him; in fact, quite the reverse. She was keen to remind him of her constancy. Later in the summer, before Katherine's baby was born, she replied to a message or a letter from him in which he had apparently apologized for not fulfilling a promise. It is not clear exactly what this promise was, and Elizabeth made light of it, assuring him:

My lord,
      You needed not to send an excuse to me, for I could not mistrust the not fulfilling of your promise to proceed for want of goodwill, but only the opportunity serveth not; wherefore I shall desire you to think that a greater matter than this could not make me impute any unkindness in you. For I am a friend not won with trifles, nor lost with the like. Thus I commit you and all your affairs in God's hand, who keep you from all evil. I pray you make my humble commendations to the queen's highness.

Your assured friend to my power, Elizabeth.[9]

This is not the language of someone who feared the person she was addressing. The letter has a dignity and gravity that counterbalance the lurid tales told later about Elizabeth and Thomas Seymour. Nothing else of any correspondence between them survives. Elizabeth continued to exchange letters with the queen as the date for the baby's arrival drew ever closer. Their peace, it seems, was made. But Elizabeth never saw Katherine or Thomas again.

ONCE SHE HAD LEFT their household, the queen and her husband set about repairing their fractured relationship. The preceding months had not all been difficult, and Katherine's pregnancy was a source of great joy and hope. She must have conceived in November and might have suspected, but not been entirely sure, that she was carrying a child when she and Thomas spent Christmas at Hampton Court with Edward VI. Whatever their domestic tensions, the couple had by no means lost sight of their ultimate goal of an official role in the king's upbringing. Thomas continued to pay out sums of money for the boy's personal use, telling him 'ye are a beggarly king' because he had little direct resource to reward friends, servants or entertainers at court. This embarrassing gap in Edward's finances was soon being filled by his uncle via the helpful Fowler. Thomas failed, however, to get the king to sign a bill naming him as Governor of the king's person. Feeling that he was being pushed into putting his signature to something he did not fully understand, Edward told Thomas that he must follow the proper parliamentary procedures. He also asked John Cheke, his tutor, for advice and was assured that his response was the correct one. Thwarted and angry, Thomas retreated.[10] Yet still he and his wife did not give up their quest.

But in the early summer of 1548, Thomas Seymour's primary concern was to ensure that Katherine gave birth to his heir (he was convinced the baby would be a boy) in the most comfortable and pleasant surroundings, with all the state that befitted a queen. So, in mid-June, Katherine set out for Sudeley Castle, her husband's property in Gloucestershire, to prepare for the birth of her child. She was often unwell at this time, her only known pregnancy, and she was old by Tudor standards to be having a first child. Her cousin Nicholas Throckmorton described her in his poem as 'past middle age' and said she 'barren was before'. Morning sickness and tiredness caused her much discomfort and even late in the pregnancy she was still suffering – and by now she was very large. Elizabeth wrote to Katherine on 31 July, thanking her for thinking of her and acknowledging 'what pain it is to you to write, your grace being so great with child and so sickly'. She was clearly pleased to read that Katherine 'wished me with you till I were weary of that country' and assured her that 'although I were in the worst soil in the world, your presence would make it pleasant'.[11]

This letter shows that, despite the circumstances of their parting, the queen and her stepdaughter missed one another greatly. However, Katherine had taken Lady Jane Grey with her to Sudeley and the younger girl was a source of comfort as well as providing a focus for the queen's maternal skills while she awaited the birth of her own child. A large retinue of ladies and gentlemen accompanied the queen and Jane, turning Sudeley into a court of its own. Thomas undertook some hasty building work so that the castle could accommodate his wife and her servants, but he did not have time to make the extensive changes with which he has often been credited.

It was a lovely, tranquil spot on the edge of the Cotswolds, a complete contrast to the bustle and noise of London. Sudeley is just outside the ancient town of Winchcombe, whose origins went back to Saxon times. The castle itself also had a long history, being mentioned in the Domesday Book, though its past was chequered. An earlier owner, William de Tracy, was one of the knights who murdered Thomas Becket; and Richard III, as duke of Gloucester, had used the castle as his campaign head-quarters before the battle of Tewkesbury, in which Katherine Parr's grandfather had fought. Much of its current appearance and appointments in the mid-sixteenth century it owed to improvements made by Richard when he became king. He added the banqueting hall and the state rooms and might have spent more time there if he had reigned longer. Henry VII gave the castle to his uncle, Jasper Tudor, but after Jasper's death it reverted to the Crown. Sudeley remained in royal ownership, though it was not much used. Henry VIII made one visit with Anne Boleyn in 1535 and when Edward VI gave it to Thomas Seymour it was in need of refurbishment. Thomas spent £1,000 (about £340,000 today) getting it ready for Katherine, but pressure of time did not allow him to make any major structural changes.

Sudeley, with its fine walks and beautiful garden, was an ideal location for the queen to pass the last three months of her pregnancy. In the spring and summer it is especially attractive. But Katherine had not skimped on her establishment when she exchanged London for Gloucestershire. Her entourage at Sudeley included her new almoner, Miles Coverdale, her doctor, Robert Huicke, a full complement of maids-of-honour and gentlewomen, as well as 120 gentlemen and yeomen of the guard. The duchess of Somerset, who was also pregnant (a coincidence, but a further competitive element between the Seymour brothers) might be the wife of the most powerful man in the land, but she could not boast such an attendance: Katherine was still a queen.

Yet as the final preparations were being made for Katherine and Thomas to go down into the country, there was the sudden threat of naval hostilities with France The prospect that her husband might be called away to fulfil his duties as lord admiral alarmed Katherine: 'I am very sorry for the news of the Frenchmen', she wrote to him from Hanworth. 'I pray God it be not a let to our journey. As soon as ye know what they will do, good my lord, I beseech you let me hear from you, for I shall not be very quiet till I know.' Fortunately, this anxiety, coupled with the continuing struggle to get her personal jewellery returned from the duke of Somerset (a dispute that was still festering nearly eighteen months after the death of Henry VIII) did not quite overshadow her continued joy in her pregnancy. The unborn child was, she told Thomas, very active: 'I gave your little knave your blessing, who like an honest man stirred apace after and before. For Mary Odell [one of her ladies] being abed with me had laid her hand upon my belly to feel it stir. It hath stirred these three days every morning and evening so that I trust when you come it will make you some pastime. And thus I end bidding my sweetheart and loving husband better to fare than myself.'[12]

Thomas was delighted with her description of the active son he believed would live to take up his father's cause and set right the injustice done to his parents. He told her:

> the receiving of your letter revived my spirits, partly for that I do perceive you be armed with patience, however the matter will weigh [here he was referring to his efforts to prise Katherine's possessions from his brother], as chiefest, that I hear my little man doth shake his poll [head], trusting if God should give him life as long as his father, he will revenge such wrongs as neither you nor I can, at this present, the turmoil is such. – God amend it!

There was, though, better news of foreign matters: 'As for the Frenchmen, I have no mistrust that they shall be any let of my going with you this journey, or any of my continuance there with your highness.' He would be with her at her time of travail and had some advice on how she might ease the pangs of delivery: 'I do desire your highness to keep the little knave so lean and gaunt with your good diet and walking, that he may be so small that he may creep out of a mousehole. And I bid my most dear and well-beloved wife most heartily well to fare.'[13]

These letters reveal a great deal about the underlying affection between Thomas and Katherine, a love that had survived ridicule, family and political pressures, as well as temptation and jealousy. At Sudeley, as the weeks passed and Katherine's confinement drew ever closer, all that remained to complete their happiness was the birth itself. They may have had enemies, but they also had well-wishers who had cause to remember Katherine's friendship and pray for her safe delivery. Her elder stepdaughter, Mary, wrote from Newhall in Essex on 9 August and said that she was taking the opportunity of a visit from the queen's brother to add another letter to the many she had already sent, as she understood that he 'intendeth to see your grace shortly'. The next day she hoped to begin the journey to her Norfolk estates, but ill-health had delayed her. She was conscious that she would be further than ever from the queen but she hoped 'with God's grace, to return again about Michaelmas, by which time, or shortly after, I trust to hear good success of your grace's great belly'.[14]

While she waited for that success, Katherine fitted out a beautiful nursery for her baby. The room overlooked the gardens and Sudeley's chapel, a fair and peaceful aspect. It was hung with tapestries and decorated in the queen's favourite colours of crimson and gold. Beside the baby's cradle, with its pillows and quilt, was a bed with a scarlet tester and crimson curtains and a separate bed for the nurse. The child was already provided with plate for a table service and fine furniture. As the summer of 1548 drew to its conclusion, the queen continued to follow Dr Huicke's advice and walk regularly in the castle grounds. Yet despite the imminence of her own child's arrival, she was still thinking about the situation of English politics and the theft, as she perceived it, of her stepson's rightful possessions. Sir Robert Tyrwhit remembered that she had said to him during one of her perambulations: 'Master Tyrwhit, you shall see the king when he cometh to his full age, he will call his lands again, as fast as they be now given from him.' She assured Tyrwhit that Seymour would give up Sudeley Castle, if the day came that the king required its return.

For the present, however, Sudeley was her home and refuge. She had endured an uncomfortable pregnancy and an emotional, uncertain time since the death of Henry VIII. But the end of her confinement was apparently more straightforward. On 30 August, Katherine gave birth to a healthy girl. The baby was named Mary, after the queen's elder stepdaughter. Any disappointment that the parents might have felt that this was not the anticipated little male avenger of their wrongs was completely swept away by the joys of parenthood and relief at Katherine's safe delivery. She and Thomas were old to be having a first child, and their delight was made plain when the proud father wrote to his brother (who already had two children from his first marriage and nine from his second) about his sweet little girl. The duchess of Somerset had trumped Katherine a few weeks earlier by giving birth to yet another boy, but her husband was circumspect, even encouraging, in his response to Thomas:

> We are right glad to understand by your letters that the Queen your bedfellow hath had a happy hour: and, escaping all danger, hath made you the father of so pretty a daughter. And although (if it had so pleased God) it would have been both to us, and we suppose to you, a more joy and comfort if it had been this the first son; yet the escape of danger, and the prophecy and good hansell [promise] of this to a great sort of happy sons, the which as you write, we trust no less than to be true, is no small joy and comfort to us, as we are sure it is to you and to her Grace also.

The use of the royal 'we', an affectation that did not endear Somerset to other members of the Privy Council, was something that his brother had come to expect. And by the time the duke's letter, written on 1 September, reached Sudeley, Thomas Seymour had far more serious things to occupy his thoughts.

At first, it seemed as though Katherine had come through the birth well. But, alas, she had not experienced the escape of danger her brother-in-law assumed. Within a few days, she developed the fever and weakness that were the first signs of puerperal fever, the deadly bacterial complication of childbirth that afflicted so many women of her time. Lacking antiseptics and antibiotics, newly delivered women were at the mercy of a lottery of life and death. Understanding of hygiene was very basic and Dr Huicke, as he tended to Katherine during and after the birth, did not have at his disposal the scrubs, gloves and sterilized instruments of our times. It made no difference whether you were a queen or a peasant. Katherine had been given the best of care while she carried her child, but there was nothing that could be done for her now.

Thomas may have clung, for a while, to the hope that the fever would pass and she would rally. Most probably her ladies, and Katherine herself, knew otherwise. As her condition worsened, she suffered bouts of delirium, interspersed with periods when she was calmer and collected. But, clearly, she realized, before her doctor confirmed her worst fears, that she was dying. After a troubled night, she called Robert Tyrwhit's wife, Lady Elizabeth, to her bedside on the morning of 3 September. This lady's recollection of the queen's words at that time have passed down to us as a deathbed denunciation of Thomas Seymour, but it should be remembered that here was someone who disliked Seymour intensely, wanting to leave an overwhelmingly negative impression. Nevertheless, her account reveals the hidden anguish that Katherine had suppressed, but which now came to the surface as she struggled to accept what was happening to her.

When Lady Tyrwhit arrived in Katherine's chamber, the queen asked her where she had been so long, and then said that 'she did fear such things in herself, that she was sure she could not live'. Seeking to reassure her despairing and frightened mistress, Lady Tyrwhit replied that she saw no likelihood of death in her. But Katherine was not placated. In fact, she became more disturbed, despite the fact that Thomas was holding her hand and trying to soothe her. 'She then . . . spake these words,' recalled Elizabeth Tyrwhit, 'partly, as I took it, idly [in delirium], "My Lady Tyrwhit, I am not well handled, for those that be about me careth not for me, but standeth laughing at my grief, and the more good I will unto them, the less good they will to me."' This rebuke was clearly intended for her husband but he strongly denied it, answering, 'Why, sweetheart, I would you no hurt.' Katherine replied: 'No my lord, I think so', but she pulled him closer, saying in his ear, 'but, my lord, you have given me many shrewd taunts'. Lady Tyrwhit went on to say that the queen spoke these words 'with good memory and very sharply and earnestly, for her mind was far unquieted. My Lord Admiral, perceiving that I heard it, called me aside, and asked me what she said, and I declared it plainly to him.' Though there are evident contradictions concerning Katherine's lucidity in this account, Lady Tyrwhit was determined to drive her point home. She admitted that Thomas was distressed enough by his wife's accusations to suggest that he lie down on the bed beside her so that he could 'pacify her unquietness with gentle communication', but she wanted it known that Seymour's attempts were counter-productive. Katherine had reproved him, 'very roundly and shortly', claiming that she would have liked a full consultation with Dr Huicke the first day she was delivered, 'but I durst not, for displeasing of you'. In other words, the queen was so far afraid of her husband's reaction if she had a private session with her doctor that Thomas's unreasonable jealousy had brought her to the point of death. Too distressed to listen further, so she claimed, Lady Tyrwhit left this heartbreaking scene. But others who were there, she vowed, could back up what she had remembered.[15]

None, however, seem to have done so, though that is not to say that the account is fabricated. Katherine had ample reason to lament her husband's thoughtlessness and his outbursts of temper. Her reproofs also suggest strongly how devastated she had been by his behaviour with Elizabeth. But his own evident concern for Katherine in her extremity is quite clear and there is no reason to suppose that Dr Huicke could have done anything further that might have prevented the childbed fever that was ravaging her body and mind. In fact, he may well have caused it. Yet however distressed Katherine was on the morning of

3 September, Thomas does seem to have succeeded in calming
her. She herself, accepting the inevitability and fast approach of
death, remembered, in the end, only the love she had long felt
for him. She sent for Huicke and John Parkhurst, the chaplain
who had served her while she was married to Henry VIII, and
dictated her will, being too weak to write it herself. All her
property and possessions were left to her husband. The queen
'wishing them to be a thousand times more in value than they
were', gave Thomas complete authority to dispose of them as he
saw fit. Katherine made no profession of religious faith in her
will, nor did she mention her baby. Of little Mary Seymour, lying
in her splendid cradle, there was no word. Nor is there any record
that she asked to see her daughter as her life ebbed away.
Presumably she believed that Thomas would be a good father to
their child and was content to leave Mary in his care.

Katherine died in the early morning of 5 September. Her
body was carefully wrapped in layers of cere cloth, a waxed cloth
used to help prevent decay, and encased in a lead envelope in her
coffin. She was buried in the chapel of Sudeley Castle, within
sight of the windows of her daughter's nursery. Jane Grey was
the chief mourner for a lady she seems to have held in great
affection. The service was short, in English, as Katherine would
have approved, and over in a morning. Not for Katherine the
processions and funeral masses that saw her third husband to his
grave. Instead, psalms were sung in English by the choir, three
lessons read, and offerings made in the alms box for the living,
not the dead. This point, a key element of the reformed religion
that Katherine had done so much to promote, was emphasized
by Miles Coverdale in his 'very good and godly sermon': 'they
should none there think,' he admonished them, 'that the offering
which was there done, was done anything to benefit the dead,
but for the poor only; and also the lights, which were carried and
stood about the corpse were for the honour of the person, and
for none other intent nor purpose'. Then he delivered his sermon,
said a prayer, and 'the corpse was buried, during which time the

choir sung Te Deum in English And this done, the mourners
dined and the rest turned homeward again.'[16] This simple
ceremony has been described as the first Protestant burial of an
English queen. It was certainly a stark contrast to a Catholic
funeral service, though the singing of the Te Deum, even in
English, demonstrates that the old forms had not quite been
swept away completely. But Katherine Parr, wife to four husbands, who had lived through thirty-six years of some of the
greatest changes England has ever seen, was gone.

However regretful they may have been in private, none of
Henry VIII's children made any public utterance on their stepmother's passing. When it was suggested to Elizabeth that she
write a letter of condolence to Thomas, she declined, on the
grounds that she might be thought to be wooing the widower.
Whether this reticence was caused by a genuine desire to discour-
age Seymour, or concern that the Privy Council could misinter-
pret her intentions if the letter became public, is hard to say. Her
caution, though, is ample evidence that Katherine's admonitions
when they parted in May 1548 had been taken to heart.

THOMAS SEYMOUR was stunned by Katherine's death. Despite
the known dangers of childbirth, and his wife being old for her
first experience of motherhood, the possibility that she might not
survive seems simply never to have crossed his mind. In his shock
and grief he turned to his family, going back to London to spend
some time with his brother at Syon House. Somerset's home, full
of children and with Duchess Anne the proud mother of yet
another son, cannot have been an easy place for Thomas to come
to terms with his loss, even if their quarrels were temporarily
suspended. His immediate thought was to abandon everything –
send Jane Grey back to her parents, disband Katherine's household, acknowledge that his dreams had been in vain: 'with the
Queen's Highness death, I was so amazed', he wrote to Jane's

father, the marquess of Dorset, 'that I had small regard either to myself or to my doings'.

His despair very soon gave way to a more considered assessment of how he would approach life without Katherine. There was no need for Jane Grey to leave and he would keep on most of his wife's ladies. He would not throw to the winds everything they had sought to achieve together. This revived ambition was mingled with sadness and a sense of responsibility towards the substantial number of people who had been dependent on the queen. Seymour told Dorset that he hoped to meet him to discuss Jane Grey's future as soon as possible but that 'I must repair unto the court, as well to help certain of the Queen's poor servants, with some of the things now fallen by her death, as also for my own affairs.'[17]

How his own affairs might be moved forward concentrated Seymour's mind as he came to terms with Katherine's demise. It was important not to lose sight of what had been their primary goal – to be put on an equal footing with his brother in the upbringing and management of the king. Much as Thomas liked life in the country, he recognized that he needed to be at court. And he speedily realized it was important to keep Lady Jane Grey with him, if his plans for her marriage to Edward VI were ever to succeed. He asked his own mother, who was currently caring for little Lady Mary Seymour, to look after Jane: 'my mother shall and will, I doubt not, be as dear unto her, as though she were her own daughter', he sought to reassure the Dorsets. But the marquess and his wife Frances needed some persuading. Seymour was compelled to visit them in person, at their home, Bradgate, in Leicestershire. Using all his charm and plausibility, he was determined to obtain their agreement that he should remain Jane's guardian. He had even taken with him his friend Sir William Sharington, who soothed Frances's fears while Thomas worked on her husband. Jane herself does not seem to have minded returning to Seymour's care: 'you have been towards me a loving and kind father', she wrote at the beginning of October. 'I shall be always most ready to obey your godly [ad]monitions and good instructions as behooveth one on whom you have heaped so many benefits.'[18]

This success boosted Thomas's confidence. He believed that there was everything to play for and that ultimate success might yet be his. And he thought he had friends: Dorset, Katherine's brother, Northampton, and her brother-in-law, William Herbert, as well as the earl of Rutland. And then there was Sharington, the head of the new mint at Bristol. Sharington and Seymour had known each other for years. Both had served with Sir Francis Bryan and Sharington had been in Henry VIII's Privy Chamber as well as Katherine Parr's household while she was married to the king. Sir William owned the beautiful Lacock Abbey in Wiltshire, not far from the Seymours' home at Wolf Hall. He was considerably older than Thomas and appeared to be wealthy and influential. Sharington certainly knew how to make money – quite literally – for he was a fraudster and embezzler on a large scale, and his role in Bristol gave him ample opportunity to cover the fact that he was hugely overstretched in his personal finances. As an associate he was shady and as a friend, it would turn out, completely unreliable. But then, so were the other men who Thomas believed to be on his side.

As the autumn of 1548 progressed, relations between the two Seymour brothers deteriorated once again. Katherine's death had briefly brought them together but now the distance between them seemed to grow wider by the month. Thomas, sensing, quite rightly, that Somerset's popularity on the Privy Council was substantially diminished compared with his position a year ago, tried to win allies to his cause. The reasons for his failure to do so must remain a matter of conjecture. Some may have had to do with personal dislike, or misgivings at his increasingly intemperate tone. His fundamental argument about the separation of the offices of Protector and Governor had both logic and historical precedent on its side, so it may well have been the man, rather than the idea, that met with a frosty reception. He required the support of king and parliament to bring about this change. Both presented major problems. Access to Edward was increasingly difficult. The king was 'guarded, monitored, taught and governed every hour of his life'[19] and it was difficult, even for an uncle who provided presents of pocket money, to penetrate this cordon to any lasting effect. In fact, it was easier, as Seymour himself once said, in a remark he later had cause to regret, to remove the king physically. The security arrangements for Edward at this time were surprisingly lax, especially at night.

Parliament presented other difficulties. Any bill would have to be sponsored by the king and, by his own admission, Thomas was not a natural parliamentarian. Surprisingly, he did not count himself an effective speaker. This may have been no more than fear of his inability to curb his temper when challenged, but it may also point to some insecurity with a large audience and a big occasion. He was an effective letter-writer but evidently did not count oratory as his strong suit.

The lack of response to his schemes did not deter Thomas. He seems to have scarcely noticed. There were other avenues to be pursued. One of the most interesting and attractive of these was the search for a new wife. He was reported as saying (though admittedly the source was third hand) that 'he would wear black for one year, and would then know where to have a wife'. This statement has been used as evidence of his heartlessness and scheming but it should be recalled that his late wife had married again after the deaths of Lord Latimer and Henry VIII in far less time than a year. Rumours of his intentions soon began to circulate among the Privy Councillors. They were not amused, and, indeed, somewhat incredulous, that Thomas might seriously think of marriage with either of the king's sisters. But though he did not broadcast his plans openly, he was undoubtedly contemplating such a match.

Of the two, Elizabeth was clearly the preferred choice. She was younger, better-looking (though Mary, at thirty-three, remained presentable) and not so obviously tied to the old religion. Seymour, who knew women well, probably sensed that the intimacy there had been between them could easily be rekindled. The business side of such a match also had a strong appeal. Thomas Parry remembered, in his rambling confessions, that Thomas had questioned him at length about the size of Elizabeth's household, her lands and where they were, and how much income she derived from them. He then offered the princess his house in London, 'stuff and all', as Parry put it, 'with such kindness and gentleness' that Parry decided to broach the matter with Elizabeth herself. There must, he thought, 'be some matter betwixt them', an underlying affection that had remained after Katherine's death. Seymour added to this impression by announcing that he would try to see Elizabeth: 'I remember my Lord Admiral said, when her Grace came to Ashridge to lie, it was not far out of his way; and that he might come to see her in his way up and down; and would be glad to see her there then.'[20]

The date of this conversation was not made clear, though other exchanges between the two men, all concerning Elizabeth, took place in mid-December 1548. Again, Thomas reiterated his desire to see the princess if she came to court. Any other meeting could not properly take place without the Protector's consent, and much as Elizabeth might have desired to see Thomas, she was conscious of this restraint. By this time, towards the end of the year in which his wife had died, Thomas was playing with fire. He had earlier denied to Lord Russell that he was pursuing either of the king's sisters. Russell told him, on the way to parliament, that he 'was sorry to hear rumours that he made means to marry Mary or Elizabeth, which would be his undoing . . . he denied attempting any such thing'. Thomas was clearly troubled by what had been said, because a few days later he pressed Russell to reveal who had claimed he was going to marry again. Russell replied: 'I declined, but advised him against it.' This counsel only made Thomas bolder. 'He replied that it was convenient for them to marry, and better within the realm than abroad, and why should not he or another made by their father marry one of them. I [Russell] told him that it would be the undoing of anyone, particularly him who was so near the king. The king might be suspicious like his father and grandfather, and suppose that if the admiral married his sister he wished for his death.' They then argued about the financial advantages of such a match, disagreeing about particulars, and left the matter unresolved. Russell clearly thought he had made his point, but went straight to the lord chancellor, Richard Rich, to relate what had been discussed.

The anger that had burned in Thomas since Henry VIII's death began increasingly to cloud his judgement. He had always spoken first and thought afterwards. Even Katherine had found him hard to handle and she had supported his ideas and sense of grievance. He hated being told that he had lost his power now she was gone and continued to fight for her jewels, asking Mary for help in identifying the pieces that were rightfully the queen's. Again, the princess prudently refused to be drawn into his affairs. Thomas was not deterred. He would prove wrong those who thought his prospects diminished. Not all power resided in London. He owned a great deal of land, a source of men who could fight, as well as income. With those men at his back, he could bring down the government. Or so he claimed. Whether he really intended armed insurrection is doubtful. He had no coherent plan of action to back up his statements, and no friends of any influence. Nor did he have the funds that such a course would have required, though the ever-resourceful Sharington might, at an earlier point, have provided him with counterfeit coin. A sum of £10,000 had been mentioned. Now Sharington himself was under suspicion, a fact noted by Thomas Seymour's enemies – of which he had a growing number.

They came for him at 8 o'clock in the evening of 17 January. Rumours about the circumstances of his arrest were in circulation ten days later in Europe, where they were met with much interest and further speculation. This international dimension to Thomas

Seymour's downfall is sometimes overlooked, yet it formed part of what appears to have been an orchestrated campaign of propaganda once he was shut away in the Tower. On 27 January the imperial ambassador, François Van der Delft, was in Calais, awaiting a crossing to England. The version he had heard was that

> the admiral of England, with the help of some people about the court, attempted to outrage the person of the young king by night ... the alarm was given by the gentleman that sleeps in the king's chamber, who awakened by the barking of the dog that lies before the king's door, cried out "help! Murder!". Everybody rushed in, but the only thing they found was the lifeless corpse of the dog. Suspicion points to the admiral, because he had scattered the watch that night on several errands and because it had been noticed that he had some secret plot on hand, hoping to marry the second daughter of the late king, the Lady Elizabeth, who is also under grave suspicion.

He would, he told Charles V, find out more when he got back to London, as at the moment he had nothing more to go on 'beyond the information of those who repeat common report'.[21] Three days later, Charles V wrote from Brussels to say that the news was common currency there, too. But by this time Thomas was supposed to have plotted the death of Mary Tudor as well. The emperor had also heard of the accusations that Thomas had sheltered pirates and been paid off in kind, and as he had recently exchanged harsh words with the English ambassador to Brussels on this very subject of piracy he was concerned not to give the impression that he had somehow had forewarning of Seymour's schemes. Such a comment was typical of the very cautious Charles V.[22]

William Paget subsequently backed up the story circulating in Calais, when, on being pushed by Van der Delft about why Seymour had been arrested, said the Privy Council had felt compelled to act 'when the admiral was finally discovered within the palace late at night, with a large suite of his own people and the dog that keeps watch before the king's door was found dead'.[23] The death of this animal is the one constant in the versions of this incident that later circulated. It has been claimed that Thomas, finally moved to desperation, decided to kidnap Edward VI under cover of darkness, knowing he was inadequately guarded, and quite possibly with his nephew's connivance. Carrying a pistol, he is said to have shot the dog when it persisted in barking, thus alerting members of the king's household and alienating Edward. It is worth noting, however, that neither the imperial ambassador's first report nor Paget's explanation makes any mention of the fact that Seymour was armed or exactly how the dog was killed. Nor were any specific charges relating to this incident included in the accusations against Thomas. But by the time of Van der Delft's interview with Paget, on 8 February, the campaign to besmirch the admiral was firmly in place. As Paget, ever the master of the pithy phrase put it, he had been 'a great rascal' and that was how the Privy Council wanted him to be remembered.

In fact, his arrest was not a spur-of-the-moment decision rendered unavoidable by nocturnal forays near the royal bedchamber; there had clearly been discussions about it over some days, but Thomas did not fully appreciate his danger. The marquess of Northampton, Katherine Parr's brother, recalled that: 'The night before he was committed to the Tower, the admiral called me and seemed perplexed, declaring that the council had secret conferences that day in the garden, but he could not learn their effect; he could get nothing of the Lord Privy Seal [Lord John Russell, who had warned him against an alliance with either of the king's sisters]. He thought they conferred to see if they could get anything against him from Sharington, who was more straitly handled for his sake.'

He was certainly correct in that analysis, though he was not the only one who might have been concerned over revelations of their dealings with Sharington. Various people close to Seymour owed the fraudster money, including his brother, Somerset, his brother-in-law, William Herbert, and even the duchess of Suffolk, some of whose jewels and plate Sharington held as surety for her debt.

For his part, Thomas professed not to be worried: 'But he cared not,' Northampton recalled, 'for he was able to answer all charges. The protector was in fear of his own estate and was very jealous because the admiral was better furnished with men about him.' This last was an empty boast. Thomas had no contingent of men he could call upon to defend him at this crucial juncture. But the mere reference to such a possibility may have been the final straw that caused the council to act. Parr must have seen him on the 17th itself, when Thomas told him he expected to be called before the council to answer charges from Lord Rutland. 'He would question Rutland before all the other lords, saying he would answer all things at his liberty, and not be shut up when he should not answer.'[24] He had, though, omitted to mention the fact that he had told the councillors that his appearance before them was conditional on William Paget remaining at Seymour Place as surety for Thomas's continued freedom. Such a deal was a bold offer but not one the council was likely to indulge.

His self-confidence was sounding increasingly forced. During his journey by river to the Tower Thomas was advised 'Sir, arm you with patience, for now . . . it shall be assayed.' He replied, 'I think no. I am sure I can have no hurt, if they do me right; they cannot kill me, except they do me wrong: And if they do, I shall die but once: and if they take my life from me, I have a master that will once revenge it.'[25] The first question raised with him was whether he had conferred with anyone about changing 'the order of the person of the king's majesty'. This Thomas emphatically denied. He admitted commenting to Rutland about Edward VI's precocity, saying that he thought his nephew 'would be a man three years before any child living', and that this 'towardness' would very likely mean that the king would want more liberty and a greater say in the direction of his own personal affairs. He had never intended this as an attack on the duke of Somerset, stating: 'And if I meant hurt to my lord's grace my brother, more than I meant to my soul, then I desire neither life nor other favour at his hand.' He repeated the essence of this explanation in a brief, disordered letter written to the Protector two days later, in which he reiterated that he had intended no ill to his brother: 'But if I meant either hurt or displeasure to your grace, in this or any other thing that I have done, then punish me by extremity. And thus I humbly take my leave of your grace.'[26] In this sad little note there speaks, for the last time, the miscreant younger brother apologizing to the elder for his bad behaviour.

But it was too late. Even the young king was pressed for evidence against his uncle. Edward divulged that Thomas had given him money and tried to get him to sign a bill for parliament. Others who had known the lord admiral, sensing the way the wind was setting, hastened to disassociate themselves from Thomas Seymour. Only John Harington, his servant, and Nicholas Throckmorton (who was not interrogated) refused to join in the stampede. Details poured forth of what he had said about the governance of the king, his bragging about private armies, his pleasure that the office of lord admiral gave him command of ships and men, his attempts to win friends through money and favours. Much of the information supplied was virtually identical, for Thomas had been neither original nor reticent in repeating his views. Whether there was also an element of collusion among the noble lords who were so eager to remember everything is an interesting question. For one person, however, there was no such possibility. Thomas's intentions towards Elizabeth formed a major part of the charges brought against him. If it could be proved that she had welcomed or encouraged marriage plans, then she would be implicated in his treason, and might expect to share his fate.

✂

ELIZABETH WAS AT Hatfield at the time of Seymour's arrest. Within days, Katherine Ashley and Thomas Parry were both themselves taken into the Tower for questioning. Deprived of the two people in whom she had the most confidence, however misplaced, Elizabeth swiftly realized her danger. Sir Robert Tyrwhit and his stern, god-fearing wife, had been sent to take charge of her. She must have sensed, if she did not already know, their antipathy towards Thomas and, by extension, their dislike of her. Both had been long in Katherine Parr's service and they knew about the horseplay and early morning visits at Chelsea and Hanworth. Sir Robert was determined to get a confession out of Elizabeth but, though she was 'marvellously abashed, and did weep very tenderly a long time' when she learned what had happened to Ashley and Parry, Tyrwhit could get nothing of any substance out of her. In fact, he suspected that she and her servants had made a pact to say nothing that would be incriminating.

At the age of fifteen, surrounded by those determined to break her and false friends (Lady Browne was still in Elizabeth's service, but 'Fair Geraldine' was happy to act as a spy on her mistress), the princess had to suppress her emotions, keep a clear head and live on her wits. She may have been a king's sister, but she was still legally a bastard and she was powerless. There was no throne beckoning in those bleak January days of 1549, only disgrace, and perhaps worse. Over nearly a week, Tyrwhit persisted in trying to wring out of her the confession that Somerset apparently required. But despite the fact that both her governess and her cofferer had effectively betrayed her, pouring out everything they could possibly recollect about her relationship with Thomas Seymour and her reaction to the idea of marriage to him, Elizabeth would not give way. When told that Parry had given chapter and verse about her alleged partiality for Seymour, her evident pleasure when the admiral was mentioned and her blushing at talk of marriage, Elizabeth momentarily lost her composure, calling her cofferer a 'false wretch'. She quickly recovered. At a young age, she was able to frame answers that would not trap her and she knew her rights. Tyrwhit wrote to Somerset on 28 January to tell him that he was getting nowhere: 'Pleaseth your grace to be advertised that I have received your letter . . . and according to the purpose of the same, have practised with my lady's grace, by all means and policy, to cause her to confess more than she hath already done; wherein she doth plainly deny that she knoweth any more than she already hath opened to me, which things she hath willingly written to your grace with her own hand . . .'[27]

Sensing that she was winning this war of wills, Elizabeth decided to take the fight directly to Somerset himself. She did not deny that she knew about the marriage rumours, or Thomas's interest in her lands and finances, or that there was talk that he might come and see her after the queen's death. Parry had asked her '. . . whether, if the council did consent that I should have my lord admiral, whether I would consent to it or no. I answered that I would not tell him what my mind was . . .' Neither she nor her governess, she claimed, had ever contemplated the idea of marriage, with Thomas or anyone else, 'without the consent of the king's majesty, your grace's, and the council's'. There was no improper response, not even the merest thought, of stepping outside the boundaries laid down in her father's will. This being so, she demanded full protection for her damaged reputation:

Master Tyrwhit and others have told me that there goeth rumours abroad which be greatly both against mine honour and honesty, which above all other things I esteem . . . that I am in the Tower and with child by my lord admiral. My lord, these are shameful slanders, for the which, besides the great desire I have to see the king's majesty, I shall most heartily desire your lordship that I may come to the court after your first determination, that I may show myself there as I am.[28]

Somerset did not agree to her request. In fact, he took such exception to the tone of this reply and an even tarter one, in which Elizabeth objected to the removal of Katherine Ashley and her formal replacement by Elizabeth Tyrwhit, that the princess gave him something approaching an apology, saying that she thought the appointment of a new governess would make people say 'that I deserved through my lewd demeanour to have such a one, and not that I mislike anything that your lordship of the council shall think good . . .'.[29]

By the time this letter was written, on 21 February, Thomas Seymour's fate was sealed. He had been asked, a few days earlier, how he knew that the council intended to proceed against him; he replied that he 'suspected it by diverse conjectures'. Again, he reiterated that he 'did never determine, in all his life, to remove the king out of [the] lord protector's hands, but by consent of the whole realm'.[30] Thereafter, he turned increasingly inwards, refusing to answer further questions unless his accusers faced him. Somerset informed the king of his uncle's intransigence but Thomas still refused to budge. He was never given a trial before his peers. Instead, an Act of Attainder (the same legal process that had been used to rid Henry VIII of Katherine Howard) was introduced into parliament. It passed unopposed in the House of Lords on 25 February, and in the House of Commons on 5 March, where it was opposed by only a handful of members.

In the end, the authorities had thrown everything they could at Thomas Seymour, even down to the accusation that, in connection with his wife's death, 'he helped to her end to hasten forth his other purposes'. The cumulative effect of his intentions were spelt out, reaching an inevitable conclusion: 'this marriage of your [the king's] sister, the getting of the rule and order of your majesty's mint at Bristol in to his hands, [the] 10,000 men he accounted himself furnished of, his preparations of victuals and money at your castle of the Holt [one of Seymour's properties on the Welsh borders] cannot otherwise be taken but to be a manifest declaration of a traitorous aspiring to your crown, to depose your majesty and to compass the death of your most noble person'.

The act concluded: 'considering that he is a member so unnatural, unkind and corrupt and such a heinous offender of your majesty and your laws as he cannot be suffered to remain in body of your grace's commonwealth but to the extreme danger of your highness and it is too dangerous an example that such a person, so much bound and so forgetful of it ... should remain among us'. He was to be 'adjudged and attainted of high treason and ... shall suffer such pains of death as in cases of high treason have been accustomed'.[31]

Faced with the reality of death, Thomas contemplated the wreck of his life. He had retreated into silence as far as those who condemned him were concerned and given up hope that family ties might, even at this extremity, compel his brother to exercise clemency. It must have been quite clear to him, as it was to Elizabeth, that Somerset would not save him. Later it was said that his fate was sealed by Duchess Anne, who threatened to leave her husband if he did not deal with Thomas. But while in the Tower Seymour made his peace with the God others accused him of rejecting, writing the following lines:

> Forgetting God
> to love a king
> Hath been my rod
> Or else nothing:
> In this frail life
> being a blast
> of care and strife
> till in be past.
> Yet God did call
> me in my pride
> lest I should fall
> and from him slide
> for whom loves he
> and not correct

that they may be
of his elect
The death haste thee
thou shalt me gain
Immortally
with him to reign
Who send the king
Like years as noye
In governing
His realm in joy
And after this
frail life such grace
As in his bliss
he may have place.[32]

He met his death bravely in the early morning of 20 March 1549. It took two blows of the axe to sever his head. Not content with executing him, the council now took pains to ensure that the assault on his reputation continued with a viciousness that matched the manner of his despatch. It was put about that he had written letters to Mary and Elizabeth urging them to rise up against his brother's regime and had hidden these rantings in the soles of his shoes. This accusation formed part of the sermon vilifying him preached by Hugh Latimer, a cleric who had received Seymour's financial support and had visited him in the Tower. Thomas had asked Latimer to preach his funeral sermon, presumably hoping that its sentiments would accord with those that he had himself expressed in his poem and reunite him, in death, with the wife whose own writings about the elect had expressed similar ideas. Latimer repaid his patron's trust by delivering the most thunderous condemnation in a sermon before Edward VI on 29 March. Thomas Seymour had been a popular man with his servants, the general populace of London and, for much of his nephew's life, with the king himself. So there was a need to ensure that the lord admiral was not remembered fondly. Latimer wanted his hearers to understand that bad lives tend to bad ends. He even questioned the likelihood that such a man could have repented of his sins. 'And when a man hath two strokes of the axe,' he pondered, 'who can tell but that between two strokes he doth repent? It is very hard to judge. Well, I will not go so nigh to work; but this I will say, if they ask me what I think of his death, that he died very dangerously, irksomely, horribly.' He went on to say: 'he was a man the farthest from the fear of God that I ever knew or heard of in England ... surely he was a wicked man and the realm is well rid of him'.[33]

Nicholas Throckmorton characterized Seymour's end very differently. For Throckmorton, it was other men's ambitions, as much as the admiral's, that brought about his downfall:

> Off went his head, they made a quick despatch,
> But ever since I thought him sure a beast
> Who causeless laboured to defile his nest
> Though guiltless, he, through malice, went to pot
> Not answering for himself nor knowing cause.[34]

And Harington, who languished another year in the Tower for his lord's sake, had not denied Seymour's contact with the Dorsets or his thoughts on Jane Grey's future prospects, but steadfastly refused to acknowledge that there was anything treasonable in his intent. Like Throckmorton he defended Thomas Seymour unreservedly as a

> Friend to God's truth, and foe to Rome's deceit ...
> Yet, against nature, reason and just laws
> His blood was spilt, guiltless, without just cause.[35]

But perhaps the truest, and most touching, remembrance of Thomas Seymour was pronounced by the girl with whom he had flirted and almost taken to disaster. When news of his execution was brought to her, Elizabeth remarked: 'This day died a man of much wit and very little judgement.' These few words, mingling as they do regretful tenderness and shrewd political assessment, are a fitting epitaph for one of Tudor England's most colourful courtiers. Thomas Seymour was a flawed man, but his detractors conveniently forgot that, in his younger days, he had served his king and country ably. The vilification of his reputation did the Edwardian regime little credit. He had no party, no clear strategy and no real aims beyond his obsession with the notion of separating the offices of Protector and king's Governor. Ambition, impatience and an inability to dissemble cost him dear. A more devious man would have bided his time and ensured that his support was real, not imagined. But Thomas Seymour was, in many ways, a man born out of his time. He saw himself as a sort of feudal baron, his prestige and power based on property and the loyalty of a personal following. Perhaps he was a great rascal, as Paget had declared. Yet both Katherine and Elizabeth, two of the most outstanding women of their time, loved him, despite his weaknesses. His importance in Elizabeth's development cannot be overstated, for he had awakened in her a lifelong penchant for men of roguish charm. She learned much from his fall, but she did not forget him. In one of her worst moments, when she was about to be sent to the Tower during her sister Mary's reign in 1554, she recalled that Somerset subsequently told her that 'if his brother had been allowed to speak with him, he would never have suffered'.[36]

LADY MARY SEYMOUR was left a dispossessed orphan by her father's death. She was not quite seven months old. Thomas had given her into the care of Katherine Brandon, duchess of Suffolk, Katherine Parr's close friend. His reasons for this course of action are unclear. It is hardly surprising that he would not have desired her to remain with the Somersets, who had been looking after her at Syon House while Thomas was in the Tower. Katherine Parr's own brother, meanwhile, had also fallen out with the Lord Protector over his attempts to annul his first marriage to Anne Bourchier (they were still locked together legally, despite Anne's elopement years before). His remarriage to Elisabeth Brooke, a lady of the court who had served his sister, was regarded as illegal and outrageous by the prim duke of Somerset. Northampton was scarcely in a position to offer shelter to his niece, and in any case he does not seem to have taken much interest in her. The duchess of Suffolk described him as 'having a weak back for such a burden'.[37] Anne Herbert and her husband, the survivors of many career setbacks themselves, apparently steered well clear. So Lady Mary Seymour was denied the affection of any members of her immediate family.

Thomas probably thought that the duchess of Suffolk, known for her strong religious views, mistress of large estates in Lincolnshire and the mother of two sons, would direct his daughter's upbringing in a responsible and loving environment. It was his dying wish that Mary should be assigned to the duchess's protection. But, as with Latimer, so with Katherine Brandon; he had been too trusting. The duchess of Suffolk's strident evangelical views did not encompass true Christian charity. She regarded Lady Mary Seymour as an expensive nuisance, for although the little girl came with a full complement of staff, a mini-household of her own, as befitted a queen's daughter, there were substantial costs in supporting this establishment, and after several months, when Somerset did not pay the £500 a year pension that had been agreed for Mary by the Privy Council three days before her father's execution, Katherine Brandon's patience was exhausted. She wrote an exasperated letter to William Cecil, clearly believing that his influence with the Somersets might succeed where hers had not: 'It is said', she began, 'that the best means of remedy to the sick is first plainly to confess and disclose the disease, wherefore, both for remedy and again for that my disease is so strong that it will not be hidden, I will disclose me unto you.' She was, she told him, in very straitened financial circumstances: 'All the world knoweth . . . what a very beggar I am.' And her situation was rapidly worsening, for a variety of causes, but 'amongst others . . . if you will understand, not least the queen's child hath layen, and still doth lie at my house, with her company about her, wholly at my charges. I have written to my lady of Somerset at large, that there be some pension allotted unto her according to my lord grace's promise. Now, good Cecil, help at a pinch all that you may help.' The duchess of Somerset had promised her some months ago that 'certain nursery plate' should be provided for Mary. She provided a list of the items that had come with the baby – the same ones that had been intended for the crimson and gold nursery at Sudeley Castle – and also included a letter from mistress Aglionby, the child's governess, who, she complained, 'with the maid's nurse and others, daily call for their wages, whose voices my ears hardly bear, but my coffers much worse'.[38] Even allowing for the duchess's pecuniary embarrassment (which may have been exaggerated, as was common at the time), it is a thoroughly unpleasant epistle. The picture it paints of an unwanted child, her anxious servants unpaid and her guardian describing her as a sickness, does the duchess of Suffolk little credit.

Perhaps the letter did eventually stir Somerset and the Privy Council into some sort of action. On 22 January 1550, less than a year after her father's death, application was made in the House of Commons for the restitution of Lady Mary Seymour, 'daughter of Thomas Seymour, knight, late Lord Seymour of Sudeley and late High Admiral of England, begotten of the body of Queen Katherine, late queen of England'. She was made eligible by this act to inherit any remaining property that had not been returned to the Crown at the time of her father's attainder. But, in truth, Mary's prospects were less optimistic than this might suggest. Much of her parents' land and goods had already passed into the hands of others.

Lady Mary Seymour never claimed any remaining part of her father's estate, and this is the last record we have of her. Her grant from the council was not renewed in September 1550, when it would have fallen due. The assumption must therefore be, in the absence of any further reference, that she was dead by the time of her second birthday. Childhood diseases produced high mortality rates in the sixteenth century, and it is likely that she succumbed at Grimsthorpe in Lincolnshire, still under the reluctant eye of the duchess of Suffolk. In the nineteenth century the historian Agnes Strickland, author of the *Lives of the Queens of England*, referred to a tradition that Lady Mary Seymour had survived, cared for by her governess, Elizabeth Aglionby, and that she had subsequently married Sir Edward Bushell, an Elizabethan courtier who later served Anne of Denmark, queen to James I. A Sussex family still claims to be descended from her. Such things are not, of course, impossible but it seems far more likely, in the absence of documentary proof, that Lady Mary, abandoned and unloved, left 'this frail life' at the mid-point of the sixteenth century, to join her parents in the 'bliss' that Thomas had so fervently hoped to find.

Two hundred years rolled over England. Through civil war, changing dynasties and the beginnings of empire, Katherine Parr rested in her tomb at Sudeley. The castle eventually passed into the hands of the Chandos family, staunch royalists, and suffered accordingly when the civil war ended. Left unfortifiable, it was abandoned and fell into ruin. The chapel also was neglected and the burial place of Katherine Parr forgotten, save for an over-looked manuscript in the College of Arms. Then, in the spring of 1782, a new local history of Gloucestershire was published, which caught the interest of the public. A group of visitors to the romantic ruin at Sudeley included several ladies whose curiosity was aroused by the remains of the chapel. Investigating further, members of the party 'observing a large block of alabaster fixed in the north wall of the chapel . . . imagined it might be the back of a monument formerly placed there. Led by this hint, they opened the ground not far from the wall.' To their astonishment, not far from the surface, they found a lead envelope coffin with the following inscription:

KP

Here lyeth Queen Katheryne Wife to Kinge
Henry the VIII and
The wife of Thomas
Lord of Sudely high
Admy . . . of Englond
And ynkle to Kyng
Edward the VI

Filled with curiosity, they cut two holes in the lead envelope. When they unwrapped the cloth covering the head, they found themselves gazing back across the centuries, into the face of Katherine Parr as she had looked on the night of her death in September 1548. The manner of her burial and the fact that she had lain all this time undisturbed meant that the queen was uncorrupted, her flesh still firm to the touch. At first awestruck by this sight, the ladies' excitement soon gave way to consternation. Hastily reburying the body, they did not seal it properly again.[39]

Much damage had already been done to Katherine's corpse by the mere act of opening her coffin. Decay inevitably set in, and when further investigations of the tomb took place a few years later, the face was worn to bone. But a crown of ivy had wound itself around Katherine's skull, a poignant reminder that this remarkable woman, attractive and sensual, intelligent and capable, deeply loving God as well as man, had been the last queen of Henry VIII.

Epilogue

Hatfield, 17 November 1558

Elizabeth Tudor had been living quietly at Hatfield for some time, watching and waiting. But since the beginning of the month there was a steady stream of visitors, despite the epidemic sweeping the country. The controller of the queen's household and the secretary to the Privy Council had both been to see her, as had Queen Mary's favourite lady-in-waiting, Jane Dormer, bringing some of her mistress's jewels. Just one week earlier, Elizabeth received the count of Feria, the envoy of her brother-in-law, King Philip. He found her much changed from the obliging young woman he had seen in the summer. This Elizabeth was independent-minded, imperious even, acknowledging no great debt of gratitude to Philip or anyone, save the people of England itself. And she was full of indignation at her treatment in recent years. Any thought that she would be tractable was clearly misplaced. He got the distinct and uncomfortable impression that she knew exactly what course she would take.

By 17 November the days were much colder, but Elizabeth believed in the benefits of fresh air. She continued to take her accustomed exercise in the extensive grounds that surrounded the old palace of Hatfield. They were familiar from her childhood, for she had spent much time there with both her brother and sister during the reign of Henry VIII. An energetic walker, she soon left the house behind. Legend has it that about a third of a mile away, in the wooded parkland that surrounded the estate, she stopped under an oak tree. Perhaps she was alerted by the sound of approaching horses. At that moment, as the riders drew near, she already knew what her destiny would be.

In the decade that followed Katherine Parr's death, Elizabeth had grown from a flighty child-woman into a confident (if more than a little embittered) queen-in-waiting. It was a hard and perilous journey, through an England convulsed by rebellion, intrigue and religious turmoil. Many of those she knew in Katherine's lifetime were now dead. The duke of Somerset, overthrown by social discontent and the mounting opposition of his fellow politicians, followed his brother to the block in 1552. Edward VI died after a long illness in the summer of 1553, disinheriting both of his sisters and bequeathing his throne to Lady Jane Grey. Edward's regard for his cousin suggests that Thomas Seymour's ambitions for their eventual marriage may not have been entirely fanciful. To everyone's surprise, Mary Tudor had fought courageously and successfully for the throne that was rightfully hers, while Elizabeth sat on the sidelines (again at Hatfield) awaiting the outcome.

Mary's accession meant ruin for the Dudley family, into which Lady Jane Grey had been reluctantly married in the spring of 1553. John Dudley, duke of Northumberland, who replaced Somerset at the head of the Privy Council, was executed for treason because he had supported Jane Grey and within a year Jane herself, her husband and father all lost their heads. None of this blood-letting seemed to aid Elizabeth, however. Her relationship with Mary, progressively cooling since their father's death, was damaged beyond repair by implication in the 1554 rebellion that cost Jane Grey her life. Elizabeth protested her innocence, as she would do ever after, but was imprisoned in the Tower for a few months and then placed under what amounted to house arrest. Mary, consumed by love for her husband, Philip of Spain, and committed to the introduction of a reformed Catholicism in England, eventually managed to control her dislike of Anne Boleyn's daughter, so that an uneasy peace characterized their dealings with each other in the last year of Mary's life. When England's first queen regnant realized, in the autumn of 1558, she was dying from a viral disease similar to influenza that had already taken so many other lives, she was finally prevailed upon to name Elizabeth as her successor.

Now, as the messengers from St James's Palace dismounted and knelt before her, Elizabeth had final proof that her sister was, indeed, dead: they gave her Mary's coronation ring. The story that she dropped to her knees herself, quoting Psalm 118, 'This is the Lord's doing: it is marvellous in our eyes', has no contemporary corroboration but has become part of the heritage of England. Given Elizabeth's knowledge of scripture and her ability to quote freely, it is something that she might well have said. Certainly she did tell her lords, and probably on the day of her accession, that 'I mean to direct all mine actions by good advice and council'.[1] It was an approach that would have found favour with her stepmother.

Despite the demands of the early years of her rule, which were far from easy, Elizabeth did not forget those who had been close to Katherine Parr and Thomas Seymour in the frivolous days of Chelsea and Hanworth, before the harsh realities of mid-Tudor England closed in upon them all. She was godmother to John Harington's son (also named John) and when Harington's first wife died, he married Isabella Markham, one of Elizabeth's ladies-in-waiting. In 1567, Harington gave the queen the portrait of Thomas Seymour that now hangs in the National Portrait Gallery in London.

Nor were Katherine's relatives forgotten. Anne died four years after her sister, in 1552. Buried with great pomp by her husband in St Paul's Cathedral, she founded the line of the earls of Pembroke which exists to this day. But William Parr lived on, a

Author's Note

A nineteenth-century writer described Katherine Parr as one of our best but least known queens. She is the one, in the famous rhyme that schoolchildren used to learn, who survived marriage to Henry VIII. Yet despite the occasional film and television portrayal and a handful of historical novels (none of which do her justice) this judgement of Katherine's role in English history still rings true. Her last resting place, in the chapel of Sudeley Castle in Gloucestershire, was forgotten for over 200 years until rediscovered in the 1780s, leading to a small revival of interest. For the Victorians, she was a worthy, matronly lady of unimpeachable Protestant views, who had narrowly escaped being the victim of a Catholic plot intended to add her to the list of beheaded wives of the much-married old king. In our own time, gender historians have examined her period as queen with renewed vigour, finding an all together different woman from the cosy image of the nurse who tended Henry's damaged legs.

But the real interest of Katherine Parr lies beyond any stereotypes of Protestant icon or proto-feminist. It is not exactly a rags-to-riches story – Katherine was the daughter of courtiers, but so were three of Henry's other wives – yet it is one of great drama, reflecting the extraordinary times in which Katherine Parr lived. She was a remarkable woman, who had survived much even before she married Henry VIII as his sixth queen. Like Henry, she viewed marriage as a natural and desirable state and so she married once more, finally, for love, with tragic results. She deserves to be better known and appreciated and I hope this biography will bring her to life for a wider audience.

One of the great pleasures of writing about Katherine Parr has been the opportunity to visit the places she lived and to meet the people associated with them. I should particularly like to thank Geoff and Carole Wood for letting me visit Stowe Manor in Northamptonshire, left to Katherine by her second husband, Lord Latimer. The house is much altered but some Tudor aspects still remain and Geoff and Carole are rightly proud of their lovely home. Their kindness and hospitality was much appreciated. Similarly, Charles Hudson let me visit Wyke Manor, near Pershore in Worcestershire, which has been in his family now for hundreds of years. The lock said to be of Katherine's hair which he allowed me to see is very beautiful. I must also thank Jean Bray, the archivist at Sudeley Castle, for her support and interest, and for the private tour she gave me of the castle.

John Guy and Maria Hayward gave prompt and helpful replies to requests for advice and information, and Leanda de Lisle and Susan Ronald have both talked with me about Katherine and her place in Tudor history. My thanks to all of them and to Dr Susan E. James, whose twenty years of research on Katherine and the Parr family is an important source for anyone writing about Henry VIII's last queen.

Finally, my gratitude to the team at Macmillan and my editors, Georgina Morley and Lorraine Green, for their enthusiasm and support. My agent, Andrew Lownie, is always there for his authors and, as ever, my husband, George, provided a willing ear and eye as I wrote.

Notes

Abbreviations

BL — British Library

Cal SP Spanish — *Calendar of letters, despatches and state papers relating to the negotiations between England and Spain, preserved in the archives at Vienna, Simancas, Besancon and Brussels*, ed. R. Tyler et al. (London, 1867–1954)

L&P — *Letters and Papers, Foreign and Domestic, of the Reign of Henry VIII, 1509–47*, ed. J. S. Brewer et al., 21 vols and addenda (London, 1862–1932)

NA — National Archives

ODNB — *Oxford Dictionary of National Biography*

One – The Courtiers of the White Rose

1 Both the Percys and the Nevilles originally had strong Lancastrian connections which had seen them rise to become earls of Northumberland and Westmoreland respectively. Henry IV's usurpation and the difficulties of the reign of his grandson, Henry VI, brought them into conflict with the Crown. This uneasy relationship continued throughout the Tudor era.

2 Sir William Parr, founder of the family, was a member of John of Gaunt's retinue. He married Elizabeth de Roos in about 1380, gaining, through her, one-quarter of the barony of Kendal and lordship of Kendal Castle. The title of baron, however, eluded the Parrs until it was

conferred on Katherine Parr's brother, William, in 1539. See *ODNB* entry for the Parr family.

3 Precise details of how Edward of Westminster, Prince of Wales, met his death are lacking. He probably died in the fierce fighting as his broken forces fell back towards the town of Tewkesbury itself. Though his end may not have been at the hands of the brothers of the king, as Shakespeare depicts, it was undoubtedly violent.

4 In 1464, Edward IV had required all recipients of lands, offices and annuities to pay one-quarter of their income to the Crown. This would have been a swingeing tax in times of peace but during the civil wars, when it was difficult to manage lands effectively, it was even more harsh.

5 George, duke of Clarence, the king's traitorous younger brother, had died in the Tower of London in 1478, almost certainly on Edward IV's orders.

6 Ingulph's *Chronicle of the Abbey of Croyland*, transl. Henry T. Riley (London, 1854), pp. 481–2.

7 C. L. Scofield, *The Life and Reign of Edward IV* (London, 1923), pp. 367–8.

8 D. A. L. Morgan, 'The House of Policy: The Political Role of the Late Plantagenet Household, 1422–1485', in D. R. Starkey, ed., *The English Court from the Wars of the Roses to the Civil War* (Harlow, 1987), p. 68.

9 Sir Thomas Malory, *La Morte d'Arthur* (London, 1889), preface, quoted in Derek Wilson, *In the Lion's Court* (London, 2002), p. 71.

10 Quoted in J. J. Scarisbrick, *Henry VIII* (London, 1997), p. 16.

11 Susan E. James, *Kateryn Parr, the Making of a Queen* (Aldershot, 1999), p. 17.

Two – A Formidable Mother

1 List of Maud, Lady Parr's jewels, in her will, NA, PCC 12 Thower (1530), quoted in James, *Kateryn Parr*.

2 All that remains of Rye House today is the partially restored fifteenth-century gatehouse. In the seventeenth century it was the centre of a plot to assassinate Charles II and replace him with his Catholic brother, James.

3 Elizabeth Cheyney was the daughter of Thomas and William Parr's only sister, Anne. She was orphaned at an early age and William Parr seems to have assumed responsibility for her.

4 Sir Thomas Parr's *Horae ad Usum Sarum*, Cambridge University Library, quoted in James, *Kateryn Parr*, p. 30.

5 Quoted in Charles Sturge, *Cuthbert Tunstal* (London, 1938), p. 55.
6 Sturge, *Cuthbert Tunstal*, p. 25.
7 Cuthbert Tunstall, *In Praise of Matrimony* (1518), quoted in Sturge, *Cuthbert Tunstal*, p. 59.
8 This assertion is made in Anthony Martienssen, *Queen Katherine Parr* (London, 1975), pp. 30–7.
9 Sturge, *Cuthbert Tunstal*, pp. 72–4.
10 Dakota Lee Hamilton, 'The Household of Queen Katherine Parr' (Oxford University, D.Phil thesis, 1992), pp. 311–12.
11 E. E. Reynolds, *Thomas More and Erasmus* (London, 1965), p. 135.
12 BL Additional MS 24.965, ff. 23 and 24.
13 Quoted in Martienssen, *Queen Katherine Parr*, pp. 40–1.
14 Martienssen, *Queen Katherine Parr*, pp. 42–3.
15 Quoted in Beverley A. Murphy, *Bastard Prince* (Gloucester, 2003), p. 61.
16 See James, *Kateryn Parr*, pp. 42–4.
17 Quoted in *ODNB* entry for John Palsgrave.
18 Quoted in Murphy, *Bastard Prince*, p. 76.

Three – The Marriage Game

1 William Camden, *Britannia* (English transl., London, 1637), p. 543.
2 Quoted in Gerald A. J. Hodgett, *Tudor Lincolnshire*, History of Lincolnshire VI (Lincoln, 1975), p. 1.
3 S. J. Gunn, 'The Rise of the Burgh Family, c.1431–1550', in Phillip Lindley, ed., *Gainsborough Old Hall* (Society of Lincolnshire History and Archaeology, 1991), p. 9.
4 Graham Platts, *Land and People in Medieval Lincolnshire*, History of Lincolnshire IV (Lincoln, 1985), p. 194.
5 Gunn, 'The Rise of the Burgh Family', p. 9.
6 James, *Kateryn Parr*, p. 61.
7 Maud Parr was correct when she referred to Borough as Sir Thomas in her will, but he was made a baron and entered the House of Lords shortly after his son married Katherine Parr.
8 Lady Elizabeth Burgh to Thomas Cromwell, 13 November 1537, *L&P*, 12, ii, 1074.
9 NA, PROB 11 Thower (1530), quoted in James, *Kateryn Parr*, p. 432.

Four – Lady Latimer

1 *L&P*, 7, 438.
2 Katherine Parr, *Lamentation of A Sinner*, March 1548, f.Fib-iiib, quoted in James, *Kateryn Parr*, p. 68.
3 The exterior of Snape Castle can be seen from the road and the path that takes visitors to the chapel. The chapel is open daily but the castle is closed to the public.
4 *L&P*, 11, 772, quoted in G. W. Bernard, *The King's Reformation* (London, 2005), p. 185. For detail on the wider opposition to Henry VIII, see ch. 2 of Bernard.
5 Revaluations of monastic wealth were not new, but most of the great orders in the north of England had been exempt inspection. See Bernard, *The King's Reformation*, p. 245.

Five – The Pilgrimage of Grace

1 Thomas Meynell's book, f. 1, from the Meynell MSS in Ampleforth Abbey Library, now on microfilm in the North Yorkshire Record Office, Northallerton, ZIQ/MIC 2050, quoted in Sarah L. Bastow, 'Aspects of the History of the Catholic Gentry of Yorkshire from the Pilgrimage of Grace to the First Civil War' (University of Huddersfield D.Phil. thesis, 2002).
2 *L&P*, 11, 503.
3 *L&P*, 11, i., 970, quoted in Bernard, *The King's Reformation*, p. 312.
4 *L&P*, 11, 533.
5 *L&P*, 11, 569.
6 For a detailed explanation of the oath written by Robert Aske and its proper interpretation, see Bernard, *The King's Reformation*, pp. 328–32. This gives the oath in both the original and the modern spelling; I have used only the latter. Professor Bernard notes, in particular, that the beginning of the oath has been widely misinterpreted to read that the Pilgrimage was *not* for the common wealth (my italics), when, in fact, the clause should be read as a whole. It is, indeed, a 'Pilgrimage of Grace for the common wealth' and there should not be a comma before the first 'but', as appears in Geoffrey Moorhouse's *The Pilgrimage of Grace* (London, 2002), p. 128. The editor of *L&P* 12 did not give the full text of the oath, which is in NA, SP1/108, f. 48.
7 *L&P*, 11, 760.

8 From J. T. Fowler (ed.), *Rites of Durham, being a description or brief declaration of all the ancient monuments, rites and customs belonging or being within the monastical church of Durham before the suppression, 1539*, Surtees Society 107 (1903).

9 Many other castles in the region were similarly at risk. Some, such as Skipton, were also in disrepair.

10 *L&P*, 11, 729.

11 Quoted in Bernard, *The King's Reformation*, p. 339.

12 *L&P*, 11, 909.

13 *L&P*, 11, 955.

14 *L&P*, 11, 1064.

15 *L&P*, 11, 1175.

16 *L&P*, 12, i, 1022.

17 *L&P*, 11, 1246.

18 *L&P*, 12, i, 103.

19 *L&P*, 12, i, 173.

20 *L&P*, 12, i, 81.

21 *L&P*, 12, i, 632.

22 *L&P*, 12, i, 131.

23 L&P, 12, ii, 101.

24 L&P, 12, ii, 31.

25 This visit, its background and the hostility felt by northerners is brilliantly captured in the third of C. J. Sansom's Tudor detective novels, *Sovereign* (London, 2006).

26 See Martienssen, *Queen Katherine Parr*, pp. 125–6.

27 *L&P*, 15, 776.

28 Will of John Neville, Baron Latimer, NA, PROB 11/29: Register Spert.

Six – Two Suitors

1 Charles Wriothesley, *A Chronicle of England*, ed. W. D. Hamilton, Camden Society, New Series, 11 (London, 1875–7), p. 141.

2 This confusion over the tailor's account may seem a minor cavil, but it has led to basic misunderstandings of the timing of Katherine Parr's relationship with both Henry VIII and Princess Mary. See D. Starkey, *The Six Wives of Henry VIII* (London, 2004), p. 815. There is no evidence that Katherine held any position in Mary's household. For the difficulties caused to some of her servants by late payment in Katherine's household as queen, see below, Chapter 7.

3 Undated, spring 1547, Dent-Brocklehurst MS, Sudeley Castle.

4 The Seymours were not all eager for advancement. Henry Seymour, the brother born between Edward and Thomas, lived quietly in Hampshire, dying in 1578.

5 The statement that affection would lead him to court but he would take care that interest kept him there is often attributed to Thomas Seymour (BL Sloane MS 1523, f. 36). Yet the line appears under the general heading 'The Seymors' and is not specifically referenced to Thomas. Sloane MS 1523 is a very curious collection of anecdotes and moralizing observations on Tudor courtiers (it also contains a treatise on growing fruit trees) written much later by an unknown person. Even more oddly, there is a brief paragraph on the Parrs that refers to none of the family directly but appears to accuse them of being self-interested upstarts.

6 John Strype refers to a story in his *Ecclesiastical Memorials* that Seymour had seduced a low-born woman, who subsequently became a prostitute and denounced his part in her downfall while on her way to the gallows for robbery. See Strype, *Ecclesiastical Memorials* (Oxford, 1822), vol. 2, part 1, p. 197. This story was apparently seized upon by Hugh Latimer in his general character assassination of Thomas Seymour after the latter's execution in 1549.

7 A letter jointly signed with John Dudley (later duke of Northumberland and close friend of his brother's at this time). March 1537, *L&P*, 12, i, 602.

8 Quoted in John Maclean, *The Life of Sir Thomas Seymour* (London, 1869) p. 4. This rare book is something of a curiosity. It was part of a series on the Lives of the Masters-General of the Ordnance (a post held by Sir Thomas Seymour) and only 100 copies were printed. The British Library does not have one, but the London Library does.

9 Gregory Cromwell was Elizabeth Seymour's second husband. They were married some time in 1538 and had five children before Gregory's death in 1551.

10 *L&P*, 13, i, 1375.

11 See below, Chapter 10.

12 John Foxe, *Acts and Monuments of the Church containing the History and Suffering of the Martyrs*, ed. Revd M. Hobart Seymour (London, 1838), pt 1, p. 615.

13 Quoted in Maria Hayward, *Dress at the Court of King Henry VIII* (London, 2007), p. 3.

14 S. Haynes, ed., *A Collection of State Papers Relating to Affairs with the Reigns of King Henry VIII, King Edward VI, Queen Mary and Queen Elizabeth . . . left by William Cecil, Lord Burghley* (London, 1740), p. 6.

15 Hayward, *Dress at the Court of King Henry VIII*, p. 96.

16 James P. Carley, *The Books of Henry VIII and his Wives* (London, 2004),
    p. 27. For further information on the libraries of Henry VIII, see Carley,
    The Libraries of Henry VIII (Corpus of British Medieval Library
    Catalogues, 7, 2002).
17 Ibid., pp. 31–3.
18 Bernard, *The King's Reformation*, p. 574.
19 Charles Lloyd, ed., *Formularies of Faith Put Forth by Authority during the
    Reign of Henry VIII* (Oxford, 1825), p. 215.
20 See Alec Ryrie, *The Gospel and Henry VIII: Evangelicals in the Early
    English Reformation* (Cambridge, 2003), ch. 1.
21 Lord Latimer does not appear to have been present at the battle of
    Solway Moss.
22 Dent-Brocklehurst MS, Sudeley Castle.
23 *L&P*, 18, i, 740.
24 *L&P*, 18, i, 873.

Seven – The Queen and Her Court

1   *L&P*, 18, i, 894.
2   Quoted in A. J. Slavin, *Politics and Profit: A Study of Sir Ralph Sadler,
    1507–1547* (Cambridge, 1966), p. 138.
3   *Cal SP Spanish*, 6, ii, 188.
4   Wriothesley, *Chronicle*, p. 145.
5   For details of the royal itinerary in the summer and autumn of 1543, see
    Starkey, *Six Wives*, pp. 716–17.
6   *L&P*, 18, i, 918.
7   None of these palaces survives. Hanworth was altered in the seventeenth
    century and destroyed by fire in 1797; Chelsea was demolished in the
    early eighteenth century and Mortlake also has long since disappeared.
8   The shift, or chemise (basically an undergarment) was generally used for
    sleeping.
9   For further details, see Hayward, *Dress at the Court of King Henry VIII*,
    pp. 185–9.
10 NA, E101/432/13. f. 6, quoted in James, *Kateryn Parr*, p. 127.
11 Skut had a number of private clients as well. They included Lady Honor
    Lisle, the wife of the deputy governor of Calais.
12 Susan E. James, *The Feminine Dynamic in English Art, 1485–1603*
    (Aldershot, 2009), pp. 28–9.
13 Hayward, *Dress at the Court of King Henry VIII*, p. 185.
14 The first appearance of an order for a farthingale in the accounts of the

Great Wardrobe is for one ordered for the eleven-year-old Princess Elizabeth in 1545. Mary also owned several and favoured the crimson satin chosen by her stepmother. See Hayward, *Dress at the Court of King Henry VIII*, p. 162.

15 On this and Katherine's religious and intellectual development, see below, Chapter 10.

16 NA, E315/161, f. 46.

17 Morris Addison Hatch, 'The Ascham Letters' (Cornell University D. Phil., 1948), p. 154.

18 'Narrative of the Visit of the Duke de Najera', in *Archaeologica xxiii* (1831), pp. 344–57.

19 *Cal SP Spanish*, 7, pt 1 (1544), 39.

20 NA, E101/426/3. f. 22, quoted in James, *Kateryn Parr*, p. 144.

21 See James, *Kateryn Parr*, pp. 120–1.

22 See Hamilton, 'The Household of Queen Katherine Parr', Introduction.

23 *L&P*, 19, ii, 201.

24 'The Life and Death of Sir Nicholas Throckmorton, transcribed AD 1678', in Cole's MSS History of the Family of Throckmorton, Warwickshire County Record Office, CR 1998/LCB/18.

25 See the curious comments about the Parrs in BL Sloane MS 1523: 'The common rule of favourites is to bring in all their relations about them, to adorn and support them; but a wall (if) it hath a firm bottom needs no buttress.' This is, however, a retrospective judgement.

26 For Hoby see *ODNB* entry, 2004.

27 *L&P*, 19, i, 724.

28 Starkey, *Six Wives*, p. 711.

29 BL Lansdowne MS 97, f. 43, quoted in James, *Kateryn Parr*, p. 195.

Eight – The Royal Children

1 Agnes Strickland, *Lives of the Queens of England* (London, 1852), vol. 3, p. 203.

2 *L&P*, 16, 380, quoted in Christopher Skidmore, *Edward VI* (London, 2007), p. 27.

3 BL Cotton MS Vespasian, F xiii, f. 221.

4 BL Cotton MS Nero, C x f. 6, printed in James O. Halliwell, *Letters of the Kings of England* (London, 1848), vol. 2, p. 4.

5 BL Cotton MS Nero, C.x. f. 8.

6 *L&P*, 7, 296.

7 For a more detailed account of Mary's travail, see Linda Porter, *Mary Tudor: The First Queen* (London, 2007), chs. 3, 4 and 5.

8 Simon Thurley, *The Royal Palaces of Tudor England* (London, 1993), pp. 78–9.

9 BL Cotton MS, Vespasian, F iii, f. 29, in Anne Crawford, ed., *Letters of the Queens of England* (London, 1994), p. 219. The date of 1544 ascribed to this letter cannot be correct. Katherine refers to not having seen Mary for some time and the fact that she was at her dower manor of Hanworth points to it being after Henry's death, and her marriage to Thomas Seymour; 20 September 1547 seems more likely.

10 *L&P*, 18, ii, 41.

11 *1544, 35 Henry VIII. C. 1.3 Statutes of the Realm* 3, p. 955.

12 *L&P*, 11, 203.

13 Elizabeth I, *Collected Works*, ed. Leah S. Marcus et al. (Chicago and London, 2002), pp. 5–6.

14 NA, E101/423/12.

15 David Starkey has suggested that there might have been illness in Elizabeth's household and that she had been required to wait in a form of quarantine until any danger to others was passed. See David Starkey, *Elizabeth* (London, 2001), p. 37. Katherine's apartments at St James's had been prepared for her during the time Elizabeth was actually there, though it is not clear whether the queen used them. See *L&P*, 19, ii, 688.

16 Elizabeth I, *Collected Works*, pp. 6–7.

17 Edward was at Hampton Court at the express instruction of his father the king, who apparently felt it was the safest place for him.

18 *L&P*, 19, ii. 58.

Nine – Regent of England

1 John Knox, *The First Blast of the Trumpet against the Monstrous Regiment of Women*, 1558. Elizabeth I, though not a Catholic, was highly displeased by Knox's work and his attempts to apologize to her fell on stony ground.

2 See below, Chapter 10.

3 *ODNB* entry for Thomas Thirlby.

4 NA, SP 1/12.

5 *Cal SP Spanish*, 7, pt ii, 56.

6 In his final despatch from England, Eustace Chapuys gives a detailed

account of his last meeting with Katherine which began with the queen
saying that the king had discussed the ambassador's departure with her
the night before.

7 *Cal SP Spanish*, 7, pt i, 46.
8 *Cal SP Spanish*, 7, pt ii, 156.
9 Luke MacMahon, 'The English Invasion of France in 1544' (University
   of Warwick, M.Phil. thesis, 1992).
10 *Cal SP Spanish*, 7, pt ii, 124.
11 Ibid., 68.
12 Printed in Betty S. Travitsky and Patrick Cullen, eds., *The Early Modern
   Englishwoman: A Facsimile Library of Essential Works*: Part 1, *Printed
   Writings, 1500–1640* (Aldershot, 1997), Vol. 3: *Katherine Parr*.
13 BL Cotton MS, Caligula E4, f. 55.
14 *Cal SP Spanish*, 7, 148. See James, *Kateryn Parr*, p. 183.
15 *L&P*, 19, i, 943.
16 *L&P*, 19, ii, 39.
17 *L&P*, 19, ii, 231 and 332.
18 BL Lansdowne MS 1236, f. 9, quoted in James, *Kateryn Parr*, p. 171.
19 *L&P*, 19, ii, 201.
20 *L&P*, 19, ii, 251.
21 The prayer is printed in its entirety in Travitsky and Cullen, *Katherine
   Parr*.

Ten – The Queen's Gambit

1 *Cal SP Spanish*, 8, 51.
2 The will of Margaret Neville, NA, PROB 11 Alen, printed in full in
   James, *Kateryn Parr*, pp. 417–18.
3 BL Lansdowne MS 76, art. 81, f. 182.
4 See Chapter 8.
5 Bernard, *The King's Reformation*, p. 525.
6 *ODNB* 2004.
7 The order that the new litany be used in every parish in the realm was
   made on 11 June 1544.
8 See James, *Kateryn Parr*, pp. 200–7.
9 From the preface to *The First Tome or Volume of the Paraphrase of
   Erasmus upon the New Testament*, imprinted in London at Fleet Street at
   the sign of the sun by Edward Whitchurch, the last day of January 1548.
10 Quotations are from the facsimile edition of Katherine Parr's *The
   Lamentation of a Sinner*, in Travitsky and Cullen, *Katherine Parr*.

11 These comments sit uncomfortably beside the earnest attempts of feminist historians to capture Katherine as a sort of sixteenth-century feminist icon. Much ink was spilt in the 1990s by (mostly) American academics on Katherine's writings.

12 Elizabeth I, *Collected Works*, pp. 9–10.

13 Starkey, *Six Wives*, pp. 757–8.

14 King Henry VIII's speech in parliament, Edward Hall, *Chronicle* (London, 1809 edition).

15 *The Correspondence of Matthew Parker*, the Parker Society, vol. 49, pp. 36–7, from the Parker MSS in Corpus Christi College, University of Cambridge.

16 *Cal SP Spanish*, 8, 204.

17 J. G. Nichols, ed., *Narratives of the Days of the Reformation*, Camden Society, Old Series, 77 (1859), p. 309. The writer quoted is the Jesuit priest Robert Persons, commenting many years later, and from a far from objective viewpoint.

18 The reference to Lady Lane is often mistaken for 'Lady Jane' and thought to be Lady Jane Grey. But Foxe's text is quite clear. Jane Grey probably did attend court from time to time with her mother during the period that Katherine Parr was married to Henry but apart from the inherent unlikelihood of a ten-year-old girl being involved in this desperate mission (even supposing it to be true), she does not figure in John Foxe's account.

19 The story in its entirety appears in Foxe, *Acts and Monuments*, pp. 614–17.

20 Lady Tyrwhit, however, was still alive. She did not die until 1578. Her subsequent reporting of Katherine's own deathbed is not, however, entirely reliable and her strong Protestant faith would have given her motive to embroider these earlier events.

21 Crome was something of a serial recanter, but his behaviour was prompted by a belief that reform would prosper through the survival of its adherents, rather than their martyrdom. His behaviour here follows the same pattern as Thomas Cranmer's ten years later, the main difference being that Cranmer was burnt and Crome, who survived the Marian persecutions, died of natural causes early in the reign of Elizabeth I.

22 Ryrie, *The Gospel and Henry VIII*, p. 55.

23 Foxe, *Acts and Monuments*, pp. 611–12.

24 Foxe, *Acts and Monuments*, p. 613.

25 James, *Kateryn Parr*, p. 265.

26 NA, E101/424/12, f. 157.

27 Robert Hutchinson, *The Last Days of Henry VIII* (London, 2005), p. 168.

28 *L&P*, 21, ii, 20 and 136.

29 Ibid., ii, 686.

30 Ibid., item 92, 1383.

31 *Cal SP Spanish*, 8, 370.

32 *L&P*, 21, ii, 684.

33 The names of Westminster and Whitehall were sometimes used interchangeably. Westminster had been a separate palace but was damaged by fire and abandoned at the beginning of Henry VIII's reign.

34 Hutchinson, *The Last Days of Henry VIII*, p. 220.

Eleven – The Secrets of Spring

1   NA, LC2/2, f. 4.

2   For a full description of Henry VIII's funeral, see Hutchinson, *The Last Days of Henry VIII*, ch. 10.

3   *L&P*, 21, ii, 634.

4   There has been much discussion over the validity of Henry VIII's will and whether it was altered after his death. See E. W. Ives, 'Henry VIII's Will – A Forensic Conundrum', *Historical Journal*, 25 (1992), pp. 779–804 and Porter, *Mary Tudor*, pp. 150–1.

5   The duke of Norfolk, England's premier noble, awaited execution at the time of Henry VIII's death. His fate hung in the balance during the three days before Henry's demise was announced. Discussions about it may also have played a part in the delay. Norfolk was spared the block but kept prisoner in the Tower of London.

6   NA, E101/426/3, ff. 6 and 23.

7   Historical Manuscripts Commission, *Calendar of the Manuscripts of the most Honourable the Marquis of Salisbury, K.G., preserved at Hatfield House, Hertfordshire*. Part 1, 1883, no 220.

8   BL MS Harleian 5087, f. 14, printed in Halliwell, *Letters of the Kings of England*, vol. 2, p. 25.

9   *L&P*, 19, ii, 501, item 2: 'The meetest place for the king's great ships to lie is thought to be at the Isle of Wight from whence, if the Frenchmen would stop the passage betwixt Dover and Boulogne or Calais, the king's ships may cut between them and their own coast, and so drive them to fight, or else go to Flanders or Scotland.'

10 Dent-Brocklehurst MS, Sudeley Castle.

11 Printed in James, *Kateryn Parr*, p. 404.

12 Bodleian Library, Ashmolean MS 1729; James, *Kateryn Parr*, p. 406.
13 James, *Kateryn Parr*, p. 404.
14 Bodleian Library, Rawlinson MS D.1070.4 and NA, SP 10/1, f. 43; James, *Kateryn Parr*, pp. 408 and 410.
15 BL Lansdowne MS 1236, f. 26. Porter, *Mary Tudor*, pp. 152–4.
16 Printed in Strype, *Ecclesiastical Memorials*, vol. 2, pt. 1, pp. 59–60.
17 J. G. Nichols, ed., *The Literary Remains of King Edward VI* (Roxburghe Club, 1857), vol. 1, no. 46.
18 Haynes, ed., *State Papers*, p. 61.
19 Quoted in Strickland, *Lives of the Queens of England*, vol. 3, p. 268. In fact, Anne of Cleves also took precedence over the duchess.
20 Dent-Brocklehurst MS, Sudeley Castle.
21 Haynes, *State Papers*, p. 76.
22 James, *Kateryn Parr*, p. 312.
23 The precise date on which Elizabeth and her retinue took up residence with the queen is unknown. But Katherine Ashley, Elizabeth's chief gentlewoman, is said to have teased Seymour about his marriage before it became public knowledge. See Skidmore, *Edward VI*, p. 73.
24 Haynes, *State Papers*, p. 83.

Twelve – 'This frail life'

1 William Cecil's preface to Katherine Parr's *The Lamentation of a Sinner*, in Travitsky and Cullen, *Katherine Parr*.
2 Leanda de Lisle, *The Sisters Who Would be Queen* (London, 2009).
3 Hatch, 'The Ascham Letters', pp. 283–6.
4 Throckmorton MS, stanza 67, Warwickshire County Record Office, CR1998/LCB/18.
5 Thomas Parry's confession, Haynes, *State Papers*, p. 96.
6 This and preceding quotes from the confession of Katherine Ashley, in Haynes, *State Papers*, pp. 99–100.
7 Haynes, *State Papers*, p. 96.
8 Elizabeth I, *Collected Works*, pp. 18–19.
9 Ibid., p. 19.
10 Skidmore, *Edward VI*, pp. 84–5.
11 Elizabeth I, *Collected Works*, p. 20.
12 Haynes, *State Papers*, p. 62.
13 NA, SP10/4, f. 14, printed in James, *Kateryn Parr*, p. 412.
14 Thomas Hearne, ed., *Sylloge Epistolarum* (Oxford, 1716), p. 151.
15 Haynes, *State Papers*, pp. 103–4.

16 College of Arms MS: RR21/C ff. 98–9 and MS R20.

17 Haynes, *State Papers*, pp. 77–8.

18 NA SP 10/5, ff. 5, 8b.

19 Stephen Alford, *Kingship and Politics in the Reign of Edward VI* (Cambridge, 2002), p. 99.

20 Haynes, *State Papers*, p. 97.

21 *Cal SP Spanish*, 9, 1547–9, p. 332.

22 Ibid., pp. 332–3.

23 Ibid., p. 340.

24 C. S. Knighton, ed., *Calendar of State Papers Domestic of the Reign of Edward VI* (London, 1992), no. 189.

25 Haynes, *State Papers*, p. 84.

26 Ibid., pp. 87–8.

27 Ibid., pp. 88–9.

28 Elizabeth I, *Collected Works*, p. 24.

29 Ibid., p. 32.

30 Haynes, *State Papers*, pp. 107–8.

31 Act for the Attainder of Sir Thomas Seymour, 2 and 3 Edward VI c.17.

32 John Harington, *Nugae Antiquae* (London, 1769), vol. 3, p. 259.

33 John Watkins, ed., *The Sermons of Hugh Latimer*, (London, 1926), p. 162; Strype, *Ecclesiastical Memorials*, vol. 2, pt 1, pp. 198–9, where it is noted that the last edition of Latimer's sermons, the passage accusing Seymour of stirring up sedition by writing to the king's sisters, is omitted.

34 Throckmorton MS, Warwick County Record Office, stanzas 75 and 76.

35 John Harington, *Nugae Antiquae*, 'Verses upon the Lord Admiral's picture', p. 87.

36 Porter, *Mary Tudor*, p. 305.

37 James, *Kateryn Parr*, p. 339.

38 Cecilie Goff, *A Woman of the Tudor Age* (London, 1930), pp. 175–6.

39 Reverend T. Nash, 'Observations on the Time of Death and Place of Burial of Queen Katharine Parr', *Archaeologia ix* (1789), pp. 1–9. Katherine's remains were reburied in 1862, in a tomb designed by Sir George Gilbert Scott in the restored chapel of Sudeley Castle.

Epilogue

1 Starkey, *Elizabeth*, p. 242.

Bibliography

Manuscript Sources

BODLEIAN LIBRARY
Ashmolean MSS 1729
Rawlinson MSS D1070.4

BRITISH LIBRARY
Additional MSS 19398, 32647, 33271, 46348
Cotton MSS Caligula E4, Nero Cx, Vespasian Fiii
Harleian MS 5087
Lansdowne MSS 97 and 1236
Royal MS 7D
Sloane MSS 1523
Stowe MSS 559

COLLEGE OF ARMS
R20 and RR21C

THE NATIONAL ARCHIVES (formerly the Public Record Office)
Exchequer: Exchequer Accounts various, E101, E314, E315
Lord Chamberlain's Office: Robes and Special Events, LC2
Probate: Registers Thower and Alen, PROB 11
State Papers, Domestic: Edward VI, SP10; Henry VIII, SP 1

SUDELEY CASTLE
Dent Brocklehurst MSS

WARWICKSHIRE COUNTY RECORD OFFICE
Cole's MSS History of the Family of Throckmorton CR1998/LCB/18

Primary Sources

(Place of publication for all printed works is London unless otherwise stated)

A Collection of State Papers Relating to Affairs in the reigns of King Henry VIII, King Edward VI, Queen Mary and Queen Elizabeth, ed. Samuel Haynes, 1740

Erasmus, Desiderius, *Collected Works, vol. 1, Correspondence*, transl. R. B. Mynors and D. F. S. Thomson, Toronto, 1974

Formularies of Faith put forth by authority during the reign of Henry VIII, ed. Charles Lloyd, Oxford, 1825

Foxe, John, *The Acts and Monuments of the Church*, ed. M. Hobart Seymour, 1838

Ingulph, *Chronicle of the Abbey of Croyland with the Continuations*, transl. Henry T. Riley, 1854

Letters of the Kings of England, ed. James Orchard Halliwell, 1848

'Narrative of the Visit of the Duke of Najera', *Archaeologia XXIII*, 1831

Parr, Katherine, *Psalms or Prayers taken out of Holy Scripture*, 1544

—— *Prayers or Medytacions*, 1545

—— *The Lamentacion of a synner*, 1548

Statutes of the Realm, 1101–1713, ed. A. Luders et al., 12 vols, 1810–1828

Sylloge Epistolarum, ed. Thomas Hearne, 1716

Testamenta Vetusta, ed. N. H. Nicolas, 2 vols, 1826

The Arundel Harington Manuscript of Tudor Poetry, ed. Ruth Hughey, Columbus, Ohio, 1960

The Chronicle and Political Papers of King Edward VI, ed. W. K. Jordan, 1966

The Early Modern Englishwoman: Part 1, vol. 3: Katherine Parr, ed. Betty S. Travitsky and Patrick Cullen, Aldershot, 1997

The first tome or volume of the paraphrase of Erasmus upon the newe testamente, ed. N. Udall, 1548

The Letters of Stephen Gardiner, ed. James Muller, 1933

The Literary Remains of Edward VI, ed. J. G. Nichols, 1857

The Mirror of the Sinful Soul, Marguerite of Navarre, transl. Elizabeth Tudor, ed. P. W. Ames, 1897

The Privy Purse Expenses of Princess Mary, ed. Frederick Madden, 1831

The Registers of Cuthbert Tunstall, bishop of Durham, 1530–1539, Surtees Society, vol. 1

Wills from Doctors' Commons, ed. J. G. Nichols and J. Bruce, Camden Old Series, vol. 83, 1863

Wriothesley, Charles, *A Chronicle of England*, ed. W. D. Hamilton, Camden Society, New Series 11, 1875–7

Secondary Works

Alford, Stephen, *Kingship and Politics in the Reign of Edward VI*, Cambridge, 2002

Anstruther, Godfrey, *Vaux of Harrowden*, Newport, 1953

Bernard, G. W., *The King's Reformation*, 2005

——— 'The downfall of Sir Thomas Seymour', in *The Tudor Nobility*, ed. G. W. Bernard, 1992

Bindoff, S., *The House of Commons, 1509–1558*, 3 vols, 1982

Brigden, Susan, *London and the Reformation*, Oxford, 1989

Burnet, Gilbert, *The History of the Reformation of the Church of England*, 1839

Camden, William, *The History of the Most Renowned and Victorious Princess Elizabeth, Late Queen of England*, 1630

Carley, James P., *The Books of Henry VIII and his Wives*, 2004

de Lisle, Leanda, *The Sisters who would be Queen*, 2009

Dent, Emma, *Annals of Winchcombe and Sudeley*, 1877

Dodds, Madeleine and Dodds, Ruth, *The Pilgrimage of Grace and the Exeter conspiracy*, 2 vols, Cambridge, 1915

Dowling, Maria, *Humanism in the age of Henry VIII*, 1986

Dugdale, William, *History of St Paul's Cathedral*, 1716

Fletcher, A. and MacCulloch, D., *Tudor Rebellions*, 1997

Goff, Cecilie, *A Woman of the Tudor Age, a biography of Katherine Willoughby*, 1930

Gunn, S. J., 'The rise of the Burgh family, c. 1431–1550', *Gainsborough Old Hall*, Society of Lincolnshire History and Archaeology, 1991

Hannay, Margaret P., ed., *Silent but for the Word: Tudor Women as Patrons, Translators and Writers of Religious Works*, Kent, Ohio, 1985

Haugaard, William P., 'Katherine Parr: The Religious Convictions of a Renaissance Queen', *Renaissance Quarterly*, 22, 1969

Hayward, Sir John, *The Life and Reign of King Edward VI*, 1630

Hayward, Maria, *Dress at the Court of King Henry VIII*, Leeds, 2007

Henderson, Katherine Usher and McManus, Barbara F., *Half Humankind*, Chicago, 1985

Hodgett, Gerald A. J., *Tudor Lincolnshire*, Lincoln, 1975

Hoffman, C. Fenno Jr, 'Catherine Parr as a Woman of Letters', *Huntington Library Quarterly*, 23, 1959

Hoyle, R. W., *The Pilgrimage of Grace and the Politics of the 1530s*, Oxford, 2001

Hughey, Ruth, *John Harington of Stepney: Tudor Gentleman*, Columbus, Ohio, 1971

Hutchinson, Robert, *The Last Days of Henry VIII*, 2005

James, Susan E., *Kateryn Parr*, Aldershot, 1999
—— 'Sir William Parr of Kendal, Parts 1 & 2', *Transactions of the Cumberland and Westmoreland Antiquarian and Archaeological Society*, New Series, vol. 93, pp. 100–14 and vol. 94 pp. 105–20, 1993, 1994
—— *The Feminine Dynamic in English Art, 1485–1603*, Aldershot, 2009
—— 'Two Holbein Miniatures', *Apollo*, May 1998, pp. 15–20

Jones, M. and Underwood, M., *The King's Mother: Lady Margaret Beaufort, Countess of Richmond and Derby*, Cambridge, 1992

Jordan, W. K., *Edward VI: The Young King*, 1968

Loades, D., *The Tudor Court*, Bangor, 1992

McConica, James K., *English Humanists and Reformation Politics under Henry VIII and Edward VI*, Oxford, 1965

MacCulloch, Diarmaid, *Thomas Cranmer*, 1996

Maclean, Ian, *The Renaissance Notion of Women*, Cambridge, 1980

Maclean, J., *The life of Sir Thomas Seymour*, 1869

Martienssen, Anthony, *Queen Katherine Parr*, 1975

Moorhouse, Geoffrey, *The Pilgrimage of Grace*, 2002

Mueller, Janel, 'A Tudor Queen finds her Voice: Katherine Parr's Lamentation of a Sinner', in *The Historical Renaissance: New Essays on Tudor and Stuart Literature and Culture*, eds. H. Dubrow and R. Strier, Chicago, 1988
—— 'Devotion as Difference: Intertextuality in Queen Katherine Parr's Prayers or Meditations (1545)', *Huntington Library Quarterly*, 53, 1988

Muller, James, *Stephen Gardiner and the Tudor Reaction*, 1926

Murphy, Beverley A., *Bastard Prince*, Gloucester, 2003

Nash, Reverend Treadway, 'Observations on the Time of Death and Place of Burial of Queen Katherine Parr', *Archaeologia IX*, 1789

Platts, Graham, *Land and People in Medieval Lincolnshire*, Lincoln, 1985

Pollard, A. F., *England Under Protector Somerset*, 1900

Porter, Linda, *Mary Tudor*, 2007

Redworth, Glyn, *In Defence of the Church Catholic*, Oxford, 1990

Reynolds, E. E., *Thomas More and Erasmus*, 1965

Rose-Troup, Frances B., 'Two Book Bills of Katherine Parr', *The Library*, January 1911

Ross, Charles, *Edward IV*, 1983
—— *Richard III*, 1988

Ryrie, Alec, *The Gospel and Henry VIII*, Cambridge, 2003

Scarisbrick, J. J., *Henry VIII*, 1997

Scott, Daniel, *The Stricklands of Sizergh Castle*, Kendal, 1908

Seymour, William, *Ordeal by Ambition*, 1972

Shagan, E., ed., *Catholics and the 'Protestant Nation'*, Manchester, 2005

Slavin, A. J., *Politics and Profit: A study of Sir Ralph Sadler, 1507–1547*, Cambridge, 1966

Smith, Hilda L., 'Humanist Education and the Renaissance Concept of Woman', in *Women and Literature in Britain, 1500–1700*, ed. Helen Wilcox, Cambridge, 1996

Smith, R. B., *Land and Politics in the England of Henry VIII: The West Riding of Yorkshire, 1530–1546*, Oxford, 1970

Starkey, David, *Elizabeth*, 2001

―――― *Six Wives: The Queens of Henry VIII*, 2004

―――― *The Reign of Henry VIII; Personalities and Politics*, 1985

―――― ed., *The English Court from the Wars of the Roses to the Civil War*, Harlow, 1987

Strickland, Agnes, *Lives of the Queens of England*, vol. 3, 1852

Strype, John, *Ecclesiastical Memorials*, 2 vols, Oxford, 1822

Sturge, Charles, *Cuthbert Tunstal*, 1938

Thurley, Simon, *The Royal Palaces of Tudor England*, 1993

Victoria County History of Lincolnshire (vol. 2), ed. William Page, 1906

Wilcox, Helen, ed., *Women and Literature in Britain, 1500–1700*, Cambridge, 1996

Wilson, Derek, *In the Lion's Court*, 2002

Unpublished Dissertations

Bastow, Sarah L. *Aspects of the History of the Catholic Gentry of Yorkshire from the Pilgrimage of Grace to the First Civil War*, PhD dissertation, University of Huddersfield, 2002

Hamilton, Dakota Lee, *The Household of Queen Katherine Parr*, DPhil dissertation, Oxford, 1992

Harkrider, Melissa Franklin, *'Faith is a Noble Duchess': Piety, Patronage and Kinship in the career of Katherine Willoughby, Duchess of Suffolk, 1519–1580*, PhD dissertation, University of North Carolina at Chapel Hill, 2003

Hatch, Morris Addison, *The Ascham Letters: an annotated translation of the Latin correspondence*, PhD dissertation, Cornell University, New York, 1948

MacMahon, Luke, *The English Invasion of France in 1544*, MPhil thesis, University of Warwick, 1992

Swenson, Patricia Cole, *Noble Hunters of the Romish Fox: Religious Reform at the Tudor Court, 1543–1564*, PhD dissertation, University of California Berkeley, 1981

Picture Acknowledgements

Henry VIII, Circle of Hans Holbein the Younger, courtesy of Sotheby's Picture Library.

Henry VIII, 16th Century English School © Society of Antiquities, London / Bridgeman Art Library.

SECTION TWO

Page

1 Edward VI, Studio of William Scrots, 16th Century, courtesy of Sotheby's Picture Library.

Edward VI, by Guillim Stretes, 16th Century © Musée du Louvre, Paris / akg-images.

Lady Jane Grey by unknown artist © National Portrait Gallery, London.

2 Mary Tudor at the age of twenty-eight by Master John, 1544 © National Portrait Gallery / Bridgeman Art Library.

3 Elizabeth I when Princess, attributed to William Scrots, circa 1546, The Royal Collection © 2009, Her Majesty Queen Elzabeth II.

4 Mary Tudor, Studio of Antonio Moro, 16th Century © Isabella Stewart Gardner Museum, Boston, MA / Bridgeman Art Library.

Signature of Queen Elizabeth I © akg-images.

Queen Elizabeth I in coronation robes, 16th Century English School, circa 1559–1600 © National Portrait Gallery / Bridgeman Art Library.

5 Cover of Elizabeth's translation of *The Mirror of the Sinful Soul* (MS.Cherry 36) © Bodleian Library, Oxford.

Cover of Elizabeth's translation of *Prayers or Meditations* (Royall MS 7.D.x) © British Library, London.

Mary Howard, Duchess of Richmond, by Holbein, Royal Library, Windsor, The Royal Collection © 2009, Her Majesty Queen Elizabeth II.

6 Edward Seymour by Hans Holbein the Younger, 16th Century © The Trustees of the Weston Park Foundation, UK / Bridgeman Art Library.

Anne Stanhope, Duchess of Somerset, English, 16th Century © National Gallery of Ireland.

7 Oval portrait of an unknown man (thought to be Thomas Seymour), 1543, attributed to Hans Holbein the Younger, ca. 1497–1543. Formerly attributed to Luke Horenbout, 1490/95–1544. Gouache on thin card, edge trimmed in gold (4.6cm). Courtesy Yale Center for British Art, Paul Mellon Collection (B1974.2.58).

Thomas Seymour, 16th Century English School © National Portrait Gallery / Bridgeman Art Library.

8 Katherine Parr's tomb at Sudeley and inscription on Katherine Parr's coffin, both reproduced by kind permission of Sudeley Castle, Gloucestershire.

Katherine Brandon by Francesco Bartolozzi, after Hans Holbein the Younger, stipple engraving © National Portrait Gallery, London.

Index

KE 2/13

extracts reading groups
competitions books new
discounts extracts
competitions
books new extracts discounts
events books
extracts new titles reading groups
interviews
events extracts
discounts
new books events
events new
discounts extracts discounts
www.panmacmillan.com
extracts events reading groups
competitions books extracts new
reading groups events reading groups books interviews